STEPHEN BARRY AND **MARC Z. LIEBERMAN**

DEFENDING TRUMP

A DEBATE ON THE TRUMP PRESIDENCY IN REAL TIME

iUniverse

DEFENDING TRUMP
A DEBATE ON THE TRUMP PRESIDENCY IN REAL TIME

Copyright © 2020 Stephen Barry and Marc Z. Lieberman.

All rights reserved. No part of this book may be used or reproduced by any means, graphic, electronic, or mechanical, including photocopying, recording, taping or by any information storage retrieval system without the written permission of the author except in the case of brief quotations embodied in critical articles and reviews.

iUniverse books may be ordered through booksellers or by contacting:

iUniverse
1663 Liberty Drive
Bloomington, IN 47403
www.iuniverse.com
844-349-9409

Because of the dynamic nature of the Internet, any web addresses or links contained in this book may have changed since publication and may no longer be valid. The views expressed in this work are solely those of the author and do not necessarily reflect the views of the publisher, and the publisher hereby disclaims any responsibility for them.

Any people depicted in stock imagery provided by Getty Images are models, and such images are being used for illustrative purposes only.
Certain stock imagery © Getty Images.

ISBN: 978-1-6632-0120-1 (sc)
ISBN: 978-1-6632-0581-0 (hc)
ISBN: 978-1-6632-0121-8 (e)

Library of Congress Control Number: 2020914782

Print information available on the last page.

iUniverse rev. date: 09/16/2020

We dedicate this book to our parents and grandparents, whose love and sacrifice made the fulfillment of our American dreams possible, and to our wives, whose love, support, and wisdom never waver.

Contents

Introduction by Stephen Barry xvii

PART 1
July 29, 2017–December 31, 2017

The Debate Begins: Personal Attacks against Trump 1
Charlottesville 4
Sheriff Joe Arpaio 6
Mueller and the Constitution 7
Trump versus the Clintons 12
Evaluating Trump 16
Sexual Misconduct 19
Fusion GPS 22
Sexual Misconduct? Racism? 23
More Mueller and Russian Collusion 26
Radical Islamic Terrorism and Racism 27
Tax Cuts 28
Roy Moore 29
Regulatory Reform, More Collusion, Jim Comey 31
Michael Flynn 35
More Trump-Russia Collusion 37
Recognizing Jerusalem 40
Back to Trump-Russia Collusion 41
Trump, Propriety, and the Unhinged Opposition 47
Anti-Semitism 49
The Rule of Law 51
Government Abuse of Power 55

More on Sexual Misconduct Allegations 56
FBI Misconduct 57
Conspiracy Theories about Russian Banks 59
Trump's Progress 60
Putin 62
Moving the US Embassy to Jerusalem 63
Who Is the Dictator? 65
More on Taxes 69
The Papadopoulos Story 70

PART 2
January 6, 2018–March 24, 2018

Trump's Tax Returns 73
Shithole Countries 74
The Nuclear Option 79
Strzok and Page Text Messages 80
More Regulatory Reform, More on Jerusalem 82
Back to the Mueller Investigation 83
DACA 87
Sanctions on Russia 88
Back to the Mueller Investigation 92
The Nunes Memo 96
Kaepernick and Racism 100
Back to the Nunes Memo 102
The House Democrats' FISA Memo 103
Trump's Experience 104
Evidence against Trump 105
Parkland 107
Mueller Indictments 109
Gun Control 110
Support for Trump 111
Draining the Swamp 113
Stormy 115
Meltdown Stage 116
More Putin 118

Back to Mueller 120
Trump the King 121
Moscow's Man 122
Transgender Persons and the Military 123

PART 3
April 6, 2018–June 25, 2018

Electoral Integrity 127
Toxic Environments 128
Support for Israel and the Wall 129
Useful Idiots 131
Raiding Michael Cohen's Office 133
Campaign Finance Violations 135
Trump's Business Ventures 137
Liars 138
Removing Trump from Office 140
Evidence 142
The Integrity of the Investigators 144
Travel Bans 146
Undoing the 2016 Election 147
The Healthiest President 149
Spying on Kerry? 150
Trump's Tax Liens 151
Fitness for Office 152
Trump's Predecessors 154
Pastor Jeffress and the US Embassy in Jerusalem 155
MS-13 158
Encouraging Violence 160
Back to the Animals Comment 162
Nobel Prize 163
Confidential Human Sources 164
Cohen's Russian Client 165
Roseanne Barr 167
Pardons 169
Legal Memo on Obstruction 171

More on Trump's Alleged Racism 172
The G7 174
North Korea 175
Speculation Following the First Inspector General Report 179
Family Separation 181
Hate Speech and Comparisons to Hitler 183
Hatred 186
Open Borders 188

PART 4
July 14, 2018–December 21, 2018

NATO 193
Peter Strzok 194
The Press 197
Helsinki Press Conference 198
More on the Press 201
The Efforts to Reveal Trump 204
Insults 207
Back to Collusion 208
Cohen and Impeachment 209
Manafort 210
Predictions 212
Prosecutorial (Mis)conduct 213
Personnel 215
Hillary 217
Permanent Investigations 218
Real Crimes 219
Tell the Truth and Move On 220
Selective Prosecution 221
Anonymous 224
Literally Nothing 225
Kavanaugh 226
The Avenatti Affidavit 228
Not Provable or Disprovable 230
The Republican Base 235

Back to Kavanaugh 236
The Caravans 239
Bomb Threats 240
Pittsburgh Synagogue Massacre 241
The Obsession with Neo-Nazis Continues 245
Jim Acosta 247
Interim Attorney General Matthew Whitaker 248
Trump at Midterm 250
Adam Schitt 252
Ivanka's Emails 255
Trump's Russia Crimes 257
Altruism 261
More Russia Speculation 263
Back to Mueller 264
Lying: Bill Clinton versus Michael Flynn 266
Trump Payments to Stormy 268
The Inaugural Committee 269
Why Not Accept That the Russians Interfered? 270
More about Campaign Finance Violations 271
Back to Mueller 273
Prosecutorial Abuse 274
Trump's Accomplishments 276
More about Baseless Allegations 278
Trump and His Critics 281
Syria Withdrawal 283
Defending Trump 285

PART 5
January 17, 2019–March 31, 2019

Report That Trump Told Cohen to Lie to Congress 289
The FBI's Conduct 292
Nicholas Sandmann and Trump Tower Moscow 294
Back to Trump Tower Moscow and Putin 308
Roger Stone Indictment 310
Infanticide and Northam 312

Generals and Civilian Control 314
No Collusion? 315
The Wall Emergency and Executive Orders 316
McCabe 320
Trump's Past 322
Jussie Smollett 323
China Trade 325
More on Michael Cohen and Stormy 326
Kushner's Security Clearance 327
Standards for Judging Trump 329
North Korea Summit in Vietnam 330
Kasparov 332
Ilhan Omar and Anti-Semitism 333
Manafort Sentencing 335
Lisa Page Testimony 339
The College Admissions Scandal 340
More on Manafort 341
Climate of Intolerance and Personal Attacks 342
More on McCain 347
Indecent, Immoral Schmuck? 348
What Will Mueller Find? 350
Mueller's Tactics 351
Mueller Report Summary Released 353
Accepting Mueller's Findings 356
Privilege 357

PART 6
April 4, 2019–June 26, 2019

The Mueller Report Findings 361
Animals 363
Some People Did Something 364
McGahn and Obstruction 365
Lies and Liars 371
The Meaning of the Mueller Report 373

Congressional Subpoenas 376
Back to Trump's Policies 377
Back to Trump's Supporters 380
Extreme Abortion 382
Israel and Anti-Semitism Again 384
Back to Obstruction 385
Digression to Omar 387
Back to Collusion 388
Should Mueller Testify? 389
Elitism 392
More Subpoenas 395
Political Hit Job 398
China Tariffs 402
More on Abortion 404
Continued Investigations into Trump and Russia 405
It's Hard to Say Goodbye to Collusion 406
Legal versus Political 415
More Problems with the Mueller Report 417
Iran 419
E. Jean Carroll's Rape Allegation 420
The Border Crisis 421

PART 7
July 4, 2019–September 30, 2019

Revolutionary War Airports and More on Putin 425
Trump Supporters Chant, "Send Her Back" 426
Mueller Testifies 431
Baltimore and Elijah Cummings 435
The El Paso and Dayton Shootings 439
More on Tlaib and Omar 441
The Inspector General's Report on Comey 445
Iran Shoots Down a Drone 448
Kavanaugh Revisited 449
The Democratic Candidates 451

Ukraine 453
A Digression Back to Russia 473
Back to Ukraine 474

PART 8
October 2, 2019–December 30, 2019

Ukraine, Continued 481
Withdrawal of Troops from Northern Syria 495
Back to Ukraine and Impeachment 497
More Discussions on Turkey and the Kurds 499
Back to Ukraine and Impeachment 503
More on the Middle East 506
Back to Ukraine and Impeachment 510
More Discussions on Turkey 512
Back to Ukraine and Impeachment 513
Hosting the G7 at the Doral 517
The Election 519
Impeachment Discussions Resume 521
Trump-Hating Republican 526
A Philosophical Discussion 528
Back to Impeachment 532
Back to Impeachment and Trump's Inquisitors 535
Self-Absorption 544
Quid Pro Quos 546
A Farce 548
Character 550
Rick Perry Ukrainian Gas Deal 554
Back to Impeachment 555
Netanyahu's Indictment and Adam Schiff 567
Navy SEAL Gallagher 569
Deranged 573
Ukraine Cleared? 575
Selective Outrage: Shooting at Florida Military Base 578
The Inspector General's FISA Abuse Report 579

Executive Order Defining Judaism as a Nationality 583
Ukraine: Meeting with Zelensky 584
More on the FISA Abuse Report 585
Comments on Greta Thunberg and Putin 588
Judgment 590
Back to Impeachment 591
Back to Character 593
Back to Impeachment 596
The White-Power Hand Gesture 597
Nancy Pelosi's Teeth 598
Back to Impeachment 599
More about Lies and Liars 601
Children 603
Corruption and Ukraine 604
Impeachment 607
John Dingell 608
Back to Collusion 609
More on Navy SEAL Eddie Gallagher and the Army-Navy Game 610
More Speculation about Trump's Ties to Putin 613

PART 9
December 31, 2019–April 12, 2020

The US Embassy in Iraq 617
The Killing of Soleimani 618
A Digression to Collusion 620
Back to Soleimani 621
Back to Impeachment 622
The State of the Union and Impeachment Aftermath 639
The Roger Stone Sentence 643
Giuliani and New York State 646
DOJ Declines to Pursue Charges against Andrew McCabe 648
Trump Rallies 649
Who Are the Bad Guys? 650
More on Racism 652

More on Roger Stone's Sentence	654
Matt Gaetz	655
Coronavirus	657
Back to Mueller	665
Coronavirus Press Conferences	666
Back to Coronavirus	668
Mitt Romney	672
Reopening the Economy	674
Back to Coronavirus Press Conferences	675
Politics	678
Back to Reopening the Economy	680
Further Discussion on Mitt Romney	682
Trump's Support for New York and California	683
The Coronavirus Response	685
The Case against Trump	710
Back to the Coronavirus Response	711
Questioning Dr. Fauci	715
Coronavirus and Race	717
Hydroxychloroquine	720
Democrats	722
The Pandemic Office	723
More on Reopening the Economy	724
Happy Good Friday to All!	725
The Latest on FBI Misconduct against Trump	726
Back to Reopening the Economy	728
Conclusion	731
Index	733

Introduction by Stephen Barry

President Trump has been the subject of withering attacks on his character and fitness for office from the moment he announced his candidacy for president in 2015. His critics, including Democrats, their mainstream media allies, and Never Trump Republicans, argue that he poses a unique threat to the presidency, our governing institutions, and our national character. He is accused of being a liar, racist, misogynist, traitor, and dictator-in-waiting. Every act the Trump administration takes is challenged, such as his efforts to ban immigration from dysfunctional Muslim-majority countries, build a wall on the Mexican border, and even raise taxes on the wealthy by limiting state and local tax deductions. Every effort is challenged not based on the law but based on Trump's alleged impure motives. The underlying theme is that Trump should not be permitted to exercise the powers of his office. But is any of this true?

This book presents text messages between Marc Lieberman and me on virtually every issue that has been in the news since Donald Trump was elected president. In these text messages, we debate, in real time, each development. Marc is a Never Trumper. In contrast, although I did not start out as one, I have become a staunch supporter of President Trump. Our text messages turned into a debate in which Marc presented the mainstream anti-Trump view, and I defended Trump.

Trump was not my first choice for the Republican nomination in 2016. He might have been my last choice. I did not believe he had the requisite experience or command of the issues to be president. I also did not approve of Trump's penchant for insulting his opponents. However, unlike Marc, I recognize that politics is, and always has been, personal and nasty. For example, in the election of 1884, Republican candidate James G. Blaine's supporters, referring to the allegation that Democratic candidate (and eventual winner) Grover Cleveland had fathered a child out of wedlock, composed the following rhyme: "Mama, where's my pa? Gone to the White House, ha ha ha." Trump is more direct and explicit than most and does not rely on others to do his dirty work.

At the time, I was concerned that Trump was the only Republican candidate who had no chance to defeat Hillary Clinton. I did not recognize that Trump had figured out something that most everyone else had missed: America's political elite, both Republican and Democrat, were not addressing the concerns of large numbers of Americans. In some cases, the politicians' focus on free trade, low taxes (Republicans), identity politics and race (Democrats), and support for foreign wars and interventions, among other things, was antithetical to the basic interests of voters. Because Trump spoke to the concerns of voters who otherwise were being ignored, he won. In fact, he might have been the only Republican able to do it.

Since his election, I have evolved into a staunch Trump supporter for two primary reasons. The first is that I quickly came to believe that Trump was the target of an illegal effort to delegitimize his election and remove him from office. This has been confirmed by the Department of Justice inspector general's report on FISA abuse and, as we are preparing to publish this book, the fast-moving developments resulting in the dismissal of the Flynn case and the release of the transcripts from the House Intelligence Committee's Russian collusion investigation, which shows that no Obama intelligence official had evidence of collusion. I expect that, as previewed by Attorney General Bill Barr, those responsible for those efforts will be indicted. As an American, I cannot think of anything more dangerous to our freedom than an effort by the party in power to undermine and then force out the opposition party's candidate for president.

The second reason for my support of Trump is that Trump has been successful. I discuss his accomplishments in the text messages, but I will note here that Trump's policies have achieved low unemployment, economic growth, and the destruction of the ISIS caliphate and that Trump has supported our allies and confronted our enemies, particularly China. As I write this, the country is on the cusp of reopening from the coronavirus lockdowns. The federal government's response to date might not be perfect, but by any fair assessment, Trump has done a solid job.

Marc became a Never Trumper prior to the 2016 election. Trump lost Marc when he attacked John McCain with the comment "I like people who weren't captured." Trump further alienated Marc when he allegedly mocked a disabled reporter. Marc's dislike for Trump is visceral. He believes Trump is a liar and uniquely selfish. He cannot stand Trump's constant self-aggrandizement. Occasionally, he will acknowledge that he likes certain policies, but as you will read, any credit he gives Trump is short-lived.

More disturbingly to me, Marc, despite his claims that he would support Mike Pence, Nikki Haley, or any other Republican, argues that Trump's rhetoric tacitly encourages racism. He further argues that a broad swath of white Americans are easily manipulated and susceptible to barely disguised racist messages. We have frequent arguments about this in the text messages that follow. However, the views he expresses in our text messages are right up there with Hillary Clinton's "basket of deplorables."

I believe that some of Marc's more extreme statements arise out of his frustration that Trump supporters do not see what he sees. It is inconceivable to him that so many people support a person whom Marc and those who agree with him view as immoral, uninformed, nasty, mean, and thoroughly unqualified. I have no problem with his dislike for Donald Trump. I have told Marc on multiple occasions to vote for someone else in 2020.

But I cannot support Marc's opposition to Trump based on false allegations. It has been conclusively established, although the allegations persist, that Trump has no connection to Vladimir Putin. He did not collude with Russia. More importantly, I believe that the investigators investigating those allegations knew the allegations were false but continued to investigate in the hope they would uncover a crime to which they could point to justify their actions.

Similarly, Trump did not commit an impeachable offense or, in my opinion, any offense at all by mentioning Joe Biden to President Zelensky of Ukraine and temporarily delaying the release of aid. In light of the Obama administration's investigation of Trump based on false allegations of collusion with Russia, it is impossible to believe that Adam Schiff, who repeatedly lied that he had evidence that Trump colluded with Russia, considered Trump's comments about Biden to Zelensky to be impeachable offenses.

The text messages that follow are essentially in their original form. We have made changes to improve the readability and, in a few instances, the tone but have not changed the substance in any way. These were our thoughts and opinions in real time on the events, people and controversies related to Trump. We often were reacting to new information and did not have the full picture, which was developing. An example is the furor over the confrontation between the Covington, Kentucky, high school students and Native American activist Nathan Phillips. Also, these are not structured conversations. I have tried to find the breaks in the topics, but there are many digressions within each topic.

Marc is a doctor, and I am a lawyer. We have known each other for almost fifty years and have been close friends since we were fourth-grade eight-year-olds in a small private school. We have celebrated happy family occasions and mourned the losses of loved ones. We are as close to family as you can be without actually being family. Each of us has been fortunate to have a supportive family who gave us the kinds of opportunities that have allowed us to become successful professionals.

We are grateful and proud to be Americans and have been engaged citizens. We care about our country and how it is governed. We want the United States to be a land of opportunity for all of its citizens. Before Donald Trump, our biggest arguments were over sports. Donald Trump changed that.

Some of our discussions get heated and personal. We both make statements that probably are more extreme than our actual positions. I hope readers will take that in the spirit of competition. Because we trust each other, we have been able to have passionate disputes and remain friends. I am grateful that Marc has agreed to be the vehicle for testing the anti-Trump case. He is not likely to win over many Trump supporters, nor is he likely to win friends among Trump's opponents, who might not appreciate having their views subject to debate. I hope I'm wrong about that.

Stephen Barry
May 11, 2020

PART 1

JULY 29, 2017– DECEMBER 31, 2017

THE DEBATE BEGINS: PERSONAL ATTACKS AGAINST TRUMP

July 29, 2017

Marc. He is under personal attack because he thinks he is above our American process and belittles others when he doesn't get what he wants. He is not able to enact conservative policies because he is not a conservative.

Stephen. He is under attack by assholes who belittle Americans—or should I say "deplorables." The media and political class do not like him and are trying to destroy him. I'm not certain how you conclude he thinks he is above our American process. It seems you're describing Hillary Clinton, Bill Clinton, Loretta Lynch, Debbie Wasserman Schultz—all of Trump's opponents.

Stephen. The political elite and the media do not accept the choice made by the American electorate. The leaks, the false Russian collusion, the baseless allegations. I'm disappointed that Trump is not proving up to the task of dealing with it. That being said, he should not have to.

Marc. Did you accept the electorate when they twice voted for Obama?

Stephen. Of course. I think Obama did a lot of damage to our economy, constitutional rights, and security. However, he was fairly elected.

Marc. I don't know the definition of *accept*, but Trump sure as hell did not accept Obama's presidency, did he? It's so easy debating with you. I think the score is like 75–0. Obama made some mistakes and had many policies that I totally disagreed with. It caused a vacuum that allowed someone like Trump. And to answer your question about how Trump doesn't accept the democratic process, he is a real estate developer used to breaking or skirting the law to achieve a result and paying or threatening people when he didn't get his way, just like now. He is such an egomaniac that he thinks Congress should simply do what he says rather than serve their constituents.

STEPHEN. Again, you make things up. How do you know Trump is used to breaking or skirting the law? The truth is that he has been a risk-taker who has built businesses and employed people. I don't know if he thinks Congress should do what he says, but at least Republicans in Congress assert themselves. Obama ignored Congress with no pushback from Democrats, but I guess you were okay with Obama's pen and phone.

MARC. Steve, I don't want to belabor the derogatory analogy to real estate developers. I said he is used to breaking the law, which he was proven in court or in deposition to have done by his own admission and settling lawsuits. Settling a lawsuit, according to Trump, is a sign of guilt. (See? I listen to what he says.) I did not like most of Obama's policies, but with the lens through which I view someone as reprehensible as Trump, I believe Obama is a highly ethical person.

STEPHEN. Lawsuits arise out of civil disputes, not violations of law. Settling a lawsuit has nothing to do with guilt. Business disputes arise every day, end up in litigation, and are settled. I don't view Obama as ethical. He violated the rights of Americans—the IRS, for example. He apparently used US intelligence services for political purposes. He lied about Obamacare. He lied about Iran. What an example.

MARC. Okay, so it's now 75–1. I'll give you this argument.

MARC. Who would you rather hang with while stranded on a desert island?

STEPHEN. Thanks for your generosity. I would much rather be with Trump. He would be a lot more fun and might help me make a little money. Obama is a droning bore and an egomaniac.

MARC. You can't be a droning bore and an egomaniac. Mutually exclusive.

STEPHEN. Obama is living proof.

CHARLOTTESVILLE

August 12, 2017

Marc. Watch the Virginia situation. This is a declared alt-right racist and anti-Semitic rally, and Trump gave a nonspecific tweet of condemnation against "violence." This is a group that voted for Trump, so it's hard for him to condemn their rally, for fear of losing their support.

Marc. His "condemnation" of Nazis was tepid and evasive.

Marc. Any equivocation or defense of Trump's lack of condemnation of riots that were completely started by the alt-right, the kind of condemnation many Republican senators are giving today, makes you a complete appeaser, or you just have your head in the sand. These are Bannon's people, and they are all around the country, and many are anti-Semites. Trump is trying to choose his words carefully, but he's not fooling anyone.

August 13, 2017

Marc. "Both sides—ya know, the neo-Nazis and everyone else—have to stop this!"

Stephen. I don't have all the details, but I read that Trump made appropriate remarks. I also note that right-wing violence, although repugnant, is not a significant issue. It certainly does not compare to Antifa, Black Lives Matter, or Occupy Wall Street. Occupy Wall Street was shockingly anti-Semitic. I saw it with my own eyes. I also note that it is possible the right-wing protesters were solely at fault. However, if the counterprotesters attempted to physically prevent the right-wingers from protesting, they may share some blame.

MARC. So you feel that if people assemble in Jerusalem with swastikas and some Israelis attempt to forcefully but not dangerously push them away and then someone is killed in the ensuing melee, the Israelis should share some of the blame? Orrin Hatch, Ted Cruz, and others all invoked the word *Nazis* in their rebuke. Trump didn't. And if it were a Muslim terrorist rally that started the violence, Trump would not be so measured or tepid in his condemnation.

STEPHEN. So right-wingers have no legal right to protest, and if they do, it is legal to attack them? If they are attacked, they are responsible? We have laws for a reason. If Muslims rallied, as they frequently do in London, the state would go out of its way to protect them.

MARC. Interesting how you think neo-Nazis should be allowed to spew hate unperturbed.

MARC. I think your thoughts are very misguided. When neo-Nazis rally, I have great respect for those who oppose them, regardless of their affiliation, period.

STEPHEN. I don't think that. They should be mocked, ridiculed, and opposed. Just do it legally without initiating violence.

MARC. Were you brainwashed or something? You are worried about Nazis' right to protest? Are you now part of the ACLU?

STEPHEN. I'm not worried about the Nazis' right to protest. I am worried about free speech, which is under assault from the left. It's not just Nazis who are shouted down; it's conservatives. The Nazis are not a threat. They are a small, despised, and inconsequential group. However, the idea that certain people do not have the right to speak—even if they are following the law—is a threat to our way of life.

SHERIFF JOE ARPAIO

August 25, 2017

Marc. So when a president is elected by the public, you believe that should be respected. Let me ask you: When someone is convicted of a crime, do you think that should be respected?

Stephen. What is your rule? You only respect a president if you voted for him? Regarding your question about respect for a person convicted of a crime, I have no idea what you are talking about.

August 26, 2017

Marc. Pardoning the sheriff convicted for not abiding by the law.

Stephen. I don't know what laws the eighty-five-year-old retired sheriff broke, but I know he had controversial (i.e., politically incorrect) views on illegal immigration. My guess is, it was a very good use of the pardon power.

MUELLER AND THE CONSTITUTION

August 30, 2017

MARC. Too bad he will be impeached when the Mueller report comes out.

STEPHEN. You mean the Mueller attempted coup. Are you following the story about the Pakistani programmers who were employed and paid large sums of money by Debbie Wasserman Schultz and other Democrats and were arrested attempting to leave the United States?

MARC. I am not impressed with Wasserman Schultz, particularly how she pushed her thumb on the scale, as DNC chair, for Hillary Clinton.

STEPHEN. The Pakistani programmers had access to the DNC servers—the ones the DNC refused to turn over to the FBI. Why were these guys paid large sums of money?

September 2, 2017

MARC. I have no doubt the alt-left has extremists akin to the neo-Nazis, so the attack against his "both sides" I will let slide for now, and I will concede that the mainstream press might be looking for things to condemn Trump. But I am repulsed by liars and phonies and exploiters. Trump will be proven to be that. When Trump's voice gave rise to some political attention, it was because he felt the same way about Barack Obama as I do about Trump, and he wanted the same fate for him. When it turns out Trump either broke the law or lied in defending himself, he will be removed from office, and those who gave him even tepid support will not look very good. Remember, removing the liar from office does not have the ramification of installing the left in power. But it would result in the unthinkable: it would prove you have been wrong.

STEPHEN. He didn't break any law or lie in defending himself. In the United States, there should be a crime first and an investigation later, not the other way around. Also, it is interesting how the political class is willing to ignore actual crimes—Hillary, Debbie Wasserman Schultz's Pakistani programmers—and pursue witch hunts against Trump.

MARC. He will be shown to have broken laws.

STEPHEN. Really? What laws? What crime?

MARC. Obstruction of justice.

MARC. Income tax evasion.

MARC. Bribery.

STEPHEN. Really? Like I said, a witch hunt. There is no evidence that he has done anything like that. They are looking for a crime.

MARC. Yes, they are.

MARC. Interference with a federal election.

MARC. They are probably going to show he didn't even win the election fairly.

STEPHEN. Are they looking at the DNC? Remember that bearing false witness is a major sin. The DNC may turn out to be an inside job, and the Democrats know it. Wouldn't that be something for those who hate liars and phonies?

MARC. I hate them too then. They should be arrested too! But do you have anything on Jeb Bush or Mitt Romney?

MARC. Either would have been president if the lying showman charlatan hadn't fooled so many people, even smart people like you.

STEPHEN. The public is fed up with the political class, exemplified by the DNC attempting to shove Hillary down our throats. Don't blame people; blame an aloof, entitled, and out-of-touch political class. We'll see if the Democratic and Republican parties have learned anything. It does not appear they have. If they attempt to remove Trump, things will only get worse.

SEPTEMBER 5, 2017

MARC. No doubt you agreed with the president's decision to evict people from the country.

MARC. I, like most people, don't have a great or practical solution to the immigration problem, but most members in his own party think his decree is preposterous.

STEPHEN. DACA was unconstitutional. The president doesn't make laws; Congress does. Congress should pass a law that resolves the problem. Unless, of course, you prefer dictatorship.

MARC. I know at least one person who prefers a dictatorship—that would be Donald Trump.

STEPHEN. I assume you mean Obama, who believed he could unilaterally enact and amend laws if Congress failed to do what he thought it should do.

MARC. Well, in that case, he should have been removed from office, and Trump should be removed from office.

STEPHEN. Obama was lauded as a hero for his disregard for the Constitution; Trump is being condemned for insisting on following the Constitution.

MARC. No. He is being condemned for peeing on a bed with two hookers because Obama slept on it.

MARC. He is being condemned for not unequivocally rebuking white supremacists. Condemned because he called McCain, a man who was crippled as a POW and who could have been released but stayed with his troops, *not* a hero. Condemned because he bragged about grabbing pussy because he is famous. He is disgusting.

MARC. He said he could walk down Fifth Avenue and shoot someone, and his supporters wouldn't care. You are among those he referred to.

STEPHEN. That's total bull. The peeing on the bed never happened. It was concocted by a Democratic opposition research firm. He did repeatedly condemn the white supremacists—watch his news conference. He also told the truth about Antifa. He said something stupid in a private conversation (the *Access Hollywood* tape). I hope you could withstand that scrutiny. I'm not a Trump supporter, but I believe he is the target of the political establishment, a sickening attempt to force him out of office. Notwithstanding his faults, he is doing a much better job than Hillary would have.

MARC. It happened. And when the tape comes out, none of his supporters will waver about the act or the lying about it. He said he didn't know who David Duke was earlier this year.

STEPHEN. You're a sucker.

MARC. I don't need the dossier. I knew he was an ass after his McCain comment, a racist after his ad in the *Post* about the Central Park Five and the birther movement, and a liar after the Ted Cruz JFK crap.

STEPHEN. You don't care if it's true? You don't have to like him or support him, but you should oppose him for things he actually does and says.

MARC. That would be nine-tenths of my observations above.

MARC. By the way, he's not only an asshole, but he is a coward. He pledged he would end DACA, so he should use his power to end it, period. But instead, he is "ending it" to assuage people who will believe that he, in fact, ended it, and, at the same time, telling Congress to figure it out, and when they can't, he will say, "I tried to honor my promise." By the way, I have a joke. After Seattle was destroyed in a hypothetical nuclear attack that left millions dead, CNN would open the show by saying, "Coming up, one of the most horrific events in modern times. But first, some breaking news in the Trump-Russia investigation."

September 16, 2017

Marc. At least your president is steadfast and principled!

Stephen. He's not my president. He's our president.

Marc. Wonder how many times you said that about Obama.

Stephen. I didn't like it, but I accepted the misguided judgment of the voters.

Marc. I know the feeling.

Stephen. There is a difference. In 2012, voters had a decent option. In 2016, they did not.

TRUMP VERSUS THE CLINTONS

STEPHEN. I don't believe that Trump is the rudest or grossest on the planet. He's an egomaniac, but he has many friends. Regardless, there are many public officials who have engaged in disturbing behavior. Do the names Bill and Hillary Clinton ring a bell? The contention that he is burning democracy to the fucking ground is simply baseless. It was his predecessor who regularly ignored the Constitution. You would be more persuasive if you opposed Trump for things he actually does. You can oppose him based on his character (although you appear to be offended by Trump more easily than by others who arguably are clearly worse), competence (a legitimate concern), or policy. But declaring him a terrible human being and conjuring up false accusations is tiresome.

MARC. You have been brainwashed. That's the only explanation. I think Hillary Clinton is arrogant and acts entitled. I do not agree with most of her policies. And I am sure she lied and covered up certain offenses, as do most politicians. I did not want her to win the presidency. That said, she is brilliant, as was Bill, who speeds through the *NYT* crosswords, and she knows how to conduct herself in public. To make the false equivalence of her being just as bad as Trump is as bad as comparing a nascent far-left group (BLM) that arose as a response to longstanding racism with pure evil. I find your stance so upsetting because you should know better. *Nothing* compares to Nazis. Nothing. Including a violent overreaction to evil.

MARC. I accuse him of saying he can grab a woman's pussy. I accuse him of shying away from a consistent and unequivocal denouncement of white supremacy. Are those false?

MARC. I accuse him of being a highly leveraged charlatan. Trump University? His incompetence is implied in all of his statements and actions.

STEPHEN. Hillary is brilliant? Based on what? She is wrong about virtually everything and a liar. Have you ever read anything Hillary wrote that was brilliant? Has she ever given a memorable speech? There are and have been brilliant liberals—think [Senator] Moynihan. She isn't one of them. As for Bill acting appropriately in public, if getting a blow job in the Oval Office, lying under oath, and sexually assaulting women are appropriate behaviors, I guess he's a role model. As for Hillary, smearing Bill's victims is very admirable? As for the media bullshit that Trump didn't condemn white supremacists, you should listen to his news conferences instead of relying on the media. If you believe that pointing out the undeniable fact of left-wing violence, which is a much greater threat than a handful of white supremacists, somehow undermines his condemnation of white supremacists, you have a problem with the truth, not Trump. However, by now, I know that when it comes to Trump, you don't care about the truth.

MARC. I heard everything. He could easily have been declarative in statements against the initial protesters and then, as an aside, said, "By the way, the other side isn't so innocent, but nonetheless, they were provoked by groups who have been historically unparalleled as hate organizations." You are missing the tell that shows pleasing his base was Trump's priority: when he replied, "Who is David Duke?" to Jake Tapper, when he knew full well who he was. As for Clinton, an adulterous president? What! Oh yeah, I see. As singularly astonishing as the afore-referenced Holocaust! I didn't say Bill's public conduct; I said Hillary. You referenced Trump's admission to Wharton to validate his intelligence, but when I mention Hillary's academic pedigree, you are not impressed, and if I mention Obama's, you probably assume it was affirmative action.

STEPHEN. I don't care where they went to school. I draw my conclusions from their public records.

MARC. If you have the stomach to watch any extended Hillary interview, you can see she's a pretty intelligent woman, and try hard not to argue that, because there are many thieves and murderers who are brilliant.

STEPHEN. I have heard her speak many times. She speaks in platitudes. She could not identify a single accomplishment as secretary of state. That says it all. I'm not saying she's stupid, but she is not a big or original thinker. She's a self-important narcissist.

MARC. Agreed.

MARC. When Trump ran and said, "When I am president, we are going to do lots of winning," I suppose you got excited and said, "Yes! We are going to win now!"

MARC. And you probably said, "Yes, build that giant wall, because that will stop immigrants! Yes!"

MARC. You probably got your wife to come over and join the rally crowd yelling, "Lock her up! Lock her up!"

MARC. In reality, you probably had none of those reactions, because those were the tools he used to get millions of gullible people to vote for him.

STEPHEN. Trump was not my choice in the Republican primaries. However, I appreciate that he can say "radical Islamic terrorism." I also appreciate that he recognizes that the Iran deal is a disaster and that Israel and Britain are allies. I'm glad his administration is rescinding the assaults on civil rights made by the Obama EPA and Education Department (the Obama rule that male college students accused of assault are not permitted due process). People voted for Trump because mainstream politicians think they are a "basket of deplorables" because they don't believe in climate change, transgender bathrooms, and so on. You are just as elitist as Hillary if you think Trump fooled anyone. He simply did not mock their worldview and call them racists.

MARC. You can say all of that, and it would apply to any Republican. What you can't yet see, which is staring me in the face daily, is that, unfortunately, there is a healthy bloc of people who voted for Trump but know very little about what the party stood for and only understand that poor whites should be on top again. These people hate rich New York Jews, and you can't tell me I am wrong, because you don't know them.

Marc. But I will concede that he revealed cowards, such as Steve King and most other politicians.

Stephen. The people who voted for Hillary are as parochial, knowledgeable, and self-interested as the Trump voters.

Stephen. Occupy Wall Street and Antifa are not fans of the Jews.

Marc. You had me at parochial.

September 17, 2017

Marc. Check out the video of Trump hitting Hillary in the back with a golf ball and knocking her over. You know, the one Trump just shared with millions of people. You will probably get a good chuckle about it. You think there won't be any supporters who interpret that as condoning violence?

EVALUATING TRUMP

October 1, 2017

MARC. Trump is a complete and absolute jerk, with supporters who will, for years, have to explain away how they didn't condemn him.

STEPHEN. "Trump is an asshole" is not a compelling argument. There are many politicians who are bigger jerks. Even if he is a jerk, you have to look at events on the merits, not Trump's position on them. For example, do you judge Josh McCown [New York Jets quarterback] on your preconceived notions or his actual performance?

MARC. To constantly tweet about his own importance—that doesn't bother you?

STEPHEN. Yes. However, Trump is Trump. He is the most transparent president, even if he often is a blowhard. I would like someone who, like Trump, does not speak in politician/diplomat speak but who does it in a more sophisticated way.

October 9, 2017

MARC. So I guess you think Senator Bob Corker is completely wrong.

STEPHEN. The political class—Republican as well as Democrat—oppose Trump. That is the source of his appeal to many. If I knew more about Corker, I would like him. However, the claims of any Trump opponent will be given credence over any response from Trump. I know you don't accept it, but many allegations made by Trump have proven to be true. Conversations at Trump Tower were intercepted. Comey did tell him he was not under investigation. Trump is bombastic, but he is not always wrong.

MARC. Nobody is always wrong. The group of pure Trump supporters is shrinking and starting to align with the more reasonable Republicans who see him as inept. Completely inept. You still cannot admit that. You, Stephen, consider yourself among middle Americans who are antiestablishment? Are you antiestablishment? I don't think so. The establishment is pretty good to you. You are part of the establishment. You just want lower taxes and strong Israel with such fervor that you are blind to what's happening.

October 11, 2017

MARC. When he is out of office, Trump can write a column on ethics and the press and be like a new William Buckley.

MARC. He wants to remove the license of the station CNN because they reported negatively on him. This is a guy who accuses people of things all the time! Including standing presidents.

STEPHEN. I think his intent is clear. However, you're consistent. You just want to attack him, and if you can construe something he says negatively, even if it's clearly not true, you do it. The FCC is not going to pull NBC's license, nor is Trump going attempt to make the FCC do it. He is correct that the media has faced virtually no consequences, other than a loss of credibility, for its extremely poor reporting on Trump. The Democrats and academia are the real threat to free speech. Democratic politicians sought to prevent Chick-fil-A from opening locations in Boston, Chicago, and New York because the owner made a personal donation to a group opposing gay marriage. Where was Joe Scarborough's outrage? When conservative speakers are prevented from speaking, where is the outrage? You don't make arguments; you just scream, "Trump!"

MARC. Intent is clear? Even Jason Miller, his TV shill, said he has to disagree with his statement. But for Stephen Barry, it's clear.

STEPHEN. I don't think it was a great statement, but I believe that my understanding is correct. Jason Miller is entitled to his opinion. I would be glad to debate him if you could set it up.

MARC. You can't even beat *me* in a debate. I won at "He was captured. I like people who weren't captured."

STEPHEN. You made a good decision to go to medical school. If your point is that Trump can be a dick, that's true. However, the fact that he has said outrageous things does not prove he's against free speech or many other things he is accused of.

MARC. Ha!

SEXUAL MISCONDUCT

October 24, 2017

Marc. Still think Trump is doing a fine job? The guy is disgusting and ineffective. A cancer on our country. I hate that I am right about this.

Stephen. What has he done today?

Marc. It's mounting. Nothing new. It's not even partisan now. Corker and Flake are *your* party, and they can't stand him.

Stephen. Actually, Trump is becoming more effective. I find it amusing that you cite Corker and Flake in support of your contention that Trump is disgusting and ineffective. I don't know much about either of them, but I'm certain that I agree with them on many issues. However, their decision not to seek reelection speaks to their lack of effectiveness, not Trump's. I also believe that if there is a Russia scandal, it is the Uranium One deal. Hillary says it was debunked, but I have not seen evidence of the debunking. The Obama administration approved the sale of 20 percent of US uranium interests to a Russian-controlled company while Hillary was secretary of state. The Clinton Foundation reportedely received over $100 million in donations from Russian oligarchs around the same time the State Department approved the deal in 2010. It is finally being investigated. Finally, many of the same people who refer to Trump as a sexual predator (although, to my knowledge, no one has made harassment claims against him) were friends of Harvey Weinstein, who appears to be a real predator, and Bill Clinton. What makes Trump worse?

October 25, 2017

Marc. Great point, sure. I guess you are correct: Trump, who bragged about being a sexually abusive person, is not worse than someone who merely *knows* a sex abuser. I'll give you that one. By the way, I unearthed a report you wrote in sixth grade: "Why Richard Nixon Was the Best President."

Marc. Let me ask you something: Do you think the people who took money from Harvey Weinstein or supported him by attending events should have listened to the rumors about him that were rampant? Or if they knew about his settlements, should that have supported the whispers of what had been said or even reported without much publicity?

Stephen. My point is that you don't know that Trump is sexually abusive. All you know is that he is sophomoric and uncouth. Weinstein appears to be a predator. A lot of people who find Trump unbearable and assume the worst about him were willing to overlook rumors and stories about Weinstein because they share his politics. They now are outraged by Weinstein's conduct because they have been exposed as hypocrites. If Trump did what Weinstein did, he would not be fit to hold office. However, Trump, notwithstanding his need to brag about everything, including his sexual prowess, is not accused of abusing women—unlike Bill Clinton. The former CEO of NPR took one year off to meet Republicans throughout the United States. He wrote a book about it. You should pick it up.

Marc. Bill Maher said that if you want to know how Trump will handle a matter, ask yourself, "What would a dick do?"

Stephen. Bill Maher can be funny. I agree that's funny. It's also true for Hillary, Bill de Blasio, Andrew Cuomo, and many others.

Marc. It's so funny how Trumpers refute allegations and then cite as credible the same allegations against others. Or dismiss news organizations as not trustworthy and then cite the same company's story when it suits them.

STEPHEN. It is the *Washington Post,* and it is specific.

MARC. CNN too.

STEPHEN. It shows you how solid the evidence is. The *WSJ* and Fox have been reporting it for months.

FUSION GPS

STEPHEN. Did you know that the head of Fusion GPS took the Fifth rather than answer questions at a congressional hearing?

MARC. So this story is solid, but none of those impugning the Trump organization and family are?

MARC. That's not collusion, not even close—nothing like it? But this is collusion?

STEPHEN. No, this is not collusion. This is a smear campaign paid for by Hillary and the DNC. The Trump collusion narrative is unraveling. Open up your eyes. By the way, you can continue to dislike Trump all you want but not because of collusion.

STEPHEN. Actually, Hillary and the DNC collude. They hired Fusion GPS to work with Russians to create the dossier.

SEXUAL MISCONDUCT? RACISM?

October 26, 2017

STEPHEN. I'll comment after I have the chance to look into the allegations. Not flattering.

STEPHEN. I read some of the articles. Frankly, it is hard to believe. He groped a woman who sat next to him in first class over twenty years ago. He groped a woman at a club in New York—it lasted thirty seconds. He walked by a table at a restaurant and commented on which women were not wearing underwear. I'll read them all. However, how easy is it to accuse someone of a fleeting incident twenty years earlier? Harvey Weinstein and Bill Clinton this is not.

STEPHEN. By the way, I would not be surprised if Trump has made vulgar sexual remarks. He is not a paragon of virtue and has, as you point out, acted with no class on many occasions. That does not make him Harvey or Bill. As we are learning, he has been the target of a vicious campaign orchestrated by Hillary and the Democrats.

October 29, 2017

MARC. I feel like Jews who support the Trump administration would be all rallying behind a policy of ridding the country of Muslims and illegal Mexicans—participating in it, enjoying it—but then all the officials would say, "Okay, now the Jews!" The Jewish response would be "Uh, but wait—we got him elected. Uh, Ivanka's Jewish." It's very simple: if white nationalists support Trump, you shouldn't.

STEPHEN. So if anti-Semitic Occupy Wall Street, BLM, and Antifa support a candidate, I shouldn't? Do you ever make your own decisions, or do you always rely on what others say or do? I don't care what Bob Corker thinks. I don't care that people who today might be called white supremacists supported Reagan. I make up my own mind. Trump is not a racist or anti-Semite. It is a smear.

MARC. Are there racists who support Trump?

MARC. Now, before you ask if there are racists who support Hillary or Obama, I don't want them either. Any racists adamantly support Marco Rubio or Mitt Romney? Don't think so.

STEPHEN. There are millions of voters. Some are racist, some are crazy, and some hold bizarre views. They support candidates across the spectrum. Trump is not, despite Democratic talking points, seeking the support of racists. According to the left, if you support policies they do not agree with, you are a racist. For example, the majority of black voters support voter ID laws. However, according to the Democrats, voter ID laws are racist. Think for yourself!

MARC. I do think for myself. That's why, unlike most Republicans, who follow the party line, I don't.

STEPHEN. No. You argue that I should conclude that Trump is bad because Corker and Flake think he's bad. Now you argue I should think he's bad because white supremacists allegedly support him. That does not move me. I have not seen any evidence that Trump is a racist. I would agree that he's narcissistic and sophomoric. I also agree that he is not familiar with the details of many issues. These are reasons that I question his leadership.

MARC. (1) White supremacists do support him and have been vocal about it; (2) I was against Trump when Corker was kissing his ass; and (3) I didn't say he is a racist. I said that if a racist supports the same person I do, I'm going to think twice. But he probably is a racist, given comments about tacos and Muslims.

MARC. And his ad in the *Post* about the Central Park Five.

STEPHEN. So what? Because the statistically irrelevant white supremacist community probably agrees with Trump's position on illegal immigration, that makes his position wrong? I don't know about his ad about the Central Park Five, but I am skeptical that they should have been released.

MORE MUELLER AND RUSSIAN COLLUSION

October 31, 2017

Marc. If you need help with scripting once Trump resigns, I'm here to help. Not going to end well.

Stephen. Why would Trump resign? The only evidence of collusion implicates the Democrats. It appears they paid millions to Russian agents for dirt on Trump. That's it.

Marc. Have you ever been fairly certain of something without concrete evidence? Ever connected dots? Had the Trump clan admitted the mistake of seeking to influence an election by working with another government, then this whole scandal would have been behind him. I hate liars, as does Bob Mueller. Papadopoulos has been wearing a wire. Others are already arrested. Maybe Sean Hannity and others will risk their reputations for this jerk, but not everyone is going to risk their career. He is toast, and he knows it.

Marc. Trump will not want the whole truth to come out.

Marc. And will want to spare his family. Will say he is quitting as a protest of being treated unfairly.

Stephen. I'll wait for that news to break, but I'm not holding my breath.

RADICAL ISLAMIC TERRORISM AND RACISM

November 1, 2017

Marc. Trump called the New York City terrorist "an animal." Said nothing of the sort for the Vegas shooter. And you say he isn't a racist. Another argument won by me.

Stephen. The Las Vegas shooter had no apparent motive. Trump called the shooting pure evil and called the shooter a sick and demented man. Although we don't know if he was sick and demented, it is a likely explanation. The New York City terrorist committed murder and mayhem in the name of an evil political ideology: radical Islam.

Stephen. Anyone who kills because you don't worship God the way he does is an animal. I don't know how it proves Trump is a racist. At least Trump is willing to point out that Islam is the crucial ingredient.

November 2, 2017

Stephen. It was reported tonight that the terrorist feels good about killing the people he killed. I think that qualifies him as an animal.

Marc. Agreed.

TAX CUTS

November 3, 2017

Marc. Even the tax cut doesn't help me. There is no consolation for Trump as president.

Marc. Or New Yorkers.

Stephen. Tax reform, particularly corporate tax reform, will benefit the country. Ultimately, lower rates and fewer deductions make economic sense. Also, the state and local tax deduction enables states like New York to avoid the full consequences of their irresponsible taxing and spending. The elimination of the deduction may impose discipline on blue states, like New York, New Jersey, California, and Illinois.

Marc. What about me?

Stephen. If the economy booms, you can charge more for your services, as demand will increase. Your taxes will be more rational, and your state and local taxes may be forced down.

Marc. I rationalized my disdain for Trump with thoughts of lower taxes. New York congressmen Peter King and Lee Zeldin, other people who will be indelibly smudged for tacitly approving Trump, will have lots of explaining to do. But I'm sure all the country's Trump fans will reap benefits of the increased death tax exemption, so that when they inherit $6 million or more, as is often the case, it won't be taxed until $12 million.

ROY MOORE

November 10, 2017

MARC. Amazing how certain allegations are given credibility, and some aren't, on the grounds of "Guilty until proven innocent."

STEPHEN. What specifically are you talking about?

MARC. According to Republicans, Weinstein allegations are true, but Roy Moore allegations are fake news.

MARC. Kevin Spacey true, but Roy Moore false.

STEPHEN. Kevin Spacey essentially admitted it; Roy Moore denied it.

MARC. Harvey Weinstein didn't deny?

MARC. Hillary Clinton denies whatever Fox accuses her of.

STEPHEN. You may be right about Roy Moore.

MARC. If smart people like you were vocal when it mattered, Trump would be gone by now. I will take any Republican with principle and decorum. Like a Pence—or anyone, really.

MARC. Smart people with money and power.

STEPHEN. That's not true. The entire Republican establishment opposed Trump, but it was too fractured. Also, Trump is flawed, and Bernie Sanders is flawed, but both of them tapped into a growing resentment of our political leaders. I like Jeb Bush, but I understand why rank and file Republicans revolted. Americans do not want noblesse oblige. On the Democratic side, the party's decision to make an entitled, dishonest, disliked woman of no independent accomplishments the nominee was a disaster.

MARC. Agree on the second part.

REGULATORY REFORM, MORE COLLUSION, JIM COMEY

November 17, 2017

Marc. Any Republican presidency would pursue that. He is a charlatan, a doof, a liar, a thief. Nothing he does should be touted. I hate liars.

Stephen. No one has effectively rolled back the regulatory state since Reagan, and possibly not even Reagan.

Marc. The Bushes were moderates. True?

Marc. It doesn't change the fact that you are backing a horse that is going to be put out to stud next year.

Stephen. If you hate liars, how did you vote for Hillary? Why would he be "put out to stud"? To date, there is not a shred of evidence he has done anything wrong, including alleged sexual misconduct. Several of the women cited by the *NYT* have denied that they made such allegations.

Marc. The cover-up is always worse than the crime. Whether discussing with the Russians about ways to harm Hillary with information was a crime or not, they lied about it. Kushner will be indicted. So will Flynn. And Trump will be shown to have known about discussions with WikiLeaks, which they denied. Also, the story with Flynn is real and significant criminally—conspiracy to commit kidnapping. And Trump asked for that charge to be dropped.

Stephen. No. Discussion with WikiLeaks is not a crime. Nor is denying it in the press.

November 18, 2017

MARC. Kushner, under oath.

STEPHEN. We shall see.

December 3, 2017

MARC. Let me ask you something: Do you think a career law enforcement officer, James Comey, regardless of errors he made, was lying under oath when he said that Trump asked him to see his way clear to ending the investigation on Flynn?

STEPHEN. Yes. Comey went along with calling the FBI investigation into Hillary's emails a "matter," which was a lie. He agreed to exonerate Hillary before the conclusion of the investigation. He oversaw an investigation that made every effort to avoid finding anything wrong (see the article by Andrew McCarthy comparing the conduct of the email investigation and the Russia investigation). He leaked information on his meetings with Trump, which may be a crime. Finally, Trump turned out to be truthful about Comey telling him he was not under investigation. Finally, if the guilty plea is the sum and substance of Flynn's wrongdoing—misleading the FBI about conduct that was absolutely legal and appropriate during a transition—there should have been no investigation at all. I have no confidence in Comey. He expected Hillary to win, and he compromised himself accordingly. I believe he is seeking to cover for a lot of questionable decisions he never expected to have to answer for.

MARC. He publicly states what her errors were.

STEPHEN. He covered for and hedged to protect his reputation because the FBI clearly believed Hillary should have been indicted.

MARC. So Comey made up, and then testified to the falsehood under oath, that Trump twice told him to ease up on the investigation?

Marc. The guy is a career prosecutor of bad guys.

Stephen. Trump did not stop the investigation. He could have ordered Comey to stop the investigation. He did not. Based on everything I said above, it is hard to see how Comey has any credibility on these issues.

Marc. I have a talent then that you lack. I know when someone is telling the truth. If you watch Comey's testimony and don't see it as the truth and you don't believe he was so astounded that he was moved to write down the notes after the meeting, then you are not being rational. Comey is a Republican, by the way!

Stephen. Did the FBI stop the investigation? You have a talent for rationalization.

Marc. They wouldn't be asked to, because that would have been transparent of trying to hide something. It's possible that nothing about Russia was unkosher, but you have to admit that lying about it occurred at all levels, and that is not a good thing.

Stephen. Comey would have lied about telling Trump he was not under investigation if Trump hadn't said his conversations had been taped.

Marc. For you to say that Comey lies under oath takes lots of chutzpah. Are you familiar with his past? He offered his resignation in a prior administration when he thought things weren't done correctly. Would you be insulted if someone said you were lying? Donald Trump has admitted to untruthful statements in the past and continues to lie, maintaining that he wouldn't mock a disabled person, when he did, and saying he is the least racist person in America. Ha!

Stephen. I'm familiar with Comey exonerating Hillary prior to the investigation. Another name for that would be obstruction of justice. I'm familiar with Comey agreeing to call an investigation a "matter"—a lie to protect Hillary. I'm familiar with Comey leaking government documents to damage Trump. Trump's "lies" that you cite are a matter of opinion.

I don't know if he intended to mock the disabled reporter. Regardless, it was in bad taste. Only Trump knows. I don't know if Trump is the least racist person in America, but there is absolutely no reason to believe he is a racist. Opposition to illegal immigration is not racist. Concern over admitting potential jihadists is not racist. The term *racism* is thrown out by the left to avoid debate. To the left, we all are racists the first time we express a view that leftists disagree with.

MARC. You misunderstood. Can you agree with me that Donald Trump is not the least racist person in America? There has to be somebody less racist than him.

STEPHEN. You're not serious. I refer you to *The Brady Bunch* "exact words" episode. Trump's statement was not intended as a statement of fact. He was simply making the point that he is not a racist. He is not.

MARC. Here is what happened: The Trump team spoke with Russia because they had dirt on Hillary. Then they tried to cover it up, and as always, the cover-up is worse than crime.

STEPHEN. That's not what happened. However, Hillary and the DNC paid Russian agents to put together the Steele dossier, which was used to justify surveillance on Trump.

MICHAEL FLYNN

December 4, 2017

Marc. Trump's lawyers are now saying (1) it's okay for Trump to have obstructed justice, and (2) collusion isn't a crime. Both were denied repeatedly, and now?

Stephen. You should be concerned about the investigators. There is no collusion. If Flynn had been involved in crime related to collusion, they would have made him plead guilty to it. This is a naked attempt to force Trump from office. The only evidence of wrongdoing during the campaign are the Hillary email whitewash and the fake Trump dossier. They did not expect Trump to win.

Marc. No, they didn't charge him with the major crime with Turkey because they are holding that charge over his head unless he cooperates. They included in a plank at the convention stuff they promised Russia that was anti-Ukraine.

Stephen. If Flynn was involved in a crime related to collusion, they would have made him plead guilty to it. That would prove there was a crime. Prosecutors hold the guilty plea over the defendant's head: if he doesn't cooperate, he will be sentenced for the crime he pleaded guilty to. However, Flynn pleaded guilty to a bullshit crime for which he likely would receive no sentence without a deal. Does it bother you that Hillary was not questioned under oath for her server and the destruction of emails, but Flynn was questioned under oath about perfectly legal conversations he had with the Russian ambassador? This is a cover-up and a coup.

MARC. Why do you always go to Hillary? Yes. It bothers me about her. They both should be impeached.

MARC. They are playing the long game.

MARC. Lying to the FBI is a bullshit crime?

MORE TRUMP-RUSSIA COLLUSION

STEPHEN. You don't understand. This is a coup. The investigators covered for Hillary. They used the Steele dossier to discredit Trump and to have a basis for surveillance. And yes, Flynn is in trouble because he lied, but he should not have been under investigation. I don't know why he lied, but if he had told the truth, all hell would have broken loose—over completely legal contacts.

MARC. If you are right, then please tell me why Trump is always kissing Putin's ass.

MARC. And if it is a coup, good. Freedom over an autocratic demagogue. "Oh yes, you are the best president, sir."

STEPHEN. Trump was up front about his views on Putin. He is not unusual. Obama kissed Putin's ass and got nothing for it. Who invited Russia into Syria? What do you mean that Trump is autocratic? It seems to me he has much more respect for the role of Congress than his predecessor. The government must obey the law. It did not obey the law during the campaign and is now seeking to cover it up. If Hillary had won, it would have been swept under the rug and ignored by a compliant media. If you think it is good for the United States that a corrupt group of powerful government officials are working to undermine Trump, you are mistaken. It is hard to believe, but Trump is the most honorable person in this drama. If he is removed, kiss equal justice under law goodbye. It will be like Soviet Russia. If you want to work, you will need to shut up and toe the party line. Otherwise, you will risk being ruined. Ask Tea Party groups who were at the mercy of the IRS.

December 5, 2017

MARC. When Trump is impeached and the evidence is undeniable for any rational person, it's going to look terrible for you.

STEPHEN. Evidence of what? You never support your arguments with facts. You seem to believe he should be removed from office because you don't support him and because you think he's crude. You have no problem with government officials abusing the awesome power they have. Mueller is trying to protect Comey and the FBI, and they do not care who they ruin. They are willing to risk a constitutional crisis. Trump can always be removed from office via the next election. How do we get the rule of law back?

MARC. So you are on a higher plane morally than Robert Mueller? Why don't you read his biography?

MARC. Rule of law? Wait till he is indicted. See if he and his sycophants follow that rule.

STEPHEN. What is Trump going to be indicted for? Uncovering the FBI's abuse of power? You want to give Mueller a free pass? Go ahead. I hope you never are on the receiving end of out-of-control prosecutors.

MARC. Mueller is good. Trump is bad. Simple formula. Do you want me to list how Trump is bad? I'll need another phone.

STEPHEN. In this case, Mueller is bad. He is protecting his friends.

MARC. And you always ask me what evidence I have? That is much less likely than my scenario.

STEPHEN. Really? Is Mueller Comey's friend? Did Comey seek Mueller's appointment? Did Comey exonerate Hillary prior to investigating? Did Comey agree to call an investigation a "matter"? Did Comey use the Steele dossier to support surveillance of Trump campaign officials? What about Uranium One? Why did the FBI fail to take action despite an investigation into Putin's involvement? Comey, Mueller, and company never expected to be subject to scrutiny. Now they will be.

MARC. He didn't exonerate her. He impugned her judgment needlessly. Mueller wouldn't compromise his own principles or risk his reputation on lies to cover up. Trump is a proven liar.

STEPHEN. He did exonerate her. She should have been indicted. She broke the law and obstructed justice. That's what destroying evidence—emails and hard drives—amounts to. She wasn't even questioned under oath. If Trump's a liar, what do you call a bad-faith investigation? You apparently support abuse of government power. As your friend, I hope you never are on the receiving end.

MARC. Did you think O. J. was guilty, even though Mark Fuhrman was shown to have made racist comments in his past? The investigation into Hillary, or whatever you want to call it, tainted her and made her lose the election. But since you realize that two wrongs don't make a right, you are now claiming that a Republican Comey and Mueller want her in office. Trump's own monumental mess-ups have put him in this position. One after the other.

STEPHEN. What are his monumental fuckups? Yes, Comey covered for Hillary. If he had not, he would have called the email investigation an "investigation" and would have referred to her conduct as "grossly negligent" as opposed to "extremely careless." He also would have questioned her under oath. In short, she would have been indicted. Furthermore, he would not have used the Steele dossier, which Hillary paid for, to investigate Trump. These are facts (or very well-founded allegations). So yes, Comey wanted Hillary to win or at least expected her to win.

RECOGNIZING JERUSALEM

MARC. More political grandstanding. Let's see if they really move the embassy.

December 6, 2017

STEPHEN. Today's announcement is a step forward for peace. Trump should get credit.

MARC. Unless it's for show and then they don't act on it. It is currently the policy that Jerusalem is the capital, but it kept getting deferred.

STEPHEN. No. The United States has never recognized Jerusalem as Israel's capital. That's why the embassy is in Tel Aviv.

MARC. They never recognized it because although it was stated in 1994 that they would indeed do so, it kept getting pushed off.

BACK TO TRUMP-RUSSIA COLLUSION

MARC. Oh, so this is where your administration is going down: there will be proof of a quid pro quo to take away the sanctions once in office.

MARC. A president who was aided in winning by our country's adversary. Pretty simple.

MARC. Trump brought Bannon into the White House. Bannon is not only a racist but is vociferous in backing Moore, who recently made anti-Semitic comments.

STEPHEN. Why do you think Bannon is a racist? How was Trump aided by Russia? Did the Russians force Hillary to illegally transact business on a private server? Did the Russians force her to transfer US uranium to a Russian company? Oh, they only bribed her. Regarding sanctions, Trump has not removed them. However, he clearly intended to change the approach to Putin, not unlike Obama's and Hillary's reset. Obama pulled missiles out of Poland and the Czech Republic. By the way, the Czech Republic just recognized Jerusalem as Israel's capital.

DECEMBER 9, 2017

STEPHEN. Read "The Long War on Donald Trump," a *WSJ* article.

MARC. There should be a war. He shouldn't be our president.

STEPHEN. He was elected. Does the US Constitution require the approval of the opposition candidate and her supporters in order to take office? Why have an election? Let the smart people appoint the president.

MARC. Obama was elected, and Donald Trump did everything he could to delegitimize him, just as congressional Republicans similarly tried to neutralize him. Only problem was there was nothing potentially criminal. If there had been, it would have been investigated—and hard. Just like Benghazi, which I do believe was related to his administration's failures and possibly deceit. So now it's the Democrats' turn to do the same, and it was Trump's idiocy in firing Comey that led to the special prosecutor. Had he not done that, he wouldn't be in the mess he is in now.

STEPHEN. Trump was not in a position to delegitimize Obama. However, Obama used the power of the federal government to delegitimize Trump. I believe the Obama administration did a lot of illegal things: Fast and Furious, IRS targeting of Tea Party and pro-Israel groups, possibly Uranium One, and the unmasking of US citizens, apparently in connection with Trump, by political appointees. Are you saying Trump's opponents should be permitted to engage in a politically motivated prosecution because he fired Comey? Do you think Comey was justified in leaking documents—a violation of law—because Trump exercised his prerogative to fire him? Should Trump opponents be on the team investigating him? Any story that appears to implicate Trump is rushed onto the air. However, after one year, the only things we have learned implicate Hillary, the Democrats, and the Mueller team.

MARC. Comey leaked because more than you or me, he knows when someone is asking him to subvert the law.

STEPHEN. Then he should have resigned. But Trump never asked him to subvert the law. The only one who did was Loretta Lynch.

MARC. You keep referring to past deeds of other people. Not sure why. It's all you have. Trump attempted to obstruct justice at the very least and probably sold the country out, promising to reverse the sanctions on Russia.

MARC. And Mueller and Comey have already proven, with their life's work, more honor than either one of us, so you shouldn't impugn them. Obama was an opportunist and a bit phony. Hillary was entitled, riding on the coattails of Bill. But Mueller and Comey—they are honorable and respected *and* Republicans.

STEPHEN. That's all I have? You referred to Obama, not me. I have given detailed support for my position. The only basis for your position is that you don't like him, and other people also don't like him. You believe that after he won the election, he promised to reverse the sanctions. There is no evidence that he did, but so what? He has the right to implement different policies. He has not, in fact, reversed the sanctions. He has decertified the Iran deal (talk about selling out the country). He has imposed sanctions on North Korea (another Obama failure).

MARC. No Obama fan here. But if Mueller finds bad stuff and then you drink the Kool-Aid that he somehow made it all up, I'll be disheartened. There *is* bias against Trump, but dedicated servants don't fabricate evidence.

MARC. Did you think Mark Fuhrman was a racist but still believe O. J. was guilty?

STEPHEN. As to Mueller and Comey, time will tell. All I know is that the investigation into Trump has been conducted very aggressively, in sharp contrast to the investigation into Hillary. It also appears the FBI used the Steele dossier, which was paid for by Hillary, as a basis for investigating Trump. To date, Mueller has found nothing. That's because the investigation is based on a fraudulent document paid for by Trump's opponents. Comey never thought Trump would win.

MARC. How do you know he has found nothing?

MARC. The investigation is based on the fact that Trump fired Comey.

MARC. Jay Sekulow and Stephen Barry: "He hasn't found anything, because the press hasn't reported on it, and there haven't been any more leaks. So that proves it!"

STEPHEN. The investigation is based on the false theory that Trump colluded with the Russians. It was ongoing during the campaign, apparently based on the Steele dossier. The Obama administration used the Steele dossier to put members of Trump's team under surveillance. It morphed into an investigation into Flynn's contacts with the Russian ambassador after the election—contacts that are customary and perfectly legal. The special counsel was appointed because Comey was fired (and Sessions had to recuse himself because he worked on the campaign), but these baseless charges against Trump appear to arise out of the Steele dossier, which led to the FISA warrant and the illegal unmasking. We know that he hasn't found any conspiracy yet. He has indicted Manafort and obtained guilty pleas on issues that have nothing to do with Russian collusion. The press would do anything to report evidence of collusion. They keep shooting themselves in the foot trying but have not found anything. So in your opinion, the fact that there is an investigation proves there is a crime? That's scary. Particularly for an investigation based on a fraudulent document commissioned by Trump's opponents.

MARC. So the fact that Flynn pleaded guilty is immaterial because of the means of how they gathered evidence? Are you the new Snowden? Don't fuck up, and you won't get caught.

MARC. I would never say that a crime was committed by anyone other than those who pleaded. I am saying I believe there will be evidence that unravels.

MARC. New crime. Jeter went undercover to help the Yankees.

STEPHEN. Flynn lied and pleaded guilty. He should not have lied. However, he shouldn't have been questioned for his actions during the transition. The same people who questioned Hillary and her lieutenants without putting them under oath, even though she had lied repeatedly about her server, put Flynn under oath for legal activity. There is no evidence of a crime (that wasn't created at the request of Hillary). Typically, an investigation follows the crime. Investigations are not conducted to look for crimes. The only reason you believe Mueller will find evidence of a crime is because you don't like Trump. How would you like it if the government started investigating you to see if you have ever committed a crime?

MARC. If I asked the police to stop investigating something close to me and, when they didn't, fired them, I would understand the suspicion that would be heightened.

STEPHEN. Trump asked Comey to repeat publicly what he admittedly stated privately: that Trump was not a target. In your case, it might be different if the police worked for you, as Comey worked for Trump.

MARC. Why is he asking anything?

STEPHEN. Why not? If Comey told him privately he was not under investigation, why not say it publicly? The Democrats were using the allegations to discredit Trump. Why should Trump be under a cloud if the allegations had no merit? I believe that Comey would have lied if Trump had not suggested he had taped the conversation.

December 10, 2017

STEPHEN. Where's the beef?

MARC. I didn't write the law, but according to it, you can't work with an adversarial country to affect an election.

STEPHEN. Where is the evidence? That's what the investigation is looking for but has yet to produce.

MARC. There's evidence of the first two things on the list.

STEPHEN. What evidence exists that the Russians offered help? What evidence exists that the campaign accepted help? I have not read about it.

MARC. The email to Trump Jr.!

MARC. The WikiLeaks offer.

STEPHEN. That has been retracted. He received the email after WikiLeaks disclosed it publicly. The person who emailed the campaign pointed to publicly disclosed information. Nor is there any evidence that the campaign reacted to the email. CNN apologized to Trump for the false and misleading suggestion that the campaign was given advance notice.

STEPHEN. Mueller may be an honest man. I hope he is. However, there are valid questions about why he chose the people he chose for the investigation. There are questions about the FBI's role in exonerating Hillary Clinton, the use of the Steele dossier, the fact that Hillary and Cheryl Mills were not questioned under oath notwithstanding publicly exposed lies over the server, the fact that Flynn was questioned under oath, the fact that Hillary's lieutenants were not subpoenaed and were granted immunity in exchange for nothing, and the fact that Paul Manafort's home was raided in the middle of the night by Mueller's team. Does the FBI have different rules for investigating Democrats than it does for Republicans? For Trump? This is why I question Mueller. Furthermore, Mueller has an unlimited budget. A team of partisan prosecutors with an unlimited budget can be very dangerous.

DECEMBER 12, 2017

MARC. Rex Tillerson says Russia interfered in the election.

STEPHEN. So? That's what Mueller is supposed to be investigating. The investigation technically is a counterintelligence investigation, not a criminal investigation. There have been intelligence assessments that Russia interfered—no real determination as to how. No evidence that the Trump campaign was involved in any way, which is the only thing the anti-Trump people care about. I note that the Obama administration interfered in Israel's election. He provided support to Netanyahu's opponent. It didn't work.

TRUMP, PROPRIETY, AND THE UNHINGED OPPOSITION

Marc. Doesn't it bother you that Trump repeatedly tweets misogynistically? Gillibrand "begs for it" and will do anything for money? Megyn Kelly with "blood coming out of her wherever"?

Stephen. Not proven. Trump is not always a class act. I still prefer him to Clinton.

Marc. Do you prefer him to Pence, Ryan, or any Republican in the Senate?

Stephen. No. I would prefer Pence or most other Republicans. However, Trump won, and they did not.

Marc. Rick Santorum just begrudgingly said that Trump's continual attacks on others are debilitating. This is all I am saying. You can't say you like decent people like Pence and others and at the same time refuse to clearly repudiate Trump. *USA Today* is generally nonpartisan, and they completely roasted Trump today, saying he couldn't clean the shoes of George Bush. And Bannon took the party, and Trump, down with him.

December 13, 2017

Stephen. That's not what you have been saying. I missed it. You think he stole the election, he's a reprehensible person, and he's unqualified. I can refuse to repudiate Trump. He won fair and square. The attacks on him are unhinged. He was not my choice, but I want him to succeed and do not believe he has done anything to warrant even a discussion about being removed from office.

Marc. I don't think he stole the election. The other two things, yes, that's what I think. The attacks are unhinged and hysterical because we all see what you can't.

Marc. You and others can't, and it's frustrating.

Marc. It is so clear to us that he is beyond unqualified that our being unhinged would be similar to your state of mind if you were to travel back in time to early Nazi Germany and had your warnings about Hitler fall on deaf ears.

ANTI-SEMITISM

MARC. This is who you align with. Why don't you come over to the side of people who believe in freedom and modern thinking? And no, blacks don't hate Jews like the average person in the Bible Belt does.

STEPHEN. The Bible Belt loves the Jews. I know many conservative Christians. They believe God blesses those who bless the Jews. It was conservative Christians who fought for the recognition of Jerusalem. When Occupy Wall Street was encamped at Zuccotti Park, many people there were spewing virulent anti-Semitism. Today the real threat of anti-Semitism is on the left. *Unhinged* means "not connected to reality." If you acknowledge that you are unhinged and hysterical, you are proving my point. You oppose Trump because you don't respect him, not because he has done anything as president that warrants the unhinged opposition.

MARC. One can be unhinged and hysterical and correct. If a person had a son murdered, and the assailant was found innocent, might the father act unhinged and hysterical in protestation?

MARC. Regarding Hitler, the Barry of the time would reply, "He was elected and deserves a chance to govern."

STEPHEN. That's why you are unhinged. Trump is not Hitler. Nor has he done or proposed anything that is remotely related to Hitler or the Nazis. If you believe that Trump is comparable to Hitler, nothing you say about him should be taken seriously.

MARC. I am not aligning the magnitude of their evil. The comparison is to the point that some people probably saw Hitler for what he was very early, before evidence, while others defended him as elected and entitled to power. I believe Trump is quite capable of murdering the rule of law as well as the reputation of the presidency and our country.

STEPHEN. This is a cop-out. Trump has done nothing to threaten the rule of law. In fact, he is undoing some of the damage caused by Obama. More importantly, if you reference Hitler, you are suggesting he is a lawless, murderous dictator. I agree your concern that he is harming the reputation of the presidency can be supported. However, that is a reason for opposing his reelection, not removing him from office.

THE RULE OF LAW

MARC. Firing the FBI chief, whom he previously had praised, because the chief refused to stop an investigation into his team is not only threatening the rule of law but also will be his downfall.

STEPHEN. No, it isn't. He had the legal right to fire him and to stop the investigation. He fired Comey but did not stop the investigation. It appears to me that he has more respect for the rule of law than his predecessor, who, at best, let the IRS off the hook for targeting conservatives and conducted a sham investigation into Hillary's emails (they gave sixteen witnesses immunity and drafted a statement exonerating her without interviewing her or any of the witnesses given immunity).

MARC. You will like this. I haven't respected the Republicans' tacit approval of Trump, but now I can root for them again in their fight against Bannon.

STEPHEN. Have you seen the Peter Strzok text messages? There is one in which he said, prior to the election, that he would have liked to believe that Trump could not win the election but that we "need an insurance policy." What do you think he meant?

MARC. It meant they already knew, like most people, that Trump was a bad, bad person probably owing money for years of financing to Russians, who are probably blackmailing him, and just in case people in this county voted him in, the initial sniffs of the investigation would end up playing out as a removal from office. You never consider that the FBI already knew he had some compromises, and that's where the bias arose from. Also, cops and detectives always have biases, just like you do.

STEPHEN. I just saw an interview with Alan Dershowitz. He believes that the emails evidence bias, and the defendants who have been indicted and pleaded guilty have grounds for having the indictments and pleas thrown out. Your explanation of the text makes no sense. The full text appears to express his desire to make sure Trump is not elected. That is not the role of the FBI. It is shocking.

MARC. Shocking is that you, unlike most educated people, do anything but express loathing for Donald Trump.

STEPHEN. You don't care about the rule of law. You just want Trump out. Be careful what you ask for.

MARC. Genie, with my one wish, I want Trump out of office.

STEPHEN. I hope you're never on the wrong side of the government. Especially if the government is lawless.

DECEMBER 14, 2017

MARC. By the way, would you say Republicans had a mission to get Bill Clinton out of office? Travelgate?

STEPHEN. Bill Clinton committed perjury and was disbarred. I happen to like him, but he is a money-grubbing sex addict—possibly a rapist.

MARC. Definitely a rapist. But they had it out for him before anything was proven. I'm reading the Toobin book on it. It was not a "vast right-wing conspiracy," but they were definitely smelling blood and wanted him out. Not that different from now.

STEPHEN. Very different. The Republicans did not use the government to whitewash criminal activity and gin up an investigation into a fake narrative. Clinton actually did the things that got him in trouble.

MARC. It may not be so fake this time.

STEPHEN. What's not fake is that FBI officials were discussing insurance against a Trump victory. This could be the most serious crime against our electoral system ever committed.

MARC. If he was guilty of something illegal, it doesn't matter what they wanted to do. They may have looked harder or more diligently, but they aren't going to make shit up, just like you didn't doubt Mark Fuhrman in the O. J. case.

STEPHEN. He wasn't guilty of anything illegal. We know that because—even today, more than a year later—no evidence of a crime has surfaced, nor has he been charged with a crime. It is not their job to provide "insurance" that a candidate does not win. Furthermore, the emails demonstrate that Strzok hated Trump. There is no mention that he even suspects a crime. Did you skip civics in high school?

MARC. I must have missed the lesson where the investigators give progress updates to the public on what has been established.

STEPHEN. You missed the lesson in which an FBI agent does not get to determine that a candidate—who is not even being investigated for a crime—should not be permitted to win or that a candidate—who the FBI agent apparently believes is guilty of a crime—should be exonerated for her crimes because he wants her to win.

MARC. If he wanted her to win, why, the week before the election, did he announce that she was under investigation?

STEPHEN. I'm talking about Peter Strzok. Regarding Comey, that's a good question. My guess is that he was covering his ass. He reexonerated her quickly.

MARC. Maybe you are right on this one, but you are naive if you think agents aren't affected by their bias and also naive if you think there is no one in that old boys' club who disliked an outsider like Trump, but also disliked Obama and looked for stuff on him following that bias.

STEPHEN. The FBI did not investigate Obama. In fact, it appears a lot was swept under the rug: Fast and Furious, IRS targeting, this Trump surveillance, and unmasking. Not liking someone is one thing. Bias—allowing your views to affect your judgment—is another. Providing "insurance" would be a major crime.

GOVERNMENT ABUSE OF POWER

MARC. Funny how you are so indignant about Trump's rights. Or are you trying to temper what might come out?

STEPHEN. I'm indignant about abuse of power by the government. It is very disheartening. It is not only about Trump's rights. It's about the confidence that the government does not use investigations and prosecutions for political purposes. Should you be audited, investigated, or prosecuted because certain government officials disagree with you? Or do you want to live in a free country?

MARC. I want free.

MARC. Free of Donald Trump!

STEPHEN. Campaign for his opponents in the next election. Start an anti-Trump PAC. I hope you will remain free to do so, as Trump's supporters should be able to support him.

MORE ON SEXUAL MISCONDUCT ALLEGATIONS

MARC. Yes or no: Do you think even one of the twelve woman who've charged Trump with abuse might actually be telling the truth?

STEPHEN. I have no idea.

MARC. So you think it is likely that they all were part of a plot, all exposing themselves to legal action for slander?

STEPHEN. No. I don't know anything about the allegations, the accusers, or, for that matter, how Trump conducts himself. I wouldn't be shocked if he was inappropriate with one or more women. I also wouldn't be shocked if these women aren't telling the truth, or at least the complete truth. They are being encouraged to make claims against him.

DECEMBER 15, 2017

STEPHEN. I just heard a report that Attorney Lisa Bloom, the daughter of Gloria Allred, who supposedly is a feminist attorney (but she represented Harvey Weinstein), was raising money to pay women to make claims against Trump. Interesting, no?

MARC. No, she was just trying to enrich herself.

FBI MISCONDUCT

MARC. You always talk about evidence, but there's absolutely no evidence that any bias affected the performance of the FBI in the investigation against Donald Trump.

STEPHEN. No? One investigator on the team had previously sent a text stating that the FBI leadership had an insurance policy against Trump's election. An attorney on the team congratulated Sally Yates for insubordination. If that's not evidence of bias, I don't know what is. If you were—God forbid—sued for malpractice, would you want jurors who had sent texts saying that you should have your license taken away?

MARC. As a lawyer, you should be more careful in reading what I said. I acknowledge that there was bias. I said there's no evidence that the bias affected the performance. Did you think O. J. was framed by Mark Fuhrman because Fuhrman was racist?

STEPHEN. That's ridiculous. If there is bias, the performance cannot be credible.

MARC. That's ridiculous.

MARC. So O. J. deserved to be found innocent?

STEPHEN. Your arguments don't deserve a response. They are not serious.

MARC. There is one missing link here. Neither you nor I have knowledge of what evidence has been collected. Please admit to me that it is possible there could in fact be evidence unearthed that would be so compelling that it would not be tainted by any latent bias. Correct? And of course, there might not be anything of the sort.

MARC. It's quite possible that all they did was try to cover up and lie about pseudoimproper discussions with Russia, and that's it, and that would be pretty much nothing, I concede.

STEPHEN. There is direct evidence that Peter Strzok was committed to preventing Trump from being elected. It appears the FBI leadership agreed not to conduct a real investigation of Hillary. It also appears the FBI leadership were working with Fusion GPS. Anyone involved in any of this should not only be nowhere near any investigation into Trump—an investigation they might have instigated—but should be under criminal investigation. Mueller agreed the texts threatened the credibility of the investigation. That is why he fired Strzok and withheld the info from Congress.

MARC. Good job by Mueller. It's good that the investigation is under such capable and steady guidance.

CONSPIRACY THEORIES ABOUT RUSSIAN BANKS

MARC. I think Trump was bailed out by Russian banks in the '80s, and that greatly compromised him in this position.

STEPHEN. The Soviet Union bailed out Trump?

MARC. Putin and the banks and the surviving oligarchs melded into a mafia state.

STEPHEN. If Russian banks bailed out Trump in the early '90s, explain how that compromises Trump. Did millions of dollars of donations by Russians to the Clintons compromise Hillary?

MARC. Yes, it did, and if she were president, I would have to look at that situation harder.

MARC. He is in debt to them. Hence no tax returns.

STEPHEN. He is in debt to Putin? I think you should bring your case to CNN.

MARC. Yes, he is. They have the pee tape.

MARC. There is no evidence to say there is no pee tape.

STEPHEN. Inspector Marc "Clouseau" Lieberman.

TRUMP'S PROGRESS

December 23, 2017

STEPHEN. https://www.commentarymagazine.com/foreign-policy/the-death-rattle-of-obamas-foreign-policy-record-susan-rice/.

STEPHEN. This should be very enlightening for you.

MARC. Obama had a terrible administration.

STEPHEN. And you voted to continue it, except with an even worse leader.

MARC. Yes. Trump and his obsequious minions kissing his ring are much more disgusting.

STEPHEN. I don't know what that means, but I know we will have economic growth, we will support Israel without apology, we will speak the truth at the United Nations, we will reduce the regulatory stranglehold that the federal government has over us, and more.

MARC. All things that would have been done with another Republican aside from Trump and will continue to be done once he's out of office.

STEPHEN. No, none of it would have happened if Hillary had been elected. No other candidate would have recognized Jerusalem. No other candidate would have permitted our UN ambassador to speak the truth like Nikki Haley. No other candidate would have had as much success with China on North Korea because no other candidate would have threatened to destroy North Korea.

STEPHEN. The other candidates I'm talking about are the Republicans. Tax reform probably would have happened, but the massive deregulation would not have. Conservative judges would have been appointed. Trump is different.

MARC. Trump is the architect of none of this.

MARC. No doubt he has smart people, the same that any Republican would have had.

December 24, 2017

STEPHEN. He is doing it. No one else would be. It's sad that you preferred Hillary, who would have doubled down on Obama's delusional, damaging, and dishonest policies.

MARC. I don't think she would have. She would have been centrist like Bill.

STEPHEN. She always was to the left of Bill, and Sanders pushed her further left. In any event, no Gorsuch, no deregulation, no tax reform, more pressure on Israel, more FBI and IRS abuse of power, no investigation into Obama outrages, no 3-percent-plus economic growth.

MARC. All the eventualities you listed under a hypothetical Clinton—none of those are true under Jeb Bush. And he would have united the country more for certain than Trump.

PUTIN

MARC. Do you believe that Putin is vicious and evil and has stolen millions of dollars from corruption?

STEPHEN. Bush would have been far better than Clinton. I would have preferred him. However, I have to acknowledge that he would have been much less direct about North Korea, the United Nations, Israel, deregulation, and so on.

MARC. Do you believe that Putin is vicious and evil and has stolen millions of dollars from corruption?

MARC. I had you at *do*.

STEPHEN. Putin is a gangster.

MOVING THE US EMBASSY TO JERUSALEM

MARC. There is saying stupid things, and then there is being a complete POS.

STEPHEN. I'm not sure why Trump's comments make him a complete POS. We all will be better off. This reform and the related deregulation will allow business to generate wealth. On an individual level, the tax reform is relatively modest for the top earners. It will hurt me. Do you consider Peter Strzok or Andrew McCabe a POS for abusing their power? They are the ones who are anti-American.

DECEMBER 27, 2017

MARC. So you think the naming of a landmark in Israel after Donald Trump was a unilateral offer from Israel? Ha!

STEPHEN. What is your point? The Israelis are grateful. They should be. All Jews should be, even those who otherwise hate Trump.

MARC. What he did still is not vested or actual. Anyone can say anything. The embassy isn't moving so fast and probably won't even be. But the larger point is that he only does things, all things, for himself. He said, "If I do this, I want a monument."

STEPHEN. It is undeniable that he has his downside. Harry Truman referred to New York as a "kike town" and was the first person to recognize Israel. Which is more important?

MARC. I will admit that I could back a jerk, depending on future events. Even him. If he blew away a tormenting country, for example. I am not all liberal.

STEPHEN. The embassy will move to Jerusalem. Trump's announcement put the Palestinians on notice that he is not going to be cowed by their threats. More importantly, the lack of reaction from Arab states who are working with Israel more closely than ever sends the Palestinians the message that they should stop dreaming of destroying Israel.

MARC. Okay, this I like!

WHO IS THE DICTATOR?

December 29, 2017

Marc. Your guy believes he can do whatever he wants with the Justice Department. I enjoy living in a democracy. Do you? Maybe you just want some low-tax pro-Israel dictator?

Stephen. You seem to have things backward. First, the president is the head of the executive branch, which includes the Justice Department. The Justice Department reports to and is subject to the direction and control of the president. The president is and should be accountable for the conduct of the Justice Department. This is not controversial, and it is democratic. Second, it was Trump's predecessor who abused the awesome power of the Justice Department. Obama politicized justice. The IRS was given a free pass. Hillary was given a free pass after Obama expressed his opinion that Hillary did nothing wrong—that could be characterized as obstruction of justice. How about fining businesses to fund left-wing groups? Sessions is restoring respect for the law. Or restoring respect for democracy.

Marc. Are you citing Obama's transgressions to mitigate the same ones Trump committed? They all do it? Because if you aren't, then citing them has no pertinence. If I said to you, "Is [former Major League Baseball player] Jim Leyritz guilty of drunk driving?" then you would say, "No, but you know who is? Ted Kennedy."

Stephen. No. Trump is doing the opposite. The Trump Justice Department—to the extent in his control—is restoring respect for the law. He is not using it to shake down his political opponents. I cited Obama to point out that your allegations are baseless with respect to Trump. However, it would have been useful if more people had expressed outrage over Obama's abuses. If they had, Trump might not have been elected. Furthermore, you call Trump a dictator but apparently do not know any relevant facts. If you did, you would know that he is restoring democracy, not threatening it. If you are concerned about dictatorship, you should be very grateful that Trump won.

MARC. You cited Obama to point out that my allegations against Trump are baseless. Got it.

STEPHEN. Obama is a better example of a dictator; Trump is not.

MARC. Dictators build and ask for monuments to be built in their own name. And they demean and even harm journalists. And they brag about their own accomplishments.

DECEMBER 30, 2017

STEPHEN. Dictators ignore constitutional restraints on their authority, such as making or amending laws without congressional authority—DACA, Title IX "guidance" on sexual harassment, delaying or suspending provisions in Obamacare. Dictators use the power of the government to favor their friends and harm their opponents—IRS abuse, Hillary's emails, the Trump-Russia investigation, illegally funneling money received by fining business to left-wing groups (funds not appropriated by Congress). All these examples are things that put your freedom at risk. Regarding journalists, Obama used the power of the government to spy on journalists. Look up James Rosen. There were others. Being a braggart is not being a dictator. Attacking a press corps that is out to get you and often proven wrong in the process is not an attack on freedom of the press; spying on journalists is. You don't like Trump because you believe his manner of speaking, bragging, hyperbole, and nasty personal attacks are beneath the dignity of his office. I understand your feelings. However, because you have a defensible low opinion of him does not mean he's a dictator. He has reversed Obama's dictatorial practices and has much more respect for the Constitution. Obama was a much greater threat to democracy because the adoring mainstream press shared his goals and overlooked his abuses of power. That's how dictatorship arises.

MARC. Are you correlating executive orders with dictatorship?

STEPHEN. Do you even read what I say? I gave you a number of examples that have nothing to do with executive orders.

STEPHEN. Furthermore, executive orders that go beyond legal authority are lawless.

MARC. You are pointing out examples from eight years. In one year, I have many. Many of the things you wrote are characteristic of presidential administrations. You just don't hear about them.

STEPHEN. Give me one real example of the Trump administration ignoring Congress, spying on journalists, abusing the IRS's power, spending unauthorized funds, or doing something equivalent.

MARC. The evidence isn't out yet, but he is spying on many people, because that's what he does: blackmail people.

STEPHEN. I asked for one real fact, and you provide baseless speculation. Name one person the government is allegedly illegally spying on at Trump's direction.

MARC. How would anyone know that at this point? You can't just take one thing that Obama did and use that as the barometer. Can you tell me one time when Obama twice asked the FBI director to ease up on an investigation and then fired him when he didn't get the response he wanted?

MARC. Trump is friends with Robert Kraft. Nuff said.

STEPHEN. I gave you examples of systematic disregard for the Constitution by Obama. Real threats to our freedom. Obama weighed in on ongoing investigations. He publicly stated that there was no evidence of wrongdoing at the IRS. He indicated that Hillary did nothing wrong, and coincidentally, the DOJ exonerated her prior to investigating. Trump fired Comey—a perfectly legal action—because Comey refused to say publicly what he admittedly said privately. However, Trump did not terminate any ongoing investigations, all of which have continued.

MORE ON TAXES

MARC. Would you read something sent from the *Washington Post* or CNN? I'm paying $25,000 *more* in taxes this year. He is a bait-and-switch carnival huckster.

MARC. And he ruined the Republican Party. He ran on helping the average guy and on bullshit things like the wall.

STEPHEN. Yes. I do read articles from the *Washington Post*. I have a subscription to the *New Republic*, which is very liberal. Tax reform will help the average guy. Our tax problem is that New York is the tax capital of America. The wall is not bullshit—ask Israel.

STEPHEN. Also, we will begin to see the results of corporate tax reform in 2018. A lot of corporate money—American and foreign—should be invested in the United States. If this happens, Trump will be a two-term president.

MARC. I'm not sure it will remain "the economy, stupid," as Carville coined. Especially if Trump is impugned in some fashion, but maybe someone else comes in and continues whatever aspects of Trump's tenure were successful and popular.

THE PAPADOPOULOS STORY

MARC. The dossier wasn't what opened the FBI investigation. Report today: Papadopoulos got drunk and spilled beans. In the news today.

STEPHEN. It appears the dossier was the source document for the investigation. I haven't heard the Papadopoulos story, but in order to spill beans, there need to be beans to spill. Also, if Papadopoulos was cooperating with prosecutors, we would not learn what he is telling them. Let's see.

MARC. There's no proof of it yet, or there's no news yet, but here's what happened. It's not just that Russia went to the Trump team and said, "We have dirt." Kushner will be shown to have worked with Russia and helped them with information to place fake ads and all that. That is the definition of collusion, and there are laws about this regarding influencing an election. This is a very plausible likelihood and also a crime. Maybe it didn't happen, or maybe it did but there isn't proof.

DECEMBER 31, 2017

STEPHEN. What is your evidence that Kushner will be shown to have worked with Russia and helped them with information to place fake ads? Why would the Russians need Kushner's help to place fake ads?

MARC. I can't tell you the evidence, or it would be an insider-information violation.

STEPHEN. I finally understand. What better cover for a crack government investigator than posing as you friendly neighborhood doctor? You are only a few blocks from Trump Tower.

MARC. Yes.

PART 2
JANUARY 6, 2018– MARCH 24, 2018

TRUMP'S TAX RETURNS

January 6, 2018

Marc. Still think Trump is an intelligent man?

Stephen. My view hasn't changed. I believe that he is generally uninformed or underinformed, and he's extremely narcissistic, but he appears to have common sense, particularly compared to Hillary or Obama, who have been consistently wrong about critical issues: North Korea, Iran, the economy, and more.

Marc. I never asked you this, but understanding that proof is required to make an allegation stick, doesn't merely his reluctance to reveal taxes make you think there is something he is hiding that will impugn him in some fashion?

Stephen. I don't know. However, I know that there may be personal or business information that the media will make a big deal about. Think Mitt Romney and the way his work at Bain was twisted. Some things may legitimately be personal. A lot of the people who want to see Trump's tax returns are not curious about Hillary destroying evidence that was under subpoena.

SHITHOLE COUNTRIES

JANUARY 11, 2018

MARC. If you continue to support Trump, it's actually disgraceful.

MARC. [*Attaches a* New York Post *article on Trump's Shithole Countries comment.*] This is the *New York Post*, who loves Trump. I have been telling you this for a year now. Bad guy. Racist.

STEPHEN. Trump's comments were ill-advised. Another example of poor judgment. However, you voted for a woman who referred to half of the American population as a "basket of deplorables." Trump's predecessor mocked certain Americans as clinging to guns and religion. I'd rather have a president who questions whether we should be accepting immigrants from dysfunctional countries than a president who despises half the American population.

MARC. I figure about half of Trump supporters will defend Trump's comments, so therefore, she actually was right about 25 percent of the American population.

STEPHEN. So you share her contempt for your fellow Americans?

MARC. I share contempt for anybody who defends calling black countries shitholes and white countries desirable.

STEPHEN. I am not defending his choice of words, but that's not what he said.

MARC. He said, "Why do we have to have people keep coming from the shithole countries? Why can't we have people from Norway coming?" At first, I thought he just called Haiti a shithole country. Then I heard the context, which was far worse, and it only corroborates what I and others have been telling you and others.

Marc. But I understand how you feel, because you thought it was okay for him to say there were very fine people among white supremacists.

Stephen. Haiti is a shithole. Most African countries are shitholes. That's why people want to leave. Regarding Charlottesville, not everyone opposed to taking down statues was a white supremacist. The altercation was initiated by Antifa. Those are just facts.

Marc. Norway was the contrast. Norway, a symbol of the Aryan race.

Stephen. Trump is not a racist. There simply is no evidence in his long public life. He clearly is against our current immigration policies and guilty of poor word choices.

Marc. The Central Park Five ad he placed was racist (and by the way, I think those kids were guilty).

Marc. Lawsuits against him in Brooklyn projects.

Marc. Haiti abstained from the UN Jerusalem vote. Norway voted against us.

Marc. He called NFL players sons of bitches.

Stephen. The players who took a knee were wrong and very disrespectful to the fans. I have known several Haitians and like them very much. Norway, like many European states, is pro-Arab and has a history of anti-Semitism. I have no problem allowing Haitians to immigrate. I have no problem with Norwegians. I'm in favor of legal immigration. I agree with Trump that the goal of immigration policy should be to benefit the United States. However, I am more open to giving people from shithole countries a chance.

MARC. Republican senator Tim Scott denounced the comments. Not just that they were "ill-advised."

JANUARY 12, 2018

MARC. There will be no more Republican agenda after 2020. The only reason he may be doing this is because he knows he is toast, and he needs some small group of people who will defend him.

STEPHEN. That's not surprising. I don't normally coordinate my comments with Tim Scott. Nor is it surprising that he would denounce the comments. The comments are worthy of being denounced.

MARC. He is now nuts. He claimed he didn't say those things, but Graham or Cotton won't defend him, and Durbin is very decisive and credible.

MARC. Now we have Cotton saying he "doesn't recall" hearing the word but Graham confirming it. What obsequious, immoral people.

JANUARY 13, 2018

MARC. Trump is a degenerate who is likely being blackmailed by Russia. I will be right, and you will be wrong. Is this likelihood becoming a little more plausible to you?

STEPHEN. He's not being blackmailed by Russia, and his reference to "shithole countries" is not presidential but is being blown way out of proportion. It was a private meeting, and many things said in private should not be repeated.

MARC. It is plausible that he is indeed in deep shit.

MARC. It's not the word. It's the fact that he contrasted Haiti and Africa with Norway! Hello! Stop covering for him! And Tom Cotton is finished now before he got anywhere.

MARC. "I don't recall"!

MARC. If a politician said "dirty Jews" in private, would that be a pertinent distinction?

STEPHEN. Trump didn't say "dirty Jews" or any racial or ethnic slur. He simply called countries that are unquestionably dysfunctional "shithole countries." You read the worst into everything Trump says and does. It was a dumb comment and understandably upsetting to people with ties to those countries. However, the Haitians I know have no desire to go back to Haiti, because it is dysfunctional and dangerous. It is a legitimate question as to why we would allow people from dysfunctional countries to immigrate here pursuant to a lottery and then allow their relatives to immigrate.

MARC. You call it understandably upsetting to people with ties to those countries. Those people have very little voice or power. Had a politician disgraced Israel in a vulgar fashion, people would be apoplectic.

STEPHEN. Obama betrayed Israel at the United Nations. He attempted to humiliate the prime minister. Very little outrage.

STEPHEN. Obama also turned over billions of dollars to Iran, Israel's mortal enemy.

JANUARY 14, 2018

MARC. He didn't merely inappropriately verbalize countries that are shitholes as shitholes, but he questioned why the United States would want the *people* who want to leave those countries. Correct?

STEPHEN. No. Not correct. He was talking about the lottery and chain migration. Why would you allow random, unvetted people from a dysfunctional country to immigrate and then allow their relatives to follow them? This random process means we don't have control over the people who are coming here. This is opposed to basing immigration on whether the person seeking to immigrate would benefit the United States.

MARC. I see the point, but the last post has to have lots of subjectivity.

STEPHEN. The lottery and chain migration were the topics under discussion. The subjectivity resides in the suggestion that the comments were racist. By the way, if you were Trump, would you ever have another private conversation with Dick Durbin? How does repeating private conversations out of context and drawing inflammatory conclusions help Dreamers? The Democrats want to force Trump to accept legalization of the Dreamers without a wall and without ending the lottery. That way, they can deny Trump a victory on immigration and piss off Trump's base.

THE NUCLEAR OPTION

January 21, 2018

MARC. I know Harry Reid once used the nuclear option—why doesn't Trump, beyond threatening? Is there a political downside?

STEPHEN. The downside is that next time the Republicans are in the minority, they will not be able to block legislation. However, I don't believe there is a strong case for the sixty-vote requirement on the merits. Also, next time the Democrats are in the majority, they will change the rule anyway. Therefore, we should end it now.

MARC. When Reid changed it, how was it changed back?

STEPHEN. It wasn't. He only changed it for appointments to federal courts.

MARC. So you can change it anytime you want?

STEPHEN. The Senate can change the Senate's rules by majority vote.

STRZOK AND PAGE TEXT MESSAGES

January 22, 2018

Stephen. The FBI claims to have lost five months of text messages between Peter Strzok and Lisa Page: December 2016 through May 2017, covering the time period in which the FBI interviewed Flynn and in which Trump fired Comey. Also, text messages show that Loretta Lynch knew Comey would exonerate Clinton, which directly contradicts Comey's testimony before Congress. Does any of this concern you?

Marc. Whenever I ask you about anything regarding Trump, you just deflect with "Obama. Hillary." Does it concern you that Donald Trump wants only white people from Norway to come into this country? Maybe it's not so bad; I can't think of anyone in history who favored Aryans!

Marc. He is a clueless figurehead with no skills except duplicity. Anything the FBI might have done to prevent him from winning, as fruitless as it turned out, was to protect us. I am in favor of a coup when it is to get rid of someone like him.

Stephen. I answer you directly. You never respond to me. It appears you are okay with government agents conspiring against a candidate for president and seeking to undermine an election. You don't believe in the rule of law or in civil rights. If you really mean what you say, you're a traitor.

January 23, 2018

Marc. Police officers on every corner have their own views yet do their job generally well. I don't believe that these agents were influenced at all. Of course they hate Trump. What thinking person wouldn't? But for you to imply that their personal communications mean the product of their investigation is illegitimate should sound as baseless as what you would say about repeated (and so far futile) attempts to discredit the investigation ahead of the imminent charges that are going to make Trump look like as much of a traitor as, or maybe even more of a traitor than, Marc.

STEPHEN. I apologize for calling you a traitor. That would only apply if you root for the Patriots. On the merits, you are absolutely wrong. The government used a piece of unsubstantiated opposition research to conduct surveillance on the presidential candidate from the opposition party. The government also used it to conduct this investigation, which, not surprisingly, has turned up zero evidence of collusion. This is the most egregious interference in politics that ever has occurred. Everyone involved should go to jail. This undermines democracy. This says nothing about turning a blind eye to Hillary's felonies.

MORE REGULATORY REFORM, MORE ON JERUSALEM

STEPHEN. Another reason it is good that Trump is president: "The CFPB Has Pushed Its Last Envelope."

STEPHEN. https://www.wsj.com/articles/the-cfpb-has-pushed-its-last-envelope-.

MARC. You mean it's good that a business-oriented Republican is president?

STEPHEN. There were only two choices, as difficult as it is for you to accept. Trump was the far better choice. If Hillary had won, Richard Cordray still would be pushing the envelope, and we all would be less free. Also, read the article in the *WSJ* about Mike Pence's remarkable speech to the Knesset in Jerusalem, the capital of Israel. Nothing like that ever would have happened under President Hillary.

MARC. Pence didn't write it.

MARC. I am not an ideologue. I don't want my country run by a schmuck, and I don't want to be part of a party that would expel eight hundred thousand young adults.

JANUARY 24, 2018

STEPHEN. The point about Pence is that the Trump administration recognized Jerusalem as Israel's capital and does not hold Israel responsible for Palestinian terror and failure. Regarding the Dreamers, Trump has offered a deal—a deal that the overwhelming majority of Americans agree with—for legislation that will legally (as opposed to an unconstitutional executive order) address the Dreamers status. If the Democrats reject the deal, they will be responsible for the Dreamers' not being legalized.

BACK TO THE MUELLER INVESTIGATION

MARC. (1) Was racism endemic in the LAPD in the '90s? (2) Did Mark Fuhrman say the N-word? (3) Should O. J. have been found guilty? If you answered yes to all three, you are correct and also have zero argument against the evidence to come.

STEPHEN. I'm not certain about the relevance, but I doubt racism was endemic in the LAPD. My point to you is that there are examples of obstruction of justice that warrant far more attention than the "evidence" supporting the Russia investigation.

MARC. You don't know the evidence collected to date.

STEPHEN. Which is telling after more than one year.

MARC. They don't announce it!

STEPHEN. It would be big news.

JANUARY 25, 2018

MARC. If Trump bucks the right wing of the party like this immigration proposal, I'll have some new respect.

MARC. Trump tried to fire Mueller last June. Ha-ha-ha. So screwed.

STEPHEN. Trump didn't fire Mueller last June. Nor has anyone ever identified the alleged crime Mueller is investigating. Nor is there any evidence that Trump or anyone connected to him colluded with Russia. Nor is there any evidence that Putin favored Trump. There is evidence that the Russians expected Hillary to win. There is evidence that certain

FBI officials acted improperly. This sad saga will conclude with FBI officials in jail.

January 26, 2018

Marc. Doubt that. Firing and then considering firing the people investigating your affairs is consciousness of guilt.

Marc. The FBI keeps us safe. Your attitude promulgates a distrust in an important institution, all because of your pride and continued idiotic defense of an idiot.

Stephen. It is the conduct of the Obama FBI and DOJ leadership that is the source of the distrust, not the slow process of exposing it. It is very convenient to argue that evidence of serious wrongdoing should not be investigated because it would cause distrust of those responsible for the wrongdoing. I'm not defending Trump. I'm defending the rule of law.

Marc. Is it possible that Trump tried to ignore the rule of law by trying to end an investigation? Is it possible that James Comey is accurate when he says Trump asked him to?

Stephen. Trump did not ask Comey to end the investigation; he asked him to give Flynn a break. Nor did he fire Mueller. He has the constitutional authority to have done any of those things. Therefore, even if he had done it, it would not implicate the rule of law. It would have been a political land mine for him. However, FBI and DOJ officials whitewashing Hillary Clinton and using Clinton campaign propaganda to investigate Trump is very dangerous. Even the politicized intelligence reports that concluded that Putin favored Trump—which, if you read the Masha Gessen article ["Russia, Trump, and Flawed Intelligence," *New York Review of Books*, January 9, 2017], the intelligence assessment is not at all convincing—are dangerous. Whether or not Trump is qualified to be president, he clearly has more respect for civil rights than Obama or Clinton.

MARC. *Clearly* has? He doesn't *even* have, but even if I am wrong, nothing is clear. If you uncovered proof that Obama asked Lynch to stop the investigation, or if Fox did, you would be beating that drum all day, even though you say he has the constitutional right to do it.

STEPHEN. Why would you stop an investigation if you preordain the outcome? They pretended to do an investigation so the FBI could clear her. That is a travesty of justice. The evidence that that happened is overwhelming.

MARC. After Trump resigns, I'm all for taking out Hillary.

STEPHEN. You don't get it. There is no evidence that Trump did anything wrong. The fact that Marc doesn't like him is not a crime. The fact that unsubstantiated and nonspecific allegations have been made doesn't mean there is wrongdoing. I'll try to get tickets for the inauguration for his second term. You can congratulate him personally.

MARC. There *is* evidence. You just don't know about it yet.

STEPHEN. You don't understand how the system is supposed to work. There is supposed to be an alleged crime first and then an investigation. For example, evidence that Hillary was using an unauthorized and unsecured server to conduct classified government business is evidence of a crime warranting an investigation. The only evidence that Trump colluded—and presumably engaged in illegal conduct in connection with collusion—appears to be the Steele dossier, which was paid for by Hillary and not verified by the people who peddled it to the media. That does not warrant an investigation. Speculation that Trump's a bad guy and therefore must have done something bad is not a basis for an investigation. No event has come to light that suggests there is something to investigate.

MARC. Are you saying this doctor doesn't understand the legal system? What are you? A lawyer or something?

MARC. Let me ask you something. I know you are not a card-carrying member of the ACLU. What would you say if our government, without cause, investigated a Palestinian terror organization and then found clear evidence of a plot to attack? Then it was revealed that the investigation was only sparked by suspicion. Would that undo or invalidate the evidence of the terror attack and derail a prosecution?

STEPHEN. That's a loaded question. I would hope that a Palestinian terror organization is under surveillance for national security reasons. A better question is how you would view being the subject of a federal investigation for fraud on the grounds that you have high family expenses and, as a result, must need money and probably are dishonest. That's what is happening here.

MARC. I think that for anyone actually guilty of a crime, the question of the cause for investigation should be moot.

STEPHEN. There has to be a crime. No one has ever identified the "crime" that is being investigated. It is a fishing expedition.

MARC. Do they have to announce it to the world?

STEPHEN. The crime generally is a public event. What is being investigated? Should you be investigated for the purpose of determining whether you ever committed any crimes?

DACA

January 27, 2018

Stephen. Trump offers to make 1.8 million DACA recipients citizens, and the Democrats call it racist. Who are the liars?

Marc. I didn't read the bill, but there was some twist to it that was anti-immigration.

Stephen. I don't think so. It legalizes Dreamers—the Democrats' supposed top priority—and it provides for the end, but not immediately, of chain migration and funding for the wall. Democrats don't want to resolve the Dreamers. They want it to remain an issue—at the expense of the Dreamers—and they certainly don't want Trump getting credit. If you were a Dreamer, whom would you blame if this deal does not get done?

Marc. I tend to agree with you on this, from what you are saying.

SANCTIONS ON RUSSIA

January 29, 2018

Marc. Does it concern you that Trump just informed Congress that Russian sanctions are not needed?

Marc. The scum has infected the government.

Stephen. No. I read that, pursuant to a law passed last year (under Trump), the sanctions are available to punish countries who make weapons purchases. Apparently, billions in planned or announced purchases have been abandoned. Therefore, the law is working, and secondary sanctions were not imposed. In addition, sanctions may be imposed against countries that are evading the law.

Stephen. More importantly, Andrew McCabe was forced out today after FBI Director Wray reviewed the FISA memo, which probably will be made public this week. He may be fired. Others may follow.

Marc. The vote to impose sanctions was near unanimous. Perhaps you enjoy an autocracy.

January 30, 2018

Stephen. You really don't know what you are talking about. You can disagree with his decision, but Trump was acting in accordance with the law.

Marc. So 99 percent of everyone in Congress voted to impose sanctions, he reluctantly signed it (if you recall), and you have zero suspicions that his reluctance to now enforce those sanctions has anything to do with the possibility that Russia is controlling him?

STEPHEN. No. That's ridiculous.

MARC. You and Fox place Trump above everything.

MARC. The only credible people are those who are willing to change their views. You aren't. I have.

STEPHEN. You never make an argument based on facts. The truth is that you know nothing about the law that provides for the sanctions or the reasons why secondary sanctions (sanctions against governments dealing with Russia) should or should not be approved. I do not share Trump's views on Putin. However, I cannot conclude that Trump's decision not to impose secondary sanctions is right or wrong. However, I can conclude that the law on which it is based has effectively reduced weapons sales by Russia.

MARC. You admit that Trump has unusually friendly views toward Putin but think it's a stretch to say that that influenced his sanctions decision. He has unilaterally decided against the will of the Congress and the people. It's not whether he is allowed to do it by law. It's common sense that this is just another example of the autocrat he wants to be, at best!

STEPHEN. He is not an autocrat if he is exercising his authority under the law. Thus, he is carrying out the will of Congress as set forth in a statute passed by Congress. This is in contrast to Obama, who took actions, like the Iran deal or DACA, not approved by Congress. Furthermore, I didn't say he has "friendly" views toward Putin. He appears to believe that it is in the United States' interest to have better relations with Russia. He further appears to believe he can work effectively with Putin.

MARC. You're a lawyer, and you don't even know the law. Congress passed a law. The White House backpedaled today, saying the sanctions will be enforced!

STEPHEN. You never bother to get the facts. The administration had no obligation to enforce secondary sanctions, though I agree, based on my limited knowledge, it is a good thing to do.

MARC. "No obligation"? The vote was five hundred something to like four. And he signed it. You don't need knowledge to insist he enact this. You need a second-grade education.

STEPHEN. You don't understand how laws work, but at least you're consistent. Trump is giving a great State of the Union.

MARC. Who ever gave a bad one?

STEPHEN. The Democrats sat for the recognition of Jerusalem.

STEPHEN. Here is a passage from a news story on the sanctions: "The 2017 legislation allows Trump to postpone imposing sanctions on people or entities if he determines they are largely scaling back their transactions with Russia's defense or intelligence sectors, as long as he notifies the appropriate Congressional committees at least every 180 days that the administration is seeing such progress."

STEPHEN. https://www.commentarymagazine.com/foreign-policy/europe/russia/hysteria-and-incompetence-russia-sanctions/.

JANUARY 31, 2018

MARC. I didn't see anything in the article about 180 days and being allowed to postpone sanctions.

STEPHEN. I'm glad you read the article so carefully. This is from the article: "The law provides the administration a 120-day grace period for the imposition of new sanctions on unspecified targets if the president can claim that those targets have already substantially reduced their business activities in the Russian defense and intelligence sectors. In a statement, the State Department declared 'that foreign governments have abandoned planned or announced purchases of several billion dollars in Russian defense acquisitions,' therefore satisfying that requirement."

MARC. You said 180.

STEPHEN. Report me to the bar.

MARC. Did you say that clause just became law? You said a 2017 law.

STEPHEN. This is from the law passed in 2017. The law the Democrats are mischaracterizing to support their phony Trump-Russia narrative. They count on people like you—educated and intelligent people—to never investigate the facts.

MARC. I still don't understand where that all came from, but it was probably, my guess is, put in by Trump so he could obfuscate the sanctions, and yes, I don't really know what *obfuscate* means.

STEPHEN. Notwithstanding Obama, who made unilateral changes to laws passed by Congress, the president cannot "put in" something with regard to the law. Furthermore, it would be very problematic for a law to automatically impose sanctions without review. It would tie a president's hands. For example, the president was able to waive the law requiring that the United States move its embassy to Jerusalem to allow the president to make judgments on the impact of the move on US foreign policy. Every president prior to Trump exercised his authority to waive the law. Thankfully, Trump did not.

MARC. I'm not liberal when it comes to Israel.

BACK TO THE MUELLER INVESTIGATION

MARC. Christopher Wray was picked by Trump and is not part of any supposed deep state. It's plausible and even likely that the Mueller report will be accurate and damning, and this memo and the so-called deep state are part of discrediting something that is accurate. You have to admit this is possible.

MARC. Devin Nunes is the head of an investigation into Russian involvement, yet he is working with the White House to discredit the investigators! How is that different from bias against Trump?

STEPHEN. Anything is possible, but what is your basis for believing that Mueller's report will be damning? I don't even know what he is investigating. There has never been any evidence that Trump or his people did anything illegal. Typically, there is a crime before there is an investigation. For example, Hillary was investigated because it was disclosed that she maintained an unauthorized and unsecured server to conduct business, which, in every case except hers, is a crime. The Watergate investigation arose out of a crime: a break-in at DNC headquarters. No event has occurred that suggests any crime. However, there is evidence of malfeasance at the DOJ and FBI, with respect to both the Hillary email and the Trump-Russia investigations. For example, the Bill Clinton tarmac meeting with Loretta Lynch; the offer of immunity to suspects for information that could have been subpoenaed; the permission granted to Cheryl Mills, a witness, to serve as Hillary's lawyer; the dossier and the efforts to hide its provenance; the apparent use of the dossier to obtain a FISA warrant, which was used to spy on the opposition party's candidate; and the Strzok and Page texts. If the Obama administration used unverified information assembled at the direction of Hillary's campaign to discredit and spy on Trump and to trigger the Mueller investigation, that would constitute the worst political scandal in US history, and the people involved should go to jail.

MARC. Your last sentence has some validity *if* the dossier claims are untrue, and you don't know, nor do I. Because if you had a loved one killed, and damning evidence was clear and convincing but discovered illegally or on a hunch and was thrown out by the judge, you would go berserk. But you are missing something huge. You continually miss it. It is a crime to lie to the investigators. And they have clearly lied, as has been shown, and those who admitted it are going to tell the whole scope.

STEPHEN. I'm not missing anything. It is a crime, but context matters. It is clear that Flynn lied about perfectly legal conversations, which the FBI already had, probably illegally, obtained. He put himself in jeopardy. However, the decision to prosecute Flynn for that crime is within the prosecutor's discretion. It is hard to see how the same people who concluded that no reasonable prosecutor would prosecute Hillary determined that Flynn should be prosecuted. Papadopoulos is irrelevant. The decision to prosecute him also is not compelling to me. Finally, Manafort is in trouble for unrelated business. Again, the same people who gave everyone around Hillary immunity appear intent to prosecute Trump associates for any reason they can find. This is not justice. By the way, if you ever are interviewed by federal law enforcement, be very careful. It is very easy to accuse someone of lying to investigators if that is the goal.

FEBRUARY 1, 2018

MARC. I read more. The FBI uses lots more than the Steele dossier to get the surveillance, but they can't say what or how without revealing intelligence and methods that are precious. They have fewer reasons to commit crimes or lie about it than career prevaricator Donald Trump.

STEPHEN. No one except the FBI, DOJ, and House investigators know what the FISA warrants were based on. The FBI first attempted to stonewall Congress. The House memo, which apparently details the FISA process, was prepared after the FBI was compelled to comply with the House's lawful subpoena. Having been forced to disclose the FISA information, the FBI then sought to prevent the release of the memo on national security grounds, as you note. However, your information is not up to date. The FBI is no longer arguing national security; they are claiming the memo is incomplete and therefore misleading. When the memo is released, we will be able to evaluate it. I hope the memo and supporting documents are released. Based on what already is known about the FBI's handling of the Hillary email investigation, your confidence in them is very naive. You also seem to believe that the FBI should not be subject to any oversight at all. They alone should determine the propriety of their actions. That ended with the death of J. Edgar Hoover.

MARC. Republicans staunchly defended the FBI until Donald Trump. It's an understatement—in fact, it's stupid to even put into words what the FBI does positively for us, but now the narrative is that they are rogue, trying to overthrow the government. And maybe they were, in fact, motivated to scrutinize Trump because of documented (accepted by most every Republican) Russian interference in the election.

STEPHEN. This is not about the FBI. This is about the FBI leadership and the Obama White House. There is evidence they abused their powers. Either you don't care about potential serious and illegal activity, or you don't care as long as it is directed at Trump. If Russia interfered in the election, we should know. But that has nothing to do with Trump, except to the extent that Hillary caused the FBI to use Russian propaganda to obtain FISA warrants against Trump associates.

MARC. What this *is* about is you trying to reconcile the fact that his administration is good for the economy and great for Israel with the fact that you will have to defend for years that you defended a figure who will go down in history as a laughingstock. When people ask your opinion on where to eat, they will interrupt and say, "Wait—what does he know? He defended Trump." And if I am wrong, you can ignore my dinner suggestions as well.

STEPHEN. This does not apply to you, but I believe that those who supported Obama will have a lot more to be embarrassed about, particularly if the abuse of the FISA process and the unmasking of Americans blow up, which I think they will. To be clear, Obama's major achievements, Obamacare and the Iran deal, are disasters and morally suspect. His regulatory overreach and usurpations of legislative authority were unconstitutional. I'll take Trump any day of the week, even on his worst day.

THE NUNES MEMO

MARC. I bet he doesn't release the memo.

STEPHEN. If he does, you agree to wear a Make America Great Again hat in public.

MARC. No. Because he probably will.

STEPHEN. The *WSJ* reported it may be released tomorrow.

MARC. I still think they'll hold off. He likes to play games.

STEPHEN. That's a definite possibility. The best argument for releasing the memo is to take these allegations out of the realm of speculation and set out the facts. I believe there has been wrongdoing, but the question is whether it's Armageddon-type wrongdoing or poor judgment with respect to certain discrete matters. The fact that Wray has supported the FBI leadership indicates he is concerned that the agents who are named will be unfairly tarnished. However, it also is possible that it is closer to Armageddon. I would be totally opposed to destroying individuals over small or questionable decisions. That's what has happened to Flynn.

MARC. The only reason for the complete rush to release this despite concerns from the FBI (which cannot *only* be self-serving) is to discredit Mueller or Rosenstein or, worse, serve as purpose for either's dismissal. You are already walking it back.

MARC. And Nunes was put up to this by the administration.

MARC. And he recused himself.

STEPHEN. I'm not walking it back. I believe there is wrongdoing. However, I agree that if there isn't any major wrongdoing, it will fizzle out, as it should. But there is a lot of evidence of wrongdoing. If it turns out to be true, people should go to jail.

February 2, 2018

Marc. All the guys attacked in the memo are Republicans! They didn't want Hillary!

Marc. Carter Page was under surveillance before Donald Trump was even running for president! Ridiculous.

Stephen. Did you read the memo?

Stephen. Carter Page has never been accused of any wrongdoing, despite being under surveillance.

Stephen. The memo is damning. They used the dossier to obtain the warrant. Although they knew the dossier was opposition research paid for by the Democrats, they did not advise the court. They cited an article from Yahoo! News corroborating the dossier without advising that it was based on the dossier. They did not mention the connection between Fusion GPS, Christopher Steele, and the DOJ. They did not mention that the dossier has not been verified. On these lies, the president has been caught up in surveillance and has been under investigation. As usual, your comment that everyone in the memo is a Republican is uninformed.

Marc. I don't take credit for being fully informed. I take credit for recognizing BS in every walk of life. I have BSP.

Stephen. You don't want to know the truth if it is not consistent with your preconceived notions. The FBI and DOJ abused their powers to place Trump associates under surveillance. This is a gross violation of civil rights. If you're okay with this, you're okay with secret police, gestapo, and KGB. The US government cannot be permitted to spy on

American citizens, let alone the opposition party candidate for president, based on knowingly false and misleading information. This is an outrage.

MARC. I'm going to wait until somebody I see on TV makes an equally compelling counterargument and then plagiarize and get back to you.

MARC. The memo crashed the stock market.

MARC. You always say, "There is no proof." I read there is no proof that McCabe said the dossier was basic for the FISA request.

STEPHEN. According to the memo, McCabe testified before the House committee in December that the surveillance warrant would not have been sought without the Steele dossier information. McCabe's testimony was not public, but there is a transcript. I have no doubt the transcript will confirm that he made the statement.

MARC. I'll get back to you when I *Steele* more ideas.

STEPHEN. I suggest you go to the Maxine Waters website. She's a good source for the Democratic view.

MARC. I am a Joe Manchin Democrat and John Kasich Republican. You are a Steve Bannon Republican.

MARC. Papadopoulos was the reason for the surveillance. Ha-ha. That's according to the memo.

STEPHEN. That's not what it says.

STEPHEN. How did you do on reading comprehension?

MARC. I thought it was a good memo, and if I had to write a book report on it, I would say that I recommend it to all my friends. I rate the memo a 10.

STEPHEN. What other memos do you recommend? I like them under ten pages.

MARC. The Penske file.

MARC. The memo alleges no crime. You always fall back on that.

STEPHEN. That's not its purpose. It's not an indictment.

FEBRUARY 3, 2018

STEPHEN. The emails show they gave Hillary a pass because they believed she would win. I believe the FBI took the criminal step of placing Trump's campaign under surveillance because they believed: (1) Hillary was going to win, and (2) Trump would contest the election or challenge the FBI's whitewash of Hillary's server. Therefore, they wanted a way to distract Americans from Trump's claims by putting him under a cloud.

MARC. Hey, the FBI probably didn't want Trump to win, and it probably influenced them. Influenced. Big deal. It's not worse than Watergate! And it doesn't undo what Mueller is doing now. Period.

STEPHEN. It's up there with Watergate. Nixon would not have had to cover up a break-in if he could have had the FBI put McGovern under surveillance. Remember, his campaign sought to eavesdrop on the DNC.

MARC. It's not up there with anything.

KAEPERNICK AND RACISM

MARC. What happens to Peter Strzok's secret society? Throw enough things on the wall, and something will stick. And just to protect that piece of crap.

MARC. Racist jerk. Called Kaepernick a son of a bitch. This is America. You are free to speak your mind and peacefully protest.

STEPHEN. There was spying on the opposition party's candidate for president. I guess you would be okay with Trump spying on Schumer and Pelosi. Your comment about the secret society is ridiculous. The Republicans didn't make that up. Lisa Page said it. Your idiotic comment describes the Russia probe. Your comment about Kaepernick also is ignorant. He is free to protest, and people who don't like it are equally free to criticize him. That doesn't make Trump a racist. It makes him opinionated.

MARC. He never takes on white athletes who criticize him. And you know very well that those texts joke sarcastically about a secret society, and Ron Johnson claimed it as fact and had to walk it back.

MARC. See him taking on Greg Popovich? When and if he runs again, he will have his head handed to him on a silver platter by any male who debates him.

MARC. Your best defense ought to revert to "I don't like him, but I don't like the alternative." That's where it should start and stop.

STEPHEN. Do you even think before you text? Trump takes on everybody. Do the names John McCain, Bob Corker, and Jeff Flake ring any bells? I'm glad you've completed your investigation into Page and Strzok and proven that her comment was a sarcastic joke. You would never give Trump the benefit of the doubt. I note that there is no question that a group of high-level FBI agents met in Andrew McCabe's office and discussed having an insurance policy. The FISA surveillance looks a lot like an insurance policy to me.

MARC. I will give him the benefit of the doubt. Jerusalem capital. I like the immigration compromise. As for thinking before texting, no, I don't. That's the beauty of the purity of the reply.

BACK TO THE NUNES MEMO

MARC. I'll let Trey Gowdy make my point for me. He said the memo in no way discredits Mueller's probe. Thank you.

STEPHEN. I didn't say that it should impact the Mueller investigation. I agree that Mueller needs to finish. However, it never should have been started.

MARC. Aren't you an ends-justify-the-means kind of guy?

MARC. Trey Gowdy is changing teams just like Corker. Because they don't need to be reelected. What's your excuse?

STEPHEN. I'm the opposite. I care about the means, unlike most Democrats and liberals. Gowdy is not seeking reelection, but I doubt he is changing teams.

FEBRUARY 5, 2018

MARC. You said the memo was damning. You were right. Oh, wait—did you mean against the Russia investigation and the president's critics? Ha-ha-ha. I saw five Republicans agreeing the Russia probe was unrelated to the memo!

FEBRUARY 6, 2018

STEPHEN. As a political matter, the Republicans are not going to tie the memo to Mueller. The FBI obtained a warrant to place a Trump campaign volunteer under surveillance based on Hillary propaganda. If this doesn't bother you, it should. The government used its vast power to affect a democratic election. If Trump hadn't won, we wouldn't know about it. It's not going away.

THE HOUSE DEMOCRATS' FISA MEMO

FEBRUARY 10, 2018

MARC. What's your take on the memos? Should one be released and not the other?

STEPHEN. The memo should be released, but I suspect the Democrats put in classified information for the sole purpose of forcing the administration to request changes. They want to claim the White House is being partisan. I hope you remember that they claimed the Nunes memo was going to jeopardize national security, but that turned out to be totally untrue.

MARC. Are you getting excited for the Trump parade? Play hooky from work, eh?

MARC. Are you concerned that the buffoon gave away key Israeli intelligence to the Russians? Are you concerned that he clearly wants to be a worshipped dictator? Are you concerned that he cares nothing about woman's rights and sides with two men who signed multimillion-dollar settlements on harassment?

TRUMP'S EXPERIENCE

MARC. I watched a documentary on him. As you probably know, he lost millions and didn't know what he was doing other than how to manipulate his image and work media. Licensing his name. Starting *The Apprentice*. This doesn't make you able to be anything close to president. It makes you know how to be a celebrity.

STEPHEN. I have no problem with a military parade. We have had them in the past. I would be concerned if he gave away Israeli intelligence, but I know that Trump is very supportive of Israel and is trusted by the Israelis. Therefore, your argument falls apart. There is no basis for your opinion that Trump wants to be worshipped or a dictator. It's your bias speaking. Finally, Trump appears to care about women at least as much as his detractors. In practice, he empowers them.

MARC. You have a lot of confidence in him.

STEPHEN. He had as much preparation for the job as did Obama, who was immersed in anti-Americanism (Jeremiah Wright, Bill Ayers, Bernadine Dohrn, and more). I agree that his career did not recommend him for president. That's why he won.

MARC. Obama served eight. Trump will have served two. It's all coming out. And the Republican Congress is going to start distancing themselves.

STEPHEN. http://www.nationalreview.com/article/456287/grassley-graham-memo-affirms-nunes-memo-fisa-steele-dossier.

STEPHEN. I hope you read this.

2/10/18, 10:03 p.m. MARC. I read as far as the part that acknowledged that the Nunes memo was tame. Not according to you or Fox.

EVIDENCE AGAINST TRUMP

MARC. You don't know that Steele isn't correct. And it's funny how you always say there is no evidence of X, but you only know what is leaked, and Mueller doesn't leak. I'm waiting for you, in all your imperiousness, to undermine Mueller. Ever read his biography?

FEBRUARY 11, 2018

STEPHEN. Read the article.

MARC. What would you say if there was a suspected Palestinian terrorist living in New York City? Some guy came to a police station and said, "There is a guy who just moved here, and a friend of mine heard that he was planning to blow up the Empire State Building." No evidence. And a rogue portion of the NYPD fabricated evidence to get a warrant and went in and found that plot and explosives. You're gonna be outraged about the fact that they had no basis for the warrant? So I think your indignation is transparent in wanting to dilute what you fear is going to come out. And yes, while the investigation continues, the Democrats in control at the time can be investigated alongside the current one.

MARC. And also, do you believe that both the ex-wives of Porter are lying and exposing themselves to slander?

MARC. You have criticized me for calling Trump a bad guy, despite repeated statements that encompass a myriad of vile traits. Let me ask you: When he says that Roy Moore and Rob Porter have to be given consideration because, after all, they say it isn't so, how come he doesn't ascribe the same credibility and deference to the women? It's disgusting.

STEPHEN. Your hypothetical has a flaw. There is evidence: "A friend of mine heard he was planning to blow up the Empire State Building." That is worth being checked out, although if the police can't corroborate it after looking into it, it would die. Regarding Trump, I have no fear about what is going to come out, either with the Democrats' memo or with the Mueller probe. It is the Democrats and, shockingly, the media who do not want to know what the FBI and, ultimately, the Obama administration were doing in connection with the Hillary and Trump investigations.

February 17, 2018

Marc. I thought there was no evidence of Russian involvement in the election? I thought it was a hoax?

Stephen. No one has ever made that claim. There is no evidence that Russia hacked DNC emails or Podesta's email account. More importantly, there is no evidence that Trump or his campaign colluded with the Russian government to break US laws or in any manner at all. The only Russian collusion that has been uncovered is through Christopher Steele.

PARKLAND

February 18, 2018

MARC. I know I should let this go. I am telling you with 100 percent conviction that Trump not only is a mentally ill individual but also clearly had or has autocratic designs. If you had a child or nephew harmed in that school, you would be apoplectic at his statements. And regarding his response to Russia messing with our election, it is the epitome of defensiveness and selfishness. You can tell me all you want about Obama and Hillary and Israel and Republicans and taxes. But you cannot continue to defend this abhorrent individual. Abhorrent on many levels—the adultery is at the bottom level (don't want to cast stones there).

STEPHEN. I don't know what you are talking about, but I know it's not based in reality. Trump's comments about the tragedy—at least the comments I heard—were appropriate. Considering the Democrats' efforts to delegitimize his election through this Russia bullshit, his reaction is understandable. Furthermore, Russian efforts to interfere, which Obama was well aware of, are a foreign policy issue, not a criminal issue. It looks to me like the Democrats have used Russia to undermine Trump. That's what should bother you. I believe Obama and Hillary officials will go to jail.

MARC. It's appropriate to say that had the FBI spent less time investigating Russian interference, they would have been able to stop the shooting? That's appropriate? It's delusional.

STEPHEN. He made very appropriate comments about the shooting. His comment about the FBI was a political shot, but the FBI has a management problem. It is evident in its mishandling of the FISA process and its inexcusable mishandling of the tip regarding Nikolas Cruz.

MARC. There's a flip side to investigative journalism and honesty. You think Israeli intelligence never made a mistake that nobody will ever know about?

MARC. Why do I have to keep outthinking you?

MARC. You watch too much Fox.

MARC. And aside from their mistake, you don't publicly and continually undermine your own country's intelligence for selfish gain!

STEPHEN. You haven't made a single compelling argument. The FBI failed to respond to an incredibly specific tip. If the FBI had responded, seventeen people could be alive today. There is no excuse. Trump is not undermining the FBI; the FBI has undermined itself. Nevertheless, Trump clearly has provided support to law enforcement. He has reversed his predecessor's anticop agenda. Finally, whatever the issue, you conclude that Trump must be at fault. The facts never matter. You don't simply disagree; you accuse Trump of being evil or racist or a piece of shit. Therefore, you never have any credibility.

MARC. Issue: shooter kills seventeen people at a high school. Fault: not Trump. So there is the proof that you were wrong in your last text.

MUELLER INDICTMENTS

MARC. Do you feel he mischaracterized the essence of the indictments by claiming they exonerated him?

MARC. This shows a real firm grasp of the 1979 legal agreement.

MARC. The fact that he tweets *anything* is ridiculous, if not self-destructive.

STEPHEN. I know. It's always Trump's fault. I agree that the indictments show Trump had no connection to the Russian information warfare. Of course, having no real basis for an investigation, it is hard to exonerate someone from disinformation. The Democrats will never give up—as long as Mueller continues his investigation. Maybe an indictment of Christopher Steele will do the trick. I assume you are referring to the Obama Iran deal, not 1979. Obama sent cash that was outside of the deal. Trump's tweets are his way of bypassing the hostile media.

GUN CONTROL

February 21, 2018

Marc. Where are you on gun control? Maybe we have common ground.

Stephen. I do not oppose stronger background checks or limitations on the sale of certain weapons. However, I do not believe that any achievable gun control would have any impact. I favor stronger stop-and-frisk in high-crime areas. In New York, stop-and-frisk took thousands of guns away from criminals. I also favor better security at schools, as Israel does. That would be money much better spent.

Marc. I'm refreshingly, for your sake, not passionate about a specific solution.

SUPPORT FOR TRUMP

February 28, 2018

Marc. Are you working on your talking points about how you could have backed this lying and collapsing administration? You might want to stay ahead of the story and admit with clarity that you were wrong to advocate for Trump before it's you in the ash heap that will be present on the coming months.

March 2, 2018

Stephen. I disagree with tariffs. I agree that he made statements about guns that are contrary to the Second Amendment. I also disagree with his criticism of Sessions and IG Michael Horowitz. I understand that Horowitz is very well regarded. I have no opinion on Jared Kushner but believe that Trump would be better off without him. All this being said, I do not expect to agree with Trump on everything. However, Trump has done a lot that I do agree with. We, as a country, are better off because of the policies he has put into effect.

Marc. What if the tariffs were a spurious decision only to take the heat off?

Stephen. Take your medication.

Marc. Do I have to take *another* helping of truth serum?

Marc. You need more Geritol.

Stephen. I take Ageless Male.

Marc. And Grecian Formula.

MARC. And Vicks 44D and VapoRub.

MARC. Doan's pills for the back.

MARC. Midol.

MARCH 3, 2018

STEPHEN. Have you been in my medicine cabinet? You forgot MyPillow.

DRAINING THE SWAMP

March 7, 2018

Marc. Your point is mature and well thought out: corruption is okay because everyone does it. What happened to draining the swamp? Trump is as filthy as anyone.

Stephen. I don't recall saying that corruption is okay. For the record, it is not. Are you saying Trump has been corrupt as president? What are you talking about?

Marc. Letting Icahn know he was placing a steel tariff. Letting company biz influence foreign policy. Paying hush money for an affair and lying about it. Much more.

Stephen. Surprisingly, it is not illegal for Congress or the executive branch to act on inside government information. Nevertheless, I agree that it is totally inappropriate for government officials to take advantage of such knowledge. Trump would advance good governance by dealing with it, although I do not expect him to do it. The alleged affair happened well before he was president, and Trump's behavior was an issue in the campaign. Trump is draining the swamp. That is why there is so much opposition to him. He does things that the Washington elite says can't be done—deregulation, Jerusalem, DACA, tariffs—and he acts quickly. He steps on their toes and doesn't listen to them. He calls them out.

March 9, 2018

Marc. If 10 is "I'm always right, and Trump, aside from saying stupid things, is perfectly acceptable and doing a fine job overall" and 0 is "I was wrong, and Trump is clueless and potentially very dangerous," where are you on that scale?

Stephen. 6 or 7 [I must have meant 3 or 4].

Marc. That's my boy!

Marc. The cracks are forming in the steely facade.

Stephen. Trump has flaws. He creates too much chaos. However, we are better off with him than we would have been with Hillary—Nikki Haley, Israel, ISIS, tax reform, deregulation. I hope he gets his deal on DACA.

STORMY

March 16, 2018

Marc. Regardless of the significance or pertinence, you cannot actually believe that Trump did not have an affair with Stormy Daniels. And if you believe it to have occurred, does his general lack of any accountability about anything concern you at all?

Stephen. I wouldn't be surprised if it's true, but it was years ago. He has had three wives. He was cheating on Ivana with Marla Maples. If Stormy Daniels took money to keep whatever took place confidential, she should keep it confidential.

MELTDOWN STAGE

March 18, 2018

Marc. Trump is in complete meltdown stage. Remember when you parroted what his lawyers said: "Trump is not under investigation"? He sure is, and he knows what they are finding, and firing Mueller is his only play left, a bad play. The narrative of Comey fabricating everything is much more ridiculous than anything in the Steele dossier. Is it possible Comey and McCabe didn't follow protocol? Yes, but that doesn't exonerate anything Trump may have done long before anything the FBI did.

Stephen. You're going to be disappointed. Trump isn't melting down; the criminal conspiracy against him is melting down. It's going to get worse for McCabe, Comey, Brennan, and maybe even Obama. For example, Comey testified in May 2017 that he did not leak and did not authorize any leaks. McCabe said yesterday that he leaked with Comey's approval. They are going down.

Marc. And of course, in your world, Trump is innocent of every accusation and suspicion, yet despite being completely innocent from the start, he has incessantly tried to besmirch and discredit.

Marc. Trey Gowdy (they don't get more Republican than that) told the president today to "act innocent."

Stephen. He is innocent. There was no collusion. This has been a Hillary, Obama, and FBI leadership conspiracy to discredit him. It is a subversion of democracy. People should and will go to jail. By the way, the fact that Trump did not collude with Russia doesn't make him a better president (or worse). It simply means he should be permitted to govern without being subject to a politically inspired and criminal witch hunt.

MARC. May not have been collusion. Obstruction of justice for sure because it's already out there from Comey (and no, he didn't make it up) and from people you don't even know. He is mounting a huge case. But worse, he is compromised by Russians big-time, and his actions might be treasonous. And the reason everyone wanted to discredit him is because everyone knows this but can't prove it. And by the way, if you, like all of Fox nation, are going to eventually claim that any testimony from the Comey clan is not valid because they may have lied about certain things, how the hell can we believe Trump, who undoubtedly, to your own admission of likelihood, silenced Stormy and had an affair and can't even admit *that*?

STEPHEN. There is no obstruction of justice. There is no case against him. There is no crime. There is a criminal conspiracy against him. Trump's affair with Stormy Daniels in 2007 is irrelevant.

MORE PUTIN

MARC. What is your explanation for his consistent refusal to speak negatively about a ruthless Putin?

STEPHEN. The Trump administration has armed the Ukrainians and fired on Russian troops in Syria. In 2012, Obama promised Medvedev (Putin's puppet) that he would have more flexibility after his reelection, invited Russia into Syria, and did nothing in response to Russia's annexation of Crimea, and in October, Obama, in a TV interview, said Russia had no ability to impact the election and told Trump to stop whining and make his case. The only thing that changed is that Trump won the election. Trump might have believed he could work with Putin. He might still believe it, but he is tougher on Russia than Obama.

MARCH 20, 2018

MARC. Would you like me to convey your congratulations to Putin on his victory?

STEPHEN. Tell him to say hello to the ayatollah too.

MARC. Nice to know you support an ignoramus who would offer congratulation to someone who didn't *win* anything.

STEPHEN. He didn't give Putin billions of dollars, like Obama gave the ayatollahs. He didn't invite Putin into Syria. He didn't refuse to arm the Ukrainians. Who are the ignoramuses?

MARC. I'd like to congratulate Adolf Hitler.

STEPHEN. Devastating comeback.

March 21, 2018

STEPHEN. I assume you were equally as contemptuous when Obama congratulated Putin in 2012. Also, the European leaders who congratulated Putin must also be ignoramuses.

MARC. Did you read that his own people wrote to him, "Don't congratulate him"?

BACK TO MUELLER

MARC. "So what if the Russians were blackmailing him and driving his policy? Obama—same thing. You think Hillary wouldn't be blackmailed?" (Stephen Barry, July 31, 2018).

MARC. "The evidence Mueller laid out was all fabricated. They are framing him. Just like the way they framed a very innocent O. J.!" (Stephen Barry, June 1, 2018).

STEPHEN. I'm not familiar with the evidence that Mueller has laid out. Enlighten me.

MARC. Your quotes are in the future.

STEPHEN. Okay. I don't think Mueller will investigate Comey, McCabe, Hillary, etc. The evidence will be presented by a different prosecutor. Like O. J., they are guilty as sin.

MARC. No, when Trump's sins are revealed, everyone will think those people are heroes.

TRUMP THE KING

STEPHEN. You support government violations of civil rights? I assume you support the IRS's targeting of conservatives. Like in Russia, the government should decide who has the right to speak and who has the right to be elected. Like in Russia, the government's opponents should be accused of imaginary crimes. Trump is being investigated for "crimes" based on Russian lies packaged by Hillary Clinton's campaign. You should be outraged. One day you will be.

MARC. I support overthrowing by any means someone who wants to be king, will not adhere to the rule of law, and is so innate at duplicity that he has been fooling smart people such as yourself. Just as I would have supported people who tried to take out Lenin when he was just an emerging autocrat.

STEPHEN. You live in a fantasy world. Trump has been giving power back to Congress, the states, and the people. He is restoring freedoms usurped by the federal government under Obama. Your belief that he wants to be king is delusional.

MARC. My belief is that he was videotaped peeing with hookers, and he doesn't want that exposed.

STEPHEN. Based on what? Your own fertile imagination?

MARC. Uh, no, a report from a seasoned agent, Trump's now documented sexual indiscretions, and the way Russians work, combined with a baffling obsequiousness toward Russia that isn't understood by anyone except Sean Hannity, Jeanine Pirro, and Stephen Barry.

STEPHEN. Thanks for confirming. Pure speculation.

MARC. It's speculation. But it's impure!

MOSCOW'S MAN

MARC. General Ralph Peters, who called Obama a pussy and Clinton despicable, just roasted Fox and Trump. Calls Trump "Moscow's man."

STEPHEN. Okay. If Ralph Peters said it, it must be true.

MARCH 22, 2018

MARC. There is an opening on Trump's legal team now that his attorney quit.

STEPHEN. I can't afford a pay cut, but thanks for the suggestion. Maybe he'll hire Dershowitz, who has been outspoken in his opposition to the Mueller probe.

TRANSGENDER PERSONS AND THE MILITARY

March 24, 2018

MARC. Are you happy that we won't have trannies in the military now? Are you antigay too? Have you come to the realization that the person you defend is an utter buffoon with zero ideological backbone?

STEPHEN. I'm not antigay, but I have no position on transgender persons serving. I note that there are very few transgender persons, and the military's purpose is to fight, not to serve as a petri dish for social issues. Also, I don't agree with gender fluidity. I don't agree that young persons should be encouraged to undergo sexual reassignment surgery, which now happens. I believe someone who truly wants sexual reassignment has serious emotional problems. They may really be suffering, but that doesn't change the fact that gender is not a choice. I further note that allowing transgender persons to serve is not the same as the desegregation of the military. As race (like gender) is not a choice, laws based on race are unconstitutional and morally wrong; blacks were required to serve and have served in large numbers and with distinction in every conflict.

MARC. Just so you know, I haven't turned bleeding-heart liberal. If you vandalize a car; cops come and tell you, "Hands up"; and you don't listen and instead run away, you're gonna get shot.

PART 3
APRIL 6, 2018– JUNE 25, 2018

ELECTORAL INTEGRITY

April 6, 2018

Stephen. Trump may be overstating the problem, but there is voter fraud. The Democrats downplay it because they benefit from it. That's the main reason they oppose voter IDs. It's curious that you worry about the integrity of the electoral process but fully support the ongoing investigation, which was based on unverified information compiled on behalf of the Democratic Party.

Marc. *May* be? I'm not worried about the electoral process. Worried about someone lying to the public repeatedly.

Stephen. He's not lying. There is electoral fraud. It's not new. I doubt it's millions, but in some places, it is rampant. I assume you know nothing about the issue but assume that because Trump says it, it must be false. Do some research.

Marc. Even Fox hadn't reported anything about millions of false votes. And yes, everything he says—every word out of his mouth—deserves scrutiny. But since he occasionally says things that are accurate and things I agree with, you are incorrect once again. I'm not incorrect, because you acknowledge that he indeed has exaggerated.

Stephen. Do research. Saying that voter fraud doesn't exist is a lie. I guess that's okay because it's not coming from Trump.

TOXIC ENVIRONMENTS

April 7, 2018

Marc. This is the climate that someone like Donald Trump creates. That people tolerate offensiveness like this.

Stephen. The delusional left, not Trump, creates a toxic environment. Remember Kathy Griffin, various people calling for or hoping for Trump's death, the mocking of Melania Trump's accent—it goes on and on. Trump's opponents are the real fascists. Good people like yourself are "useful idiots."

Marc. Wrong, because I am not the left. That's where I have the credibility, because most people are intransigent. I want Pence!

Stephen. I didn't say you're on the left. I said you're a useful idiot of the left. You parrot their accusations, which you take at face value.

Marc. Maybe.

Marc. Even the right knows Trump is a moron. Nobody wants to admit they are wrong.

SUPPORT FOR ISRAEL AND THE WALL

STEPHEN. This is your big mistake, or maybe blind spot. Trump is not a moron. The difference between Trump and other politicians is that he does not play by the rules. For example, he recognized Jerusalem, despite the conventional wisdom that it would cause a backlash. The truth is that it was a step in the right direction. He is right about border security. He is going to win that argument. How foolish does California look? I could go on.

MARC. He doesn't know anything about or care about Jerusalem. People like Friedman tell him what to do and would have also told Pence what to do if he were the POTUS. I am not opposed to border security, but a wall of that length is ridiculous.

STEPHEN. How do you know that Trump doesn't know or care about Jerusalem? Useful idiot. How do you know what the length of the wall should be? Israel's wall has been a complete success. In addition, it also is symbolic of the nation's commitment to border security.

MARC. Trump did nothing his whole life toward Israel. Or anything out of generosity for anyone except his family.

STEPHEN. Again, a nasty, unsupported comment. He clearly did things for other people. Regarding Israel, what did Obama do? What about Hillary or even Pence?

MARC. Pence isn't a billionaire. (Actually, neither is Trump.) I concede that the other two did nothing for Israel. I guess that makes them deficient.

MARC. My comment is supported until you show me anything he did pre-politics in philanthropy toward Israel.

STEPHEN. Your comment is baseless and irrelevant. Based on Trump's relationships with big supporters of Israel, my guess is he has supported pro-Israel causes. When Jared Kushner or David Friedman is raising money, there's no chance they would not go to Trump. However, it's irrelevant. He has assembled a pro-Israel foreign policy team. He recognized Jerusalem. He appointed Nikki Haley, who has been more honest and direct about UN bias than any predecessor, also against conventional wisdom. These are facts.

MARC. Nikki Haley for president.

MARC. Mike Pence for president.

MARC. Marco Rubio for president.

MARC. Rick Perry for president.

MARC. Paul Ryan for president.

USEFUL IDIOTS

MARC. The useful idiot is one who thinks Trump is great because he isn't an ordinary politician. That doesn't make him great.

STEPHEN. That doesn't make someone a useful idiot. That's an opinion. It may turn out to be wrong, or it may turn out to be right. It may end up somewhere in the middle. A useful idiot is someone who buys into false propaganda. For example, the 1980s nuclear-freeze movement. The Soviets used credulous Americans and Europeans to argue for unilateral Western disarmament. In this case, the left is relying on otherwise rational citizens to support the removal of the duly elected president, based on baseless allegations placed into the public domain by the opposition party, using US intelligence and law enforcement agencies. This is one of the most egregious abuses of government power in the history of the United States. They call him, without a shred of evidence, racist and more. They call him a threat to democracy, when he actually is restoring democracy. They are relying on you, the otherwise rational citizen, to parrot this nonsense. I can understand opposing Trump based on policy or even his style. I can accept dislike of his use of Twitter. But if you say he's a racist, a Nazi, a Manchurian candidate, under Putin's thumb, or a moron, you are a useful idiot.

MARC. I was on record as anti-Trump before anyone had to influence me. The McCain comment—what was that? "Tough talk"? Was it refreshing? And the mocking of the reporter with cerebral palsy. Reprehensible on both counts. Pretty easy conclusion.

STEPHEN. I get it. I understand your opposition to Trump. I agree that in both cases, Trump was classless. However, because he was classless in those cases (and others) doesn't mean he colluded with Russia. It doesn't mean he's an autocrat or a moron. He is what he is, but he was elected to do certain things, and he's doing them. He may be successful (to date, he's had success), or he may fail. Even if he succeeds on the issues he ran on, I believe that a person, like you, who believes he does not have the temperament or class to be president has every right to oppose. However, you should oppose him for those reasons, not a fake Russian scandal or baseless claims that he is a racist or an autocrat. Furthermore, no one was more classless than Bill Clinton in getting a blow job in the Oval Office and directing his staff to lie about it. Obama repeatedly lied about important things. Obama may be more of a gentleman, but his lies and his use of government agencies to affect the election are more dangerous than anything Trump has said or done.

MARC. I don't like people who think they are above the law. Who are not accountable? He should have said, "Yes, I had affairs after Baron was born—none of your business." But as always, he lies. I would not have criticized him for having an affair, as the Republicans did Clinton in 1998. Regarding Russia, all his team were caught or will be caught lying. Why? Why lie?

STEPHEN. Clinton had an affair in the White House. That is much more relevant than an affair ten years before being elected, which is nobody's business. No one has been caught lying about anything relevant, except McCabe. The fact that the special counsel threatened to prosecute for inconsequential "lies"—which, in the case of Flynn, were not considered to be lies by the FBI agents who interviewed him—tells you more about the investigation than it does about the "crime."

RAIDING MICHAEL COHEN'S OFFICE

April 9, 2018

Marc. FBI is going to take this clown down and then imprison all people who have texted friends in his defense.

Stephen. Comey?

Marc. No.

Marc. Comey is a man of the highest ethics and integrity.

Stephen. It doesn't appear that way to me.

Marc. At least Trump looked presidential today. Nixonian presidential.

Marc. FBI has a search warrant approved by a Trump appointee. Such a buffoon, saying the FBI "broke in." Casting aspersions on investigators.

Stephen. I don't know the details, but it appears to be a stunt. Absolutely unnecessary.

Marc. It's necessary when you have a group of bold-faced liars. He obviously hushed Daniels with Trump's involvement, and he obviously went to the banks under false pretenses.

Stephen. So what?

April 10, 2018

MARC. Don't worry; Trump will be okay. I'm sure Michael won't be arrested and won't turn evidence against Trump to save his hide.

STEPHEN. Useful idiot. Now it's not Russia; it's a consensual affair that Trump had ten years before running for office (which he denies) and the woman's acceptance of money to keep silent. None of that's illegal. It certainly is not getting a blow job from a subordinate in the Oval Office and directing your staff to lie. It is not spying on the opposition candidate in a US election based on "opposition research." Instead of undermining the credibility of our democracy, why don't you simply support another candidate in the next election?

MARC. It's everything. That's the point. I don't want a lying, rotten, phony person as president.

STEPHEN. Then why did you vote for Hillary, who outdoes Trump in each of those categories?

April 11, 2018

MARC. I suppose the US attorneys in New York, people who prosecute terrorists and white-collar crooks, are all putting aside ethics to take down the president? More of the witch hunt to look for things that don't at all exist?

STEPHEN. So you believe every president should be under continuous investigation? Supposedly, he was being investigated for allegedly colluding with Russia to hack Hillary or break some other law. Now he's being investigated for a $130,000 payment that allegedly violates campaign laws. I note that Obama paid a fine in the amount of $375,000 for accepting millions of dollars of illegal contributions. This appears to be crazy.

CAMPAIGN FINANCE VIOLATIONS

MARC. He is being investigated because where there is smoke, there is fire. Because for years, people knew him as a slimy schemer, but they didn't have the interest in going after him until he proved to be a threat.

MARC. Edwards was investigated and charged with the same thing.

MARC. Pence! I am the only one who isn't partisan. I hate Trump for who he is and what he did to win the presidency, which included rallying the David Dukes of the world. He assuages people like you by making Jerusalem the capital and lowering taxes. "I'm good!"

STEPHEN. I'm going to research Edwards. Nevertheless, your text applies to Hillary, in whose case the government ignored a smoking gun—the private server—and overlooked destruction of evidence: the deletion of thousands of emails and the physical destruction of the hard drives and phones. Trump may be "slimy," but it was no secret. Assuming he slept with Stormy Daniels ten years before the election, it was admittedly consensual on her part and, unlike with Edwards, did not involve a love child and a wife dying of cancer (much slimier). So I ask you: Is this worthy of taking down the duly elected president? No way.

MARC. Cheating on a wife who has a one-year-old versus cheating on a wife with cancer? That should be a question on the game show *Men*. The latter is more understandable to me—sorry.

STEPHEN. No love child. However, I am interested in the Lieberman hierarchy of cheating. Someone needs to set standards.

MARC. https://nypost.com/2018/04/11/mistress-governor-groped-slapped-and-shoved-me-during-unwanted-sexual-encounters/?utm_campaign=iosapp&utm_source=message_app.

MARC. I suppose this is a witch hunt also.

April 12, 2018

STEPHEN. According to Stormy Daniels, she had a consensual relationship with Trump over ten years ago. What do allegations that Eric Greitens forced himself on this woman have to do with Trump? It sounds more like Bill Clinton.

MARC. That his cries that this is a witch hunt are as hollow as those of Trump. And how Trump has created a culture of unaccountability and denial. I listen to Hannity and Gingrich crying about how Cohen and Manafort had their doors taken down in the middle of night and so on. Do you think they would be crying about impropriety if it was a Clinton raid?

STEPHEN. There wasn't a Clinton raid. She was allowed to designate Cheryl Mills, who was knee deep in the emails, as her attorney.

TRUMP'S BUSINESS VENTURES

April 14, 2018

MARC. [*Attaches an excerpt from an article on Trump's business career.*] Can you throw a bone to your old friend and, for the sake of my sanity, so I don't think I'm living in a *Twilight Zone* episode, tell me that there is some merit to the content of this paragraph?

STEPHEN. I'm not in a position to defend all of Trump's business ventures. However, businesspeople are not stupid. If Trump was so corrupt, no one would deal with him, including NBC. Also, like all businesses, Trump's businesses have been sued, but that proves nothing other than the existence of a private dispute. Also, with the possible exception of Trump University, I do not believe Trump ever has been prosecuted for criminal actions. However, now, in retrospect, Trump is the most corrupt businessman? Give me a break. By the way, how did the Clintons get rich? What business were they in? That's right: selling their connections to the US government. Pure corruption.

MARC. And if Hillary had been installed as president, I'm sure she would've been subject to the same scrutiny.

STEPHEN. Luckily, we will never know. However, I doubt it. The press certainly would not have covered it.

LIARS

STEPHEN. In order to rebut a true story that McCabe directed the FBI to stand down its investigation into the Clinton Foundation, McCabe leaked a conversation in which he appeared to oppose the decision to stand down. He lied about authorizing the leak, which no one at the FBI corroborated. Liar.

APRIL 19, 2018

MARC. When they asked Trump why he reversed and refused to enact the sanctions that Haley promised, he said, "Nobody has been tougher on Russia than me."

APRIL 20, 2018

STEPHEN. Who's lying? McCabe? Comey? Both of them?

MARC. Are you crazy? That's a rhetorical question. Listen to the tape of Trump pretending to be John Miller and telling the *Post* that Trump is worth $400 million and not $200 million. Trump going down.

MARC. By the way, his latest lie is "I never told Comey to steer clear of the Flynn probe."

STEPHEN. I'm not crazy. They are liars.

MARC. Are you telling me that Comey, who, like anyone, may be caught in a lie, tells more lies than Donald Trump? I challenge you to give a yes-or-no answer.

MARC. Even you don't want to answer that. 'Cause the answer is no.

STEPHEN. Comey has engineered a false prosecution. Huge lie.

STEPHEN. By the way, "Nobody's been tougher on Russia ..." is an opinion. It can't be a lie.

MARC. If I state publicly that I know more about being a general counsel than you do, is that an opinion? It's so easy to win arguments with you. The truth is on my side. You are backing a slimy sludge.

April 22, 2018

STEPHEN. Yes, it is an opinion but not one that would have too much support. Trump has a much better argument.

MARC. A delusional opinion is probably worse than a cold-blooded lie.

STEPHEN. So far, the evidence is that Comey, McCabe, Loretta Lynch, Brennan, and Clapper are all liars. Their lies are criminal.

REMOVING TRUMP FROM OFFICE

MARC. https://www.theguardian.com/media/2018/apr/22/michael-cohen-sean-hannity-property-real-estate-ben-carson-hud.

MARC. This is who you get your talking points from?

STEPHEN. I get my information from a wide variety of sources. When I hear something, I try to check it out, which, it appears to me, you never do. You're entitled to dislike Trump. You have real reasons for your dislike of Trump: his comments about McCain, his mocking the handicapped reporter, the *Access Hollywood* tape. Assuming that you're right and that Trump is the big asshole you believe he is, make the case that he should not be reelected. However, that doesn't justify the Obama administration's use of intelligence agencies and the DOJ against Trump. What happened in 2016 is the worst abuse of government power in US history. If we're lucky, it will be prosecuted.

MARC. Obama's party is not in office now, and if Trump leaves, he will be replaced by someone in his party. Any one of the Republican nominees would have beaten Hillary, and I would be a Republican. It isn't just Marc, a Republican of clear mind, who detests Trump.

STEPHEN. You're willing to overlook Obama's interference in the election? If it had been Romney and not Trump who was the subject of the interference, would you overlook it? If you were accused of wrongdoing based on a complaint manufactured by a competitor and prosecuted, would that be okay?

MARC. Why are you wasting any energy on being upset about what the *former* president's administration might have done? I am expending energy to get this guy out of office.

STEPHEN. The current president has been under an investigation into so-called collusion that was manufactured through the prior administration's abuse of intelligence and law enforcement in connection with the election. You apparently do not value your freedom. In fact, you seem to believe it's okay to violate Trump's civil rights and the civil rights of the people who elected him because you would have preferred a different result. Trump is not going to be removed from office, but if that were to happen, it would be a coup. There very well could be civil unrest that would be unlike anything we have seen since the Civil War. What's your rule, Marc? The American electorate can elect anyone they choose as long as you approve? Will it be okay for Trump to use intelligence and law enforcement to manufacture criminal investigations into his 2020 opponents? Why take a chance that his opponent might win? Is that the banana republic you want to live in?

MARC. Would it be a coup if Trump was lying and in fact involved in criminal activity? You sound like an Edward Snowden liberal. Or an ACLU member. Would you appeal for a convicted murderer who might have had his confession coerced?

APRIL 23, 2018

STEPHEN. Yes. There was no crime. He is being investigated based on false allegations from his opponent and the Obama administration. Now the investigation has turned to anything Mueller and his team of seventeen prosecutors and dozens of FBI agents can find. Would you want an essentially unlimited team of prosecutors and investigators looking through everything you ever have done and then coming up with theories—like campaign finance—that clearly are bullshit? A coup.

MARC. How would you like it if your emails were hacked and a competing business enabled the hacking?

EVIDENCE

STEPHEN. This is the disconnect. There is zero evidence that Trump had anything to do with the hacking of the Democrats' emails. No evidence. None. The entire allegation is fiction based on the Steele dossier, enabled by Obama's abuse of government power.

MARC. Would you concede that there is absolutely evidence that people connected to Trump had something to do with it? Both evidence we don't know and also commonsense inference, like "There is going to be some big new coming out" right after the Trump Tower meeting? And Trump Jr.'s emails and Roger Stone lying about knowing Assange.

STEPHEN. No evidence. There is evidence that Donald Jr. took a meeting that he should not have taken. There's no evidence that anything resulted from that meeting. There was hours and hours of testimony regarding a twenty-minute meeting. Mueller's seventeen prosecutors and dozens of agents have had ample time to investigate. There is nothing. Not even Comey references it. Furthermore, if Trump had been colluding with Putin, why would that meeting have even occurred? The stupidity of the allegation is mind-boggling. A better question for you is this: Why did the Democrats refuse to permit the FBI access to the servers that were hacked?

MARC. Okay. And now the most salient point I've ever raised: How do you know what evidence exists?

MARC. And when that evidence comes out, you will never concede you were wrong; you will just say it was fabricated.

STEPHEN. After more than one year, with the government and Mueller leaking like sieves, there is no evidence. In your demented view, the absence of a crime and the unsurprising fact that there is therefore no evidence of a crime suggest to you that there was both a crime (Trump conspiring with Russia to hack Hillary or something like that) and that

Mueller has evidence of it. Is it in Comey's memos? Or in the Steele dossier? How long should this charade continue? The balance of Trump's term? His second term? The House investigation concluded that there is no evidence of collusion. Is that not enough? This is an outrage!

MARC. He didn't reveal anything yet. Who says there is no evidence? And for every *WSJ* article you send, there is a *NYT* article I can rebut it with.

STEPHEN. The House investigated and found no crime or evidence of a crime. If Mueller is looking at Stormy Daniels, there is no evidence of collusion. As for the *WSJ*, it's the substance, not the provenance, that matters. Show me something from the *NYT* that makes a good argument. I doubt it exists, but I will read it. As to the article I just sent to you, it is incontrovertible that Comey claimed to Trump that he doesn't leak, and then he admittedly leaked. He failed to advise Trump that the dossier was a Hillary product. Why? Does the *NYT* have different facts?

THE INTEGRITY OF THE INVESTIGATORS

MARC. So basically, Trump, aside from vulgarities and stoking racial hatred, did nothing worthy of investigation and only finds himself there because lifelong law officers with great reputations all are lying?

STEPHEN. I disagree that he has stoked racial hatred. That is the Democrats' stock in trade. He is being investigated because the Clinton campaign and Obama administration concocted this Russian collusion narrative and used the Steele dossier compiled by a paid operative from unidentified Russian sources, which was leaked through the Obama administration, which then placed the Trump campaign under surveillance. These are high crimes.

MARC. Don't denigrate Steele. He risked his life long before there was a Trump candidate, and he continues to live in peril. And I believe that Trump was in that hotel and that he lied about being overnight and is obsessed with it instead of dismissive of it. You don't really believe that Comey lied in those memos?

STEPHEN. Yes. He said he doesn't leak, and then he leaked. That's not an opinion. Why shouldn't I denigrate Steele? He is a foreign national interfering in a US election at the behest of one of the candidates. As Democrats like to point out, that's illegal. Furthermore, he was played by his unidentified Russian sources, peddling propaganda. He should be in jail.

MARC. So I assume nobody in the Fox atmosphere ever received leaked information, and Devin Nunes et al. never leaked.

STEPHEN. Comey's leak is criminal. The FBI is supposed to prosecute leaks, not make them.

MARC. When people accused Trump of impropriety and potential illegality by telling Comey to steer clear of Flynn, you and others used to rebut with "What's wrong with that?" Now Trump denies he said that. I wonder why.

STEPHEN. Comey's notes indicate that Trump argued that Flynn didn't do anything wrong, not that he should not be investigated. In any event, it appears Flynn was not treated fairly.

MARC. Why would you assert that a criminal peddling influence to other countries wasn't treated fairly?

TRAVEL BANS

April 25, 2018

MARC. Elena Kagan asked the solicitor general arguing in favoring the travel ban what would happen if a future president ever felt that Jews were a threat and wanted to ban them, and he said to the effect that "If that's what the president deems, it would be okay."

STEPHEN. That's the law. Of course, no president would do that. Are you saying the threat of Islamic terror is a fiction of Trump's imagination? Are you saying the threat of Jewish immigration is equivalent to the threat of Muslim immigration? By the way, Trump has not banned Muslim immigration. He has restricted immigration from certain Muslim-majority countries. No restrictions on Indian Muslims or Indonesian Muslims, for example.

MARC. "Of course, no president would do that"? The "president" of Germany once did.

STEPHEN. I meant an American president. If it happens, America would no longer be America.

APRIL 26, 2018

MARC. That's what happening.

MARC. Are you more excited about [quarterback Sam] Darnold falling to the Jets or President Trump's poised and collected interview on *Fox and Friends*? I know you would be proud of the latter.

STEPHEN. I'm not convinced about Darnold.

UNDOING THE 2016 ELECTION

April 27, 2018

Marc. But you are convinced the shrill, shrieking, fearful fool of a president is in good shape? What about when he said Michael Cohen was his lawyer for only a fraction of his business?

Stephen. I'm convinced Trump has been the subject of a concerted effort to undo the election.

Marc. I agree. Could it be because he is a lying jerk who has engaged in criminal behavior his entire life? This concerted effort is no less a threat to our system than banning individuals from certain countries or making an equivalence between Nazis and people who oppose them.

Stephen. No. The effort to remove Trump, if not punished, will do more to undermine our system than anything, except possibly the secession of the Southern states prior to the Civil War. The only legitimate way to remove Trump is to not reelect him. Using the government intelligence apparatus to leak unverified allegations, abusing the rights of American citizens through unsupportable secret investigations, and investigating nonexistent crimes to force out the duly elected president is a criminal abuse of the apparatus, and it undermines our freedom. Your ignorant allegation that Trump has engaged in criminal activity his entire life is your delusion, not reality. If it was true of anyone in 2016, it was true of Hillary.

Marc. Somehow, I don't think you would write this if they wanted to remove Obama.

Stephen. I would have said exactly the same thing. I believe that Obama abused the Constitution on numerous occasions. IRS targeting of conservatives, use of intelligence to smear Trump, unmasking, DACA, amending Obamacare without Congress, the Iran deal—all these actions were reasons to vote Republican. I never would have supported impeachment for any of these actions, although all of them, particularly the use of US intelligence and law enforcement to smear and undermine the opposition party's presidential candidate, are impeachable offenses.

MARC. See? You are so partisan you couldn't even write, "If Obama was subject to the same treatment, I would have felt the same way." You had to reflexively bash him.

STEPHEN. I didn't bash him. If you want to know what it sounds like to bash, read your texts and emails.

MARC. Nothing wrong with bashing if done properly. For example, anyone I bash is deserving of it. By the way, check out the faces of the *Fox and Friends* anchors as Trump ranted. They were like *Fuck, we are so screwed*.

APRIL 29, 2018

MARC. You do realize that oppressive and authoritarian regimes denigrate free press. It's one thing for Trump to declare, "The press is out to get me," but to tell the public, "The press hates *you*"? If anyone has been, and continues to be, neglected by government, it's the middle class. Trump is actually brainwashing dumb Americans—not you, unlike what you call me. He is a cancer and a nascent dictator, and the media has every right to find evidence to take him down. I agree there's no true sign of it, other than obvious proof that his supporters have lied and continue to lie.

STEPHEN. You are so uninformed and foolish. Trump fights the press; he doesn't investigate it, like Obama did. Trump doesn't rewrite laws, use intelligence against his opponents, or use the IRS against Americans for getting involved in politics. The real threat to your freedom is from the Democrats and the left. The "case" against Trump is built on one lie on top of another. It is falling apart around you, but you refuse to see it and don't seem to care.

THE HEALTHIEST PRESIDENT

May 2, 2018

Marc. Just curious whether Trump's ordering his doctor to say he's the healthiest president of all time makes you question his credibility or validates in any way what I have repeatedly told you is his despotic tendency.

Stephen. How does Trump saying he is the healthiest president indicate he is despotic? Did Obama's claim that he was a better speechwriter than his speechwriters and so on (he went through several jobs in which he claimed to be better than the people in those jobs) make him despotic? If not, why not?

Marc. It wasn't a claim! And you know it. He told the doctor to represent that in the doctor's report. This information came from the doctor, who only turned on Trump because Trump raided his office because he let on that Trump used Propecia.

Stephen. This is really an issue for you?

Marc. Totally! I always had a thing against bullies. This is totally a case of the emperor having no clothes. Maybe you are just a more trusting person.

Marc. This is a guy who rails against unfair criticism yet tried to tarnish the image of Obama with birtherism.

SPYING ON KERRY?

MAY 6, 2018

MARC. https://www.theguardian.com/uk-news/2018/may/05/trump-team-hired-spy-firm-dirty-ops-iran-nuclear-deal.

MARC. You always talk about "threat to our liberties." Does this story concern you? Probably not, because it was an Israeli firm.

STEPHEN. Notwithstanding the credibility of the report, I'm not certain what you believe would be wrong with investigating the ties that Obama officials had to Iran in connection with the indefensible Iran deal. You have no problem with Hillary hiring a British spy to troll Russian sources for dirt on Trump—which only turned up disinformation. Once again, you miss the more problematic story: Kerry meeting with the Iranians.

MARC. You are inconsistent. Even if Trump may have committed crimes, you're against the investigation because the FBI seemed bent on taking him down. With Kerry, you focus on his transgression, not the investigation, and then you say something to effect of "It's not so bad; I'm sure you wouldn't have a problem with it if it was ops against Trump," but you have already told me it was unilaterally wrong for them to do just that. You are inconsistent. If you are so principled in your outrage, then it should be across the board. As for the credibility, the reports are always right. You know that.

STEPHEN. The problem with Hillary's opposition research is not the fact that she did opposition research. It's the fact that the government used unverified information that she paid for to investigate Trump. That's a big difference.

STEPHEN. The reports almost always are wrong when it comes to Trump.

MARC. He is a grifter sleazeball who doesn't deserve your respect or defense.

TRUMP'S TAX LIENS

MARC. He already pleaded to income tax fraud.

STEPHEN. That's your opinion [that Trump is a grifter sleazeball]. He also was elected president. If he is not afforded due process, there is no due process. In the future, who is going to decide whom should be treated fairly and whom should not? You? I'm not aware that he was charged with or pleaded guilty to income tax fraud. I'll check it out, but I do not believe it happened. Again, you thoughtlessly believe any negative statement about Trump.

STEPHEN. A quick internet search does not support your mindlessly repeated allegation.

MARC. https://en.wikipedia.org/wiki/Legal_affairs_of_Donald_Trump.

STEPHEN. I read it. It doesn't make the claim that Trump pleaded to income tax fraud. You're very careless.

MARC. Tax lien. I grant you superiority in the legal department.

MARC. Can we say he has kind of a slimy business past?

MARC. Huh?

MARC. Is that careless to say?

STEPHEN. Lots of people have tax liens. It is a function of having to file dozens of complex tax returns in multiple states. These are disputes over the correct amount owed. It is not an indication of wrongdoing.

STEPHEN. At least you admit that you don't know what you are talking about, although it is obvious in virtually every exchange we have. The sad thing is that you don't care.

FITNESS FOR OFFICE

MARC. If you are implying that Trump might be merely a brash talker with a good, selfless heart, you are wrong, and I can say that without evidence.

STEPHEN. I'm not saying that at all. It is irrelevant to my point. If you believe he is unfit to be president, go ahead and make your case. Just don't base it on false allegations of Russian collusion or obstruction or campaign finance violations. As for me, I see his flaws, but I believe Hillary is by far more unfit and would have harmed the country.

May 8, 2018

MARC. He is unfit to be president. Having never served or had his kids serve in the military, he said that a POW who was held captive for years and who suffers life-altering physical and psychological injuries was not a war hero and that he liked people who "weren't captured." Is that good enough?

MARC. An evil or backward person says something like that.

STEPHEN. He actually is fit—meeting the requirements for the office. Your problem is not with Trump but with the people who elected him. You think they made a mistake. However, he is a far better president than his predecessor.

MARC. He isn't fit really on any level. Being voted in doesn't make him fit.

STEPHEN. No, meeting the requirements for the office makes him fit. Maybe you would prefer Iran, where the ayatollahs decide who may and may not stand for election. You could be Ayatollah Lieberman.

May 9, 2018

STEPHEN. While you're focused on Michael Cohen, North Korea released three American hostages; unemployment, including black unemployment, is at an all-time low; government revenues are at record levels; the Iran deal is dead; and, as of next week, the US embassy in Jerusalem will officially open. Of course, all of this pales in comparison to whether Michael Cohen did work for Novartis.

May 10, 2018

MARC. From the years 2008 to 2016, I am sure you will concede that by chance, something good must have happened in this country, yet it didn't stop Fox from constant ridicule of the president.

TRUMP'S PREDECESSORS

STEPHEN. Fox criticized Obama. He was a terrible president who made bad decisions and abused his authority. They may have ridiculed the statement "If you like your doctor, you can keep him" and his justifications for turning over hundreds of billions of dollars to Iran. However, I do not recall anyone personally ridiculing him. They certainly did not investigate imaginary crimes, although they did call for the investigation of real crimes, such as IRS targeting of conservatives and pro-Israel groups.

MARC. Someone said he was illegitimate because he was born in another country. Forgot who said that. They couldn't criticize him personally because he isn't a rotten person.

STEPHEN. That's true. The birther allegations were pointless. However, Fox News did not report them as if they had validity. There was no investigation. Obama was criticized for his actions. He also obstructed the Hillary email investigation and the IRS targeting investigation, and it appears he authorized the investigation of the opposition party's candidate for president. What a great guy!

MARC. Do you think George Bush I and II and Mitt Romney were quality people? That's all I am asking.

STEPHEN. Yes. I also think that Obama is, on a personal level, perfectly fine. It's his ideas and policies that were very troubling. Remember, he humiliated Netanyahu and bent over backward for the Iranians. He also ignored the Green Revolution and tried to unseat Netanyahu.

PASTOR JEFFRESS AND THE US EMBASSY IN JERUSALEM

May 13, 2018

MARC. [*Attaches a tweet about Pastor Jeffress's presence at the opening of the US embassy in Jerusalem.*] Got a clever retort for this baby?

May 14, 2018

STEPHEN. My guess is that Jeffress is not an anti-Semite, except in the minds of smug elitists.

STEPHEN. http://www1.cbn.com/cbnnews/israel/2017/december/an-anti-semitic-cesspool-of-racism-robert-jeffress-unloads-on-un.

STEPHEN. Are these the comments of an anti-Semite?

MARC. Not everything he has ever said is anti-Semitic!

STEPHEN. Not having heard of him until yesterday, now you are an expert on him? I have heard him. I also understand that he, as an evangelical Christian, believes in Jesus and believes that those who do not believe in Jesus will not be saved. That being said, evangelicals recognize that Jews are the chosen people. I'm not an expert on evangelical theology, but the smug and uninformed views of elitists who look down on evangelicals are worthless.

MARC. Did I say I was an expert on him? I asked for your response. Why is this guy even involved?

STEPHEN. Because he is an outspoken supporter of Israel and the decision to move the embassy to Jerusalem.

MARC. Once again, you are so right, and I am so wrong.

STEPHEN. I am right. Unless, of course, being a religious Christian makes you a bigot. Is that what you believe?

MARC. Saying that you are screwed if you're Jewish in the eyes of God is okay? He has that right to that opinion, yet he was selected to appear at such an event?

STEPHEN. It is no different from the Jewish view of Christianity.

MARC. Oh, I see. You think there will be a rabbi speaking at a Vatican City ceremony? It's tiring winning these arguments. I rest my case!

STEPHEN. Jeffress is a supporter of Israel presiding at a US event. Furthermore, Jeffress likely has a relationship with Netanyahu. As for your belief that you won the argument, ignorance is bliss.

MARC. "People of Vatican City, today we welcome the new pope. We have brought Rabbi Stern to say a few words. Rabbi, the floor is yours."

MARC. I do a much better job of arguing these points than you could regarding medicine.

MARC. My wife said Roberts and Thomas ruled in my favor in *Lieberman v. Stubborn Steve*.

STEPHEN. She has a conflict of interest.

MARC. Elena Kagan doesn't know who I am, and she also said my Vatican argument was valid.

STEPHEN. Her name, Elena, is too close to your sister, Elaine—also a conflict of interest.

Marc. Ha! Clever retort. Okay, I'll give you a point for that. The score is now 75–1 in my favor.

Stephen. As I said, ignorance is bliss.

Marc. This guy is more convincing than you [forwards a video].

Stephen. I'm glad you appreciate his point. I note that your focus on Robert Jeffress entirely missed the point: the United States has moved its embassy to Jerusalem to the great joy of the people of Israel. No one is upset about Jeffress except Trump haters.

MS-13

May 17, 2018

MARC. [*Attaches a tweet.*] Do you think you or I had ancestors who spoke Yiddish in New York City? This is precisely what I am rallying against. Yes?

STEPHEN. What evidence is there that Trump has empowered white people? Are you saying that but for Trump, no one would say bigoted things? Is Trump responsible for violent rhetoric directed at cops? Is he responsible for Kathy Griffin holding his severed head or Shakespeare in the Park depicting his murder? Are you saying it is bigoted to advocate against illegal immigration or for the deportation of illegal immigrants? The implication of what you are saying is that you are a bigot if you espouse Trump's position on immigration. You think the worst of Trump. You think he is an anti-Semite, even though he has embraced his daughter's conversion, provided more support to Israel than any other president, and pardoned Sholom Rubashkin, whom I met this week. Rubashkin, an Orthodox Jew and owner of a kosher meat-processing company, was the victim of prosecutorial misconduct by the Obama DOJ and treated unbelievably harshly because he is a religious Jew. Trump righted that wrong. Somehow, you think Trump is an anti-Semite. Same with his supposed racism, which is based exclusively on his position on illegal immigration. There is absolutely no evidence that he is a racist.

MARC. I didn't say *anti-Semite*. In favoring "strong borders," he has spewed rhetoric. He claimed he didn't know who David Duke was. He didn't condemn the KKK in Charlottesville (he could have slammed them *and* Antifa but instead cited "fine people"). His comment yesterday was reckless. I saw the exchange. He should have said in referring to the gang, "*They* are animals." He said, "We have people coming into this country who are animals." He didn't add, "For instance, MS-13." Slamming all Mexicans, slamming all Muslims, slamming all people from terror countries—you might be right; he *is* a genius in his ambiguous talk. He instills a sense of nationalism that is more than just sparking pride. It is sparking vigilantism.

STEPHEN. All of your comments reflect your anti-Trump bias. For example, Trump's familiarity with David Duke is certainly less problematic than Obama and other Democrats taking pictures with Farrakhan. Trump did condemn the KKK, but he recognized that not everyone who opposed the removal of the statue was a KKK member or Nazi, and he criticized Antifa, who clearly contributed to the violence. These are facts. Your parsing of his comments yesterday is idiotic. He clearly was talking about MS-13. He never has slammed all Muslims or all Mexicans. That simply is your extrapolation of his comments.

MARC. Wrong. It's not anti-Trump bias. It's Trump hatred. I see who he is more than you do. I realize I can't prove that to you, but when the shit hits the fan, your pro-Trump bias will be on display as the charlatan has you and others defending him.

MARC. "And some Mexicans, I *suppose*, are good people," he said. Are you kidding me?

ENCOURAGING VIOLENCE

STEPHEN. Your charge that he has sparked vigilantism is simply a charge. There is no proof. If you want an example of speech encouraging violence, look at Black Lives Matter, who chant to kill the police and are lauded by the Democrats.

MARC. He pretended he didn't know Duke. It wasn't his familiarity. I hate liars. In my core. That's why I can sniff them out.

STEPHEN. He actually has been more honest than Obama.

MARC. "Who is that guy in the back [booing me]? Someone ought to smack him," he said. "I could walk onto Fifth Avenue and shoot someone, and people would still love me."

STEPHEN. Really. That was an insightful comment. Since you acknowledge your bias or hatred, your analysis can never have credibility. Particularly because you never base anything you say on facts.

MARC. Quotes are facts, and I've given you three now. I've hated him since he said a POW was only a hero because he was captured and since he mocked a man with cerebral palsy. It's all I needed. Quite simple. Didn't bother you, apparently.

MARC. The *Access Hollywood* tape didn't bother me. You never hear me criticizing him for Stormy Daniels.

STEPHEN. Those were terrible comments. I'm not nominating Trump for sainthood, but Obama's animus against Israel bothers me more than Trump's nasty comments. He certainly has flaws.

MARC. I can understand and respect you for preferring Trump and liking things that he did.

MARC. But I see those terrible comments and many more as indicative of him as a person.

STEPHEN. He's a loudmouth and a bully, but personally, I have met people who know him and like him. He raised decent children.

MARC. I'll grant you that.

BACK TO THE ANIMALS COMMENT

May 22, 2018

Stephen. I disagree. What would you call Nazis who threw people into ovens? What would you call Khalid Sheikh Mohammed, who beheaded Daniel Pearl and organized 9/11? What would you call the ISIS fighters who put people in cages and drowned them? How about Central American gang members who kill someone, cut their heart out, and behead them? Calling them "animals" is morally edifying.

Marc. I see your point. I think *monster* would be an equally descriptive term but not as charged.

Stephen. It is amoral to compare the Nazis' (or Islamists') reference to Jews as animals based on their religion and Trump's reference to vicious criminals as animals based on their sickening behavior.

NOBEL PRIZE

MAY 24, 2018

MARC. He is spouting off about a Nobel Prize for himself for talking about scheduling a meeting. That provides no insight about self-centeredness? Attacking Amazon and Bezos because he owns the *WaPost*—no insight into vindictiveness? "You aren't a war hero if you were captured"—no insight into callousness? Bragging that his own relatively empty inauguration had the most attendees ever—no insight into mendacity?

STEPHEN. I think the South Korean president talked about the Nobel Prize. Regardless, Trump did the right thing today. He increased our chance of the denuclearization of North Korea. He certainly has made the world safer. By withdrawing from the Iran deal, he showed that he is seeking real progress, not phony deals. He proved it again with North Korea. I point out that the fact that comparing the time frames in which Trump commented on two different matters tells you nothing about his views on race, and you respond by bringing up his comments about McCain, Amazon, and the inauguration. None of those comments have anything to do with race either. If you are arguing that Trump can be rude and a bully, I agree. That doesn't make him a racist. Again, he is clearly not a saint, but he is becoming more effective every day.

CONFIDENTIAL HUMAN SOURCES

MAY 26, 2018

STEPHEN. Former Obama officials Brennan and Clapper acknowledge that the FBI placed a confidential human source in the Trump campaign but claim that a confidential human source is not a spy. What do you think?

MARC. Law enforcement relies on informants. I don't think it's clear that they "placed" anyone.

STEPHEN. The FBI had a spy, Stefan Halper, spying on the Trump campaign. Clapper, Comey, and Brennan object to calling him a spy. The call him an informant or confidential human source. It is semantics. Also, they claim the FBI informants have strict rules. It is bullshit. They refuse to identify the reason that would justify undermining the integrity of the US presidential election. They have none. Their actions were illegal and should be the biggest political scandal in US history.

MARC. When the report comes out about what was going on, you will either have a valid point or sound like a member of the ACLU.

COHEN'S RUSSIAN CLIENT

MARC. What's your spin on this? Just some made-up crap? No Russian interference? This guy is a known Putin crony.

STEPHEN. I didn't read the article, but this occurred after the election.

MARC. Eleven days before.

STEPHEN. The inauguration.

STEPHEN. Michael Cohen might have been seeking business, as he did with Novartis.

STEPHEN. It is not a crime to represent Russians. Ask the Podestas.

MARC. I just did. They now say that it is.

STEPHEN. They say it is what?

MARC. A crime.

STEPHEN. A crime to represent Russians? A foot fault—like registering as a lobbyist?

MARC. It's only the tip of the iceberg. Russia wanted Trump in and worked with his campaign before the election to do something about it. This statement alone was considered ridiculous and vehemently denied by the Trump administration. Now it's admitted to and defended as "So?" It's a law that a foreign entity cannot help influence an election.

STEPHEN. The crime is the Obama administration's surveillance of the Trump campaign. A meeting between Michael Cohen and a Russian businessman after the election is not evidence that Trump colluded with Putin prior to the election. It might show that Cohen was seeking to parlay his connections to Trump into consulting and lobbying work. The only person we definitively know colluded with Russia to impact the election is Hillary (and the DNC) through Christopher Steele. As you know, Steele got his disinformation from Russian intelligence sources. Furthermore, the evidence presented in the intelligence assessment regarding Putin's preference for Trump is very flimsy. Putin, in response to a question, referred to Trump as "colorful," which was mistranslated as "brilliant." He also said he would welcome better relations. Other than that, he said nothing. I refer you to Masha Gessen's article on the intelligence assessment. She speaks Russian and is anti-Putin. She also is anti-Trump, but she believes in the truth.

ROSEANNE BARR

MAY 29, 2018

MARC. Do you think it's right to refer to an African American as a monkey?

STEPHEN. Whom did Trump refer to as a monkey? What was the context?

MARC. He didn't. But Rosanne did, and her resurrection has been celebrated recently as a Trump supporter. She has galvanized a part of the population who felt ridiculed for liking Trump. Worse than a single individual, Trump has, at the very least, permitted a kind of loose attitude toward basic decency with many things he has said and, at worst, given tacit approval for a certain group of people to say racist things. That's all. Just watch for this. He most certainly has not been the unifier that people hoped for after Obama (who also was not a unifier). I just want someone decent who is a healer.

STEPHEN. It is not a fact that "Trump has, at the very least, permitted a kind of loose attitude toward basic decency" or "given tacit approval … to say racist things." I can appreciate the argument that he is coarsening public discourse but point out that he is attacked and ridiculed on a daily basis. His intelligence and mental competence are questioned. He is accused of treason. Kathy Griffin held up his severed head on TV. Therefore, public decency is under attack from all sides. Furthermore, Democrats routinely call Republicans racist. Therefore, I reject the charge that he has somehow given approval to say racist things. We've been hearing about alleged racist dog whistles for years. For example, support for voter ID laws is allegedly racist. Questioning "Hands up; don't shoot" is racist. The left accuses Trump of tacit approval of racism not because of racism but because they disagree with him on immigration and other policies. However, black and Hispanic Americans are doing far better under Trump.

MARC. This is one of your more compelling arguments. I'll give you this one. The score is now 75–2 in my favor. By the way, you spelled *questionable* wrong after "intelligence and mental competence are."

STEPHEN. Your scoring of these debates is reminiscent of East German figure skating judges scoring for Americans. By the way, as you already know, I did not say "questionable."

MARC. I did know that! But you already know what I meant! Your training in the law gives you an edge.

PARDONS

May 31, 2018

Marc. You think Trump might be abusing power by pardoning criminals simply to make a statement?

June 1, 2018

Stephen. No.

Marc. Dinesh [Conservative Commentator Dinesh D'Souza] admitted he broke the law and was prosecuted by Preet [U.S. Attorney Preet Bharara]. You don't think that figured into it?

Stephen. Dinesh's prosecution was politically motivated. No one other than Dinesh has been sent to prison for a $20,000 campaign contribution. It was a travesty of justice.

Marc. Okay, I don't know the story.

Marc. What about Rod Blagojevich or Martha Stewart?

Stephen. I don't know about Blagojevich, but the Martha Stewart prosecution was unfair.

Marc. Really? She definitely had insider knowledge.

Stephen. I don't remember the details, but I recall thinking that no one should go to jail for what she did.

Marc. Now you are reasoning with the compelling nature of one of my texts.

June 3, 2018

Marc. Yes-or-no answer: Do you believe a president—any president—could conceivably be caught on camera taking bribes or plotting to kill someone and then pardon himself?

Stephen. A president may have the constitutional authority to pardon himself, but pursuant to the Constitution, the pardon power does not apply to cases of impeachment. Therefore, a president in that situation could be removed from office. Of course, Trump has not plotted to kill anyone and has not been accused of taking bribes. Furthermore, Trump has the same authority as Clinton or Obama to pardon someone who happened to make a movie critical of Obama and was later convicted of making $20,000 in illegal campaign contributions.

LEGAL MEMO ON OBSTRUCTION

Marc. Giuliani walked back the crazy claims of that "memo" meant to embolden his base.

Stephen. I haven't heard the news regarding this issue.

Marc. Big story. Trump's team ostensibly sent a memo to Comey stating absolute powers that essentially preclude the president from being under investigation. The belief is that they leaked the memo so the public would be influenced.

Stephen. I read that the memo stated the president cannot obstruct justice by taking actions that he has the constitutional authority to take, like firing Comey. I heard that it also said that the president, as head of the executive branch, cannot obstruct himself. Not having read the memo, I can't comment on it, but I agree that the president cannot obstruct justice by exercising his constitutional authority. However, I believe a president could be guilty of obstruction of justice if, like Clinton, he commits perjury or directs others to commit perjury.

MORE ON TRUMP'S ALLEGED RACISM

June 5, 2018

Marc. This is the problem [referring to an attachment].

Stephen. It might make you feel good, but it tells you nothing about Charlottesville, the anthem dispute, or Trump.

Marc. Totally does. That he picks petty strategic battles to fool dumb people. You base your arguments on reasoning and facts, granted, but dumb people will think that all NFL players are bad because most are black, a few kneel, and they canceled going to the White House and didn't honor the king.

Stephen. He picks issues that strike a chord with a large number of Americans. Your statement that "Dumb people will think players are bad because most are black …" is dismissive and insulting. You are arguing that people who are offended by rich athletes acting disrespectfully are stupid or racist or both. I disagree.

Marc. There are racist blacks and racist whites. There are dumb Republicans and dumb Democrats. But Obama, whose policies I didn't agree with, did not goad liberals or incite their base instincts, and despite the rise of the alt-left, it pales in comparison to the history of anti-black and anti-Jewish behavior. There is absolutely no reason why Trump could not have forcefully, and without having to be questioned, condemned Nazis and condemned a statement that a black woman looks like an ape. He remained quiet because his silence is garnering adulation from the only people who support him and because he is bent on not doing what people tell him he should do or what convention dictates. That might have an occasional constructive upside but not across the board. The national anthem issue is ridiculous. People didn't care until he said something that appealed to their base loathing that they are struggling while athletes are privileged.

MARC. The dumbass president who preaches and lectures about patriotism can't even remember the words to "God Bless America."

STEPHEN. If you don't believe that Obama was divisive, you were not conscious during his term.

MARC. It took evil to awaken me. Obama, like most politicians, was ambitious, to say the least, and megalomaniacal at worst, yet in my opinion (since it is not a fact), he is another class of human being from this piece of garbage. And I am not the only one who thinks that.

STEPHEN. I am awake. Open your eyes!

THE G7

JUNE 10, 2018

MARC. Not one person in this country, including on Fox, said that Russia should be included back into the G7. So that means Trump is either 100 percent wrong or smarter than every person in this country.

STEPHEN. Most, if not all, of Roosevelt's advisers opposed Lend-Lease based on their belief that it was a waste of resources because of the inevitability that England would surrender. Fortunately, Roosevelt was the president, not his advisers. Virtually everyone opposed George W. Bush on the surge. Fortunately, he was the president. We elect our presidents to lead, not to follow the consensus. Trump may be wrong on bringing Russia back, but he will be evaluated on all the decisions he makes.

NORTH KOREA

June 12, 2018

MARC. https://twitter.com/jeffblix/status/.

STEPHEN. No one ever said that Fox commentators are particularly knowledgeable or consistent. That's why I evaluate issues on my own, to the extent possible. That being said, there is a huge difference between Kim meeting with Obama, who was a weak, apologetic appeaser, and Kim meeting with Trump, who threatened to destroy Kim's regime. Think of Nixon going to China.

MARC. Perhaps Trump is crazy like a Fox.

STEPHEN. Trump certainly is not an appeaser, but it remains to be seen if he can negotiate a deal that requires North Korea to denuclearize in a reasonable time frame and is verifiable.

MARC. You have to admit that the spurious move reeks of self-promotion more than altruism.

STEPHEN. Which "spurious move" are you referring to?

MARC. Agreeing to a nuclear disarmament plan after a short solo meeting.

MARC. You have to be worried he is being bribed or rewarded, if not threatened, to do this.

STEPHEN. We do not have an agreement, but if we are successful, it will be a huge achievement. I have no idea what your basis is for that speculation.

MARC. He sure made it seem to really gullible people that they *do* have an agreement. Trump said Kim was impressive—long before there was a Trump, everyone you respect considered him a murderous, repressive thug. I am sure some people said about Hitler, "But hey, you have to give it to the guy ..." You wouldn't respect someone like that.

STEPHEN. One thing at a time. If North Korea denuclearizes, we can pressure the regime on human rights. Trump, however, as he states repeatedly, is concerned, in the first instance, with the security of Americans. Regarding dealing with repressive thugs, whose approach appears to be better: Obama's or Trump's?

MARC. Do you actually think that as of two months ago, North Korea was any threat whatsoever to us?

STEPHEN. Yes. They are developing missiles that can reach the United States. They have fired missiles over Japan. They have threatened us. What am I missing?

MARC. Oh, I dunno—maybe that nobody has ever attacked anyone with nukes since 1945 and won't because they don't want to end the world. And for once, I have you trapped, because if North Korea was ever a threat to do something so cataclysmic, might they perchance be devious enough to simply sign a treaty and then not abide by it?

STEPHEN. You're right. No civilized nation would ever gas millions of people. No one would ever fly airplanes into office buildings. Why would anyone do that? It's called miscalculation. I have no doubt that North Korea will not easily agree to a verifiable deal. Trump may lose on this. We shall see if the administration can pull it off. I don't think we will be worse off.

MARC. Those examples would not be, and were not, retaliated with total and complete annihilation.

MARC. Nuking a country would be.

STEPHEN. Your point was that there is never going to be a nuclear attack. I hope you're right, but I would rather not take that chance. We need to address the North Korea threat.

MARC. My point is that no treaty would ever stop anyone from doing the unthinkable. You know it, and I know it, and Trump knows it. Cozying up to a world adversary for ostensible gains is not kosher.

STEPHEN. Verifiably dismantling their nuclear weapons would stop them. South Africa, Libya, and Ukraine dismantled their respective nuclear arsenals. They are no longer nuclear powers.

JUNE 15, 2018

MARC. You have to admit I have been right about a few things. I've been telling you that Trump wants to be a dictator. Today he said to a reporter on video, "Kim Jong Un, when he speaks, people put their hands up [in "Heil Hitler" deference], and I want my people to do that." It's what he said, Steve! And that Kim Jong Un is a talented guy whose people love him!

STEPHEN. It was reported in the *Washington Post*. Trump claims the statement was made sarcastically. I think the claim that Trump wants to be a dictator is ridiculous. He has shown more respect to our institutions than Obama did. I am more troubled by his praise for bad people, like Putin and Kim. However, he has been tough on Putin. He has been tough on Xi Jinping. I hope he holds Kim's feet to the fire. We shall see.

MARC. It wasn't reported. It aired, and watch it. It's not a joke. Watch it!

MARC. You hope he is tough on Kim? He is tough on Canada!

STEPHEN. That's why he was elected, not to do what every other candidate would do. I don't know enough about tariffs, but I would like to know why it is okay for Canada to place tariffs on US dairy products. Maybe there is a good reason (at least from the Canadian perspective), but Trump's position is "Don't expect us to take it." He may have a point. Regarding his comments, I will watch the clip, but even if he sincerely made a stupid comment, it does not establish that he wants to be a dictator. As I said, he has shown more respect for our institutions and the rule of law than Obama. The IG report is damning. I plan to read it myself next week.

SPECULATION FOLLOWING THE FIRST INSPECTOR GENERAL REPORT

June 16, 2018

Stephen. Do you still believe that Comey has more integrity than Trump? The Inspector General's report is only the first step. It should end with each official who took part in undermining our democracy in prison. I'm talking about Comey, Brennan, Clapper, Strzok, and Page (Lisa, not Carter). I have no doubt that Obama, Hillary, Lynch, and others were involved. I hope the lazy, uneducated POS voters who supported Trump in 2016 support him in 2018.

Stephen. I saw the clip of Trump's comment [regarding Canada]. He made it in the context of speaking with the press for almost an hour, including many hostile reporters. Just like any would-be dictator.

Marc. "So what if he lied that there was no pee-pee tape? It still doesn't mean he was being blackmailed! So what that they have emails showing that Trump was lying about knowing about a quid pro quo with Putin? So what if he committed treason? Obama also did. Trump was framed just like O. J.!" Things Stephen will be saying next year.

Stephen. Hillary committed real crimes and should have been indicted. With Trump, there was no crime, but the FBI attempt to find one. With Hillary, the FBI ignored destruction of evidence. The IT person who destroyed evidence was given immunity after admitting he lied. Paul Manafort was sent to jail (by an Obama appointee) for allegedly reaching out to potential witnesses, even though he has not been found guilty of anything.

MARC. You are so indignant about improprieties and illegalities with Hillary. But you won't be when Trump's come to light. What you should be saying is "They all do this stuff; it's no big deal." You should be embracing transgressions of Obama and Hillary, because otherwise, you will be shown to be selective in your indignation.

STEPHEN. No such improprieties and illegalities have come to light, despite dramatic midnight raids, use of foreign intelligence powers, and more.

MARC. Is it possible those raids have indeed produced incrimination, but the process is so methodical that it has not yet come to light?

MARC. Methinks so.

MARC. They wouldn't drag it out for no reason on the hope that something turns up.

STEPHEN. There is nothing. They are hoping for a Democratic Congress.

MARC. Mueller?

STEPHEN. Yes. That way, the Democrats will impeach over anything, even a parking ticket. Trump won't be removed from office, but the impeachment will be used to delegitimize him. I don't think it's going to happen, because I think the Republicans will retain Congress. If the Republicans retain Congress, the investigation will end. If the Democrats win and impeach, all things being equal, the Democrats will ensure Trump's reelection.

FAMILY SEPARATION

June 20, 2018

Marc. Glad to lend no support to this administration and their reprehensibly inhuman actions.

Stephen. Inhuman? Really? As usual, you have no idea what you are talking about and are a useful idiot for Democratic propaganda.

Marc. If there was no problem with the separation of families, why is Trump now announcing a change to the policy?

Stephen. Because of politics.

Marc. I commend the president for ending this policy! See? I give credit where it's due!

Marc. But unfortunately, it's too late. They made a bad, bad mistake. Will go down in history as connected to some of the worst atrocities ever witnessed. Republicans will get toasted in the fall.

[Stephen. No, it's not an atrocity. The children held by the government are well cared for. Laws and court decisions made it illegal for the government to leave the children with parents who are detained. Furthermore, the government cannot immediately send the family back. Therefore, if the government cannot separate families, the families, which entered the United States illegally, are simply allowed into the country. This encourages people seeking to enter the country illegally to bring children with them. The children are not always the biological children of the adults they are traveling with and are often at risk of abuse. Instead of fixing the problem, the Democrats successfully politicized the issue and, as usual, have made the problem worse. They succeeded because useful idiots like you are quick to call a humane policy—one likely to eliminate the utility of bringing children into the country illegally—an atrocity.

MARC. And yet Trump caved to the useful idiots instead of standing his ground. Why is that?

MARC. I guess he lets idiots push him around. Who listens to idiots anyway?

STEPHEN. Because the Democrats' bullshit narrative got traction with the public, as it did with you, and the zero-tolerance policy became too politically problematic. Trump stands his ground better than most politicians, but too many Republicans were running for cover. As to who listens to idiots, I'm committed to our lifelong friendship no matter what your IQ is.

MARC. As I am to someone who listens to racists.

MARC. Useful racists.

MARC. Why doesn't Trump cut off the Republicans?

STEPHEN. Ask Bob Corker or Jeff Flake.

MARC. Every Republican who isn't going for reelection sees things as I do. Those who need the votes of racists to stay in power see things differently.

STEPHEN. You're impervious to facts and reason. Therefore, you resort to name-calling. Do you really believe that Americans who support enforcement of our immigration laws are necessarily racist? Why? I look forward to receiving your explanation.

HATE SPEECH AND COMPARISONS TO HITLER

MARC. There is a huge swath of white male Americans who are unsuccessful and uneducated and blame anything and everything for their cycle of poverty. This is exactly what Hitler seized on to exploit narrow-minded Germans into scapegoating Jews. Trump proves my point with actions and inactions that I have often brought to your attention. Regarding immigration, there is a fine line between, on the one hand, having legal immigration and deterring an influx of migrants and, on the other, rhetoric referring to impurities and infestations and animals.

MARC. By the way, Trump said the other day he had no authority to stop the separation of families. And now he signs an executive order stopping it. This is why nothing this man says is credible, and this is why it's not only Democrats who are useful idiots.

STEPHEN. A "huge swath of white male Americans" are racist? How many? Twenty million? Fifty million? This is a disgusting allegation. Those who live in glass houses should not throw stones. If you believe that, you are an elitist fool. Furthermore, this idiotic statement is an assertion; it does not prove that people opposed to illegal immigration are racists. I note that blacks and Hispanics also oppose illegal immigration. Are they racists too? Trump was seeking to force Congress to deal with the issue. The Democrats are committed to playing politics with the issue. I believe that Trump ultimately will win. The American people support him on it.

JUNE 23, 2018

MARC. I really don't understand how you don't see the parallels. You are obviously knowledgeable, but Trump is not being clear with his verbiage in making a distinction between, on the one hand, terrorists and gang members and, on the other, the greater whole of Muslims and Mexicans, respectively. And this is energizing the less knowledgeable of the masses into a generalized hatred of each group.

STEPHEN. There are no parallels. What is the basis for your belief that the "masses" have a generalized hatred of Muslims and Mexicans? By "masses," I assume you mean white Americans who oppose illegal immigration. Aside from opposition to illegal immigration, is there any evidence of generalized hatred? I see hatred for Trump and Trump supporters, but I don't see evidence of generalized hatred toward Mexicans anywhere in America. Also, you confuse cause and effect. Americans don't oppose illegal immigration because of Trump. They supported Trump because he clearly opposed illegal immigration.

MARC. All I know is that Trump's language *is* the parallel.

STEPHEN. Parallel to what?

MARC. Hate speech!

STEPHEN. If I disagree, I hope you will let me know how I might express myself. Apparently, disagreement equals hate speech. Regarding *Mein Kampf* [Marc had shared a comment posted on the internet comparing Trump to Hitler and referencing *Mein Kampf*], which I read in college and which still sits on my bookshelf, I don't know where to start. All I can say is that you should read it. I have no doubt you would rethink that comparison. I doubt the person making it actually read *Mein Kampf*. No one who actually read *Mein Kampf* would find anything Trump has said about anyone or any group to be remotely comparable.

MARC. I can see that you are much more well-read and knowledgeable. I just have a very high emotional intelligence.

STEPHEN. No. You just hate Trump and are willing to believe anything negative that is said about him. That's not intelligence; it's blind hatred.

MARC. I thought he was a character. I immediately recognized from his actions (like reinventing himself as a conservative) and comments that he was not a genuine or nice person, and his business failures are well documented. I felt he was less entitled to be president than the previous two unentitled presidents.

STEPHEN. I fully understand your reasons for not supporting Trump. You can question whether he is genuine or whether he has the right temperament to be president. I also can understand your desire to support someone else who you feel would be a better president. However, I don't see how comparing him to Hitler, cheering on the abuse of his civil rights, accusing him of nonexistent crimes, and so on is appropriate. Support his opponents in 2020.

HATRED

June 24, 2018

Stephen. Sarah Huckabee Sanders was asked to leave a restaurant in Virginia because she works for the president. Seth Rogen refused to take a picture with Paul Ryan and berated him in front of his children at a fundraiser for Alzheimer's. And you think the hate is coming from Trump?

[6/24/18, 7:54 a.m.] Marc. Yes. They hate what he does, what he says, and what he stands for.

Marc. How is asking her to leave different from telling gay people you don't want to make a wedding cake for them?

Stephen. No. They are ignoramuses. The baker agreed to sell them a cake but not to make a special cake, because he believed it was contrary to his sincerely held religious beliefs. In the case of the restaurant, it is simple refusal to engage in a civilized manner with a person who has a different political opinion. In the case of Rogen, Ryan is not Trump. It just proves that it is not Trump but conservatives that the left hates.

Marc. Didn't follow the Rogen stuff.

Marc. A guy on Fox this morning, during a debate with a black liberal, told him he was out of his "cotton-picking" mind. Even if Trump didn't intend it, he has loosened the bounds of decency and emboldened racists. Hard to argue that statement. You agree there are people who are anti-nonwhite, don't you? They are becoming energized, and maybe you aren't concerned because they are not yet directly or outwardly anti-Semitic.

Stephen. I saw the comment. It was inappropriate, but it does not prove that David Bossie is a racist, that Trump is a racist, or that Trump has loosened the boundaries. The guy he was debating was calling Trump and Republicans racists and using that old Democratic standby of "racist dog whistles." Interestingly enough, Nancy Pelosi saying that MS-13 all have humanity does not constitute support for MS-13, but opposition to illegal immigration is racist. I further note that before Trump, the left was comparing Bush to the Nazis and calling for the murder of police officers, which, by the way, has resulted in actual murders of police officers.

OPEN BORDERS

MARC. I am no liberal when it comes to policing. I was even on George Zimmerman's side. But I do have a question for you, and this one actually is an open question: What's your take on Trump saying that illegals should be immediately deported without any due process?

STEPHEN. I don't know. However, subject to more information, I assume we could stop a person from entering the United States at a border checkpoint if they do not have the right to enter. Therefore, it makes sense that we should be able to deport someone who entered illegally and require them to apply for permission from outside the United States. Due process is a constitutional protection afforded to US citizens. There may be court decisions that extend it to people legally in the United States and even to people with a colorable claim to enter the United States, but due process for illegal immigrants, if it exists, is not the same as for US citizens. Trump's position on illegal immigration is not unreasonable. He wants to prohibit entry to people who do not have the right to be here. The Democrats appear to want an open border. Which policy do you prefer?

MARC. I would be okay with a closed border, but it can't be a spurious executive order that is totally political.

STEPHEN. What makes it spurious? Trump has made clear that his goal is to prevent people from entering the United States illegally. That's his policy and his politics. Do you believe that Trump should not pursue his goals unless the Democrats approve?

MARC. When he just comes out one day and announces something, many in his own party cringe.

STEPHEN. He is not a typical politician, and many in his party don't like it. There are times when his uniqueness clearly is a benefit, as when he recognized Jerusalem, and there are times when it may not be beneficial.

STEPHEN. I did a little research, which appears to confirm that the Fifth Amendment due process protections do apply to persons who are here illegally (but not to persons outside the United States). Therefore, I agree that Trump is wrong to call for deportation without due process. I note that the Obama administration was criticized for deporting illegal immigrants without due process pursuant to a program called Stipulated Removal.

PART 4
JULY 14, 2018– DECEMBER 21, 2018

NATO

July 14, 2018

Stephen. Trump knows that our allies are our allies and that Russia is an adversary. But is it wrong to insist that our allies pay more for mutual defense? We pay 70 percent of NATO's budget. Is it wrong to question why Germany would enter an energy deal with Russia that enriches Putin and gives him leverage, when they could obtain energy from us? So Germany is not paying for its defense, which we subsidize, and is paying Putin for energy instead of buying it from us. How is Trump wrong to raise this? How is insisting that Germany get its energy from us instead of enriching Putin helping Russia? Think for yourself!

Marc. He can insist on all that without threatening to leave NATO and without criticizing our allies' leaders (and then being told he shouldn't and doing an about-face the next day). You have to admit, he has zero credibility. The charade with North Korea. The lack of criticism for Russian interference. The most plausible explanation remains, with lack of evidence to the contrary: he owes Russia something. Don Jr. and Roger Stone have been caught in lies.

PETER STRZOK

STEPHEN. Trump's predecessors also tried to get our allies to step up but were unsuccessful. He has raised the stakes. He believes that the allies need NATO more than we do. He might succeed. He might not. I don't see why he should be criticized for trying a different approach when the conventional approach has not worked. Also, tough love doesn't mean we are not allies. Therefore, his kind words make sense. Again, we will see if his approach is successful, but he is asserting US interests. Regarding North Korea, we will see if he succeeds, but he certainly changed the dynamic. There remains no evidence that Trump or the Trump campaign colluded with Russia. The new indictment is further proof of the lack of evidence. In contrast, the evidence of FBI and DOJ misconduct in the investigation of Trump continues to build.

MARC. Right. Misconduct. Like calling Trump names, like many Republicans who know and work with him do. Funny how Trump "says stupid things" or "jokes," but Peter Strzok's texts are proof of a conspiracy.

STEPHEN. He was the lead investigator, and he promised to stop Trump from being elected and texted about an insurance policy against his election. If he had not been part of the investigation, his anti-Trump and pro-Hillary comments would have been personal opinions. But he was the lead investigator! If you were being investigated by the FBI and the lead investigator made similar comments about you at the outset of the investigation, would you believe the investigation was going to be fair? No way. And you would be right.

MARC. "Promised to stop." How is a text a promise versus the asinine things Trump says weekly?

MARC. You think the lead investigator of the NYPD looking into whether a young black kid is guilty with some early semblance of even a fleeting connection to the crime isn't going to be biased and looking for evidence? That's what investigators do!

MARC. It's a huge, insulting leap for anyone to say this guy who might have privately hated Trump would concoct evidence!

STEPHEN. If you think it is okay for an investigator investigating both presidential candidates to believe that one—who clearly committed crimes—should win one hundred million to nothing and to vow to stop the other candidate, you should be forced to take a remedial course in citizenship and basic fairness. Regardless of whether Trump is the worst person ever to be elected, he was the victim of a conspiracy orchestrated by the US government. It is a much bigger threat to our freedom than a foreign government hacking DNC emails.

MARC. What is your evidence that he was a victim (victims are harmed) of anything other than people thinking he is a con man? Tell me something that was done to the victim.

STEPHEN. Strzok's texts. FISA abuse. Government informants. Unmasking. The whitewash of Hillary Clinton.

MARC. What would your law school professor have said if "Strzok's texts" was the answer to the question "Which actions victimized Donald Trump?" The emerging civil libertarian in you should really be consistent across all people, not just entitled fools fed with a silver spoon.

STEPHEN. I was wrong. Trump is only one of the victims. The others are the rule of law, democracy, and Trump's supporters.

MARC. You are probably right; if not for the vast conspiracy Trump, might have won the presidency. You think there wasn't similar bias to convict Bill Clinton from the Republican-led FBI? Why are you so upset that he was the victim of a conspiracy, given that he remains solidly in power? Some conspiracy!

STEPHEN. It is fortunate that Trump won, notwithstanding the undemocratic and illegal actions of the government. Otherwise, we never would have known what took place. Trump's election was the flaw in the plan. Bill Clinton lied under oath. He also directed other people to lie. That was the source of his problem.

Marc. I win these arguments even when I stay away from my belief that evidence will surface that impugns Trump as a criminal. When that happens, you will probably say, "It's not fair. His rights were violated!" Or "That is not him on the tape! It's an actor!"

Stephen. If you think you won this segment, it is only because all the kids receive trophies. If you still believe that Trump is guilty, notwithstanding that the evidence shows the government tried but failed to make a nonexistent case, you are like the leftists who believe that the Rosenbergs were innocent. As I have repeatedly said, oppose Trump, support his opposition, and campaign for other candidates, but accept that he is the duly elected president, and be careful about the massive abuse of power in 2016.

Marc. And your last sentence puts you on the board! It's what I'm doing.

THE PRESS

July 16, 2018

MARC. You are aware and do believe that Putin has had journalists killed. Therefore, saying something like "The press is the enemy of the people" is very dangerous.

STEPHEN. The press is largely an arm of the Democratic Party. It provides nonstop coverage to Michael Avenatti but has zero interest in the US government's interference in the 2016 election. This is not new. Remember Abu Ghraib [a scandal at a military prison in Iraq during the Bush Administration]. However, if the press is going to take partisan positions, then they, by definition, oppose the other party. With Trump, it's partisan reporting on steroids. I don't trust the press to be evenhanded. The anti-Trump press is not serving the interests of the American people.

MARC. Is the *New York Post* part of the press? Fox? *WSJ*? Is more of the mainstream established press anti-Trump and anti-GWB? Yes. But when you combine "The press is the enemy of the people" with "Putin isn't a bad guy," you have no defense.

STEPHEN. There is a partisan conservative press, but it is not nearly as influential as the mainstream press, which falsely claims to be nonpartisan.

HELSINKI PRESS CONFERENCE

MARC. Great job by Trump today. America first!

STEPHEN. I know it may appear that I have nothing else to do but follow all things Trump, but I do have a job. Unfortunately, I won't be able to comment until I have time to learn what took place. But don't worry; I'll be back.

STEPHEN. Based on the limited information I have, it appears Trump gave a terrible press conference.

MARC. If you were implying that sometimes people can say the wrong thing, then I'm sure Peter Strzok agrees with you.

STEPHEN. No. Peter Strzok didn't say the wrong thing. He undermined the rule of law and interfered in a presidential election. It appears Trump cannot separate actual Russian interference with the baseless allegations that his campaign colluded with them. Nevertheless, he should be able to recognize that Russia is an adversary and that Putin can't be trusted.

MARC. That's a pretty big thing that our commander in chief "should be able to see."

MARC. If it was the first moronic, idiotic thing he has said in public, I could cut him some slack. It's probably the thousandth. And since, according to one principle, the most obvious explanation is usually the correct one, he's totally being blackmailed by the Russians. No, I have no evidence of it, but that doesn't make it less of a likelihood.

MARC. Maybe life is so great for you that you are in a bubble of comfort and wealth and health, and Trump as president doesn't enrage you. I'm in that bubble, and it nevertheless infuriates me.

STEPHEN. I think Trump's position on Russia is ridiculous and potentially damaging to our interests. However, he has taken a much harder line with them than the Obama administration. Trump's views on Russia are, in my opinion, naive but are not nearly as dangerous as Obama's weakness was. Nor are they as embarrassing as Obama's obsequiousness to Iran. Remember Iran's detention of our sailors. Trump is not perfect and not always good, but he still is better than the alternatives.

MARC. A tepid comment like "better than the alternatives" is not consistent with the kind of incessant defense you provide. And regardless of his policies or those of his predecessors, paramount in his role as a leader is what he says publicly. Obama is done and wholly irrelevant, and your invocation of his name points out the impotence of your argument: "But he did it. What about …" Face it head-on. Cavuto and others on Fox ripped him. One called him treasonous.

STEPHEN. Everything has to be looked at in context. I find Trump's defense of Putin embarrassing, but we were weaker with Obama and would have been much weaker with Hillary. Why are Trump's comments treasonous, but Obama's apologies for American foreign policy are a strategy? It's that Trump's critics think he's a fool, not because of a qualitative difference. And to the extent there is a qualitative difference, it favors Trump.

MARC. Even Lou Dobbs is ripping Trump.

STEPHEN. I agree. I'm not defending Trump's position on Russia. I think he has damaged his standing with his base. But I believe the reaction to him is different than it would be to anyone else who took a position as stupid as this one, as Obama often did. Trump is an interloper in the US political system and is treated like one.

MARC. If Obama had said that, he'd have been impeached immediately.

STEPHEN. He gave $100 billion to Iran and was not impeached. Get real.

STEPHEN. He also told Putin he'd have more flexibility after his reelection.

STEPHEN. As I watch the news, I believe the reaction to Trump's press conference is a big overreaction. I need to do a little reading, but I note that the Democrats and the media are invested in Russian collusion. It seems to me their reaction is related to their belief in their phony narrative. The attacks on Trump are the true disgrace.

MARC. Newt Gingrich said it was the worst day of his presidency. Period. He has been an apologist.

MARC. Stephen, he stood up in front of the world and said clearly that he believed Russian word over that of US intelligence.

STEPHEN. That may be true, but I wonder if you ever had an independent thought on politics. I agree the Russians sought to disrupt our election in 2016, as they did in 2012 and 2008. Nothing they did in 2016 actually impacted the election, which doesn't mean we should not deal with it. If Hillary had won, it would not be an issue. Furthermore, I can't help but think the Democrats fear discovery of their collusion with Russia. What do you think was in Hillary's missing emails—wedding plans?

My bigger concern is Russia's annexation of Crimea. We cannot accept it.

MORE ON THE PRESS

July 17, 2018

Marc. Was it independent thought when Trump said that he didn't think McCain was a war hero simply by having been captured and that he liked people who weren't captured? To that point, he had intrigued me.

Stephen. You often base your arguments on "So and so said this" or "So and so said that." You don't often examine an issue independently. Your reason for disliking him is the exception that proves the rule.

July 19, 2018

Marc. Press being the "enemy of the people" is a phrase used by dictators throughout history. Don't you find it strange that Putin and Kim Jong Un are admired by Trump and think that maybe he wants to be like them?

Stephen. Much of the press is unhinged. They are not reporting news. They simply are against Trump. They are committed to destroying him. Why shouldn't he call them enemies? For example, it is possible to criticize Trump's press conference with Putin without calling it treason, 9/11, Pearl Harbor, and so on. Objectively, his Russia policy has been stronger than Obama's. He has armed Ukraine, placed troops in the Baltics, and attacked Russians in Syria. Furthermore, Russia's interference in the election occurred while Obama was president, and in October 2016, Obama assured us that an American election could not be hacked and mocked Trump for suggesting it. Where is the press's interest in the Obama administration's actions? What did Brennan do when the Russians were interfering? Nothing, except attempting to frame Trump. No media interest. If you recall, Obama was caught on an open mic telling Medvedev that he would have more flexibility after his reelection. Then he did nothing. Is there a story there? The press doesn't think so.

Obama turned over $150 billion to a government that has "Death to America; Death to Israel" rallies, and Trump is the traitor? Where was the press? You are concerned that Trump calls the press enemies but are not concerned that the press is partisan and is actively working against Trump. I guess you will continue to root them on until the day comes when they try to destroy someone you support.

July 20, 2018

Marc. Are you saying the press is the enemy of Donald Trump? Yes! But which of the following two statement is more likely? (1) The press is the enemy of the people—actively opposed or hostile to the people, or (2) Donald Trump wants to be a uniquely worshipped dictator whose main goal is his own self-aggrandizement, thus invoking a statement that implies he is more important than a basic tenet of our freedom. Think for yourself! You are what we liberals call a useful idiot for Donald Trump.

Stephen. Read your own stupid analysis. The press is feeding lies to the American people. Whose interests are they serving? Not the American people's interests. Your statement number two is a product of the press. The idea that Trump wants to be a uniquely worshipped dictator is such nonsense it is hard to believe that a friend of mine who I know to be intelligent could accept it.

Marc. They aren't feeding lies to the people. Did they lie when they reported that Donald Trump kissed Putin's ass?

Marc. You have to admit, if Obama unilaterally had gone to Moscow and North Korea and conducted himself with the same BS, there would have been calls of "Traitor!" and for impeachment.

Marc. Haven't you seen the clips wherein people go around the room declaring how great Trump is to his face? That is messed up. Having a parade for himself? Come on! That's the easiest conclusion. I can't wait until this crap all comes out. You are defending a really bad, lying guy.

MARC. And I didn't need the press to tell me that. Saying McCain is not a hero? Right there.

STEPHEN. Obama was caught on a hot mic telling Medvedev that he would have more flexibility after his reelection. This means he was telling the American people one thing and Putin another thing. He also pulled American missile defense out of Poland and Czechoslovakia because Putin objected. He refused to supply Ukraine with weapons to defend itself against Putin. He wasn't accused of being a traitor. Trump has taken steps to counter Putin, and he's the traitor? Are you simply ignorant of all these facts (which you would be if you get your news from the mainstream media), or are you simply a fool? In regard to excessive self-regard, Obama declared his election the moment when the seas would recede and so on. Obama received a Nobel Prize for nothing. He declared himself to be the one we had been waiting for. He also stated he was a better speechwriter than his speechwriters. He went ahead with the Iran deal, notwithstanding the opposition of Congress. However, Trump is somehow more of a narcissist? Give me a break.

MARC. I can't win any arguments with you on your knowledge detail. Only on instinct. Hey, are you in Cape Cod?

STEPHEN. It's beautiful. We're here through Sunday. We highly recommend the Chatham Bars Inn. We're heading to the pool shortly.

MARC. I've been there. We are in Martha's Vineyard next week.

STEPHEN. Have a good time!

THE EFFORTS TO REVEAL TRUMP

July 24, 2018

Marc. Instead of a daily harangue from me, I thought I'd just check with you weekly. Trump still doing a great job by you? No concern that he might prove to be as compromised or stupid as people like me think?

Stephen. He's not compromised or stupid, but he is the victim and target of the Obama administration's abuse of its intelligence and law enforcement powers. This effort to undermine Trump should sicken all Americans, even those who don't like Trump.

July 27, 2018

Marc. There is a difference between an organized campaign to smear someone and a concerted effort to reveal who someone is and what he has done. And there will be corroboration of the recent allegations and additional incrimination on Cohen's tapes.

Stephen. Is there a question as to who Trump is or what he has done? You believe it is a legitimate function of the government to reveal who the opposition candidate really is? So the Trump administration would be within its rights to investigate Democratic candidates to reveal who they are? Or only in the event the government makes allegations that the candidate might have done something that may or may not be a crime? If you ran for office, would it be appropriate to investigate your relationships? You didn't do anything illegal, but it might reveal who you are. You may or may not be right about Trump's fitness for office. Regardless of his fitness, there may be nothing that would convince you he is the right person to be president. I respect your views on that. I don't respect your view that it's okay to ignore Trump's civil liberties or that the government should be encouraged to trample his rights in the hopes of finding wrongdoing. If it can happen to him, it could happen to any of us.

MARC. One small difference. If I ran for office to represent the entire country and someone asked me about my relationships, I wouldn't lie. He has repeatedly lied and has a very checkered past beyond. Now you are such a civil libertarian. I am sure you aren't that concerned with human freedom when it comes to how Israel treats Palestinians. I won't debate you on that topic, but I happen to be a one-state-Israel Bibi fan, so I can be consistent when I place the security of our country first over a criminal's civil liberties.

MARC. And by the way, not once have I ever invoked anything personal into the discourse. That wasn't very nice.

STEPHEN. You miss the point. Having known you my whole life, I know you have integrity. Regardless of that and of the total irrelevance of your personal decisions, it could be used against you. I was trying to make a point, not impugn you. I'm very happy for you. It should make you consider how Trump must feel about how ten-year-old personal decisions that are not in any way illegal are being used to attack him.

MARC. I think the bar is raised when you run for president. He usurped it, essentially, like Obama. Each of them exploited people to gain the presidency.

MARC. You can't play the victim card for him when he held himself up to be scrutinized.

STEPHEN. I'm not playing the victim card. I'm pointing out that he is being breathlessly accused of having a complicated personal life, as if it is a surprise or a crime. He also is accused of lying about his discussions with his lawyer about how to deal with extortion. Even for a candidate for president or a president, attorney-client communications are privileged.

MARC. As you know, they waived the privilege.

MARC. It would have stayed privileged.

STEPHEN. Trump didn't waive the privilege, and it's his privilege.

MARC. [*After not answering Stephen's call.*] I would never pretend to talk on the phone to avoid someone, and there, my friend, is one of my first lies in years!

STEPHEN. One time, when we were on the phone, you said, "I could make up an excuse to get off the phone, but we've known each other a long time, so I'll be honest. I don't want to talk anymore." Total honesty.

INSULTS

August 4, 2018

MARC. You told me it was wrong to call Trump a racist. In the span of two weeks, he has called Maxine Waters, Don Lemon, and LeBron all "dumb." Would you concur that this is improper and, if not entirely representative of his actual beliefs, could be misinterpreted by the less enlightened among his supporters as fact?

STEPHEN. I agree with him on Maxine Waters. I don't know enough about Lemon but have seen him make outrageous comments. I disagree about LeBron but don't know what LeBron might have done that Trump reacted to. Trump is an equal-opportunity insulter. It would be racist to treat blacks differently.

STEPHEN. I would prefer if Trump was more dignified. However, he is mercilessly attacked. He fights back.

MARC. When we were kids, did you agree when I called a disabled kid retarded when he stuck his tongue out at us during the Knicks game, when I was rooting for the Nets? Trump is the president. How about he accept the criticism and be above it? Or object or rebut with substance and not insults? The fact that voters enjoyed him calling every opponent, including their own leaders, like Cruz and Rubio, or their wives, short or ugly doesn't make it right.

STEPHEN. I just read the comment Trump made about Lemon and LeBron. It was not nice. It doesn't make him a racist, but it is not appropriate.

BACK TO COLLUSION

August 10, 2018

STEPHEN. The DOJ was working with the Democrats and Clinton campaign on the dossier. This means the government was working with one candidate for president to damage the other candidate. Does this concern you? If not, why not?

MARC. It is definitely on my list of concerns. Along with (1) arranging with a non-ally nation to take down a candidate, (2) changing the plank in the Republican platform at the last minute as a quid pro quo, and (3) lying to congressional investigators and the public. I have about ten more, but I'll get back to you when time permits.

MARC. Oh, and the Steele dossier is probably all true.

STEPHEN. The difference is, there is actual evidence of government collusion with the Democrats as well as a conspiracy to frame Trump. There is no evidence that Trump had any connection to any actions taken by Russia. Zero.

COHEN AND IMPEACHMENT

August 21, 2018

Marc. Michael Cohen pleaded guilty to a campaign finance violation. Do I not know anything *now*? You believe in following rules and law?

Stephen. It's bullshit. It is not an illegal campaign contribution to pay Stormy Daniels, regardless of the guilty plea. Moreover, the amounts involved are drops in the bucket. Obama accepted millions in illegal contributions and received a slap on the wrist, as is usually the case.

Marc. He's going down.

Marc. Where is your spine? This guy is a criminal, and only his presidency is protecting him.

Stephen. Why? What high crimes and misdemeanors? Once again, you thoughtlessly repeat things you read. The prosecutors threatened to ruin Cohen and to prosecute him for things another man who didn't work for Trump would not be prosecuted for, so he pleaded guilty. This is a travesty. The real crimes were committed by Brennan, Strzok, etc. Be patient. You will see.

MANAFORT

August 22, 2018

STEPHEN. It's a witch hunt. Manafort may rightfully have been convicted, but he was prosecuted on transactions that occurred around ten years ago because Mueller wants to pressure him for dirt on Trump. That's an abuse of a prosecutor's power. It also is the polar opposite of the DOJ kid-gloves treatment of the people around Hillary. Mueller is seeking to find a basis to remove Trump from office and to avoid scrutiny of the very real crimes committed against his campaign. Manafort and Michael Cohen are collateral damage. It simply is wrong.

MARC. Manafort was hardly found guilty of merely innocent, meaningless crimes. Don't diminish it.

MARC. Are you going to defend a murderer if it comes out in a future investigation of a Palestinian mastermind? You are so high and mighty. You should be incensed at white-collar crime.

STEPHEN. The crimes are irrelevant. The government previously declined to prosecute Manafort. That was before he served on Trump's campaign. Also, Mueller gave Gates a pass for the same conduct. I agree that Manafort put himself in a vulnerable position by engaging in conduct proven to be illegal. However, that doesn't change the fact that he was prosecuted because of his role in Trump's campaign. Abuse of power.

MARC. When are you going to get through your stubborn head that Trump always only cares about his own hide? He is praising Manafort for "not breaking," and he called John Dean "a rat." Come on!

MARC. Who said they previously passed on prosecuting Manafort?

MARC. This is the tip of the iceberg. Everyone knows it. Manafort changed the platform at the convention.

STEPHEN. The transactions for which Manafort were prosecuted occurred ten years ago. I understand that the government reviewed them but did not take action. There must have been an agreement to toll the statute of limitations. I'll find the source. Tip of what iceberg? This is a witch hunt. They want to run Trump out of town.

MARC. If you had vermin in your house, would you like to run it out?

MARC. I suppose Chris Collins and Duncan Hunter, if the reports are accurate, as they usually are, were victims of revenge against Trump because they endorsed him?

STEPHEN. That's not what the people who voted for Trump consider him [referring to Marc's use of the term "vermin"]. They (including me) are more concerned about this effort to find any reason to undo the election. I know nothing about Collins or Hunter.

PREDICTIONS

August 23, 2018

MARC. Checkmate. Don't question my criticism of this monster.

MARC. You would make an excellent defense attorney.

MARC. I'm curious. Do you come in each day with talking points out on your desk: "Here is how we are going to defend *these* accusations"?

MARC. "If I am impeached, the stock market will crash, and people would be very poor." People will be very poor? Are you kidding me?

STEPHEN. Before the 2016 election, Democrats and their media sycophants predicted economic Armageddon if Trump was elected (the predictions might have come after the election but before the inauguration). Other than the fact that they were spectacularly wrong, what's the difference between the Democrats and Trump?

PROSECUTORIAL (MIS)CONDUCT

MARC. Consistent with what I have always said, he has a uniquely self-centered view of the world. He believes it revolves around him. It's what dictators think. Stop defending him; you are wearing out your efforts.

STEPHEN. He is not uniquely self-centered. He is responding to injustice. Mueller is out to get him and is threatening people with jail and financial ruin to get them to cooperate. He is not acting in good faith.

MARC. He wouldn't be able to get people to cooperate if they hadn't broken the law themselves! What are you missing? Manafort and Cohen are victims? Come on. Even the one holdout juror on ten counts couldn't avoid a guilty verdict on eight counts.

MARC. You always lecture me. You should read Mueller's biography. You have some nerve to criticize his ethics.

STEPHEN. They are victims. But for their connections to Trump, they would not have been prosecuted and threatened. The fact that Manafort is guilty is irrelevant. Compare the treatment afforded to Manafort and Cohen to the treatment of Cheryl Mills and Huma Abedin. They lied to investigators and participated in felonies, but the DOJ declined to prosecute them. I don't care about Mueller's biography. I can see what he's doing: ignoring certain crimes (Fusion GPS, Steele, FISA abuse, unmasking, informants) and conducting dramatic raids against Manafort and Cohen. There is a lot more. As usual, you base your opinion on a description of his biography, not an evaluation of what is actually happening.

MARC. He is an investigator. You look for evidence. Getting criminals to flip is standard practice that you and I and Americans and Israelis have benefited from. He isn't making things up. I am not sure you are intimating that, but you eventually will.

Marc. I wouldn't be surprised if Trump is connected to the mob. He is just thoroughly polluted. He was elected by a large percentage of uneducated people as well as educated people whose primary concerns are their pocketbooks and a pro-Israel stance or people who hated Hillary more. You don't want to admit you are wrong and probably never will. You just keep digging a deeper hole. Sessions (today) and Corker (yesterday) know more than you, and they aren't taking this guy's crap. And Trump, with the entire Congress in the majority, has accomplished nothing that any other Republican would've. But don't worry; impeachment from the Senate will only come if evidence warrants it. He probably is going to resign before that.

Marc. By the way, though I don't think you'll answer this because you'll have no answer, are you implying that it would have been fair to let Manafort's crimes go untried? I challenge you for a yes-or-no answer.

Stephen. The government did let them go until Manafort became connected to Trump.

Marc. How do you know they let him go? They probably didn't even know what sleaze he was until he partnered with Trump, who, by the way, was supposed to bring in the best people. Ha! (Aside from Haley.)

Stephen. Because he wasn't prosecuted.

Marc. Even you know that's lame. Maybe they hadn't investigated, and maybe once he became head of the campaign, he held himself up to higher scrutiny. Or they were gathering evidence.

PERSONNEL

STEPHEN. That's not how it works. They are desperate to justify the actions taken prior to the election. Mueller is abusing his power. The head of the Soviet secret police under Stalin said, "Show me the man; I'll show you the crime." That's what this is about. Trump has brought in great people: Mike Pompeo versus Hillary and Kerry; Nikki Haley versus Samantha Power; Bolton versus Susan Rice; Mick Mulvaney in the Office of Management and Budget; Ryan Zinke in the Interior Department; and the White House barber. During the campaign, Trump had a difficult time finding an experienced campaign manager. Manafort had experience.

MARC. He had a hard time finding a campaign manager because nobody wanted to associate with someone with such a bad business reputation—unpaid bills, Trump University, lying during depositions.

STEPHEN. Don't embarrass yourself.

MARC. Stephen Barry, staunch supporter of Donald Trump.

MARC. Voted Republican his whole life and would take Mike Pence as president tomorrow but continues to hope that no additional evidence of wrongdoing is unearthed against Trump.

STEPHEN. I'm a staunch supporter of justice and fairness.

MARC. Me too! Fairness isn't "He was elected, so he gets to stay in office." If you fuck up and then lie about it, you can't lead the country.

STEPHEN. You mean like Benghazi?

STEPHEN. Where people died.

MARC. That was bad. Unlike you, I don't make excuses for everything. Someone should have been more accountable for that.

STEPHEN. I don't make excuses, but I also don't make hysterical allegations.

HILLARY

STEPHEN. By the way, you voted for one of the people responsible for Benghazi and other misconduct.

MARC. You defend a guilty person [Manafort] for tax evasion. He was found guilty on eight counts by a woman who had a MAGA hat in her car.

STEPHEN. Apparently, some people who fuck up and lie about it are, in your opinion, fit to lead the country.

MARC. Hillary was incompetent. Trump is incompetent and mendacious.

MARC. I was faced with the same hard choice and went with someone I believed to be phony and entitled but not evil.

MARC. Clinton wouldn't have wanted to be a queen.

MARC. You say I don't know much to earn credibility.

STEPHEN. I'm not defending Manafort. My point is that he is a pawn to get at Trump. That is an abuse of power. The families of the Benghazi victims, the people of Haiti, and the women abused by Bill might disagree about Hillary not being evil.

MARC. Evil would be if she'd planned the attack. She was negligent and derelict.

STEPHEN. Regarding Benghazi, we could have sent help, but the military was told not to go. That's more than negligent.

STEPHEN. In your view, everything Trump does or doesn't do disqualifies him. That can't be possible.

MARC. Nope. He held a beautiful ceremony yesterday for a dead soldier. Well done!

PERMANENT INVESTIGATIONS

August 24, 2018

MARC. A nice Jewish man who happens to run Trump's finances was granted immunity. Trump is toast. And when all the crap comes out (if he doesn't resign preemptively), all you will say is "It doesn't matter that he did X, because they were really targeting him!"

STEPHEN. There still is no evidence of any wrongdoing. But I get your point. From now on, every president will be under permanent investigation until prosecutors find evidence of wrongdoing. Along the way, the prosecutors will investigate all people affiliated with the president in the hope of making them talk. Welcome to the banana republic of the USA.

MARC. I think they knew this at the very beginning, as there were tons of crap and clues in his history. No president has any shit like this. None. Had Hillary won, I am sure this whole process that you call a witch hunt would have occurred via the House Committee.

MARC. Trump's interview on Fox had to have been scary even for you: "People will be very poor if I'm impeached." I think Trump never wanted to win and never thought he could win. He has ruined his children's lives. And they probably will be indicted with the information that will come out from the financial guy. The crimes may well not have been collusion and likely happened before he was president. It won't matter.

STEPHEN. You're delusional.

REAL CRIMES

STEPHEN. Why don't you focus on the real crimes committed against Trump, for which there is actual and substantial evidence?

MARC. You sound like O. J. saying he was going to look for the real killers! By the way, do you think the LAPD, seeing the evidence without clear, incontrovertible proof, set out to prove O. J. guilty? You bet they did. Point for Marc!

STEPHEN. No. How many FBI and DOJ employees have been demoted or fired or have resigned? The difference is that crimes were actually committed. For example, it is not disputed that Hillary paid millions (as opposed to $150,000) to Fusion GPS and Steele that were not reported as campaign expenses. I'm waiting for the indictment.

MARC. They are totally going to get to that in another week or so after Trump resigns to save his corrupt sons.

MARC. I say get rid of Trump *and* Hillary!

STEPHEN. But you voted for Hillary.

TELL THE TRUTH AND MOVE ON

MARC. Rich Lowry wrote that Trump should just admit what is obvious: that he lied about Stormy and payments and all that.

MARC. I voted for Hillary because I didn't want Trump to win. Because I knew he would be the kind of president who says, "Without me, you will be very poor."

STEPHEN. I agree he should tell the truth—whatever it is—and move on.

MARC. Maybe he should have said that a year ago and the same with the Trump Tower meeting. When you lie, you raise suspicions.

AUGUST 25, 2018

STEPHEN. Trump is facing an unprecedented situation. As for the Trump Tower meeting, Glenn Simpson, the head of Fusion GPS, had dinner with Natalia Veselnitskaya, the Russian lawyer who met with Trump Jr., on both June 8 and June 10. She met with Trump Jr. on June 9. He testified that he did not discuss the Trump Tower meeting at either dinner. Who are the liars?

AUGUST 26, 2018

STEPHEN. https://www.cnn.com/2017/09/19/politics/mueller-manafort-pressure-decade-investigation/index.html.

STEPHEN. This article confirms that the Justice Department determined not to prosecute Manafort.

SELECTIVE PROSECUTION

MARC. If Donald Trump is completely innocent of all charges or even simply guilty of not reporting the payoffs to women, then I concur that the selective prosecution is unfair and not a wise practice for this country. However, if there is more to the story, particularly additional real criminality and potential exposure that Russians have knowledge of, then the reconsideration of the Manafort prosecution and other means to unearth those facts (which have been rumored and even suggested by Eric Trump) is completely understandable. If there are only claims of lying about election fraud regarding payoffs, I will apologize and admit I thought wrongly. If they charge him with more serious shit, you should consider moving off your stance of prioritizing Trump's rights.

AUGUST 27, 2018

STEPHEN. Trump's comments about McCain were terrible. I thought so at the time and still think so. Trump was not elected to be a gentleman but as a rebuke to the establishment. Trump is an imperfect vessel, but he is addressing a real problem: the disconnect between the political class and ordinary Americans (and not only Republicans). You should consider that McCain himself was a darling of the press when he opposed Republicans but was mocked as Obama's opponent, as were nice guys like W. and Romney. Furthermore, a lot of people think all politicians are full of it and feel Trump is fighting for them.

MARC. One more thing. Trump is a disgusting, vile person. You know it; I know it. Everyone knows it.

AUGUST 28, 2018

STEPHEN. The people attacking him are vile.

September 4, 2018

MARC. Let's see if your powers of defense can reconcile these conflicting views. Or am I vile for attacking him?

STEPHEN. For disagreeing with him, no. For attacking him, yes.

MARC. I guess I'm a vile person then. Who do you think is more likely to actually be vile? Trump or me?

STEPHEN. You're not vile, but you are a poor advocate. Personally, Trump often is not nice. However, he is under withering attack. He responds in kind and sometimes inappropriately. I don't see him as uniquely bad.

MARC. We are way beyond Trump being "not nice." He acts like and says things that indicate he believes he is above the law and much more important than he believes. He said, "I could shoot someone on Fifth Avenue, and my backers wouldn't care." You are among them. Chris Collins and Duncan Hunter were being looked at for a long time, and he is actually saying that the Justice Department shouldn't be playing favorites.

STEPHEN. The Justice Department has a rule about bringing charges prior to an election. They are not supposed to affect an election. If the charges were under investigation for a while, the DOJ could have waited until after the election, allowing the Republicans to have a chance in a special election. I don't know the facts, and there may be good reasons for putting Republican voters in a bind. I have not seen any evidence that Trump believes he is above the law. In fact, it is the opposite. His opponents appear to have committed gross violations of many laws and civil rights and are seeking to avoid accountability. They will not.

MARC. It's not a rule.

STEPHEN. It is a practice. If they bring charges before the primaries, the party can choose a different candidate. Now Republican voters are in an unfair position. Their candidate has been charged with a crime. If the DOJ did not have information prior to the primaries, it is improper to affect the election. Remember, the congressmen are presumed innocent—just like Hillary. The problem with Hillary is that the Democrats decided to go with her notwithstanding evidence that she had committed felonies. That's why the Obama DOJ could not indict her.

September 5, 2018

Marc. I'd rather be a vile attacker of a powerfully dangerous person, with my powers of intelligence and inference intact, than a stubborn mule who puts his head in the sand and is unwilling to admit he was wrong.

Stephen. You're all emotion and no logic.

ANONYMOUS

MARC. When it comes out that it's Pence or Kelly who wrote the anonymous op-ed, the Republican Congress will listen.

MARC. I suppose Woodward and the *NYT* just make all this up?

STEPHEN. If you don't respect someone, don't work for him. When it comes to attacks on Trump, I trust what I can verify.

MARC. The only thing you'll be verifying is that on this one issue we have debated, this one long argument, despite many things you are no doubt dead-on correct about, you were abysmally incorrect.

MARC. Report after report after report has been consistent. These are longstanding, credible sources who collectively, based on the quantity of reports, if occasionally imperfect, have legitimacy that far outweighs Donald Trump's.

MARC. [*Attaches a photo.*] The people behind him are who support Trump because they don't know better. Not you.

LITERALLY NOTHING

September 17, 2018

Stephen. Lisa Page testified that at the time Mueller was appointed, the FBI had no evidence of collusion—"literally nothing." We also know the FBI was leaking information from the FISA application—a crime—and talked about using the leaked information as a pretext for interviewing people. Trump has declassified the FISA application and other documents. The conspiracy against Trump is being blown wide open.

Marc. Yes, but even if they weren't kosher in their pursuit, they didn't fabricate evidence of wrongdoing or lie to investigators. With Manafort and Cohen about to enumerate and substantiate all kinds of stuff, the White House has only one play left, and it won't work. So when you ask me about civil liberties and such, no, if someone is breaking the law, I am not particularly concerned about the means with which they are taken down. See? I'm not a liberal!

KAVANAUGH

MARC. Kavanaugh is a liar. The woman will be compellingly credible, and he will withdraw.

STEPHEN. They didn't fabricate evidence? They provided a court information that they knew was not credible. They leaked that information to create the false impression that there was evidence of wrongdoing and to justify a baseless investigation. Manafort and Cohen are sideshows. Manafort may bring down Democrat lobbyists, but he has nothing on Trump. A lot of Obama officials will go to jail. It is hard for me to believe that you really believe what you say. You say that Trump wants to be a dictator, yet it was the Obama administration that used the DOJ and FBI to try to subvert their political opponents. Regarding Kavanaugh, you support character assassination? The accuser does not remember key details, yet she knows she was groped by Brett Kavanaugh. She does not even know the year. At best, it is a case of mistaken identity. At worst, it is a setup. The woman claims she had no intent to come forward, but she hired a Democratic lawyer and took a polygraph in August. This is very sad and is going nowhere. It's a disgrace.

SEPTEMBER 18, 2018

MARC. Let's choose sides. I have minorities, women, and Jeb Bush. You have Paul Manafort, white nationalists, and the Bible Belt. Those are fair sides! Israel is not playing.

STEPHEN. I have the US Constitution, justice, and fundamental fairness, and you have abuse of power, the wanton violation of civil rights, and lying. By the way, Manafort may be guilty of tax evasion, but he did not seek to subvert our democracy. I can say with certainty that I'm not on the same side as white nationalists, a numerically insignificant group, on the only issue that relates to their beliefs: equal justice under the law. By your analysis, you are with Antifa thugs who oppose free speech and Black Lives Matter thugs who are responsible for the deaths of police officers. They are not numerically insignificant.

THE AVENATTI AFFIDAVIT

SEPTEMBER 26, 2018

STEPHEN. I read her affidavit, and it is not compelling, except as a smear.

MARC. How come nobody is talking about all the women who came out of the woodwork to denounce Judge Gorsuch?

STEPHEN. Because Kavanaugh will change the ideological balance of the court. Read the affidavit carefully, and ask yourself whether there are specific facts—which party, where, what date, who was present. She claims she went to parties at which gang rapes occurred. If that happened more than once, who would go back? Everyone, including the many friends who have supported Kavanaugh, would have heard about it. This is a smear.

MARC. By the way, never do you give even one inch. So you think these woman are *all* lying? The problem for Kavanaugh is not ultimately going to be that he was raunchy (which his yearbook substantiated). It's that he is lying about it. He should have just said, "I was wild, and now I'm not."

MARC. Who are you to question what she says? So everything you ever state is accurate, and you don't lie or concoct, but *all* these other women do? What about Stormy Daniels and Jennifer the *Playboy* Playmate? Everyone dismissed them, and they were proven to be right. Where there's smoke, there's fire. When the women called out Weinstein, I didn't hear you impugning their integrity. Kavanaugh is toast. You'll see. They are going to withdraw him.

STEPHEN. Yes. I think Dr. Ford, Ramirez, and Swetnick are either lying or mistaken. I am reacting to nonspecific claims regarding events that allegedly occurred over thirty-five years ago that are impossible to prove or disprove. Ms. Swetnick alleges that other unnamed girls—not her—were the victims. Who are they? These allegations would be insufficient to support any type of claim. However, you think Kavanaugh is obligated to disprove them? You must be a fan of Joe McCarthy.

STEPHEN. The allegations against Weinstein were specific, serious, corroborated, and overwhelming. No one who was a friend of Kavanaugh in high school, college, or afterward knows anything about any of this. This is very sad.

MARC. How do you explain that his yearbook lists him a member of a club that was named for all the people who slept with a specific woman? Wait until this woman speaks. She will be more credible than a guy who claims he was a virgin despite a yearbook filled with debauchery.

MARC. Let him get approved. And then let him get impeached.

MARC. This from an alumnus of Stuyvesant. I don't even see it as a question of innocence or guilt. This is not a criminal proceeding, and there is no burden of proof. Why would women come forward with such horrific and traumatic stories and subject themselves to being pilloried in the media (always blame the victim!) unless there was a whiff of truth (more than a whiff)? Gee, he drank a lot in high school (and did much worse) and was sexually frustrated—that's it. Oy. And the freaking apologists who come out of the woodwork with "Boys will be boys"—wow. Hope they don't have daughters. Besides, I think every effort to stonewall this guy is merited, and fuck every Republican senator on the Judiciary Committee. Merrick Garland. Mic drop.

NOT PROVABLE OR DISPROVABLE

STEPHEN. He will not be impeached, because these claims, related to events that allegedly took place over thirty-five years ago, are conveniently not provable or disprovable but are not corroborated by the people who knew him at the time. Why would these women do it? I don't know, but if they succeed in preventing his confirmation, they will be heroes on the left. The person who wrote the text you forwarded to me wants to believe these women, but she is wrong about them being pilloried; they are being lionized. She clearly is angry that Republicans have the power to appoint judges, but no one smeared Merrick Garland. The Republicans, as the Senate majority, simply exercised their constitutional prerogative not to confirm.

MARC. I agree there is an incentive for them to fabricate, and I agree they would be heroes. See? You never cede anything, nor can you even state that maybe the women are all telling the truth. The reason these things can emerge at the last minute is because the visibility is raised, and that can move people to action. Even you have to agree that any defense based on "The Brett I know would never" is empty because charming, seemingly nice people do stupid things. Note, by the way, the number of defenders of Kavanaugh who concede, "And even if he ..." You lose the argument when you go there.

STEPHEN. It's possible he did a stupid thing, but participation in a gang rape is much more than a stupid thing. Regarding the use of "even if," it is not clear to me what "even if" would be. The allegations are too amorphous. Aren't you skeptical that these claims are not provable? As the Democrats have said, they simply have to be believed unless Kavanaugh can disprove them. When did Kavanaugh transition from an alcohol-fueled rapist to a pillar of the community? 1983?

MARC. Being $200,000 in debt? Something is fishy.

STEPHEN. Is Kavanaugh $200,000 in debt? What are the details? Most mortgages are larger. He also probably sends his children to private schools. As a longtime public servant, he probably is not rich.

MARC. I am enjoying listening to Trump's press conference. He can be likeable, like when an abusive husband shows a little tenderness to his attention-starved wife.

SEPTEMBER 27, 2018

STEPHEN. Kavanaugh will be confirmed. I'm truly disappointed in you. I can no longer take your moral outrage at Trump seriously.

MARC. So you believe that all the women aren't credible, and the timing is suspicious, but the two men who last night claimed *they* were the ones who abused her—that rings true, right?

STEPHEN. No, not right. Senator Graham reported that the men who came forward are not reliable. If a woman came forward today and claimed you attempted to rape her at a party somewhere in Forest Hills sometime in 1982, what would you do? If a reporter asked me about you, I would tell them I never saw you act that way. I imagine all of your friends would say they are not aware of you ever acting that way. So it would be everyone who knew you and spent time with you against an accusation made by a relative stranger. Who wins?

OCTOBER 6, 2018

STEPHEN. Kavanaugh has been confirmed. A victory for a fine man and well-respected judge. More importantly, a victory for fairness over smears, evidence over bald and completely unsupported allegations, and process over mob rule. Thank God!

MARC. I agree wholeheartedly, and I hope the satisfaction is healthy for you!

STEPHEN. I hope you're serious. It would be healthy for you too.

MARC. Had he simply said, "Look, I did some really stupid things when I was in high school"—not "I was a virgin"—"and college, and I learned from them, as evidenced by my life. I don't want to dignify what those terms in the yearbook meant, because they're disgusting, and I look back with shame on them, and I've learned from them. If you allow me this chance, I will use it to continue to prove my maturity and worth, as I've done for years," this would have been over weeks ago. And not "It's the Clintons!" and "What goes around comes around." Unlike distinguished, admirable people like Neil Gorsuch, whom I truly do respect and who has gained respect just like Romney and Bush in juxtaposition to those in the lineup today, Kavanaugh will always know that he was shamed for crying "like a little baby in diapers," as Trump has said about other "criers," and he will always be known as a liar under oath. He will be laughed at in public. He will be ignored in the courtroom. Can't wait for someone to say in front of the court, "I don't want to listen to what that judge has to say," and suffer the contempt. Worst of all for him, there will be report after report of people backing up what Ford told them, on high-visibility networks. While you disagree with all this, in keeping with the state of play to not yield an inch, you probably enjoyed how Ford, who most every Republican said was credible and probably suffered from "some attack from someone," was mocked by the president. Because you probably thought she was a complete and total vicious fabricator.

STEPHEN. You're very good at repeating Democratic talking points but not very good with marshaling facts. The Democrats announced their opposition to him as soon as he was announced. Certain Democrats referred to him as evil upon his nomination. The Democrats then manipulated Dr. Ford and leaked totally unsubstantiated allegations. Despite zero evidence that supports her claims, the Democrats rushed to announce that they believe her. In essence, the Democrats accused him of attempted rape. Nevertheless, you believe he should have responded by being impartial. No judge or human being is expected to be impartial in evaluating claims against themselves. The Democrats attacked him, and he responded. Furthermore, the allegations are false. Not one person confirmed any aspect of any of the stories. Dr. Ford initially told the *Washington Post* that the attack occurred in the mid-1980s, when she was in her late teens. That changed to 1982, when she was fifteen. Dr. Ford said she doesn't like to fly, but she flies all the time. Dr. Ford refused to turn over her therapist notes or polygraph data to the committee. A friend of Dr. Ford contacted Leland Keyser to ask her to change her testimony. On the other hand, people have come forward to support Kavanaugh's testimony about his yearbook, including Renate Dolphin and students who played devil's triangle. I note that the focus on the yearbook is simply idiotic. You should listen to Susan Collins's speech.

MARC. Why in God's earth would you believe the people who came out last week saying what devil's triangle meant?

MARC. I know I'm right. You don't have to tell me I'm wrong. I'll take Mike Pence as president tomorrow and Amy Coney Barrett on the Supreme Court.

STEPHEN. Why not? They [the students who played Devils's Triangle] don't even know Kavanaugh. You can discount it, but it is a reflection on your closed-mindedness.

MARC. I'm not a Democrat, and I already wrote that had the Dems won on Kavanaugh and then tried to block the open seat for two years, that would have been ridiculous. I respect people like Flake and Kennedy of Louisiana, who at least speak with respect.

MARC. My closed-mindedness? In wanting Pence as president? I'm the only one who will give an inch.

Marc. And I suppose the Renate alumni club was because, as they now claim, they all admired her?

Stephen. Renate commented. Are you aware? She also signed a letter in support of Kavanaugh.

Marc. Commented that she was upset when she learned what *alumni club* meant. You tell me I'm gullible? Not once did I say that he should be denied because he "probably" did it (and he probably did). He took an oath to be on the court and wasn't truthful. I was also the guy who said that it was wrong for a Parkland dad to sneak up on him after the hearing and try to shake his hand.

Marc. Cried like a little baby.

Stephen. What did he lie about? I haven't seen it. He was asked about inside jokes and testified carefully but honestly.

THE REPUBLICAN BASE

October 8, 2018

Marc. I am sure you enjoy being part of the Southern Strategy. You are on the wrong side of history.

Stephen. Are you calling me a racist? Do you believe that anyone who disagrees with you is a racist? Do you believe that rank-and-file Republicans are racists? If so, you're a fool. Take a look at the cities governed by Democrats—Detroit, Baltimore. They are the enlightened ones?

Marc. I'm in neither party. Both are disgusting. I believe you are part of an organization that is filled with mostly white, mostly non-Jewish, and mostly intolerant men.

BACK TO KAVANAUGH

MARC. Max Boot, who knows more than you about politics, a senior fellow, a lifelong conservative, left the party, a party with the useful idiots, to use your term, who believe things Trump says—like "Kavanaugh was proven innocent," for example.

STEPHEN. Thanks for letting me know. I will seek Max Boot's approval before I make up my mind on any issue. Regarding Kavanaugh, I would love to know a single piece of credible evidence that implicates him.

MARC. Implicates him for lying under oath? Devil's triangle is not a drinking game, and don't cite the flunkies who drew up that eleventh-hour letter avowing that it is a quarters-like game. The Renata club wasn't an appreciation club. He said he didn't watch her testimony, when he did. He's not fit for the Supreme Court, as evidenced by his crying like a baby; saying, "What goes around comes around"; and criticizing Democrats, when he said he would be apolitical. I spend my life in medicine, and you spend yours drawing up documents, writing, and defending, yet I make more compelling cases!

STEPHEN. You would be laughed out of a courtroom. You have no idea what facts are. You have no idea what evidence is. Devil's triangle is illustrative. Kavanaugh testified that it is a drinking game. As he is the author of the yearbook entry, that is evidence of what he meant. No one with any knowledge of the entry testified that it means anything different. Opponents of Kavanaugh's nomination, who have absolutely no knowledge of the entry, assert it means something else but cannot offer any evidence to support their assertion. Others who are familiar with devil's triangle confirm that it was in fact a drinking game, corroborating Kavanaugh's testimony. The only evidence offered regarding the meaning of *devil's triangle* is that it was a drinking game. Judge Lieberman, who considers himself so fair-minded and reasonable, would reject the only evidence put forth and conclude that Kavanaugh lied because Judge Lieberman wants to believe that Kavanaugh lied.

MARC. Renate club?

STEPHEN. Again, the only person who knows what he meant testified to his meaning. Is there contradictory evidence? Renate was one of the women who signed a letter in support of Kavanaugh. Although she did not appreciate the yearbook comment, she confirmed that she never had sex with him. Kavanaugh apologized for the comment, although a fifty-three-year-old federal judge should not have to explain a comment in his high school yearbook. It is ridiculous and would be laughed out of any courtroom. What would be problematic is a woman who makes a claim that she was sexually assaulted thirty-six years ago and relies on notes from a therapy session to demonstrate that she reported the claim six years ago but refuses to turn over the notes.

MARC. The only person who remembered what happened that night testified to its meaning. She didn't turn over the notes because they included sexual details, and it would have meant nothing. The senators, as lame as the Ottawa Senators, said the anonymous claims would have merit only if the woman came forward, and she did. Then they said she had no corroboration, and if she had, they would have said, "Uh, it's she said, he said."

MARC. This is the kind of clear legal analysis you get when you subscribe to my newsletter, *Straight Law*.

STEPHEN. Again, you are wrong. The only evidence that there was such a night was her testimony. However, she could provide no details. Kavanaugh and Mark Judge denied that that night occurred. Her friend Leland Keyser stated she never attended a party with Kavanaugh. Ford could not produce any evidence that corroborates her story. In addition, Ford changed her story, which originally claimed that night occurred in the mid-1980s, when she was in her late teens. She lied about her fear of flying. Regarding the notes from her therapy session, you cannot in any fair process cite them and then refuse to produce them. That's what Joe McCarthy did. Also, she refused to turn over the materials related to her lie detector test. I was involved in a trial before a federal judge in which one of the witnesses for the other party told the judge he didn't want to answer a question. The judge told him he didn't have to answer, but if he didn't, the judge would dismiss his party's case. Finally, unlike with Bill Clinton, Harvey Weinstein, Matt Lauer, and Bill Cosby, no credible person emerged to make similar claims. Instead, people from every stage of his life came forward to vouch for him. Based on the record, it is impossible to conclude that she made a credible allegation against him. No law enforcement agency would investigate this claim.

THE CARAVANS

October 24, 2018

Marc. I don't think the so-called caravan is a threat to people.

Stephen. The caravan is a huge threat. Think about it like this: a crowd converges on Fenway Park tonight and demands to enter the stadium. Should they be let in? By the way, the crowd includes Yankees fans, a threat to all red-blooded Sox fans.

Marc. Ha!

BOMB THREATS

MARC. I didn't hear all of Trump's comments, but I heard him say the media had to stop with the vicious attacks. That would be the same as if Trump was shot and, on the day of the shooting, I said, "Well, he shouldn't have been so divisive." Some idiot would probably say that, as Trump essentially did today, but not a thoughtful person.

STEPHEN. Trump condemned violence and vowed to capture the perpetrators. He could not have been more direct. Apparently, that is not sufficient for you. On the other hand, Democrats, like Booker and Waters, have been encouraging mobs, and the media has debated whether it is appropriate to call a mob a mob. Hillary and Holder have threatened incivility. The Democratic senators invited a mob into the Kavanaugh hearings. However, Trump is at fault.

MARC. Pointless.

PITTSBURGH SYNAGOGUE MASSACRE

OCTOBER 27, 2018

MARC. Maybe the shooter in Pittsburgh was a rabid Bernie Sanders Black Lives Matter person.

MARC. It's actually very simple, and it boils down to this: I would not want to be supporting anyone who also is supported by white nationalists. Nor would I want to be supporting anyone also supported by Black Lives Matter. And that's why I choose to be a Jeb Bush and Mitt Romney supporter.

STEPHEN. I hope you are not suggesting that Trump is in some way responsible for this attack.

MARC. If I'd wanted to say that, I would have said that, rather than suggesting it. He is not. What he is in all ways responsible for, perhaps without intention, is promulgating violence. All of his policies can be supported and understood and stated in a responsible and intelligent manner, just like the way you have often been able to cogently distill down and properly communicate. But not so the president. Condoning and even celebrating the Montana candidate who body-slammed a little Jewish reporter, Ben Jacobs, is exactly the kind of message, intended or unintended, that makes bad people feel supported in their hate. No need to respond, because it will just be some irrelevant tangent about BLM or Hillary Clinton.

STEPHEN. I'm glad you are being honest. All views other than yours are irrelevant. I guess that's easier than defending your views. In this case, it appears your point is that Trump and Trump alone supports hate. If Jeb or Romney had been elected, would they have been responsible for a mass murder? They certainly would have been accused of it. Remember Gabby Giffords? Would the Democrats have attacked them on immigration? Would the Democrats have encouraged mobs and called Jeb or Romney a Nazi? Maybe leftists would even have held up severed heads or, as they did with W., imagined assassinating him. Before Trump, BLM marched in New York City chanting, "What do we want? Dead cops. When do we want it? Now." Trump certainly has not risen above his opponents. Whether he has made things worse is debatable. However, people like you who find him uniquely at fault in the face of the overwhelming evidence that it is not true, denying reality, will ensure a Republican victory a week from Tuesday.

October 28, 2018

MARC. The attack yesterday was essentially the congregation's fault because they didn't have armed guards? Really? Even if there is a kernel of truth there, you don't say such a thing hours after it happened! You know how I've told you I want Pence as president? It's because even though I am imperfect, I am basically a moral person. As someone wrote, you cannot have an immoral person be a moral leader. Anytime Trump says what he should be saying, it's a statement written for him that is said in a reluctant, dour tone, and usually, his words in the following days dilute the statement. And I repeat: How can you support someone who is feverishly supported by white nationalists? I don't support Bernie Sanders! And no, if a centrist were the president, now nobody would charge him with not doing enough to combat the hate, because he would have already clearly and convincingly repudiated it.

STEPHEN. How can a person who voted for Hillary Clinton state that a moral person cannot have an immoral leader? That's very amusing. Also, you criticize Trump for his comment about armed guards? He didn't say it was the congregation's fault. That's your spin. Go ahead; twist his words. It only strengthens his support.

MARC. He said if they'd had guns, the outcome would have been "much better." Hello! When asked about guns on that tarmac, you say, "This is not the time for questions like that." Are you familiar with the fact that Jews have often been blamed for causing their own victimization? I voted for Hillary because I believed, and still believe, her to be less immoral than Trump.

MARC. I'm not an ideologue, and I always yield to you that you make Trump's policy points better than he does and say I would vote for Mike Pence. I had zero issue with Neil Gorsuch and major problems with Kavanaugh. I'm consistent in wanting a moral leader and would vote against my own financial interests to prove the point.

STEPHEN. In Israel, the congregation would have had guns and maybe even guards. If you believe Hillary is moral, you are willfully ignorant. She's a power-hungry, conniving liar. If you have major problems with Kavanaugh based on a smear campaign devoid of evidence, you are very easy to manipulate.

MARC. All you do is twist my words. Probably every time. If you understood the way English works, you'd see that "less immoral" implies that I find her immoral. I'm against Kavanaugh for his high school yearbook words and the words of his college roommate combined with his conduct and words during the hearing. Oh, you're the one who has been manipulated. I'm the one who thinks for myself. Because who would vote for Mike Pence and a moderate Democrat?

OCTOBER 30, 2018

MARC. By the way, are you also a nationalist?

MARC. Oh, if you had a corporate celebration the night of the Pittsburgh attacks, would you blare "Happy" out of the speakers and yuk it up?

Marc. Oh, last question—a short, easy one. If a TV star ran for president; attracted the support of an interesting mix of white people angry with their lives and looking for people to blame, white nationalists, and wealthy people who care only about low personal and corporate taxes and a strong stance on Israel that any Republican would offer; and then proved to be a misogynist and abettor of racists and blamed Jews in worship for being attacked because they didn't have guards, would you sit silently because you weren't strong enough to admit even the slightest bit of concern amid a national climate reminiscent of 1932 Germany?

Stephen. When the president is proven to be a misogynist and abettor of racism, I'll answer your question. I also would recommend that you brush up on your knowledge of 1932 Germany. Although Hitler did not become chancellor until 1933, neither Hitler nor, in all likelihood, his predecessor condemned anti-Semitism, supported a Jewish state, or had Jews in their families. As for the climate, Trump has never shared a stage with Louis Farrakhan, as Bill Clinton and others recently did. The fact that Trump's opponents call him a racist doesn't make it so.

November 4, 2018

Stephen. By the way, Trump's approval rating among black Americans is at 40 percent.

THE OBSESSION WITH NEO-NAZIS CONTINUES

MARC. https://forward.com/fast-forward/413488/gop-candidate-no-peace-in-israel-until-jews-muslims-convert-to/.

MARC. This is a member of your party!

STEPHEN. So what?

MARC. It's an example of how you are delusional that right-wingers who "love Israel" also love Jews. It's an example of how, if things continue on the curve they're on, the anti-Muslim and anti-Mexican climate is going to swallow up other minorities. But somehow, you are too blind to see that being aligned with neo-Nazis with Trump is not a good thing.

MARC. I'll wait till you go back to the people who tell you what to say.

STEPHEN. Once again, you are showing your ignorance. I don't have time to explain it to you now, but I will.

STEPHEN. I'm not aligned with neo-Nazis, and I'm not aware that there is an anti-Mexican or anti-Muslim climate. There is a recognition that certain Muslim groups, including the Iranian government, al-Qaeda, ISIS, Hezbollah, and Hamas, are terrorist organizations and threaten Israel, the United States, and the West generally. No one is anti-Mexican, but many oppose illegal immigration. Muslims and Mexicans in the United States are almost universally treated with respect. All you are saying is that those who disagree with you on certain policy choices are racists. That's a very compelling argument. Regarding the religious Christian who believes in Christian doctrine, it doesn't disturb me. If I have to choose between a religious Christian and an antireligious atheist, all things being equal, I'd go with the Christian. Finally, your comment about me talking to the people who tell me what to say is funny. It may have worked in third grade, but I know why I think what I think. It's not clear that you do.

MARC. You are aligned with neo-Nazis in terms of your support of Donald Trump. Is that an accurate statement?

STEPHEN. No.

MARC. You tell me that I am a useful idiot, so I can say that you are reading talking points. I have a growing antipathy for indecency in all forms. Immigration has needed reform for years, but that doesn't mean someone who finally tries it inhumanely should be revered.

STEPHEN. I'm not aligned with neo-Nazis. Nor is Trump. There is no significant neo-Nazi movement in the United States. It is irrelevant.

STEPHEN. Trump has not taken any action that is inhumane.

MARC. Separating families.

STEPHEN. It is not inhumane. The families make the choice to enter the United States illegally. The separation of children from parents who break the law is a function of parents breaking the law. The fact that the Democrats won that political battle doesn't establish that the policy was inhumane, only that the Democrats successfully characterized it as inhumane. They could work with Trump to fix the law and stop encouraging illegal immigration, but they won't. They prefer props to helping people.

NOVEMBER 5, 2018

MARC. President O. J. Nixon is pretty nervous right about now.

JIM ACOSTA

November 8, 2018

STEPHEN. Jim Acosta was completely out of line, but you take issue with Sarah Sanders? I saw what Acosta did. The intern attempted to take the mic, and he physically refused to let her take it.

MARC. I saw it too. Physically? He was rude. All I know is that your vaunted Ben Shapiro agrees with me!

STEPHEN. If a player refused to hand the ball to a referee the way Acosta refused to hand over the mic, the player would be ejected. Acosta has been banned. That's the right result. I'm glad you're listening to Ben Shapiro. Maybe you'll learn something.

MARC. I learned that unlike you, Shapiro disagrees with occasional actions and statements of the president, just as I occasionally agree with them. That's balance. You, on the other hand, never yield on a point and never give an inch, which lessens your credibility.

STEPHEN. I do not always agree with Trump. When I do not, I do not conclude that he's a racist or is implicitly encouraging racism or that his actions are qualitatively worse than his critics'. My credibility is based on the validity of my arguments and assessments of facts. Once again, your argument is that someone agrees with you. You and Ben Shapiro take issue with Sanders's statement that Acosta put his hands on the intern. He did not let her take the mic and shook her off. I think Sanders's characterization is fair. If you believe he was rude but not physical, I think you're wrong, but it is not all that important.

INTERIM ATTORNEY GENERAL MATTHEW WHITAKER

MARC. I heard the press conference midway, which I think was after the incident, though I didn't know about it as I listened. I thought Trump sounded avuncular and reassuring and pragmatic. I enjoyed listening to him. I have a hunch that's the real guy, and his handlers turn him into a divisive demagogue. It may be the other way around at this point—I don't know. But then he appointed someone who liked him from TV to acting attorney general. Now it's going to be back to the old stuff. If he had nothing to hide regarding Mueller, he wouldn't need this guy.

STEPHEN. He appointed Sessions's chief of staff. A real guy. It's temporary.

MARC. That real guy said that Sessions was right to recuse himself from the Mueller investigation because of the appearance of impropriety.

STEPHEN. Okay, I'm missing your point. I like Sessions and think Trump was unfair to him. Sessions did a great job of implementing Trump's agenda.

NOVEMBER 9, 2018

MARC. Some guideline says Rosenstein is supposed to be the interim. Trump went around that because this guy, who was nothing in government except a US attorney, said as a pundit that the Mueller investigation should be starved. He also denied Russian involvement in the election of 2018 until recently. He was chosen by Trump to oversee an investigation in order to protect Trump, and that is not what an attorney general is for. We need checks and balances and separation of powers.

MARC. It's pretty obvious Trump is afraid the report will impugn his family.

STEPHEN. By the way, your analysis of Whitaker is devoid of facts and based on conspiracy theories.

MARC. Maybe the last article was, but I heard his voice say that "someone" should strangle the investigation.

TRUMP AT MIDTERM

November 14, 2018

MARC. Proud to have Donald Trump as our president? What a complete and utter laughingstock.

STEPHEN. What are you talking about?

MARC. Nothing new. He's a big baby who doesn't go to Arlington on Veterans Day, watches TV all day, and undermines all our institutions. He calls elections he and his party lose rigged but not the ones he and his party win. He lost tons of seats in all the swing states that voted for him in 2016. He hired for acting attorney general someone for a specific reason the whole world knows. He is radioactive; nobody wants any part of him anymore. He is done, and it's actually better he isn't impeached, 'cause it's now a long, humiliating torture.

STEPHEN. As usual, you're thoughtlessly spouting bullshit. It's funny; it is the Democrats who cannot accept losing elections. That's the premise for the Mueller probe and the disgrace that is Broward County. By the way, O. J. is going to hire Mueller to find the real killers as soon as he finds evidence of Trump-Russia collusion. Fortunately, O. J. is in no rush.

MARC. The prestige you have gained in defending Trump will age in Nixonian and O. J. fashion. Bret Stephens and Ben Shapiro are already reviving from the hypnotic state they found themselves in.

STEPHEN. The Trump administration is doing a good job. Trump is unconventional but refreshingly honest. He has his issues. He brags. He exaggerates. He is crude. However, so are his critics. And most of them have been abject failures. Judge Trump by the same standards as everyone else, and he looks fine.

MARC. Refreshingly honest, exaggerator, crude, unconventional—those descriptions are more apt for a sociopath than a president of the United States. If he was able to deliver the country unparalleled security, harmony, and wealth, maybe those terms and characteristics in the POTUS would be worth tolerating.

NOVEMBER 16, 2018

MARC. There's only one way to explain this: people who aren't millionaires, consumed with Israel, or blinded by hate are disgusted with Trump. Feel free to explain another way.

STEPHEN. You're right. Trump is controlled by rich, scheming Jews. Thank God that guy shot up the synagogue in Pittsburgh. If there were only more like him. I hope you realize the idiocy of your last comment. I'll also note that most of the people who attend his rallies are neither Jews nor rich.

MARC. Uneducated white men love Trump. People with education who voted for Trump out of antipathy for Obama or Hillary have now left the party, at least symbolically on Election Day. Given the economy is doing well, please explain so many flipped House seats in nonrural areas.

MARC. The educated people who left the party exclude the groups I mentioned, who proclaim as accomplishments "Trump moved the capital of Israel! Trump lowered corporate taxes!"

STEPHEN. Okay, Jews and stupid racists support Trump. Great analysis. By the way, did you see Kamala Harris compare ICE agents to the KKK? I guess that's the educated view of the world. Also, Trump is popular with people who appreciate that the economy is booming, including white working-class people who now have jobs. Also, people who believe that our laws should be enforced, especially at the border; people who believe in religious freedom in the United States; and people opposed to identity politics support Trump, as well as people who believe in constitutional judges. There are reasons to support him. My favorite is that it drives you crazy.

ADAM SCHITT

November 18, 2018

Marc. I suppose you won't express even the slightest disgust at Trump calling Adam Schiff "Adam Schitt." Or do I have no sense of humor?

Stephen. I don't think it's helpful, but Schiff has been promoting the fabricated claims that Trump colluded with Russia. That is much more consequential. But I guess making false allegations against a president you don't like is okay.

Marc. Oh, okay.

Marc. You couldn't possibly have replied, "It's not helpful." Couldn't bring yourself to avoid a defense of such a vile statement. Last night, he said there should be more decorum in the White House. Again, that was his statement just last night.

Stephen. You're ridiculous. There are two sides, and according to you, one has a free pass, and the other is vile.

Marc. The president of the United States called a congressman "shit," and you don't think that is corrosive and, given his platform, yet another thing for anti-Semites to run with?

Stephen. No. By the way, Schiff is a political hack, but he is a congressman and should be treated with respect. Trump is the president and should be treated with respect, but he is not by Schiff or any of his Democrat colleagues.

Marc. I think this issue highlights where we differ. If Trump's actions were all enacted by a responsible, presidential President Trump, including things I have argued against, I wouldn't be close to this animated against it. I wasn't against Obama when he took many stances I disagreed with, like backing Michael Brown or being anti-Israel. I love the presidency, and I also hate mean people. You aren't mean when you believe someone committed a crime he might not have. I didn't even think Trump was mean with the birtherism, which at the time didn't bother me because I never found the tone corrosive or racist—he might have made those same claims against a liberal president of Asian or European lineage. Just have a little decency! It's not indecent to maintain the things Schiff does, or was it so when Trump maintained the birther movement? But the repeated nonpresidential statements continue.

STEPHEN. Schiff is indecent. He peddles claims that he must know are false. He and other Democrats have questioned Trump's mental competence. In addition, they routinely call him a racist and anti-Semite. From what I have seen, Trump's critics and opponents aren't qualitatively different from him. Despite the claim that he lies more than anyone else, he is the most candid and transparent president we ever have had. Again, can't say that about his detractors.

MARC. Schiff doesn't believe his claims are false. You can disagree with him or believe his claims to be false, but on what basis could you assert that he believes his claims to be false?

STEPHEN. I disagree. He knows they are false. At some point, there has to be evidence. He cites nonsense. If he's not a liar, he's a malicious fool.

STEPHEN. The Democratic leadership made up the alleged collusion. That is the crime.

MARC. If Russian illegals hacked and stole information and then peddled it as a weapon to WikiLeaks with approval or involvement of Trump's team, you don't think there is a problem with that? Because that proof will exist.

STEPHEN. You're right. If Mueller will just investigate every person involved with Trump, he might find something someday. That's the American system. I hope the next president is under immediate investigation for imaginary crimes. By the way, you're not concerned that several top-ranking DOJ and FBI officials have been fired for involvement with real crimes.

November 20, 2018

MARC. Just a friendly tip: you might want to start thinking of ways you will be able to explain your alliance with Donald Trump. It's not a good look to any outside your insular group.

STEPHEN. I have a tip for you. You're the one in an insular group. A group that is thoroughly incapable of distinguishing fact from fiction and simply believes anything that confirms your bias.

MARC. I'm not like the rest, because I had no bias until he started with statements that were uniquely and completely reprehensible, like McCain's not being a war hero. You probably have a defense for that too: "He says stupid things." When is something beyond stupid and instead irreparable? And I'll tell you what: the Israeli government that says, "The Saudis were wrong, but …," would be singing a different tune if the Saudis ordered a hit on a prominent Israeli citizen.

IVANKA'S EMAILS

MARC. "Uh, but that's different. She didn't know. Right? How could she have known?" It's not like her father ran for president with a daily diatribe against Hillary Clinton for this.

NOVEMBER 21, 2008

STEPHEN. Another good point. I wasn't aware that Ivanka is secretary of state, set up an unsecured private server to conduct government business, transmitted classified information, destroyed thousands of emails, destroyed hard drives, and lied about it. Now that you have pointed that out, I have to agree with you. Don't be such a dope.

MARC. Oh, so the higher you are in government, the more serious your gaffes are? Oh, I see.

STEPHEN. That is true. However, Hillary did not commit a gaffe. She subverted the law, lied about it, and destroyed evidence. The security risks associated with the secretary of state being compromised far exceed the risks associated with Ivanka Trump's limited role. Also, Ivanka did not set up a private server, did not transmit a large number of emails, did not transmit classified emails, did not lie about it, and did not destroy evidence. Otherwise, it's exactly the same. If you don't see the difference, I will invoke the Twenty-Fifth Amendment to the Orthopedic Constitution and have you removed from your practice.

MARC. Ha. You can't be so adamant about someone being reckless with emails and then completely defend what Ivanka did, even if it wasn't as egregious. It's like making repeated statements against a person for armed robbery, and then that person is nabbed for petty larceny, and you defend their actions as "not that bad." Trump is attacking the army and the chief justices, so everyone sucks, and he is great?

STEPHEN. It's not the same thing at all. Ivanka sent emails at the start of her government service. There is a learning curve. You have to train yourself not to use your personal email. Ivanka's actions deserve a "Be careful, or you will get in trouble." Hillary was in government a long time and purposely subverted the law and national security.

MARC. I am impressed at your latent skills as a defense attorney. You have an answer for every asinine thing he says and does!

STEPHEN. This is not a response to anything Trump did or said. This a response to the asinine comparison of Ivanka Trump's foot fault to Hillary's intentional violations of the law.

MARC. All depends on what Mueller has. Trump is a known quantity. Everyone knows he's crooked, a total ass, and a pathological liar and has no moral center—this doesn't bother 40 percent of the country. No new information adds much.

STEPHEN. No one knows that.

STEPHEN. I hope you had (and are having) a happy Thanksgiving.

MARC. You too!

TRUMP'S RUSSIA CRIMES

November 26, 2018

Stephen. https://www.nationalreview.com/news/monica-lewinsky-bill-clinton-told-me-to-lie-about-affair-in-sworn-affidavit/.

Stephen. If you want to know what obstruction of justice by a president is, read this article.

Marc. I have been watching this series and have said many times that he should have been impeached based on her being an intern and his fooling around with her in the White House. Trump is going to have a whole array of credible facts revealed that won't necessarily cause him to leave office but will render him fully impotent and unable to run again at best.

Marc. He will be shown to have lied to the people on many fronts (not under oath, so not a crime). He will be shown to have borrowed crazy sums from Russia and Saudi Arabia, which has shaped his decisions. That will not look good to the more intelligent of his supporters.

Stephen. Right. I'm glad Mueller is keeping you fully up to date on his progress. By the way, what decisions about Russia are you speaking about? He has been tough on them. Your accusations are thoughtless drivel.

Marc. His saying, "Putin is not a bad guy"; not agreeing with the consensus that Russia interfered; and kissing Putin's ass in front of the whole world.

Stephen. That pales in comparison to arming Ukraine, calling out the Germans for buying Russian natural gas, and taking other military steps regarding the Baltics and more. Russian interference had nothing to do with the outcome of the election. It might have happened and should have consequences, but it was irrelevant. However, the FBI and other Obama national security agencies interfered, and we are still dealing with this phony Russian collusion.

MARC. If there is financial proof of substantial loans to Russians, would that make you concerned that Trump was literally and figuratively indebted to Russians?

STEPHEN. I have no idea. If Trump borrowed money from a party in Russia and has paid it back or his business is paying it back, that is called finance. We'll see.

NOVEMBER 29, 2018

MARC. Serious question. I would really appreciate a straight answer. If Donald Trump is truly running for president on an America-first agenda, do you actually have zero problem with that, given that as he was poised to win the nomination, he was lying that he had terminated business dealings with Russia, when he hadn't? He was trying to build a huge Trump Tower Moscow, and a well-sourced report says they promised a $50 million penthouse for Putin! And this has nothing to do with Trump continually kissing Putin's ass?

MARC. Rich Lowry of the *National Review* is "appalled."

STEPHEN. If the penthouse story is true, that's bad.

MARC. You are back! My rational friend!

NOVEMBER 30, 2018

STEPHEN. https://apple.news/ANt6qMQ2CTAuwUwtjYpU7qQ.

STEPHEN. Marc, read this article by Mark Penn, a longtime pollster and strategist for both Bill and Hillary. It lays out a compelling case that Mueller is abusing his power to create the appearance of wrongdoing. I hope you are rational too.

MARC. Penn turned from Hillary to Trump. He is more biased than anyone. He and Andrew Stein, Jews for Trump, started a BS campaign saying they thought Hillary would run again. Just to rile people up.

MARC. Forget Mueller. Do you believe Trump tried to enrich himself with Trump Tower Moscow? That story is consistent with everything I've been saying. Read *my* article. He said, "America first," and was trying to build a tower in Russia and lying about it.

MARC. Just read it. It looks like it was written by an eighth grader, and it doesn't fulfill that promise of the tease of "You won't believe what's coming next."

STEPHEN. Trump was a real estate developer. There is nothing inappropriate about doing a project in Russia. If he promised Putin a free apartment, which I do not believe actually happened, that would be bad, even if there was a legitimate reason to do it.

MARC. (1) He wants to build a billion-dollar building in Moscow and talks with Putin cronies. (2) He tells the American people he has no dealings with Russia and continually lies about it instead of saying, "I'm a real estate developer; there is nothing inappropriate about doing a project in Russia." (3) Early in his campaign until today, he's been submissive to Russia. (4) He changes the plank at the convention in favor of Russia. (5) Russia hacks the election. What are you missing?

STEPHEN. The Russian development was reported at the time it was taking place. He did not lie about it. He has been accused of colluding with the Russian government to hack Hillary's servers. He denies that, and there is absolutely no evidence of it. He has been much tougher on

Russia than Obama. I don't know what "Russia hacks the election" even means. As far as I know, they are accused of posing as Americans and making social media posts. What are you missing?

MARC. "Russia, if you are listening, please find the missing thirty thousand emails."

MARC. Hacked the DNC emails.

ALTRUISM

DECEMBER 2, 2018

MARC. We each take turns telling each other things. It's my turn. All Trump ever has cared about professionally is money. Period. He doesn't have an altruistic bone in his body. Papadopoulos was just reported as having told a friend he was working on a deal with Russia that would make him a very wealthy man. Trump is caught in serious lie after lie, and he is going to be shown as having been involved in an arrangement with Russia that allows Russia to exploit him and have leverage over him, if not directly expect a quid pro quo. It is clearly the reason he inexplicably has refrained from ever speaking negatively about Putin. This is hard to refute. It's not proof, but it is a highly likely scenario. It's not going to be pretty, and as for Mueller, I don't care if he overreached or if anyone overreaches to uncover shit like this. No, I don't care about civil liberties more than I do criminality, and neither did you before Trump. You backed the wrong horse. You should have been a wary Republican like Bret Stephens, not Sean Hannity.

STEPHEN. You can speculate all you want. You don't know Trump. You have no basis for your judgment regarding Trump's altruism. It is simply consistent with your irrational hatred of Trump. As far as I know, Trump has not been caught in any lies. Again, you continue to believe that Russia has leverage of some kind over Trump. You have no evidence, only your belief that it must be true. I reiterate that the only proven liars are McCabe and Strzok, and there is evidence that Comey and other Obama officials lied as well. We shall see who is right.

MARC. Did you ever make a conclusion about what kind of person someone was without knowing them, only based on their statements?

STEPHEN. Yes, but I would like to know on what basis you have concluded that Trump has no altruism. You jump on any story or information that confirms your bias. You do not consider any contrary evidence. Therefore, I have no doubt your conclusion about Trump based on statements that you believe confirm your view of him is simply a rehashing of what you believe. It is not an analysis of Trump's actual record or life.

MARC. Self-promoter! Fair statement?

MARC. He is the definition of that!

STEPHEN. I think that's fair.

MARC. *Self-promoter* is the antonym of *altruistic*!

MARC. Bam!

STEPHEN. No, it isn't.

MARC. Do I get my honorary law degree now?

MARC. It kinda is.

STEPHEN. No politician would be altruistic under your definition. Nor would any orthopedic surgeon.

MARC. I know his charitable record for such a billionaire: not good.

MARC. I've got an opening here, and I am going to drive a truck through it!

STEPHEN. Go ahead. Make sure you don't drive off a cliff.

MORE RUSSIA SPECULATION

MARC. Still on dry land. Here is what may have happened: in order to build the Trump Tower, they needed the financing from a bank that was under sanctions. Trump and his people (Flynn among them) were reassuring the Russians that sanctions would be dropped if and once he became president. If this is indeed the case, that's a checkmate on a Nixonian level.

STEPHEN. Or Hillary and the Democrats sought to create a narrative that Trump was colluding with the Russians, which could be described as "an insurance policy." The virtue of this version is that there is evidence that it occurred.

MARC. Page 17 of your manual on how to defend Trump: "When you have no point, in the final days before you have to say, 'I was wrong,' invoke the name of Hillary or Obama."

MARC. This stuff isn't made up. Where there is smoke, there is fire. If he wanted to be president, a complete dissociation with business was necessary, as it involved an adversarial nation.

MARC. You know it; everyone knows it. The question is, was it just a stupid move and innocuous aside from the duplicity or worse?

STEPHEN. Trump-Russia collusion has nothing to do with a business transaction that did not take place. It has everything to with Hillary's failed campaign. Thoughtless repetition of the bullshit spread by Hillary's campaign and the Obama administration doesn't make it real, no matter how much you want to believe it.

BACK TO MUELLER

MARC. So if Mueller has everything documented, which it sure seems like he will, would collusion still be a story concocted by Hillary? The guy was double-dealing at best, and at worst, he was sacrificing the security of this nation by cozying up to a thug that every Republican, even those who back Trump, like Lindsey Graham, loathe! Even you said Helsinki was bad, and now we likely know one of the reasons.

DECEMBER 3, 2018

STEPHEN. Trump did not collude with Russia, but Hillary hired Fusion GPS to get disinformation from Russian intelligence sources. That's a fact. The FBI used Russian intelligence disinformation as a basis to investigate Trump. Everything you believe is propaganda.

MARC. Collusion is small potatoes now. It's much worse. The basis for the investigation is secondary to what is uncovered.

STEPHEN. Nothing has been uncovered, except wrongdoing at the DOJ and FBI.

STEPHEN. I'm glad you were born Jewish. If you hadn't been, you would be easy pickings for anti-Semitic propaganda. There are people who are just as certain that the Jews control the banks and media as you are that Trump committed some yet-to-be-determined crime. Their beliefs are based on the same evidence that you assert: "Everybody knows." I know you have a brain. Use it.

MARC. I am seeing all the dots, and like many, I follow them, as well as my own deductions, in connecting them. You too are following propaganda.

STEPHEN. None of your dots are real. You connect propaganda dots.

December 4, 2018

MARC. Michael Flynn had nineteen interviews with Mueller, and Mueller recommends no jail time! You know what that means! Ha-ha-ha. So Flynn implicating everyone is just propaganda, eh?

STEPHEN. It means this whole thing is a farce. There is nothing in the report on Flynn about collusion.

LYING: BILL CLINTON VERSUS MICHAEL FLYNN

MARC. Kenneth Starr was not hired to prosecute Lewinsky.

DECEMBER 5, 2018

STEPHEN. Clinton directed people to lie about Lewinsky. Clinton lied about a tawdry affair. Flynn was involved in Trump's campaign and transition. He is charged with nothing except lying to investigators after the fact, even though the investigators who interviewed him did not believe he lied. This is a disgrace.

MARC. What's wrong with lying to federal investigators?

MARC. I looked up *disgrace* in the dictionary: "e.g., when the CIA director appointed by Trump lays out for Congress that Saudi Arabia's leader ordered the hit, Trump's biggest supporters dress him down by saying that anyone who can't see what is obvious needs to have his judgment questioned, and the current administration equivocates about it."

STEPHEN. He didn't lie. He was threatened with prosecution for lying. That's a big difference.

STEPHEN. Saudi Arabia is about politics. Khashoggi is terrible, and MBS is a thug and should go. I think Trump could handle it better, but he is no different from all of his predecessors. There is nothing new.

MARC. Bill Clinton's lying was about politics.

STEPHEN. Bill Clinton obstructed justice. He directed people to lie under oath. That is not politics.

MARC. Donald Trump obstructed justice. At the very least, he asked the Justice Department not to investigate Michael Flynn.

STEPHEN. Trump could have ended the investigation of Flynn, which he did not do, and it would not have constituted obstruction of justice. That is his right. However, under no circumstances does a president have the right to direct someone to commit perjury.

TRUMP PAYMENTS TO STORMY

December 8, 2018

Marc. You have to admit that if there is proof on tape or testimony from the Trump Organization CFO that he knowingly used Trump Organization money to pay off women who were making claims against him, it's, to a lesser extent, election fraud and, to a much greater extent, tax fraud. The bigger issue here is the Russians floating the idea of paying Trump hundreds of millions of dollars in exchange for dropping sanctions, making statements against NATO, and more. You can't say there is no proof, because the report was only now previewed. And by the way, the Steele dossier is getting corroborated piece by piece. You still want to cry, "But it's not fair they investigated him!" as your defense?

Stephen. Keep dreaming.

Marc. Oh yes, it's so far-fetched and ludicrous. It's actually a commonsense inference.

Marc. The Trump Organization did pay for that, and they also broke the reimbursement up into monthly payments to disguise it.

Stephen. The campaign finance laws do not apply to payments made by Trump to Stormy Daniels. Trump's efforts to resolve an attempt to extort money from him is not a campaign finance violation. If Cohen made the payment and was reimbursed, that is not a violation. However, even if there was a violation by someone, the normal response would be a fine for the candidate, not a $30 million investigation over a $150,000 payment. I haven't read the memos yet, but I hope to do so.

THE INAUGURAL COMMITTEE

December 13, 2018

Marc. The *Wall Street Journal* is all over your guy. I suppose all that is reported, all that is alleged, and all that is pleaded to is garbage and part of a left-wing conspiracy? How did it ring when Hillary deflected the similar deluge against Bill as a vast right-wing conspiracy?

Stephen. I read the *WSJ* every day. I don't know what you're talking about. Did you read the editorial about the FBI's tactics against Flynn? It was a disgrace.

Marc. There's new reporting that inauguration funds were misused.

Stephen. Don't you find it odd that everything related to Trump is investigated? Especially when you consider things the DOJ has chosen not to investigate in the past?

Marc. A special counsel was appointed. Just like Starr, who investigated everything Clinton, as you know.

WHY NOT ACCEPT THAT THE RUSSIANS INTERFERED?

MARC. I have a simple question for you, one you will have no good answer for: When all of Congress on both sides agreed and accepted the finding that the Russians interfered in the election, why do you think Donald Trump continues to publically and continually refuse to accept that finding?

STEPHEN. The federal judge overseeing the Flynn case ordered Mueller to produce all the FBI reports on the Flynn interview by 3:00 p.m. tomorrow. Flynn was interviewed on January 24, 2017. The FBI report on the interview originally relied on by Mueller is dated in August. However, the report was referenced by Comey and McCabe as being written contemporaneously with the interview, as they are supposed to be. This could be big. Regarding Russian interference in the election, it was irrelevant. Nothing compared to the FBI's interference. Trump clearly objects to the false implication that Russia had anything to do with his victory. Russia is a red herring for gullible useful idiots.

MORE ABOUT CAMPAIGN FINANCE VIOLATIONS

MARC. Trump lied to the American people in saying he knew nothing about these payments. He not only knew, but he was involved in them. If you lie once, you lie often. If Comey was caught in a lie, you'd be apoplectic.

MARC. Flynn admitted to lying, as did Papadopoulos.

STEPHEN. Comey has been caught in many lies and was fired. Trump may have lied about whether he knew about the payments, but the payments are also a fake issue. It is not illegal for Trump to make the payments. It's a personal matter. The fact that Flynn pleaded guilty to lying is more about the FBI's and Mueller's abuse of their power, as is now evident, than about any actual lying. Open your eyes.

December 14, 2018

MARC. Trump knew the payoff to the woman was wrong and knew about the scheme to reimburse Cohen. Felony and conspiracy.

STEPHEN. There is absolutely nothing wrong with the payoff. The extortion against Trump was wrong. If you believe that anyone else in America would be accused of a felony under these circumstances, you are kidding yourself.

MARC. Weak point. You are admitting it was a felony.

STEPHEN. I'm saying that no one would be accused of a felony. Cohen pleaded guilty to something that was not a crime and not related to the business conduct that got him in trouble. But for Trump, Cohen might not have been prosecuted at all. He certainly would not have been criminally charged with campaign finance law violations.

STEPHEN. By the way, for the 2016 campaign, Clinton raised $1.2 billion, and Trump raised $647 million. Thus, the payment to Stormy Daniels represents about 0.2 percent of the money raised by Trump. Even if it were clearly illegal, like millions raised by Obama, it would be treated as a civil violation for any candidate except for Trump. Furthermore, if Trump listed it as a campaign expense, he would be investigated for using campaign funds to pay a personal debt. This is nonsense.

BACK TO MUELLER

MARC. I agree to a small extent (you never agree with anything I say other than conceding his unpolished nature). But when it is shown that Russia influenced Trump's public statements, policies, and stance against Ukraine in the platform at the convention, he is done! And please acknowledge that Trump was always an oily businessman and person and that all career federal prosecutors might indeed be biased against him, but they all don't concoct evidence.

STEPHEN. They have in this case, and I don't know what it means to be an "oily businessman." He is, in my opinion, a self-promoter and a good one.

MARC. Oh, they invented all the evidence and should be blamed for all the lying, and there's no culpability among the thirty-three indicted by Mueller. Sure.

STEPHEN. He convicted Manafort on totally unrelated matters. He convicted Cohen on unrelated matters and compelled him to plead guilty to campaign finance violations that are not crimes. He indicted a group of Russians who have no connection to Trump and who will never appear for trial. The FBI entrapped Flynn, and then Mueller ruined him financially for a guilty plea to lying about a perfectly legal activity—a conviction that may be thrown out based on the FBI's and Mueller's abuse. He also convicted Papadopoulos for lying about perfectly innocent conversations and got him sentenced to two weeks. That's a really strong record for someone who has spent $30 million to date. On the other hand, Comey, McCabe, Strzok, Ohr, Lisa Page, and Baker all have been fired, demoted, or forced out. That tells you everything you need to know about this ridiculous investigation.

MARC. If Flynn's activity was perfectly legal, why did he lie?

STEPHEN. He didn't lie. He pleaded guilty to lying. Two different things.

MARC. Oh, I see.

PROSECUTORIAL ABUSE

MARC. Something done all the time: pleading guilty to a crime one didn't commit. Got it!

STEPHEN. You have no idea how much power prosecutors have to destroy your life. Flynn willingly met with the FBI to discuss perfectly legal conversations. The FBI advised him he did not need a lawyer and asked him not to bring one. Months after the conversation, he is accused of making an untrue statement. There is a possibility the guilty plea could get thrown out based on prosecutorial misconduct. However, at the time, Flynn may have felt that pleading guilty was a better option than going to trial, facing further investigation into his business dealings, and bankrupting himself. It shouldn't be that way, but it is.

MARC. You didn't answer. If Flynn and Papadopoulos lied about perfectly legal activity, why did they lie?

MARC. Flynn was supposed to be defense secretary and, as someone just said on TV, someone supposed to be aware of threats far and wide, yet he was hoodwinked into a meeting and claims he didn't know he couldn't lie to the FBI?

DECEMBER 15, 2018

STEPHEN. Whether or not Flynn or Papadopoulos consciously lied or misspoke or have a different recollection is unknown. The point is that we know that if the information they provided to the FBI was exactly consistent with what the FBI or Mueller believed to be accurate, there would have been no crime. However, Mueller wants to get Trump. He tells Flynn, "I will prosecute you for lying"—which does not mean he would win, but it would be extremely costly and risky for Flynn—"or you can plead guilty and cooperate." It is abuse.

STEPHEN. Flynn agreed to meet with the FBI because he thought they were on the same side. If the FBI had said, "You are under suspicion," I'm sure he would not have met without a lawyer.

DECEMBER 16, 2018

MARC. You can lie if you aren't under oath—it's okay!

MARC. "We didn't do it. We probably didn't do it. Even if we did it, it's not illegal." Convincing!

STEPHEN. Do you even know what Flynn supposedly lied about? Or are you talking through your you-know-what?

MARC. They didn't "break into" Cohen's office, as you know. It's called a search warrant. Giuliani implied today that Trump didn't actually have affairs with the two women (of course he did), and while most everyone says that's no big deal, Giuliani said that the relatively small amount of money paid to these women suggests they weren't telling the truth. Come on! Regarding Flynn and Russia, you do realize that no evidence has been released directly other than what wasn't redacted. They have everything on Trump or his sons. He is done. Finished. Even without impeachment, he won't get the nomination. Corker and others will challenge him, and they will be unburdened to do what you and his powerful supporters should be unburdened to do: tell him to get the ef off the stage, as he is embarrassing himself, his supporters, and the country. The swamp is thicker than ever, Mexico ain't paying for the wall, and the tax cut means things only for people like you (not me).

TRUMP'S ACCOMPLISHMENTS

December 17, 2018

Stephen. If I had realized that Mueller has personally advised you about the redacted evidence, I would have given more credence to your position. I assume you have agreed to maintain the confidentiality of the redacted information; therefore, I won't ask you to disclose it. Regarding the payments to the women, do you believe paying off women who are seeking to extort money in connection with alleged affairs that took place ten years earlier is a campaign expense? It's ludicrous. Also, the payments, if they were made by a donor, constitute less than one half of one percent of the money the campaign raised. If taking millions of dollars from foreign donors, which clearly is illegal, is resolved by a fine, why would these payments ever be a felony? Only because it's Trump. Trump isn't embarrassing himself. The economy is stronger because of tax cuts (which have screwed me big-time) and deregulation, more people are working, wages are up, and our foreign policy is rational (we are not giving hundreds of billions to our enemies, and we are supporting our friends). If you think Trump is the problem, would you prefer Macron? You are elitist, and whether it is Trump, Brexit, or the yellow vest protests, there are millions of people who are fed up. Trump may have his faults, but his critics are worse. I support Trump because I hate the abuse of power and unfairness he is dealing with. He wasn't supposed to win, and the elites are seeking to undo it.

Marc. There is some truth to things you have written. You could say those payments weren't a campaign expense, except Rudy said, "Can you imagine if those reports came out a month before the election?" By the way, you have to admit that it is possible, despite your stated cynicism, that Trump's universally acknowledged obsequiousness to Putin is consistent with the reports about Trump Tower, the revision of the party platform, and what could be a quid pro quo or even blackmail from Russians.

MARC. Also, you know how I told you I believe that Trump wants to be king and dictator, and you say that's ridiculous? He said that *Saturday Night Live* should be investigated for being one-sided against him.

STEPHEN. I agree that Trump should not speak about investigating *SNL*. But Trump is not going to take any action against NBC or *SNL*. His comments simply highlight *SNL*'s bias. I don't agree with *SNL*'s position but have no problem with the show. Regarding Trump's "obsequiousness to Putin," I don't agree that it is universally recognized. In fact, the reality is that Trump has made Putin's position a lot harder. Putin had no opposition from the United States at all until Trump became president. Finally, China, not Russia, is the biggest threat to a liberal democratic world order. Trump is the first president to challenge them.

MORE ABOUT BASELESS ALLEGATIONS

December 18, 2018

Marc. Now Flynn's team has dispelled any of this BS that he was treated unfairly. By the way, Judge Jeanine lauded this judge last weekend.

Marc. Trump is so effed!

Marc. The Trump Foundation board of directors hadn't met since 1999. And you ask why I think Trump is a fraud? Wake up!

Stephen. Nothing has changed. Trump is being investigated for anything and everything. The Russia probe is not investigating a crime, as there never was any evidence of collusion. It is simply an effort to force Trump out of office. It's a disgrace.

Marc. You'll be saying the same thing after he resigns.

Marc. You probably think Woodward and Bernstein were a disgrace for how they attacked Nixon.

December 19, 2018

Marc. I guess you and Fox listeners know more about this case than Judge Emmet Sullivan, the one who told Flynn his conduct approached treason?

Stephen. The judge apologized and acknowledged that he was factually incorrect. He apparently thought Flynn was acting as a registered foreign agent for Turkey at the same time he was acting as national security adviser. However, he was not. Regardless, based on what I know, Trump is being investigated based on baseless allegations about Russian collusion, and the prosecutors are pulling out all the stops to connect him to a crime. This should never happen in the United States. You think it's appropriate because you don't like Trump. Instead of corrupting our justice and intelligence institutions, you and all Never Trumpers should focus on the 2020 election. Unless, of course, you want riots in the street like Paris.

Marc. The judge only apologized about that one distinction, not taking away from a strong rebuke. We are a country of a rule of law, but you guys are "That wasn't that much of a crime. That wasn't that big of a deal. Hillary Clinton did worse."

Marc. Trump worked for years in a quasi-legal, swampy way, like many people who are not under investigation. If he is selectively targeted, it's not because people don't like him. It's because he is the president!

Stephen. You make my case for me. In the United States, you don't investigate people; you investigate crimes.

Marc. Trump signed a letter of intent and then campaigned for president while promising better relations with Russia. Then he told voters he had nothing to do with Russia. That's the definition of *conflict of interest*. He's so eager to make the project happen that he just kissed Putin's ass publicly.

Marc. And today he pulled out of Syria against the advice of our own military!

December 20, 2018

Stephen. Having now read a more complete report on the Flynn sentencing hearing, it is clear the judge invited Flynn to withdraw his guilty plea. He was frustrated that Flynn's lawyers declined.

MARC. Interesting take. He did ask him to clarify that his plea was not coerced and that he knew his lie was a crime, no?

MARC. What about Trump going rogue on Syria withdrawal?

STEPHEN. It is possible that Flynn or his son has legal exposure in connection with the lobbying work he did for Turkey, as evidenced by the indictments of his associates. He may not want to upset the deal. It also is possible he lied about his conversations with Kislyak, but based on his description of the conversations, he appeared to be generally accurate in describing perfectly legal conversations. The point is that Mueller is using every bit of leverage he has to get Trump. It is a disgrace.

TRUMP AND HIS CRITICS

MARC. Not once have you ever used the term *disgrace* for any of the almost monthly disgraceful things Trump does.

STEPHEN. I don't see Trump as that different from his critics. He is attacked as a traitor, mentally incompetent, antidemocratic, and antiwoman. He fights back. If I were an adviser, I would encourage him to be more dignified and not to be petty. However, if he followed that advice, he still would be attacked, as the Bushes and Reagan were. In his way, he is the most honest president in my lifetime. He tells you exactly what he plans to do. I thought it was great that he accepted responsibility for the possibility of a government shutdown. No one else does that. I note that Schumer was smirking when Trump said he would take responsibility, because Schumer would never in a million years be so forthright. You think Trump is in a slimy business, but he made his money through building buildings, licensing his name, casinos, and TV. In contrast, the Clintons got rich by selling government influence. Which is more legitimate?

MARC. Not sure why you always mention Clinton. Am I going to defend Stalin by saying that Hitler was worse?

STEPHEN. Trump does not exist in a vacuum. You seem to think he is uniquely bad. My question is, what makes him so bad?

MARC. I'll tell you. He is uniquely selfish and a braggadocio, obvious compensations for inadequacy. Being blunt and brash only gets you so far. You need substance. He has none.

STEPHEN. No substance? He pulled out of the Paris Climate Accord. He recognized Jerusalem. He passed tax cuts. He met with Kim. He has compelled the Europeans to provide more funding for NATO. He has slashed regulations. He has a clear stand on immigration. He has challenged Chinese economic warfare. It seems to me there is a lot of substance.

MARC. I cannot believe you think he is responsible for any of that. He has handlers with those interests who told him what to do.

STEPHEN. No one advised him to recognize Jerusalem or to meet with Kim. He was told not to pull out of the Paris Accord or the Iran deal. However, every president takes advice. How is he different?

MARC. Meeting with Kim was asinine and unproductive. ISIS defeated? Nobody is in favor of this, and Mattis said, "I'm done."

MARC. Please stop defending Trump. He retweeted a *Green Acres* parody with the market down four hundred points, and his cabinet dawdles.

SYRIA WITHDRAWAL

MARC. The Republicans are turning on him. He is done.

STEPHEN. The country and economy are in better shape than they would have been if Hillary had won.

MARC. Stop with the Hillary crap. Who cares? You don't have to justify your vote. That was three years ago. How you can defend his actions, recent actions in particular, is beyond anyone. Are you watching the news? Even Fox!

MARC. The secretary of defense resigned and schooled the president in his letter.

DECEMBER 21, 2018

STEPHEN. It has nothing to do with justifying my vote. The point is that you criticize Trump for everything and anything he does, based on a standard you apply to no one else. If you apply that standard to others, they do not meet it either. So be honest: Trump is not uniquely dishonest—in fact, he is extremely honest about policy—or lacking in substance. You simply do not like him. Therefore, instead of seeking to overturn the last election, which you, not I, can't get over, focus on supporting a candidate to unseat Trump in 2020.

MARC. I can get over it because it'll be over soon. Funny how you have stopped defending his actions and have reverted to your go-to comments that invoke Clinton. You can't defend the Syria move, and you can't defend the obvious influence Russia has over him. Regarding Israel, he knows nothing about Israel. He knows nothing about anything. I wouldn't call G. W. Bush a rocket scientist, but he exuded decency.

STEPHEN. Now you believe he should be removed from office because you disagree with his decision on Syria, which you attribute to Russian influence? What is the evidence of Russia's obvious influence over him? How do you know he knows nothing about Israel? The Democrats believe settlements are an obstacle to peace. They also believe that Israel regularly responds to attacks with disproportionate force. They claim Israel is an apartheid state. Do they know more than Trump? You sound like an uninformed but all-knowing undergraduate.

MARC. Look at the macro, not the micro. I'm not trying to convince you. I've been trying to tell you, to warn you, that when this guy is out of office and everything is revealed, you are going to lose all credibility, based on your ignorance. And you similarly are warning me that Trump's misunderstood, unorthodox style is actually a magic touch and that at the end of the day, I will have been proven to be the ignorant one. I predict that your only recourse will be "So what that he committed (crime, crime, crime, crime, crime)? It's not fair! Everyone has committed crimes if you look hard enough."

DEFENDING TRUMP

STEPHEN. What is going to be revealed? Is there going to be Mueller II? Mueller hasn't accused Trump of any crimes, and he is doing his best to make things that are not crimes appear to be crimes (e.g., Stormy Daniels). You are a good Bolshevik: "Show me the man, and I'll show you the crime." Trump, as a president, is a wild card. To date, he has been a huge improvement over Obama. However, his impulsivity may backfire. If he takes actions that turn out badly or if I disagree, I can imagine supporting someone else, but not the Democrats, who I believe are far worse.

MARC. What does "Mueller hasn't accused him of any crime" mean, when he hasn't released his report?

STEPHEN. Don't hold your breath.

MARC. You should be saying, "I'll take any Republican *now*."

STEPHEN. Why? Because you imagine, based on your fervent dislike, that Trump has committed crimes? Or because he supports policies you disagree with?

MARC. I actually agree with many of his policies, but I am viscerally upset, as you can see, with his constant self-aggrandizement. I hate people like this in all walks of life. He became the nominee (just to take Clinton out of this) because his demeaning personal attacks were so amusing to people who have nothing in their lives but to live vicariously through his calculated and phony disdain for political elites. His tweets reveal his imbecilic nature (whereas you claim him to be smart).

STEPHEN. He is mercilessly and personally attacked and has been since he entered the 2016 race. He is often inappropriate, but more often, his critics are worse, and they attack his supporters too.

MARC. Maybe he is mercilessly attacked because he deserves to be! You think Obama wasn't attacked? He was attacked by Trump, among others—for playing too much golf and wearing a beige suit!

MARC. I'd say you have about three days to get out from Trump and admit you are wrong and have been wrong, lest waiters in Delray, in the year 2035, question your lunch order with "Wait—are you sure you are in a position to choose that meal correctly? After all, you did defend Donald Trump until the end."

STEPHEN. I defend Trump because he is attacked unfairly. It has nothing to do with whether he is or is not a good president. He has to defend himself against a totally false claim: Russian collusion. His real crime was winning a primary election and a general election that our pompous political class, whom he holds in contempt, did not expect him to win. What they don't understand is that Trump won mainly because a critical mass of Americans are fed up with a political class who worry about nonsense like transgender bathrooms and not the lives of ordinary people. The same thing is happening in the United Kingdom and France. You don't get it. The people out to get Trump are ruining our country.

MARC. If Bernie Sanders had been elected president in 2016, you'd be singing a much different tune, as he would be attacked by all the Trump defenders, and then you would be the one not getting it. Do you always defend those who are attacked, regardless of their performance? Really?

STEPHEN. You have one of the most well-developed internal senses of fairness of anyone I know. Yet with Trump, it doesn't function. I would disagree with Sanders on most things, but I would not support an investigation based on a false allegation originating from his opponents that turns into an investigation into everything he has done and everyone who has worked for him.

PART 5
JANUARY 17, 2019– MARCH 31, 2019

REPORT THAT TRUMP TOLD COHEN TO LIE TO CONGRESS

JANUARY 17, 2019

MARC. https://www.buzzfeednews.com/article/jasonleopold/trump-russia-cohen-moscow-tower-mueller-investigation.

JANUARY 18, 2019

STEPHEN. That's not good.

STEPHEN. If it's true. And if it's coming from Cohen, it's suspect. In fact, every fact about Russia is suspect.

MARC. The markets have been going up in the face of this inevitably. Do you think the markets will drop big?

MARC. There is going to be evidence. Probably McGahn.

MARC. They won't be able to say everyone's lying.

STEPHEN. I think it's bullshit. Trump's project in Moscow—which didn't happen—is not relevant to anyone except conspiracy theorists who only care about Russian connections if it's Trump. It would not be relevant even if Trump proceeded with the project. Russians do business here, and Americans do business there. That being said, if he directed someone to lie to Congress, that is not good. I doubt it. It was not necessary. The big bombshell this week is that Bruce Ohr advised the FBI and DOJ leadership in August 2016 that the Steele dossier was connected to Clinton and that Steele was biased. It's funny how this Buzzfeed story comes out right after that.

MARC. Even if his building the tower could be deflected as not being a conflict or not influencing his foreign policy as president, if the report is correct, he will be impeached or resign. And the latter story proves there were people who didn't like Trump—many hated him. That doesn't mean the information that originated from bias is irrelevant.

STEPHEN. The bottom line is that Trump did not collude with Russia to influence the election. However, Hillary did, and the FBI and DOJ interfered big-time, which is the scariest part of this. Not only that, but it appears Comey and others have lied under oath to the FISA court and Congress. Any effort to impeach Trump will ensure his reelection.

MARC. Did you copy and paste that from last year? If there is proof he violated the law by suborning perjury, he is done. Ben Shapiro agrees.

STEPHEN. I don't agree.

MARC. Meaning senators would not be moved on that? Maybe. But I think they will.

MARC. The incoming attorney general who was advising Trump was on record during the confirmation hearings as saying that suborning perjury was obstruction of justice.

STEPHEN. I agree that directing someone to provide false testimony to criminal investigators during his term would be a serious issue. The question you should consider is, on what basis would a practicing attorney follow such a direction? I would not do it, nor would anyone I work with do it. I can imagine discussions on the best way to handle that question. It is the attorney's job to make sure the responses are truthful. Also, Trump responded to written questions. What did he say? My guess is that this story fizzles. The investigation itself is the fruit of a poisonous tree—a fake narrative.

January 19, 2019

Stephen. As predicted, the Buzzfeed story has blown up. Mueller confirmed that it is not true. In fact, the story was totally unverified. In fact, I'm embarrassed I didn't recognize that it could not have been true. If it had been, Cohen would have been charged with obstruction of justice.

Stephen. Fake news!

Marc. So I guess you're saying that Mueller must be a credible source.

Stephen. On this question, he would know. Do you wonder why you are sucked in by bullshit over and over again?

Marc. Yes, Mueller is a very accurate and fair person whose word should be listened to. As for the story, you saw the words from Mueller. Sure, there is much worse, and this was all coordinated as well, though perhaps not told directly from the president. Someone wrote that Trump and his followers are eager to lap up the table scraps they are thrown, in this case from Mueller's equivocal denial.

Stephen. His statement was not equivocal. Nor does Mueller's denying the story make the investigation valid. Bruce Ohr testified to Congress that in July 2016, he briefed top FBI and DOJ officials, including Andrew Weissmann and another attorney on Mueller's team, that the Steele dossier was connected to Clinton and that Steele was biased. This contradicts the story that they did not know about Clinton and that Steele was credible. It also contradicts the time line about learning about the Steele dossier. They used it for the FISA application anyway. Also, it is the basis for this investigation. It is an attempted coup.

THE FBI'S CONDUCT

MARC. Even before Trump came along, if someone was clearly guilty of a serious crime and the process needed to be tweaked a bit to ensure conviction, I was all for it.

MARC. And you would be too if you were a victim.

STEPHEN. That's scary. Also, unless you're talking about the FBI, I'm not certain who is clearly guilty of a serious crime. It certainly isn't Trump. The investigation has lasted longer than the campaign, and it was started with full knowledge that there was no collusion. It has been an all-out effort to justify the crimes committed by the FBI and DOJ against Trump and the American people.

MARC. Or it could be that Trump is the Manchurian candidate.

MARC. Someone just posted a tweet of Trump's from a year and a half ago wherein he wanted to join forces with Putin to prevent cybercrime. Are you agnostic to the fact that the Russians hacked into our electoral process and also stole emails and published them?

MARC. Trump has been attempting to build a giant tower in Moscow, using influence that would be gained with a quid pro quo.

MARC. You are appalled by texts from FBI workers that basically say, "I can't believe this douche we have as president," which actually is understandable. But in your mind, Trump can do no wrong.

MARC. By the way, you used to say Trump is smart. I'm sure after watching his reading of cue cards, his constant spelling mistakes, and his thinking that coyotes were actual coyotes, you would concede he's a moron. I'll be, in your eyes, a magnanimous, altruistic champion of America.

STEPHEN. Your response to lies about Trump is to attack Trump and speculate that the lies must be true. The Manchurian candidate is pure fantasy. So is your speculation about a quid pro quo with respect to a deal that did not happen. Your lack of concern about the FBI's anti-Trump texts, which speak about an insurance policy against his election, is willful ignorance.

MARC. These FBI people knew what a crook he was for most of his professional life and what a degenerate, indebted, sensationally overrated, and disgustingly philandering man he was; the whole bureau knew.

STEPHEN. Really? How did they know that? Do you believe the FBI is a type of secret police, like the Gestapo or KGB, that should randomly investigate American citizens? They have been trying to prove collusion, which you seem to believe they know occurred, except they have no evidence or even probable cause. But somehow, they know he is a crook. Let me know what crimes he committed and when he was convicted. It's sad that a person as educated and intelligent as you seems to want to live in a police state (provided that you agree with the head).

MARC. Rudy implied collusion occurred in the campaign. Next argument?

MARC. The police state is the one Putin is running from afar.

MARC. See? I am one of the few people who is not an automaton ideologue blinded by a passionate agenda. I want Mike Pence for president!

NICHOLAS SANDMANN AND TRUMP TOWER MOSCOW

MARC. Okay, just tell me that these kids' behavior is unacceptable, even if it has nothing to do with Trump. Please tell me.

STEPHEN. I watched it [the short initial video] several times, and I couldn't figure out what they were saying or doing. What was going on?

MARC. "Build that wall."

STEPHEN. What behavior are you objecting to? A political rally in favor of the wall?

MARC. You didn't think they were acting like a mob and disrespecting that veteran? Mocking him?

MARC. What about the smug looks and that one guy getting in the veteran's face?

STEPHEN. I couldn't tell if the veteran was for or against them. What was the veteran saying?

MARC. The veteran was chanting at an indigenous peoples rally, and these guys surrounded him and started laughing, and the one guy was basically looming smugly, almost goading the elder to push him away. Complete disrespect and intolerance.

STEPHEN. If they were being disrespectful, that's inappropriate. However, it is not clear to me that anything at all happened. Trump and his supporters are called names, yelled at, and attacked on a regular basis. This is America, and everyone should be free to express their opinions without being intimidated. If that's what was happening, it is wrong. It certainly is not a Trump phenomenon. Too many anti-Trump people, including you, believe that the law does not apply if Trump or Trump supporters are the victims.

January 20, 2019

STEPHEN. I read your Facebook post, and you simply mischaracterized what I said. I have watched the video over again and reached the same conclusion: the video is inconclusive. Of course, you have no problem jumping to a conclusion when Trump is involved. However, if you really think I would ever support being disrespectful to any person, you don't know me very well at all. Furthermore, if you want to mischaracterize what I say to prove to your self-righteous anti-Trump followers the moral failings of people who support Trump, don't write to me.

STEPHEN. The transaction did not go forward. Nor is it illegal to build buildings in Moscow. Compare that to the Clinton Foundation, which took hundreds of millions for selling access.

MARC. He was poised to become president, and his foreign policy was influenced by this potential deal. It's relevant, whether it went through or not, and you know that.

STEPHEN. It's a made-up issue.

MARC. Made-up issue? Giuliani today basically implied Cohen's testimony that the tower talks ended in January 2016 was a lie, and it was discussed with Trump and/or Trump's lawyers. That's called collusion to lie. By the way, if Cohen was such a terrible attorney, why was he handling a $300 million project? The last thing to cap off your day of misjudgments: the MAGA high school students have had many stories of their intolerance unearthed, and their own school is considering expulsion. The fact that you make it seem like they were victims of the elder chief's aggression shows again that you don't know how to apply objective common sense to evaluation situations. You watch that video and think, *Hmm, I can't really say these kids are disrespectful little shits, because that would be conceding a micron toward the argument that Trump cultivated hate. Better say, "It looks like the Indian elder chief must have taunted the fifty teen boys."*

STEPHEN. The Moscow tower is a made-up issue. Trump is a real estate developer. He was working on a project in Moscow. That's what real estate developers do. You seem to believe he spent hundreds of millions of dollars to run for president to get approval of a project in Moscow. Are you really that gullible? There is no evidence of collusion related to the Trump Tower project or anything else. Regarding the incident at the Lincoln Memorial, you said the chief was at an indigenous persons rally. That's not true. He had been at a rally. He was no longer at the rally. You said the students surrounded him. They did not. He approached them. You said one student was "looming smugly" and goading the chief to push him away. That's not true. The chief approached the student, who simply continued to stand there. So your description of the incident is false in every respect. Furthermore, I didn't see any of the students do anything but chant along with him. They may have thought it was funny, but at sixteen, you also would have thought a guy dressed like a Native American banging a drum and chanting at you was funny. They had no idea who he was or what he was doing. However, you're willing to condemn them because they were wearing MAGA hats. By the way, the chief is an activist. He was hoping to make a video for gullible people like you. He probably succeeded beyond his wildest dreams.

MARC. Chanting along with him? You lost the argument right there. "Aw man, this guy is cool. Let's chant along with him in support. How's it go, Chief?"

STEPHEN. They didn't do anything to him. He approached them. You lose the argument because every fact you asserted was false.

MARC. He approached fifty-plus physically intimidating, raucous, disrespectful, hormonal bigots-in-training who were mocking him? Good for him!

Marc. Or they were just minding their own business, having a spirited gathering, and he decided to confront them for no reason to make the news. I don't think so.

Stephen. They were physically intimidating? Are you on crack? You don't think he approached them? It's not an opinion. Watch the video. No facts matter to you. When every fact you assert is false, you continue to maintain your position.

Marc. Trump had a $300 million deal approaching the approval stage while he was campaigning and spewing, to most people in both parties' surprise, unusually favorable things about Russia, including changing the platform and suggesting Putin's a great leader. That's made up?

Marc. They were mocking him from about a hundred feet away, so he calmly refused to be ignored and gradually walked toward them. Hey, the school apologized. I accept it. Next issue.

Marc. And I'll accept Ivanka Trump's apology as she tries to have a New York City life again after the utter humiliation of her entire family ending up under indictment.

Stephen. Trump clearly spoke approvingly of Putin. That's apparently his view. It had nothing to do with the project, which did not go forward. I'm glad you're not a businessman. Spending hundreds of millions to run for president—a race he was widely expected to lose—is not a cost-effective way to obtain approval of a project, even a $300 million one. Regarding your new argument that the Covington students were mocking the Chief from a distance and that he refused to be ignored, I guess you established that at the same time you established that the students are hormonal bigots. Because you have evidence of that in the video. The school's apology is irrelevant. It could not have been the result of an evaluation of the incident, so it must have been offered to mitigate the embarrassment caused by the reaction to the video.

STEPHEN. By the way, conservatives are pro-Israel and pro-Jewish. It is the Democratic Party and left who are at home with anti-Semitism.

MARC. I'm not voting Democrat. I'm voting for any other Republican but Trump, as I have told you many times.

MARC. Excluding any Roy Moore types.

STEPHEN. But you think conservatives who support Trump are bigots and anti-Semites?

MARC. No, the Trump fans who are bigots and anti-Semitic aren't conservative, because they are generally less well off. They are angry white people looking for scapegoats, and you should be ashamed to be part of the same team as them.

STEPHEN. I'm glad you cleared that up. I knew something had to be wrong with them. Is it possible they have a different view of Trump than you do and legitimate reasons for supporting him while being good people? Just a crazy thought.

MARC. Many, I suppose, are good people. Fair statement?

STEPHEN. I suppose.

MARC. "Until ten minutes ago, kids were able to be kids. They should have ignored him. Comported themselves better."

STEPHEN. Okay. That is not the same thing as calling them racist bigots. Nor does it excuse an adult for baiting them, which is the point of the story.

STEPHEN. Just admit you were duped. Don't feel bad; you could work for the mainstream media.

STEPHEN. One last thing: as I frequently encourage you, think for yourself!

MARC. Duped about what? They were just cheering about their school, and the Indian tricked them? If he had been a topless female who walked in front of a pack of teen boys, and then they got whooped up and groped her, would you say she started it by walking toward them?

STEPHEN. It was a false story intended to paint the students as white racists. You bought it hook, line, and sinker.

MARC. I actually didn't think they were racists. I thought they were entitled, arrogant high school punks. At first, I didn't even see the hat. Yes, I do think Trump's constantly derogatory comments against Mexicans and Indians enabled this kind of behavior.

STEPHEN. What behavior? These students didn't do anything wrong. Furthermore, Trump doesn't constantly make derogatory comments about Mexicans or Indians. If you haven't noticed, the left believes anyone who holds a position with which it disagrees is considered a racist.

MARC. Pocahontas.

MARC. By the way, Trump's real estate licensing deals generally gain him "only" a few million dollars. Why was this Trump deal $300 million?

STEPHEN. Mocking Elizabeth Warren for her ridiculous claim of Native American heritage—which she used to advance her career—is fair game. It is mild compared to the attacks on Trump. I have no idea what is meant by a $300 million deal. It could mean a lot of things, but he would not make $300 million at one time.

STEPHEN. The $300 million probably refers to the cost of the project. Trump would have had to invest or raise $300 million to build the tower. Trump would then sell apartments, offices, and stores and receive fees for managing the property or licensing his name to the management.

January 21, 2019

STEPHEN. None of these kids [Nicholas Sandmann and his classmates] were in school in 2015, so whatever happened [regarding a 2015 photo of Covington High School students], it did not involve these kids. Nor does it have any bearing on what happened at the Lincoln Memorial on Friday. Finally, aren't you tired of jumping to conclusions without knowing any facts? You have no idea what the circumstances regarding that photo are. However, you're willing to circulate it because you're a hater—a hater of white kids who attend a school in an area where people support Trump.

MARC. Maybe *you* jumped to facts? You don't have a video from before they started their school chant. More than that, they come from a culture of hate. Yes, there are militant, extreme liberals and minorities who hate Jews and whites, and yes, there are the same on the other side. In the middle, however, are many more measured whites who have a hidden pedigree, long ingrained, of hate toward minorities. That has been the Republicans' dirty secret that they keep. They want the South to help them out one day every four years, and that's it.

STEPHEN. Do you have any understanding of prejudice? Do you listen to yourself? You believe, based on a thorough investigation you must have conducted in your spare time, that Covington, Kentucky, is a culture of hate? Do you even know where Covington, Kentucky, is? What you're saying is despicable nonsense. It's like "All Jews are cheap," only worse. I may not have all the facts about what happened at the Lincoln Memorial, but I have read several accounts that are consistent with video evidence. The students' story appears to be the best description of what happened. Nathan Phillips's [the Native American activist] account was blown out of the water.

STEPHEN. Covington is a suburb of Cincinnati, Ohio, a hotbed of racism.

MARC. I am claiming that a percentage of white people in the Rust Belt and South grow up around prejudice, and this had been cooling or at least simmering for years until this president unleashed it, made it okay, and ran on a platform that said Mexicans were rapists (aside for the admission that some, *he supposed*, were good people). Trump *supposed* that *some* were good people. That is despicable! And he pretended he didn't know who David Duke was and wouldn't condemn him until his arm was twisted into one of his phony prompter statements.

STEPHEN. Your argument is embarrassingly ignorant. You believe that Americans—at least certain ones, the deplorables—were latent racists whom Trump empowered to express their racism. His opposition to illegal immigration was the signal—this is what the Democrats believe, but normal people understand that criminals take advantage of our lack of enforcement of immigration laws, which permits bad people to enter the country. I have not seen any evidence that Americans are more racist under Trump. In fact, America is probably the most tolerant country that has ever existed. You can continue to spew Democratic talking points about how Trump and his supporters are racist. Meanwhile, blatant anti-Semites are welcomed into the Democratic Party, American citizens are denounced for their religious beliefs, and the Knights of Columbus are denounced. While you're protesting fake racism and nonexistent racists, real bigots are taking over. Don't be a fool.

MARC. There are new videos. The Indian was walking through, and most kids parted the way, and the one jerk stood firm to block and challenge him.

STEPHEN. Stop it. The kids were being harassed by a group of Black Israelites, an extreme and crazy group. They were calling the kids crackers and faggots, among other things. Nathan Phillips claimed in an interview that the kids were harassing the black activists. That was simply not true. The kids did not know what Nathan Phillips was doing. Some apparently thought he was on their side and then weren't sure. I don't understand why you want to believe that a group of high school students waiting for their buses, who were being harassed by an extremist, racist black group, were the bad guys. It was bad enough they were being harassed, but then they were exploited by Nathan Phillips and then attacked by people like you. Where is your vaunted Lieberman sense of fairness?

STEPHEN. Phillips also lied about the boys chanting, "Build the wall." There's no evidence of that.

MARC. Duke lacrosse players. Everything is black or white. So they weren't completely pugilistic, so therefore, they were harmless innocents?

MARC. The black guys were not central to this. If you want to go by the video, they said a few things—that's it.

STEPHEN. The Duke students were falsely accused of rape. Apparently, you believe they were guilty of being privileged white kids. That's not a crime yet. According to Nathan Phillips, he inserted himself because the students were threatening the Black Israelites, who were actually making racist and antigay threats. Nathan Phillips either lied or got it completely wrong. Regardless, that's irrelevant, but a group of kids who were waiting for buses and said or did nothing aggressive or inappropriate are your targets. I can't believe it.

MARC. Nathan Phillips didn't do anything wrong. He is a man of peace. I believe him over the teenage kids, who fear their careers are going to be affected by the notoriety they are getting. But put your "I can't believe you" feeling in a bottle so you can capture how *I* feel when you make excuse after excuse for the mendacious, self-absorbed, and ignorant criminal, who currently is our president!

STEPHEN. You don't know anything about Nathan Phillips. He lied. That's obvious in comparing his statements to the videos. He is an activist who exploited a group of high school students wearing MAGA hats. I don't make excuses for Trump. I simply look at the facts. You obviously don't care about facts.

MARC. Fact: Trump was saying uncharacteristically obsequious things to and about Putin while at the same time running for president and denying having anything to do with Russia while at the same time negotiating a deal to build a $300 million building in Moscow that requires Putin's approval. It's not hard to connect those dots, and he is screwed. Giuliani tried to stay ahead of the story to prepare his base (which consists of 1 percent of really smart people comprised of Stephen Barry and his cronies) for the story that Trump continued communication with Russia despite having denied it.

MARC. And if the kid was such an angel, why was he wearing a 2018 swastika on his red hat?

JANUARY 22, 2019

STEPHEN. There is something very wrong with you. You live in a fantasy world.

MARC. That's not a nice thing to say.

STEPHEN. It's true. You would love to prove that high school kids who were minding their own business and being harassed by nasty adult extremists and exploited by an adult activist were really the bad guys. Why? Because they were wearing MAGA hats. With Trump, you go from one conspiracy theory to another, none of which have any basis in fact, because you don't like him.

MARC. Something wrong with me?

MARC. Here is what happened. I saw a whole breakdown and time line. The black Hebrew guys were chanting out shit, as they always do. The white boys took offense and started shouting back. It's the Hebrews' right to say what they want to say and the white boys' right to say what they want to say. Things were starting to escalate, and the Indian came over calmly and slowly chanting a song of peace. The boys were whooped up and mocking, though this background of the incident does mitigate things. Because of the things Trump has said in the past that I have cited—which are clearly racist, even if you don't think he should be called a racist—and because of the actions of people at his rallies, the hat is really a hard thing for a lot of people and an offensive statement to people.

STEPHEN. The "Indian" is an activist who exploited a group of high school students. He had a person with him filming the interaction, who reportedly said, "We have enough." The "Indian" then lied to the media about the interaction. By the way, the boys were not sure what the "Indian" was doing and certainly did not realize he was attempting to exploit the situation. There is no evidence that the boys responded to the Black Israelites or mocked the Indian. Your sole issue with boys is that they were wearing MAGA hats. It is sad that you believe supporting Trump is racist because his political opponents say he's racist. I'm offended by people who accuse me of being racist or sexist because I disagree with them. Grow up.

MARC. Have I called you a racist? I am surprised you support one, but that doesn't make you one.

MARC. Trump *is* a racist. That's the only indisputable fact. He said, "Mexicans are rapists; some, I suppose, are fine people." Suppose? He doesn't *know* there are good people in Mexico?

STEPHEN. I did not say you called me a racist. My point is that for a lot of people, I am presumptively a racist for many reasons, including the fact that I'm a Republican. I disagree that Trump is a racist. You may not like the way he presents the case against illegal immigration, but there is nothing in his history that suggests he is racist or a homophobe or any other bad thing. In fact, his policies are helping blacks and Hispanics. His support among Hispanics is way up since the beginning of the government shutdown. Again, if you believe his rhetoric is racist or encourages racism, that's your choice. I disagree, as do a lot of Hispanics. I note that every Republican, not only Trump, is accused of being racist. The only way to avoid that charge is to accept the Democrats' identity politics. No thank you.

MARC. Nothing in his history? His father was a slumlord. What about his ad against the Central Park Five (who I believe were probably guilty)?

STEPHEN. Now you're making baseless allegations against his father? If your father made racist comments, would that make you a racist? Are you a racist if you believe a black person is guilty of a terrible crime? Or is it only okay to accuse white kids in MAGA hats?

MARC. My father was a racist, as were many white men of that generation. Trump's father had documented claims against him. It's not baseless.

STEPHEN. So are you a racist because your father was one? By the way, did your father treat people differently based on race? Did he refuse to deal with blacks? When he did deal with them, was he unfair? Did he support segregated schools? What do you mean when you say he was a racist? Regarding Fred Trump, I know that you do not know anything about him. I would like to know the specific facts that justify your conclusion. Calling him a slumlord doesn't get you there.

MARC. https://www.vox.com/2016/7/25/12270880/donald-trump-racism-history.

STEPHEN. I read the article and once again encourage you to think for yourself.

MARC. I'm sure you would agree that not everything is as it seems. But you can't just use that one-sidedly. Those Covington school kids, as a group, were bad news. There are stories and videos all over the place, and I saw the whooping and stupid yelling on the video, regardless of one kid.

STEPHEN. Kids were whooping and yelling. What does that prove? Nothing. The kids, according to the interviews, initially thought Nathan Phillips was there to support them and joined in. I can easily imagine sixteen-year-old Marc joining in the chant. The kids were exploited, and people like you want to blame them. It is shameful. Virtually all the Vox article is based on recent political differences—racism as defined by the purveyors of identity politics and Trump opponents. However, my favorite one was the allegation that in the 1980s, the management of Trump Castle ordered black employees to leave the floor when the Trumps visited. I hope that is too ridiculous even for you.

MARC. Why are you listening to the interviews from the kids? Their futures are at stake. Of all the times you implied I was gullible, that takes the cake: "But, Marc, the kids say they were just minding their own business. They say they were missionaries doing God's work."

STEPHEN. You're right. The students were not at the Lincoln Memorial to meet their buses. That was just a clever ruse. They went to confront the Black Israelites, whom the students goaded into making racist and antigay taunts. Then they got lucky and found an American Indian activist to mock. How could I not see that?

MARC. You often ask why I say things without proof. Because I just know. The letter was not written by that kid!

MARC. That's called thinking for yourself! Stephen: "He must have written that letter. It couldn't be that someone might have written it for him. Those fine boys would never do that." There is also a tape in which one of them says, "It's not rape if you enjoy it."

STEPHEN. Good for him. He was vilified by a bunch of malicious idiots and was smart to get guidance on how to respond. Businesses do it every day. You don't hire public relations firms to make up a story but to effectively tell your story. You're being very mean and unhinged. Also, a boy in a group of teenage boys made a bad joke about rape. He and his friends should all be arrested. I think we've beaten this issue to death. It is clear the only thing that matters to you is that the students were wearing MAGA hats.

January 23, 2019

STEPHEN. Nathan Phillips never served in Vietnam. Unbelievable.

MARC. I'll grant you that one.

MARC. They said *vet*.

MARC. The kids were not punks. By the way, are you wearing a MAGA hat around town?

MARC. Why not? You don't find it offensive. You aren't one to back down. Be proud.

MARC. By the way, the boys could have behaved better at the very least, as they were with adult chaperones. Yet apparently, they are being invited to the White House in heroic fashion. That is a perfect example of how Trump fosters a divisive America.

BACK TO TRUMP TOWER MOSCOW AND PUTIN

STEPHEN. You seem to think I should back down from positions I take, even though the only argument you ever make is "Marc believes Trump is a racist," "Marc believes Trump colluded with Russia," "It's okay for the FBI to lie to a court in the interest of removing Trump from office," and things like that. To date, I have not seen any evidence that Trump has done anything wrong that requires this never-ending investigation. The fact that you want to believe it doesn't make it so. On the other hand, the evidence the FBI sought to manufacture a case against Trump is very strong, resulting in several firings and resignations. It will ultimately result in prosecution. That being said, I agree that Trump can be vulgar and inappropriate. I also agree that he is upending norms, which may or may not work out. I fully understand that you have good reasons for opposing Trump. I disagree that there is any reason to remove him from office, and it would be a disaster for our country if it happened.

MARC. How can you not see that his astonishing defense of Putin (saying, "He's a good leader. Everyone kills. Who needs NATO?" and believing him over our intelligence) was and is connected to either blackmail or, more likely, currying favor due to this huge tower deal?

MARC. It's a simple question that deserves a simple answer that doesn't reference something else. Answer the question. And it's hardly "Marc says," especially since you say I don't think for myself. It's most of America (*most* means more than 50 percent).

STEPHEN. Everything you say about Trump and Putin is pure speculation and not supported by any evidence. A $300 million deal to build a tower is a big deal, but that's what it costs to build big buildings. It is not unusual in any way. In fact, it's much less than similar projects in New York. For example, the Barclays Center was a $1 billion project. Regarding what 60 percent of Americans allegedly believe, would 2 + 2 = 5 if 60 percent of Americans believed it? The only thing that matters is whether there is a factual basis for the garbage thrown at Trump, not whether people believe the garbage.

MARC. It's not speculation that he was unusually, unprecedentedly favorable toward Putin, and it's not speculation that he was planning to build a tower at the same time he was running for office. Neither is speculation. It *is* conjecture that the former influenced the later.

STEPHEN. That's right. He was very clear and public about his desire to work with Putin (unlike Obama, who was caught on a hot mic promising more flexibility after his reelection) and was elected on that basis. He also has been much tougher on Putin (arming the Ukrainians, opposing the Russian natural gas pipeline, supporting increased US oil and natural gas production, attacking Assad, and more). Unless you believe that only professional politicians should run for office, what is wrong with a real estate developer working on real estate projects? The idea that Trump would betray the United States to build a building in Moscow—without a shred of evidence—is laughable. It's not like he set up a "charity" that received hundreds of millions in donations from Russians while he was in the government. Oh, I forgot: that's no problem.

MARC. Trump hasn't been hard on Russians; Congress has. How do you explain revoking the sanctions on the oligarch recently? Plain and simple, Trump was being kind to Russia against US policy only because of business relations. Because he has no conviction about anything politically and just goes where he is told by influencers.

STEPHEN. You don't know what you're talking about.

ROGER STONE INDICTMENT

January 25, 2019

Marc. Mike Pompeo has called WikiLeaks a nonstate intelligence agency abetted by hostile actors and foreign governments, including Russia. This morning's indictment shows, with documents, that a high-ranking Trump campaign official directed Stone to get WikiLeaks to release the emails hacked by Russia. The official later texted to Roger, "Well done." What's going to happen is they will get Trump to resign in exchange for not indicting his family members.

Stephen. Keep dreaming.

Stephen. Again, Stone is indicted for allegedly lying to investigators and to Congress, not for any actual crime. Who decides whether Stone lied? The investigators. I hope Stone fights it. Also, if Stone had inside information on what WikiLeaks was going to do, which he denies, what is the crime? Would it be the same crime as paying a foreign spy to get information on your opponent—which turns out to be false—from Russian intelligence sources? If not, can you explain the difference?

Marc. I love the "which he denies" and the "What would be the crime?" People deny things for a reason. Funny how you have been such a civil libertarian in defense of this shit show. I bet if a Palestinian terrorist were arrested for plans to commit terror, you wouldn't be so "Where's the crime? Where is the proof?"

Stephen. People deny allegations that are not true all the time. I hope Stone fights it, because I believe he will win. By the way, civil libertarians defend people against government abuse. You will have more egg on your face as this develops.

MARC. You would have made a great co-counsel alongside Johnnie Cochran.

STEPHEN. I make arguments. You make stupid, irrelevant comments.

MARC. That's what Johnnie Cochran said about Marcia Clark. And it worked!

INFANTICIDE AND NORTHAM

January 30, 2019

Stephen. Governor Cuomo thinks that aborting a baby at birth is okay because he is "not here to legislate religion," and the governor of Virginia believes a baby who is born alive can be killed. And you think Trump is immoral. Two Democratic governors are on record as supporting the murder of living human beings. They are sickening monsters.

Marc. Never heard of aborting at birth.

Marc. There are lots of immoral people. They aren't president.

Stephen. If Trump is defeated, it is likely the next president will support infanticide. Not surprisingly, the same people are undisturbed by overt anti-Semitism.

February 2, 2019

Stephen. There are reports that the media had a medical school yearbook photo of Virginia's Governor Northam showing him in a Klan hood or in black face prior to the November election but didn't run it. Not surprising. Why did it come out now? In defense of Virginia's now-rejected abortion law, Northam explained that under the law, an infant born alive would be allowed to die. Because of his candor on how the law would work, he became a liability to the Democrats. Prochoice Democrats never use the word *infant*. That probably explains why the photo was released now. The Democrats need to change the subject. By the way, Pelosi was asked about Northam's interview on the Virginia abortion law and claimed she did not know what he had said. Is she a liar?

Marc. Yes, she lied. They all lie.

MARC. And Northam proves my point. Casual racism is endemic in most of the country.

MARC. How many times do I have to tell you? I want Mike Pence.

MARC. I am anti-Trump.

GENERALS AND CIVILIAN CONTROL

FEBRUARY 5, 2019

MARC. A top US general says Trump did not consult him on the Syria announcement.

MARC. https://www.cnn.com/2019/02/05/politics/votel-trump-syria-withdrawal/index.html.

STEPHEN. I have reservations about Trump's decision-making process. However, the president does not have to consult with a general or any generals at all. It is the other way around. I note that Lincoln fired one general after another. Roosevelt approved Lend-Lease against the opposition of his advisers. Bush supported the surge.

NO COLLUSION?

February 12, 2019

Marc. It is looking like there will be no smoking gun or crime except lying. But why did they lie?

Stephen. The better question is, why were they being investigated? Lying is determined by the prosecutors. Although it is entirely possible Flynn or Papadopoulos purposely lied, it also is possible the prosecutors threatened to prosecute them over inconsistencies, even if they were innocent. The threat of prosecution—the cost of defense and possibly losing—leads some people to plead guilty in exchange for certainty.

Marc. Spare me.

Stephen. I know you're ignorant on these issues, and you don't accept any views that don't support yours. Ignorance is bliss. Good luck with the Green New Deal!

Marc. I will be voting Republican when they are released from their hostage situation or wake up from their trance and nominate a decent and intelligent person.

Stephen. Until then, you'll vote for a socialist anti-Semite. Good decision.

Marc. Over Trump? Correct!

THE WALL EMERGENCY AND EXECUTIVE ORDERS

MARC. Extreme policies won't go far in Congress, but stupidity and wanting to be king might.

MARC. Would you rather have a dictator who was friendly to Israel and conservative with financial policies or a democracy? You always talk about the people having spoken. We will see what they choose.

STEPHEN. The "Trump is a dictator" argument—after two years—is simply disconnected from reality. A dictator under permanent investigation by his political opponents. The Democrats and the Green New Deal are the totalitarians. I recommend you disengage your head from your anus.

FEBRUARY 14, 2019

MARC. All your talk about our liberties. Your stupid-ass king you worship is doing what kings and tyrants do.

FEBRUARY 15, 2019

STEPHEN. How is Trump acting like a king or a tyrant? Because he declared a national emergency pursuant to a law that grants him the authority to declare a national emergency? Because he is seeking to fulfill a campaign promise that was central to his election? I have no doubt his declaration will be challenged in court. Everything he does is challenged. However, there is a king who is accountable to no one: Mueller.

MARC. We all know it isn't an emergency. He said today, "I don't have to do this." Some emergency! It's not only a moronic statement; it's oxymoronic! It's his power to declare an emergency when there *is* an emergency! No, not everything he does is challenged. All he does is talk about what he did and what he may do. It's tiresome and transparent!

STEPHEN. That's so unusual for a politician.

MARC. I respect when you say, essentially, "He is dumb, but he was voted in, so he should be accepted until he is voted out." Stick with that. Anything complimentary about the man isn't a good look for you.

STEPHEN. I think he has done a good job under obscene circumstances. He has many faults, but the country is in much better shape than it would have been if Hillary had won. The economy is growing, the United States is the leading energy producer, and we pulled out of the Iran deal and the Paris Accord. I believe he has strengthened our hand with China, and he has strongly backed Israel. The Democrats want open borders, higher taxes, and the Green New Deal, and they tolerate anti-Semites. I'll take Trump every time.

MARC. Why weren't Obama's circumstances "obscene"? He faced a stock market collapse, a Republican Congress who declared a singular goal to block him, calls that he was overreaching with executive power (ha-ha-ha), incessant Fox stories emptier than current stories against Trump, and claims that he was a terrorist.

MARC. Eh?

MARC. And Marc wins the round!

MARC. He said, "I didn't need to do this." That means there's no emergency.

STEPHEN. Obama had political opposition offset by an adoring media. He should have had much more critical coverage. Remember the IRS, Fast and Furious, Benghazi, and the poor economy. Trump is facing an attempted coup, abuse of power, and the harassment of his supporters. The media looks the other way. Regarding the declaration, the Democrats want to remake the entire American economy and place it under government control to address climate change, something they have no real power to effect. Trump wants to deal with reality. I'm not in favor of the declaration, but he has the right to do it. Politically, we'll see who is right.

MARC. No, Trump doesn't have adoring media. Nah. Not Breitbart, Fox, Drudge, Limbaugh, or Levin.

MARC. He has the right to do it like Obama has the right to declare he is a Muslim!

FEBRUARY 17, 2019

MARC. Do you want to volunteer your legal skills to investigate *SNL* at the president's request? To investigate them and seek repercussions for their satire?

STEPHEN. I'm glad you're worried that Trump could abuse his power and investigate *SNL*. However, I'm disappointed that you see no problem with the Obama administration and DOJ and FBI officials investigating the Trump campaign and then seeking support to remove him from office. No abuse of power there. By the way, there will never be an investigation of *SNL* or NBC.

MARC. Did you feel the Obama administration abused power?

STEPHEN. On many occasions. Trump hasn't come close.

MARC. Why was Obama's use of executive action any more aggressive than Trump's declaring an emergency?

STEPHEN. Trump is following a statute. The statute gives the president broad authority. I think it's a bad idea because even if it is legal and even if the argument that the situation at the border is an emergency is supported, Congress has a different view. I think he should continue to advocate for more funding. Obama's abuses did not have statutory support. He abused the rights of Tea Party groups by permitting the IRS to deny them nonprofit status. He made changes to Obamacare without seeking amendments to the law. He refused to submit the Iran deal to the Senate for approval. He permitted the investigation into Trump's campaign, the unmasking of American citizens connected to Trump on the other end of conversations with Russians under surveillance, and more. Obama also unilaterally changed US immigration laws after acknowledging that he didn't have the authority. The difference for Obama is that the mainstream press cheered him on.

MCCABE

February 18, 2019

Marc. McCabe said that Rosenstein wanted to wear a secret wire and also said that he and others were trying to use the Twenty-Fifth Amendment to get Trump out. I happen to agree with what I imagine you think: it's not cool to bug the president or force him out with duplicity, beyond preexisting evidence.

Stephen. I'm glad. They wanted to substitute their preference for the actual outcome of the election. That's the same problem posed by the Mueller probe. It is not an investigation of a crime; it is an investigation of Trump—looking for crimes to justify the illegal actions taken in the run-up to the election and to seek his removal from office. That's why the unimpeded continuation of this affront to democracy is sacrosanct to the Democrats. The reality is that the Obama administration, not the Russians, interfered in the election, and the Democrats desperately want to avoid a reckoning.

Marc. Yes, McCabe was very credible.

Marc. Oh, wait—maybe you think McCabe is credible only when he provides information to support your claims, but when he says Trump said, "I believe Putin!" that didn't happen. Like Trump, who says the *Times* and *WaPo* are enemies of the people, until they have a report with even a morsel of favorability toward him; then he cites them. It's laughable. How you can believe a lifetime liar (I didn't call him a criminal or con man, just a mendacious person with a history of prevarication and BS akin to a Don King promoter) over dedicated lifetime servants nobler than you or I who served the country for years before Trump was a candidate is beyond me. Many past presidents were liars; some get caught, and some don't. Russia *did* mess with the election, and Trump lies and continues to lie about his involvement in it, involvement that might not have been illegal. It's always the lying that gets people.

STEPHEN. McCabe is a proven liar. His account of the discussions regarding the Twenty-Fifth Amendment may or may not be accurate. However, it certainly is evidence that the discussions took place. Let's hear from Rosenstein and others. Trump is right to call out the media. They act as an arm of the Democratic Party. For example, none of the networks covered the report by the Senate Intelligence Committee that found no evidence of collusion. Trump may exaggerate and brag, but he is the most transparent president we have had. He has done exactly what he promised to do. If the Democrats were so concerned about Russia, what did Obama do about it? Nothing. What did Hillary do about it? She sought dirt on Trump.

MARC. Does Fox act as an arm of the Republican Party? Of course! There are just more liberals than conservatives in the media. Fortunately, Mueller is a highly respected Republican, so we will wait for what he has to say. Oh, had the Trump campaign leadership just admitted on day one what happened, he would have easily gotten past this cloud.

STEPHEN. There is no comparison between the number who watch the networks and the number who watch Fox. In addition, the people who watch Fox are watching Fox because they are engaged conservatives. The people watching the networks are not as engaged in politics. Thank God for Fox, or there would be no dissenting voice at all. There is nothing for Trump to admit. There was no crime. Nor is Mueller investigating a crime. He's investigating Trump.

TRUMP'S PAST

MARC. Trump has some bad shit in his past. You can argue that everyone does and that it would be uncovered if it were examined closely and incessantly. But remember, Clinton was examined and lambasted and vilified for lying under oath for a trifle.

STEPHEN. What bad shit are you talking about? You have no idea. If you're talking about casinos that went bankrupt, you're faulting him for being an entrepreneur. Businesses fail all the time. Are you talking about women? Everyone was aware that he was a womanizer, and he was elected anyway. Are you talking about Trump University? That seemed a little seedy to me, but I know nothing about it. I know that everyone engaged in business, especially high-profile business, is likely to get sued. Clinton both lied and suborned perjury regarding conduct during his term in office. That's not trivial.

MARC. No, lying is not trivial.

STEPHEN. Under oath.

MARC. Right, but lying not under oath in an investigation is perfectly acceptable?

MARC. I actually came across some very disturbing evidence moments ago.

STEPHEN. Trump has not lied under oath. Clinton did—he denied doing something he actually did do. He also told his staff to lie about it. This is different from making a statement that might have been honestly provided but is contradicted by other evidence. In the latter case, the person could have purposely given false testimony or could have made a mistake, especially if the conduct they lied about was not criminal. In Clinton's case, he didn't make a mistake. He lied. Facts always make a difference.

JUSSIE SMOLLETT

FEBRUARY 22, 2019

MARC. So do you think Jessie Smollett's bogus claims are degrading toward, or representative of, black culture?

STEPHEN. Smollett's claims are an insult to blacks who really suffered under Jim Crow. Here is a guy who has had great success at a young age and is using the suffering of earlier generations to get a raise. The idiotic reaction of the media and Democratic presidential candidates to his bogus assault, like the reaction to the Covington students, should tell you that you cannot trust a single thing reported that in any way touches on Trump, including the Mueller probe.

MARC. Oh, I see. So one erroneous report annuls any report going forward? Do you believe the Robert Kraft prostitute story, or is that okay, and he is a victim of targeting? What about the guy arrested for plotting mass murder against Democrats? Phony story?

[2/22/19, 3:54 p.m.] MARC. "Should tell you that you cannot trust a single thing reported"? "Can't trust anything"? Without a doubt, that's the most asinine thing you have ever said. You are totally brainwashed. Can't trust a *single* thing that might come out? Because one guy made up a story?

[2/22/19, 4:12 p.m.] STEPHEN. It's not about Smollett. It's about the news coverage afforded to Smollett and the immediate conclusion that Smollett was a victim of Trump-inspired hate. The story was full of holes, and the Chicago PD and the Chicago media were immediately skeptical. Nevertheless, the national media and the Democrats ran with a false story and directed hate at Trump supporters for preposterous claims. The media was spectacularly wrong. They were spectacularly wrong about Covington and went after a sixteen-year-old high school student.

They have been spectacularly wrong about Trump over and over again. Therefore, I don't believe anything coming from the media unless it is based on solid reporting. Regarding Kraft, I believe he was arrested in a prostitution sting. That's a fact. I have no opinion on what actually happened or what it may say about his character. I'm disappointed to hear it.

Marc. The Trump reports have been consistently, not completely, on the money, and many have been explained, defended, or minimized. You are transparent in your preparation to refute the eventual Trump reports.

Marc. Oh, I apologize because you said "unless it is based on solid reporting." Yes, I agree.

Stephen. What world do you live in? I'll put together a list of stories about Trump that have been discredited when I have time. The bottom line is that the story the media ignores about the FBI and DOJ interference in the election is the real story.

CHINA TRADE

February 26, 2019

STEPHEN. What's your point? That Trump may have misunderstood that the memorandum of understanding (with China) is intended to be the final agreement? The more interesting point is that Trump is engaged in the transaction. Furthermore, a good deal—whether you call it an MOU or a trade agreement—is what is important. Without Trump, there would be nothing.

MARC. Nothing? Wow. Without God, there would be nothing. Without Trump, there would be nothing. Therefore, Trump = God.

MARC. "Without Trump, there would be nothing" (Stephen Barry, February 26, 2019). You started by saying Trump was the lesser of two evils. That soon became "Trump, all hail. Without you, sir, there would be nothing! You omniscient, omnipotent leader who should not be questioned."

STEPHEN. You're ridiculous. I meant there would be no deal with China, at least not one beneficial to the United States.

MARC. "Without Trump, there would be nothing!"

MORE ON MICHAEL COHEN AND STORMY

MARC. So when Cohen shows checks Trump signed while in office that implicate him in committing election fraud, which are you going to go with: (1) "Cohen is a liar," or (2) "It's no big deal"?

STEPHEN. If Trump issued a personal check to pay women making claims, it is not a campaign finance violation. In fact, there is no scenario wherein $300,000 in payments for anything is a serious crime. Certainly not more serious than accepting millions in illegal donations from foreigners, as Obama did and for which he was fined. You could not even explain why you believe it is a serious crime, but I know that if Trump used campaign funds to pay these women, you would believe he should be prosecuted for misusing campaign funds, because that's what the media tells you to believe.

MARC. The media is telling me he committed a crime. Not the payment but how it was hidden. Giuliani already admitted the payment was made to affect the election because that revelation "would look real bad right before the election."

MARC. I believe simply because it is being reported by the *WSJ* that he will provide evidence that he committed a campaign finance violation. A crime is a crime.

STEPHEN. Good. You will support the prosecution of Comey, McCabe, Strzok, etc.

KUSHNER'S SECURITY CLEARANCE

FEBRUARY 28, 2019

MARC. Trump ordered a security clearance for Kushner. That's effed up!

MARCH 1, 2019

MARC. I just got a call from the Department of Reputation. They told me that if you finally start moving away from Trump, they will forgive and forget.

STEPHEN. Thank you for looking out for me.

MARCH 2, 2019

MARC. The president's right to give top security clearance to whomever he wants? "Why shouldn't I like Kim Jong Un?"

STEPHEN. If I understand the facts correctly, he overrode White House staff who work directly for him. He did not override the CIA, which denied Kushner a higher level of clearance. By the way, the CIA also works for him. Although I do not believe it is a good idea to ignore professionals, I don't know what issues they had with Kushner. The concerns may be bullshit, like the alleged concern at the FBI that Trump is a Russian asset. We elect the president to make these decisions, not his staff.

MARC. If Obama gave a Muslim cleric security access, you and your base would be apoplectic. You make Trump better and smarter than all our institutions! Otto Warmbier was Jewish. That's even worse. What is with this Trump? What happened to "America first"?

STEPHEN. Do you believe Kushner is a security threat? I highly doubt it.

MARC. That's irrelevant, and you know it.

MARC. I ask you: Is it possible someone in the future could infiltrate an administration if not properly vetted or overruled?

STEPHEN. In response to your question, yes, even if they are vetted. My guess is that Trump knows Kushner pretty well.

MARC. If the report is true—and it is, because even Abbe Lowell took a step back from it—you have no concern about their outright lies about it?

STANDARDS FOR JUDGING TRUMP

STEPHEN. There is nothing Trump has done that warrants the treatment he receives. The transgressions that threaten democracy are the ones committed by the Obama DOJ and FBI against Trump and by Comey and McCabe after the election. In Iran, there is a Guardian Council that determines who is qualified to run for office. Trump's opponents seem to wish the United States had such a council. What do you think?

STEPHEN. I agree with Chris Cuomo [who opined that Trump supporters see no difference between Trump and other politicians]. I would add that it is not just that Trump's supporters see no difference between Trump and other politicians; it's that there is no difference. If the media held every politician to the same standards they hold Trump to, Trump never would have won.

MARC. Yes, there should be a council!

NORTH KOREA SUMMIT IN VIETNAM

MARC. What's your take on Trump having no problem with Kim?

STEPHEN. I think he's trying to get a deal. He walked away. He didn't kiss Kim's ass the way Obama and Kerry kissed the Iranians' asses and gave them money and overlooked their humiliation of American sailors. Remember Cuomo.

MARC. Wrong. He did kiss their ass the same way; he just didn't get a deal.

STEPHEN. No, you're wrong. Obama gave the Iranians hundreds of millions of dollars for a terrible deal. He also ended sanctions. Trump gave Kim nothing, except flowery praise. I agree it is unbecoming, but at the end of the day, sanctions are in place, nuclear testing has stopped, and Kim has gotten nothing.

MARC. It's probably going to come out that Trump was going to give away the mother lode, and at the last minute, somebody told him he was an asshole.

STEPHEN. Someone should have stopped Obama.

MARC. Trump said today that we have to "reclaim our heritage." Gee, I wonder who that sounds like.

STEPHEN. Who are you thinking of?

MARC. Adolf.

MARC. You don't appreciate how many anti-Semites there are in this country and how many of them are his supporters.

STEPHEN. Trump is the most pro-Israel president ever, and he is not an anti-Semite. It is just a smear. The anti-Semites are embraced by and elected as Democrats. Try to stay in the real world.

MARC. No, no. The people who go to the rallies and cheer for him, the people of the Rust Belt, the white truckers, hate Jews and couldn't give a crap about Israel. You know it. Yes, there are extreme liberals and blacks who are anti-Semitic also, but they don't have the ingrained DNA to be violent. By the way, while I will take a backseat to you on knowledge of Jewish history, don't equate anti-Israel and anti-Semitic views. There are plenty of J Street–like people who are liberal on Israel. Hey, if you want to tell me Israel is your primary love beyond the USA and you don't want to contradict Trump because you don't want to lose a finger on your power hold, I get it.

STEPHEN. You're a bigot.

MARC. You support a reprehensible human as the leader of the country. He called Comey a dirty cop. Comey made a mistake *in favor of* Trump. I am outraged on Comey's behalf.

MARC. Trump called Kim a great person and Comey a dirty cop.

STEPHEN. Comey didn't make a mistake. He interfered in the election and took it upon himself to decide who should and shouldn't be president. He should go to jail. I agree that Trump's efforts to win over Kim are hard to take. He's not a great person, but Churchill and Roosevelt called Stalin, who murdered more people than Hitler, Uncle Joe because they needed him. Trump knows what Kim is but is trying to convince him to denuclearize. It may be hard to take, and it may not work, but as I said earlier, it is better than funding a terrorist nation that seeks the destruction of Israel and the United States for a slight pause in their nuclear program.

KASPAROV

March 3, 2019

Marc. https://www.nydailynews.com/opinion/ny-oped-kasparov-korea-20190228-story.html.

Marc. Garry Kasparov is a shit ton smarter than you will ever be and a hell of a lot more worldly. Compared to me, he is even more so, which is giving you the world's all-time-best backhanded compliment.

Stephen. The article begins with "No matter how low your opinion of Trump …" It is a screed. It is not factual. Kasparov is entitled to his opinion, and I am entitled to mine. I agree that I could not match him in chess. In politics, who knows?

ILHAN OMAR AND ANTI-SEMITISM

March 7, 2019

STEPHEN. It's ridiculous [Regarding Congress' inability to condemn anti-Semitic statements by Omar]. Omar is an anti-Semite. She isn't criticizing Israel's actions. She criticizes its existence. Israel is the only country on her agenda, not the murderous Assad regime or the terrorist Iranians, who routinely execute gays. Not Saudi Arabia, which denies women basic rights. She focuses only on Israel, which, in reality, shows amazing restraint. She is an anti-Semite, and the Democrats can't condemn it.

MARC. Nor could Republicans condemn Steve King.

STEPHEN. They did condemn him by name and stripped him of his committee assignments.

MARC. Yeah, so?

MARC. The Dems are going to rip off her cap.

STEPHEN. Are you really this indifferent to real anti-Semitism, as opposed to theories that Trump is flaming anti-Semitism?

MARC. Not sure how to measure or quantify anti-Semitism. Talk to Geraldo.

STEPHEN. It's easy. Classify people who make repeated, explicit anti-Semitic statements and those who make excuses for those statements as anti-Semites.

MARC. People marched in Charlottesville chanting, "Jews will not replace us," and Trump said some of them were fine people. Spare me.

STEPHEN. He said there were people who opposed taking down the statue of Robert E. Lee who were fine people. In other words, people on both sides of the issue. He never said people chanting about the Jews were fine people. Anti-Trump idiots purposely misinterpreted his comments. Trump is the most pro-Israel president ever.

MARC. He never condemned those people or Duke, and you know it. That's a fact.

STEPHEN. Yes, he did.

MANAFORT SENTENCING

MARC. Do you feel better about the world now that Manafort got four years and time served for something you felt he never should have been prosecuted for?

STEPHEN. He was prosecuted for working for Trump. The prosecutors asked for twenty years.

MARCH 8, 2019

MARC. Really smart. Listen to me. He is a moron whom you vaunt in high esteem. I know, I know—his people told him to be friendly to Israel.

STEPHEN. You're blind and foolish.

STEPHEN. David Duke tweeted that because of her defiance of ZOG (Zionist Occupied Government), Omar is the most important member of Congress. I assume you'll agree that she's inciting anti-Semitism.

MARC. Never heard of David Duke.

MARC. So it's not fair Manafort is going to jail, because the crimes he committed would never have been found if he hadn't worked for Trump? Is that actually your position?

STEPHEN. The government chooses whether or not to investigate or prosecute crimes every day. Prior to Mueller, the government chose not to prosecute. However, Manafort's conduct gave Mueller leverage to try to get him to testify against Trump. That's why he was prosecuted. In some cases—for example, Hillary—crimes are not prosecuted. That doesn't make her innocent.

STEPHEN. By the way, I'm pretty sure you know David Duke but only when he supports Trump.

MARC. I don't know. Donald Trump said last year he didn't know him.

MARCH 9, 2019

MARC. You believe that a true piece of scum is someone to be respected and admired. For the record, I will vote Republican in 2020 when the nominee is someone else. Unlike liberal Democrats, Trump stands for nothing except self-promotion and grifting.

STEPHEN. That's your opinion. I don't even know what it means. By the way, Marc, Schiff's staff spent ten hours with Michael Cohen before he testified. What does that tell you?

MARC. And Fox gave Trump the questions for the debate.

STEPHEN. Megyn Kelly denies it. Regardless, Trump won the nomination fair and square, and none of his opponents would disagree. More importantly, to compare the Democrats' efforts to manufacture charges against Trump—efforts that are designed to cause political turmoil and undermine the president—should make fair-minded people sick. Unfortunately, people like you, who generally are fair-minded, are willing to tolerate it.

MARC. Nobody is manufacturing anything. Looking incessantly? Yes, and most people would pass that scrutiny other than declaring too may write-offs or cheating on spouses. This guy made himself a target before he was even running for president and was a person who garnered little respect and, for someone of his purported wealth, gave nothing back. Manafort was the same way—he bought $25,000 jackets while ripping off the government. They were made for each other.

STEPHEN. They are trying to manufacture crimes. Here's a refresher: in a free country, crimes are investigated, not people. The fact that you don't like Trump and, based on what you know about him, feel he is beneath the presidency doesn't mean it's true. You really know nothing about Trump. But my argument with you is not that you should like or support him. It's that you should accept that he won the election and be fair. If you believe it is fair or just to subpoena anyone associated with him and to seek to embarrass them and him, you're not fair.

MARC. He isn't exactly an opaque individual. How can I not know him? He shows the world what an asshole he is every day! And how do you know they are trying to manufacture a crime? They are looking for one. There is a difference. Hey, did you think John Gotti committed crimes? How do you know? Were you in favor of people like Rudy Giuliani investigating them incessantly back in the day?

STEPHEN. Next week, the government is going to begin an investigation into me to see if I have committed any crimes. They are going to subpoena all of my business associates and friends. It may destroy my career and friendships, but people who deal with me need to know if I have committed a crime. At the end of the day, if they find that I didn't, it will all be worth it.

MARC. If, in the initial investigation, they found that your business associates had lied, they would dig deeper.

STEPHEN. Great. You believe that in a free country, the government has the right to investigate people to look for crimes.

MARC. The president must be held to a higher standard. Trump and the Republicans before him grilled Obama and Hillary.

MARC. I didn't hear your ACLU views back then.

STEPHEN. Clinton was investigated over his involvement in Whitewater, which resulted in the failure of federally insured savings and loan. Obama was not investigated; things that happened under his administration were investigated, like the IRS and Benghazi. Those things should have been investigated. Neither of them were investigated to see if the investigators could find crimes.

LISA PAGE TESTIMONY

March 12, 2019

Stephen. Lisa Page testified that Hillary was never going to be charged with a crime, as directed by the Obama DOJ. She also testified that the FBI, after nine months of investigation into Trump, had no evidence of collusion. Soon Mueller will concur. A lot of people should, and hopefully will, go to prison.

March 13, 2019

Marc. I'll read the article and be receptive to being more vigilant on taking Democratic rhetoric more seriously. Did you see the story of parents committing crimes to get kids into college? What did you think about it?

THE COLLEGE ADMISSIONS SCANDAL

STEPHEN. I think the parents did a terrible disservice to their children, and the admissions process is a disaster. I don't think anyone should go to jail. The humiliation is enough.

MARC. What do you think about the FBI's uncovering it? Was it a witch hunt? Were they out to get these parents? Their actions enrage me on a Trumpian level. So do reparations for blacks. I am uniquely credible because I am not aligned to one message.

STEPHEN. Do you know how the FBI learned of it? They must have gotten a tip. There were many people involved in it. In fact, it probably is the polar opposite of a witch hunt. Assuming they received credible information suggesting the scheme existed, they investigated and found corroborating evidence. You're upset because wealthy and powerful parents subverted the process to the detriment of deserving students and their own children. I agree with you. I wouldn't be surprised if Felicity Huffman and Lori Loughlin are part of the resistance. If I'm right, it is another example of the hypocrisy of the self-righteous left.

MARC. Yes, hypocritical.

MORE ON MANAFORT

MARC. By the way, anything you say to ameliorate or minimize Manafort is about as ridiculous as saying that a member of the White House staff who turned up in the Mueller investigation as a murderer should be forgiven or given special treatment because his crimes would have remained unknown if not for the Mueller investigation. There were sentencing guidelines in place long before Trump came along, and he got a fraction of the low end.

MARC. Fools that he and his lawyers are, Manafort was just indicted by the New York DA, so this way, if Trump pardons him, he can't get bail. Now he is going to spill the beans.

STEPHEN. The point that you're missing is that federal prosecutors chose not to prosecute Manafort before Trump but chose to prosecute him after Trump in order to pressure him. As for beans, he has none to spill. Under the current two-tiered system of justice, certain people get prosecuted with the full force of the law, and others have their crimes overlooked. Hopefully that will change.

MARC. Yeah, sure, I guess black men just go unprosecuted.

STEPHEN. You were upset that Jeanine Pirro questioned whether Ilhan Omar is loyal to the Constitution, yet you have no problem suggesting my comment was racially motivated. I was talking about Hillary Clinton. As we now know from Lisa Page, the DOJ decided (or was ordered) not to prosecute Hillary for her multiple violations of the law and lies to law enforcement. As I said before, the decision not to prosecute does not mean she did not commit crimes. She clearly did.

CLIMATE OF INTOLERANCE AND PERSONAL ATTACKS

March 15, 2019

MARC. Why don't you stop worrying about Lisa Page and start worrying that Donald Trump declared his supporters will turn violent and that his hatred is breeding and fostering the same kind of violence against Muslims that he claims they and Mexicans perpetrate?

STEPHEN. That's funny. Are the Democrats fostering rocket attacks against Israel? You don't have to discern their anti-Semitism. It's explicit.

March 16, 2019

STEPHEN. Apparently, it was Chelsea Clinton's rhetoric, not Trump's.

MARC. Huh?

STEPHEN. Students at NYU accused Chelsea Clinton's mild rebuke of Ilhan Omar as being responsible for the New Zealand massacre. Look it up. It just highlights the stupidity of the argument. If the condemnation of anti-Semitism is responsible for a terrorist attack against Muslims, free speech would not be possible. As applied to Trump, he, unlike Omar, has never made a racist comment; he, like Chelsea, is simply accused of being racist.

MARC. Here is the problem: he said, "I have the police and the bikers, and things can get real bad. Real bad." That is messed up. He is delusional and thinks he is a dictator. He gives dictators legitimacy; you can't deny that.

STEPHEN. He's been president for more than two years and hasn't done or said a single thing that suggests he has any intent not to uphold the

Constitution or the law. Nothing. If you're concerned about dictatorship, you should be concerned about the efforts of the DOJ and FBI to make Hillary president and to undermine Trump. That's a constitutional crisis.

MARC. He hasn't because he is under investigation. Once that's over, he might be unleashed. Hillary was an institutionalist. They don't become dictators.

STEPHEN. Don't you ever get tired of making wild and baseless accusations?

STEPHEN. By the way, Obama, on behalf of Hillary, actually subverted the Constitution.

MARC. It's like I came back from the future and saw what was going to happen, and stubborn people won't believe me. By the way, Hitler didn't become Hitler right away. Yes, I am comparing Trump to an early 1930s Hitler. This guy lies constantly. Constantly. You know it; I know it. Why would you want to defend someone like that?

MARC. He's a liar.

STEPHEN. Every single person accusing Trump of collusion has been lying through his teeth.

MARC. And Trump didn't do anything to get Kushner a security clearance. Just man up and admit it if it's okay to do!

MARC. The people accusing Trump of collusion who lie—is that okay? Is that unacceptable?

STEPHEN. Interfering in an election undermines our system. Giving Jared a security clearance is a political issue, not a legal one. The collusion lie has cost millions of dollars, harmed citizens exercising constitutional rights, and polarized the electorate (which is the point). No, it's not acceptable. Trump actually is the most transparent president we have had in our lifetimes. He says what he thinks and does what he says he's going to do. Remember "You can keep your doctor"? Or, with regard to the IRS, "not a smidgen of corruption"?

March 20, 2019

Marc. I'm sure you think Trump's incessant attacks on a guy who gave his body for our country are okay because Trump is good for Israel.

Stephen. If you're talking about McCain, I haven't heard what Trump has said recently, but I have heard that McCain's associate, David Kramer, shopped the dossier around to government agencies for the purpose of undermining Trump. That was bad.

Marc. He said today about Mueller, "Out of the blue, a man comes to write a report. A man who got no votes."

March 21, 2019

Stephen. So? Trump has been the victim of the biggest political crime in American history. Mueller is a willing participant.

Marc. A citizen of New York City could have told you he was a crooked swindler long before he hit the campaign trail. When he was voted in, the law enforcement people moved to protect this country against his swindling.

Stephen. You must have missed civics when you were in school. Also, I look forward to the evidence you compiled that he was a crooked swindler. By the way, Hillary broke the law, and the same law enforcement officials, probably at the direction of Lynch and Obama, tanked the investigation. You might call it obstruction of justice. Also, they have used their power to spread lies and spend millions of dollars while trampling on the rights of American citizens. Great job.

MARC. More important than civics is human decency, particularly one's being an example when he is the most visible person in the world and a representative of our country.

STEPHEN. You're in favor of dictatorship as long as you approve of the dictator. Marc doesn't abide the results of an election unless his candidate wins.

MARC. Anyone who says that he "gave someone a nice funeral and didn't get a thank-you" is beyond any defense!

STEPHEN. Trump has been investigated for three years based on lies spread by his political enemies, including McCain. Trump is not the bad guy.

MARC. Shame on you.

MARC. You should know better. You can't even say, "That is a terrible thing for anyone to do, though it doesn't change the dynamic that he is being persecuted." So I have to tell you how a person (Trump or you) should conduct himself?

MARC. You can't give an inch. Never.

STEPHEN. McCain hated Trump. Trump responded in kind, just like you probably would. I have given plenty of inches, but I don't accept that Trump, who clearly has been the subject of political dirty tricks, should pretend the people attacking him are great people.

MARC. Then he should keep his mouth shut. And as for McCain, who earned the gravitas, perhaps you should consider why he, more than Marc, hated Trump, because he, unlike Marc or Stephen, was a hero who could have gotten out of a POW camp and chose to stay with his men rather than get bailed out. If you can't see the difference between selfless acts and selfish acts, you never will know. Trump is a douchebag who deserves nobody's sympathy. Trump University? Google it. Walking into dressing rooms during the Miss USA pageant? Google it. The only thing more astonishing is that he was rewarded with power by people who were stupid enough to vote for him.

STEPHEN. Their other choice was Hillary Clinton. I'm surprised Trump didn't win one hundred million to nothing.

MARC. You have a point there.

MARC. But was Trump a victim when he accused Obama of not being born in this country? Or are those kinds of unsubstantiated rumors allowed when they are unfair against Trump?

STEPHEN. Trump's conspiracy theories about Obama were stupid and pointless. However, that's politics. Obama's supporters and associates were not subpoenaed, investigated, and ruined in order to prove Obama was not born in the United States. Trump has been under investigation based on a hoax, and people close to him have been investigated and threatened with prison in order to get to Trump.

MARC. That's politics!

STEPHEN. No, it's criminal.

MARC. So nobody in the Trump campaign did *anything* criminal? Nothing? Didn't break one law?

STEPHEN. Not that I have seen. They didn't put together a bunch of lies fed to them by Russian intelligence and peddle them to government officials to generate a fake narrative, which provided a pretext for the government to investigate the opposition party's candidate during an election (and ignore crimes by its candidate). If you're okay with this, you're okay with the United States being a banana republic.

MORE ON MCCAIN

March 22, 2019

Marc. Trump likes Chairman Kim but doesn't like a US war hero. Your arguments are impotent.

Stephen. This is among the stupidest points you have made. Trump is engaged in diplomacy with North Korea. He and Kim are not friends. Regarding McCain, it's news to me that we are required to admire McCain. Are we also required to admire Flynn? Or only military heroes who hate Trump? If McCain tried to destroy your practice, would you say, "That's okay. After all, he is a hero"?

Marc. He was attacking McCain long before anything about a dossier. Point to Marc.

INDECENT, IMMORAL SCHMUCK?

March 23, 2019

Marc. Here is an avid supporter of Israel [photo attached] who isn't a blind bat!

Stephen. He [the person in the photo] doesn't like Trump. Good for him. He can vote for Bernie, Kamala, Beto, or whichever nonentity wins the Democratic primary and live with the disastrous results for the United States, Israel, and the world if a Democrat is elected.

Marc. Of course he doesn't like Trump. Who would like such an indecent, immoral schmuck?

Marc. You're supposed to not like him either. You're just supposed to accept him and appreciate what he does.

Stephen. I don't understand what is terrible about him. Has he been credibly accused of rape, like Bill Clinton has been? Did he start his career in politics at the home of convicted domestic terrorists, like Obama did? I did not support him in the Republican primaries because I did not believe he was well informed and did not think he would govern effectively. I don't know how well informed he is, but he is much more rational than his opponents. He takes action and has been effective. If Hillary had been elected and followed Obama's path, we would be in much worse shape in virtually every respect. If he's not reelected, we will have infanticide; support for socialist dictators, like Maduro; curtailment of free speech; and demonization of Israel and Jews.

Marc. Yes, he has been accused of rape. In fact, he admitted to it on tape.

MARC. He won't be reelected, but a Republican replacement would be elected.

STEPHEN. This is an example of your problem. The *Access Hollywood* tape is evidence of boorishness, not rape.

MARC. Believe me, Clinton raped women like Trump rapes them. Just so you know, I haven't turned into a milquetoast liberal. If you are a woman and go into a strange man's hotel room, you are stupid. Those were the situations Clinton was accused of.

STEPHEN. It's fairly certain that Mueller did not find collusion. Are you going to admit you were wrong about that? Not that there ever was any evidence of it. Read about Juanita Broderick if you want to know what an allegation of rape looks like. Specific and verifiable.

WHAT WILL MUELLER FIND?

[3/23/19, 4:23 p.m.] MARC. I don't think he will find that. I think it could be that there was no clear-cut crime. Mueller was charged with investigating the Russian intervention (evidence) and also obstruction of justice. If the report shows nothing, that should not bolster cries of "Witch hunt!" It should represent that nothing was found. And if lateral crimes are uncovered or led to, I cite Bill Clinton: Whitewater, which became lying about sex. Deep down, you cannot square the hypocrisy of the "morality" of the Republicans back then. Their own statements are incongruent with theirs today regarding behavior.

[3/23/19, 4:26 p.m.] STEPHEN. "No clear-cut crime" means there was no crime. However, there is no crime at all. The real crimes were committed by the Obama FBI and DOJ: the obstruction of justice of the email investigation and the banana republic investigation of Trump.

[3/23/19, 4:27 p.m.] STEPHEN. There will be accountability.

[3/23/19, 4:28 p.m.] MARC. Maybe there was no crime. That isn't needed for impeachment.

[3/23/19, 4:28 p.m.] MARC. Which I don't think is warranted at the moment.

[3/23/19, 4:28 p.m.] MARC. There won't be shit on Obama or Hillary.

[3/23/19, 4:30 p.m.] STEPHEN. Impeachment requires high crimes and misdemeanors. Regarding Obama and Hillary, we will see.

[3/23/19, 4:32 p.m.] MARC. Okay, you are wrong. As you know, those are not required. Correct? It's whatever they think it is. If he got up in front of a crowd and said, "Niggas and Jews are the scum of the earth," he would be impeached.

[3/23/19, 5:23 p.m.] STEPHEN. Those are the words in the Constitution.

MUELLER'S TACTICS

MARCH 24, 2019

STEPHEN. I just watched an interview with Jerome Corsi, who was questioned by Mueller but not indicted. He described Mueller's efforts to get him to plead guilty to one count of perjury. He refused. He described being questioned for eight hours a day by three prosecutors and six FBI agents accusing him of lying. He described the financial ruin. He described his fear that the FBI would raid his house. He is going to sue. I hope so. This is why Flynn and Papadopoulos pleaded guilty. Abuse.

MARC. Sorry. You don't hold a candle to Mueller.

STEPHEN. Another stupid comment.

STEPHEN. Your champions will end up in prison.

MARC. Ha.

MARC. I guess Israeli police have never been tough on a suspect.

STEPHEN. I have conducted myself ethically my entire thirty-two-year career. I'm not sure about Mueller.

MARC. Wow.

STEPHEN. Wow? What do you know about Mueller? Virtually nothing. Based on his handling of this investigation, I'm not impressed.

MARC. Do you have anyone in your life you hold in high regard for their past ethical conduct? You think they never had a lapse in judgment? Same with McCain—you think because he tried to take down Trump, that diminished a career of bipartisanship and patriotism? You can't even correctly state what is required for impeachment. Based on that erroneous statement, I'm not impressed.

STEPHEN. You're ignorant. Section 4 of article 2 of the Constitution provides for impeachment for treason, bribery, and other high crimes and misdemeanors. That is the standard.

STEPHEN. I appreciate McCain, but I do not agree with what he did to Trump, particularly his vote on Obamacare. I certainly understand why Trump would not hold him in high regard.

MARC. Trump is a con man and a pathological liar. Ted Cruz and Lindsey Graham told us. Case closed.

MUELLER REPORT SUMMARY RELEASED

STEPHEN. The case is closed. No collusion. And those who peddled that bullshit are the liars.

MARC. Tons of collusion, all documented. They may choose not to prosecute.

MARC. Kushner is going to turn on Trump.

STEPHEN. No. There is no collusion. If there was tons of collusion or, more precisely, a conspiracy between the Trump campaign and the Russians to break US laws, there would be indictments. That's why Mueller was appointed. You're upset because your anti-Trump fantasy is now demonstrably false. Now you appear to be making up a new one about Kushner. Have some class, and admit you were wrong.

MARC. You might be confusing me with other people who pushed an expectation for the Mueller probe. I have been demonstrably true in stating that Trump is someone who shouldn't be president based on his character—demonstrably because Trump demonstrates it on a daily basis. Any blindness you think I will have about an exculpatory report pales in comparison to your own blindness. And once again I say, to demonstrate that I am not participating in a political, ideological hack job, I want President Mike Pence. Pence for president.

STEPHEN. 2024.

MARC. Pence won't be Trump's running mate. They need a woman. Haley.

STEPHEN. Pence will be on the ticket. However, if he's not, she would be a great choice.

MARC. Sure looks like there was nothing there. That's why you have an investigation. The fact that they found nothing doesn't mean it was a witch hunt!

MARC. The report says there's no exoneration of collusion. That's an important distinction.

STEPHEN. The report says there was no collusion. That's it.

STEPHEN. The part of the report in which Mueller didn't exonerate him (which is not his job) referred to obstruction of justice, not collusion. There's no evidence of collusion. If there was no collusion, there could not be obstruction.

MARC. I partially agree with you, but even if he was accused of a crime he didn't commit, he could still obstruct justice by trying to shut down that investigation. It's an abuse of power to say, "I didn't do it, and you are not investigating me," because that subverts the legal process. And there probably wasn't criminal collusion, and it always resonated with me that both parties play dark, seedy games. Well, there was no witch hunt! Ha!

MARC. I guess Mueller was a good guy after all. Still not impressed with him?

MARC. I bet Fox News will be impressed with him.

STEPHEN. No. He knew that there was no evidence of collusion but harassed and ruined people to try to make a case.

MARC. Innocent people like Paul Manafort?

MARC. And liars like Flynn and Papadopoulos?

STEPHEN. Yes. Corsi was offered a deal to plead guilty to one count of lying. He refused because he did not lie. In the end, Mueller did not indict him. Flynn and Papadopoulos chose to plead guilty to avoid further harassment and financial ruin. Mueller should be ashamed.

MARC. I don't think enough has come out to make that conclusion. By the way, Flynn wanted Hillary to go to jail for doing exactly what Kushner is doing.

MARC. I guess there'll be no problem in releasing every single word of the report then, if it's so innocuous.

MARC. Maybe you know more than a career prosecutor.

STEPHEN. Mueller did not find he obstructed justice.

MARC. He equally said that he did not find that he did not obstruct justice.

MARC. I'm not a lawyer, and I stand toe to toe with you. Just leave it at the fact that it was a good day for Trump, and that's it.

STEPHEN. Agreed.

STEPHEN. https://www.scribd.com/document/402974442/AG-March-24-2019-Letter-to-House-and-Senate-Judiciary-Committees-1.

STEPHEN. It's always better to go to the source.

ACCEPTING MUELLER'S FINDINGS

March 26, 2019

Marc. You are so right about accepting due process. I guess Jussie Smollett was just totally exonerated! All charged dropped. I guess he had nothing to do with staging his own mugging!

Stephen. Do you ever tire of making stupid arguments? Mueller found no evidence of collusion. None. After two years of an unlimited investigation, nothing. Smollett is a completely different situation, but it looks like there is going to be an investigation into the dismissal of the charges.

March 27, 2019

Marc. We have to accept the decision of the prosecutor, don't we? Wait—who are you referring to about an investigation into the prosecutor's decision?

PRIVILEGE

STEPHEN. Yes. The state's attorney recused herself because she had, at the request of Michelle Obama's chief of staff, attempted to transfer the investigation to the FBI. The chief of staff was trying to help out Smollett's family.

MARC. That whole thing is a mess! I hate privilege and unfair treatment of the superrich and connected even more than Trump!

STEPHEN. That's what it looks like. By the way, I fully support privilege and unfair treatment for the superrich and connected. I won't give an inch.

MARC. Ha! This is where I am becoming more liberal. I am willing to vote against my own economic self-interests, and I'm proud to say that. Like most people, I am generally selfish, but in lieu of massive charity or empathy, I feel good about myself.

STEPHEN. The difference for you is that you don't expect favors and do not seek them. Fortunately, you don't need them.

MARCH 30, 2019

MARC. Hey, Rip Van Winkle, time to snap out of it. You are on the wrong side of history.

MARCH 31, 2019

STEPHEN. Do you ever get tired of being absolutely wrong?

MARC. Apparently not!

MARC. I'm proud that my views aren't clouded or tethered to one or two personal ideologies.

STEPHEN. I don't know what that means. However, I'm proud that I do my best to base my opinions on reality, not emotions.

MARC. It means that some people support Trump just because he made Jerusalem the capital and because some of his policies are extremely beneficial to wealthy people (granted, you won't take advantage of the $12 million threshold for estate tax inheritance). I would pay money in the form of higher taxes to see a liberal beat Trump. That's not emotions. It's called generosity.

STEPHEN. Trump raised my taxes. You're talking emotion, not facts. You don't see a connection between economic growth and the cut in the corporate tax rates? If you want to pay higher taxes, pay more. No one will stop you. However, don't impose destructive policies on the country. I guess you liked the Obama economy. Not only have I paid my fair share of taxes in my career, but I have donated generously to charities every year. That's generosity.

MARC. I don't want to pay more taxes, but I will if it means I get to have Trump out of office, and that's why I would love to have Pence in there immediately.

STEPHEN. I want to live in a free country where I have the ability to say what I think and provide for my family as I see fit and where everyone rises or falls based on their efforts.

PART 6
APRIL 4, 2019–
JUNE 26, 2019

THE MUELLER REPORT FINDINGS

April 4, 2019

Marc. I thought the report exonerated Trump? Ha-ha.

Stephen. No collusion. That's all that matters.

Marc. I thought indeed there was no collusion, but apparently, Devin Nunes says the report is not credible.

Marc. Oh, wait—I see what you're saying. It's credible when it's good for Trump but not credible when bad. Got it!

Stephen. When did I say that? Barr quoted Mueller. No collusion. No evidence of collusion.

Marc. But he didn't say there was no evidence of obstruction of justice—you know, the thing Nixon was impeached for.

Stephen. I know there was no obstruction. Everything Trump did was public.

Marc. "Ladies and gentlemen, I am announcing that I am stopping the investigation into my potential criminal behavior. This is not obstruction of justice, however, because I am being public about it. Thank you!"

Stephen. That didn't happen. Mueller investigated without interference for two years. He investigated something that did not happen.

MARC. He can't investigate something that didn't happen.

MARC. By the way, if you ask me if Trump did anything much worse than other administrations, with what I know now, I might say no. But I want to put an end to hubris and untouchability.

ANIMALS

MARC. [*Attaches a tweet from Brad Thor.*] Lifetime Republican and former frequent Fox guest. My sentiments exactly!

STEPHEN. Compelling. Brad Thor thinks Trump's an asshole. I believe he is the world's foremost authority on who is and isn't an asshole.

April 5, 2019

MARC. Is there absolutely not any scintilla of a point here?

STEPHEN. Hitler was talking about immutable characteristics. He thought if you were Jewish, you were subhuman. Trump is talking about behavior. He's saying they are animals not because of who they are but because of what they are doing. That being said, Trump could be more temperate, but he won't be.

MARC. "These aren't people." Nice try. My point is proven.

MARC. Inexcusable.

STEPHEN. Your point, like all of your points, is the same. If Trump says it, it is bad. If you are unable to see the distinction I made, it is because you don't want to see it. But if you call a cold-blooded murderer an animal, that is not the same as calling all Jews subhuman.

MARC. "These people."

STEPHEN. I don't know the context, but I know he used that phrase about the MS-13 gang members who dismembered a victim. If that's the case, Trump was right.

SOME PEOPLE DID SOMETHING

April 14, 2019

Marc. Did you think Ilhan Omar's comments about 9/11 were substantially a problem or indicative of anything about her?

Stephen. Yes. It indicates she is not particularly disturbed by the 9/11 terrorist attacks. Presumably, she sympathizes with the terrorists and their goals. I'm sure you have a simplistic comparison to Trump, so let's have it.

Marc. I'm sure his jovial nature about something so grave concerns you.

Stephen. You're defending her? She said, "Some people did something." Trump put out a video clarifying what that "something" actually was.

Marc. I'm not defending her.

MCGAHN AND OBSTRUCTION

April 18, 2019

Marc. I guess the respected lawyer for the White House (not Trump) is a liar too?

Stephen. You seem to miss the point. There was no collusion, and there was no obstruction. Regardless of what Trump ordered McGahn to do, Trump did not fire Mueller. Therefore, it is irrelevant whether he told McGahn to deny that he told him to fire Mueller. Furthermore, Trump fully cooperated with Mueller. Trump did not destroy evidence, delete emails, or smash hard drives to cover up crimes. This McGahn thing is nothing.

Marc. He's not running in 2020.

Stephen. I think he'll be reelected.

Marc. You may be right, especially if they run a very liberal liberal.

April 19, 2019

Marc. The report confirms my consistent contention that he is an unethical liar and revealed a clear consciousness of guilt, regardless of an inability to prove that guilt for various reasons. He has had successes in office, but in my mind, they don't diminish his central inability to improve over prior regimes in restoring prestige and honor to the office, nor do they make any progress in uniting the country, as difficult a task as that could be.

Stephen. The report proves he was the victim of a witch hunt based on a criminal conspiracy. As I have said from the beginning, people will go to jail but not anyone associated with Trump. The liars are the Obama officials who spied on an opposition political campaign.

MARC. So there's nothing in the report that reflects poorly on Trump, huh? He's just a poor, poor victim. Even Barr expressed concern about Russian interference, but Trump believes Putin because Putin was adamant.

STEPHEN. Trump was the target of an illegal effort, in the first instance, to prevent his election and, ultimately, to force him out of office. Mueller did everything in his power to find a crime, including scorched-earth tactics that harmed innocent people. Trump was forced to deal with an investigation into everything his campaign did and everyone associated with it, an investigation that he knew was totally baseless. Despite his justifiable frustration with dealing with the investigation, the administration did not withhold a single document or witness, except for Trump himself. No, the report doesn't reflect poorly on Trump. I look forward to seeing Brennan, Comey, and Clapper go down. It may reach Obama. They all should pay a heavy price.

MARC. Nothing is happening to those people, because Trump and his team will want to run and let sleeping dogs lie. Fox won't, but the administration will.

STEPHEN. No way. Do you ever get tired of being totally wrong?

MARC. I'm right!

STEPHEN. You will be wrong again.

APRIL 20, 2019

MARC. Smerconish elucidated that the Mueller report was never going to find Trump guilty of a crime because established guidelines precluded that since a president couldn't defend himself in a conventional, speedy manner while in office. It's so stated in the report. Yet while Mueller would be able to declare him not guilty, as he in fact did with collusion, no such wording was used for obstruction. Therefore, we can infer that Mueller believed he was guilty of obstruction. Don McGahn and Corey Lewandowski testified to that effect.

STEPHEN. Prosecutors never declare people not guilty. That is not their job. Their job is to bring charges or not bring charges. If Mueller had found Trump broke the law, he would have said so. In his report on Whitewater and Lewinsky, Ken Starr found Clinton had broken laws. The argument that Trump obstructed justice is pure fantasy. First, he did not commit an underlying crime. Second, he provided Mueller unprecedented cooperation. He gave Mueller access to every document and witness, including the White House counsel. He did not assert executive privilege in any instance. Furthermore, it goes without saying that he didn't fire Mueller. Doesn't it seem strange to you that even though Mueller found no collusion, the Democrats still claim he's guilty? Where is your sense of fairness?

MARC. Nope. He wrote in the report that he wasn't going to make a legal conclusion because it wouldn't be fair. OLC prohibits presidents from indictment. Keep in mind, Clinton was impeached for lying about a sexual affair. Trump already has lied about that, though not under oath, I realize.

STEPHEN. You're ignorant. What Mueller did was inappropriate; his job was to determine whether or not a crime had been committed. If he could not determine a crime had been committed, he should have simply said so. Instead, he suggested that certain incidents could support an obstruction charge but left it to the DOJ. My understanding is that he didn't base his decision on DOJ policy that a sitting president can't be indicted but on the question of whether a president can be charged with a crime for making decisions, such as firing Comey, which is his constitutional prerogative if the president could be shown to have corrupt intent. In any event, the DOJ—Barr and Rosenstein—determined that the scenarios set out by Mueller did not establish a basis for an obstruction charge. In other words, nothing Trump did constituted obstruction. As I noted earlier, Barr and Rosenstein certainly took into account Trump's unprecedented cooperation with Mueller.

MARC. Mueller wrote explicitly that if there was no evidence of obstruction of justice, he would state so. Barr and Rosenstein are biased. How is it that a doctor can win debates against a lawyer?

MARC. Also, most of the "fake" media reports that Trump shot down each time were true.

STEPHEN. You only win by changing the rules. What Mueller did was inappropriate. However, on its own terms, what Barr and Rosenstein concluded is that the evidence presented by Mueller does not establish obstruction. To put it another way, Mueller says, "We found that Trump did X, Y, and Z. We, the Mueller team, do not take a position on whether X, Y, or Z constitutes obstruction. Maybe it does, or maybe it doesn't. Therefore, Attorney General and Deputy Attorney General, we will leave it to you to decide." Legally, it was not a close call, and Barr and Rosenstein concluded that X, Y, and Z did not constitute obstruction. In my opinion, Mueller's team desperately wanted to find a crime to charge Trump but could not. They certainly did not want to clear Trump, which they actually did. By inappropriately suggesting there might be a basis for obstruction but knowing that there was not and that the DOJ would make the correct decision, Mueller has allowed the attacks against Trump to continue. It's unfortunate, but it will hurt the Democrats. Furthermore, the investigation into the Trump investigation will continue and will expose the real crimes that the Democrats and Mueller do not want exposed.

MARC. Maybe they suggested there might have been obstruction because there might have been, if so interpreted by Congress. Just as Republicans so acted with Clinton.

STEPHEN. That's not how it works. Congress does not make prosecutorial judgments for the DOJ. Mueller laid out his assessment of the facts. Barr and Rosenstein concluded that those facts do not constitute the crime of obstruction. Therefore, no crime has been alleged. Congress can consider whether conduct that does not constitute a crime constitutes treason, bribery, or other high crimes and misdemeanors, but it is not a serious argument to say that conduct that does not constitute a crime under federal criminal statutes constitutes a high crime or misdemeanor akin to treason or bribery under the Constitution. Also, Ken Starr, unlike Mueller, found that Clinton committed crimes. Ultimately, the Senate determined his crimes did not constitute grounds for removal from office.

MARC. Ken Starr found Clinton committed crimes, and Congress chose to act accordingly. Mueller found that Trump might have, and Congress will act accordingly. Be more economical with your words. It's like verbal diarrhea.

STEPHEN. No, Mueller did not find any crimes. He laid out scenarios for consideration by the DOJ, which determined that no crimes had been committed, which is obviously true. Congress can do whatever it wants to do, but it cannot seek impeachment based on a finding that Trump has been found to have committed a crime. As for verbal diarrhea, I'm arguing with a person who consistently talks through his ass, so I guess it's appropriate.

MARC. He specifically stated in the report that they would not be going about a process that would look for crimes, because it would be unfair to charge a president with crimes that he couldn't defend. Therefore, you can infer that the things he throws out for consideration are, in his view, crimes.

STEPHEN. The purpose of his report is to determine whether evidence exists that support criminal charges. It is binary: he either makes criminal charges, or he does not. Because he did not find any violation of any US law, that's it.

MARC. I am not sure about your first sentence's accuracy, but he deflects that by specifically asserting that he would not be considering whether a crime was committed.

STEPHEN. I plan to read the Mueller report. However, what could be more unfair than saying—after a two-year scorched-earth investigation conducted by a legal team staffed with anti-Trump partisans—"We did not find any violation of US laws, but there could be criminal violations, and Congress should further investigate," even though investigating crimes is not Congress's job?

MARC. They didn't say that. They precluded your inference by stating that they would specifically not be going through the process to determine whether a crime was committed. I'll send you the reference.

MARC. Complete vindication? Maybe for me, who has been saying what a snake he is.

STEPHEN. I don't agree with Napolitano. First, Trump did not withhold any evidence from Mueller. There were no claims of executive privilege. There was total transparency. Furthermore, what Mueller characterizes as Trump telling McGahn to lie may not be true. For example, my boss has, in moments of frustration, told me to fire someone. I knew he didn't mean it, and I didn't do it. If Trump had wanted to fire Mueller, Mueller would have been fired. If Trump said to fire Mueller but didn't follow up on it, it is because it wasn't intended to be an order. Trump may be venal, but he was the victim, under attack by his political enemies. They're the criminals, as we will soon see.

MARC. I do respect your point about the boss just spouting off and not being taken seriously.

LIES AND LIARS

MARC. When I've told you that Trump is a liar, you say, "How do you know he's a liar?" Well, he's a liar—it's all there.

STEPHEN. If it's all there, tell me all the lies he told. After that, we can stack them up against the lies about Trump by Comey, Clapper, Brennan, McCabe, Adam Schiff, and more. It's going to be quite a reckoning.

MARC. I'm not following. Are you asking me to substantiate my doubtful contention that he lies? Or are you saying that's it's okay because all the Dems lie as well? Focus, Steve.

MARC. And then, when I tell you the lies he has spread, you will tell me, "But he wasn't under oath."

STEPHEN. I'm asking you to identify the specific lies that Trump is alleged to have told. You said it's all out there, so I assume you can identify them. For example, Comey certified in a FISA warrant application that the Steele dossier was verified. That was a lie. Adam Schiff has repeatedly said he had proof of collusion—another lie. What lies did Trump tell?

MARC. [*Sends an attachment with people accusing Trump of lying.*]

STEPHEN. All you're showing me is that people say he lied. I'm not saying he didn't, but I'm asking what specific lies he told.

MARC. "I never had a relationship with Stormy Daniels."

MARC. "I don't know anything about WikiLeaks; that's not my thing."

MARC. "Who is David Duke?"

STEPHEN. Okay. He probably is lying about Stormy Daniels. I believe him about WikiLeaks and David Duke, but I don't know. None of these supposed lies are relevant to his presidency. In other words, who cares? They are certainly less relevant than lies like "If you like your doctor, you can keep your doctor" or that Benghazi was a protest against a video or that the investigation into Trump was not based on the dossier.

MARC. "I have no business whatsoever with Russia."

STEPHEN. I doubt he said that. If he did, it would have been in response to a specific question. It's funny: you know he's a liar, but you can't identify any lies he told.

MARC. He said it in a press conference—exact quote. He says ridiculous things like "I am the least racist person in the world."

MARC. And "Some people say I'm the best president ever."

MARC. [Sarah] Sanders told a complete lie that is just horrible. Regardless of your thoughts on Comey, you know he was loved by his subordinates, and she said she heard from "countless" people who were happy he was gone. Nobody would tell her that, and when interviewed, she said that she misspoke.

STEPHEN. Those are not lies. They are opinions. I don't know where you read that Comey was loved by his subordinates, but I have read or heard reports that the FBI rank and file is disgusted by Comey's handling of the Hillary investigation, Trump, and his book tour.

STEPHEN. And not from Sarah Sanders.

THE MEANING OF THE MUELLER REPORT

April 21, 2019

MARC. https://jonathanturley.org/2019/04/21/the-special-counsel-and-trumps-sage-of-self-inflicted-wounds/.

MARC. Here is a view that agrees with your view that Trump was innocent of crimes and that most damage was mere bluster but at least treats people like me with respect. You are all about Trump being the victim, never assigning him culpability for putting himself in this mess.

STEPHEN. I always treat you with respect by, for example, explaining my positions, which you referred to as "verbal diarrhea." I'll read the article.

STEPHEN. I disagree with Turley. Based on what we have learned about Comey, he should have been fired immediately. Having made the mistake of initially keeping him, Trump rectified it by firing him when he did. Turley assumes Trump would have been better off leaving Comey in place. Maybe or maybe not. Comey faces criminal liability for his role in the investigation into Trump (the false FISA application, for example), the exoneration of Hillary, and more. Notwithstanding Mueller's inappropriate comments, I have more confidence in him than in Comey. Regarding the internal deliberations within the Trump administration over whether to fire Mueller, the only thing that matters is that Mueller wasn't fired. Trump's internal deliberations are protected by executive privilege, which Trump could have asserted but did not. Finally, Trump was being investigated against a false allegation that had zero credibility. It was not legitimate. Trump's frustration and anger are completely understandable. Despite it, he allowed the investigation to proceed unimpeded. That's the real takeaway.

MARC. My belief that there was not enough evidence uncovered—as evidenced by Trump saying, "I'm fucked"—will be bolstered by the fact that despite your repeated assurances, there will be no investigation into the investigation. They will want to move away from this.

STEPHEN. In context, Trump's comment clearly referred to the impact of a special counsel investigation on his ability to get things done. Based on your track record, your certainty that there will be no investigation into the investigation makes it an absolute certainty that there will be.

MARC. Right here in the record, you will see, going back to the text transcripts from three minutes ago right above, I said *belief*. Few beliefs of mine are certain. I think that is actually within the definition of *belief*. Phrases like "I guarantee" or "I am certain" would be another story. I wish I was in law school with you!

STEPHEN. Okay, fair point. Your belief that there will be no investigation into the investigators is the best reason to believe there will be an investigation.

APRIL 24, 2019

MARC. So if a woman accused a corporate executive of sexual assault, the company decided they needed an internal investigation, and then that executive used his power to call the general counsel to fire the investigator, you don't think you would have any culpability?

STEPHEN. Apples and oranges. If a company refused to investigate a claim of wrongdoing, the company could have greater civil liability for that wrongdoing. It would be worse if there was criminal conduct. Corporate officers cannot stop the board of directors from investigating or stop law enforcement or a civil plaintiff. In contrast, the president has the sole authority to investigate or prosecute violations of federal law. He can't stop Congress from investigating him for stopping an investigation. He also can't stop the press from investigating. If you're talking about

Trump's consideration of firing Mueller, it would have been a political disaster for him but legal. More importantly, Trump did not fire Mueller or impede him in any way.

MARC. If there were transcripts of a CEO saying, "Let's deceive all our investors and analysts!" and someone talked him out of it, there would be no culpability for his intentions that he was talked out of?

STEPHEN. No. It's not illegal to consider doing something illegal. It's only illegal to do something illegal. In Trump's case, he didn't commit a crime and cooperated in the investigation into a nonexistent crime.

STEPHEN. On October 16, 2015, Obama publicly commented on Hillary's emails. He stated that she made a mistake but did not endanger national security. Is it a coincidence that the DOJ conducted a sham investigation? Today it was reported that Obama had thousands of emails from Hillary's server. Obstruction?

CONGRESSIONAL SUBPOENAS

April 26, 2019

Marc. https://twitter.com/billkristol/status/.

Stephen. Trump is challenging the legality and constitutionality of the subpoenas. He may ultimately be required to comply. However, it is clear that Congress is not carrying out its oversight function. They simply want to continue investigating Trump to try to embarrass him and to take the spotlight off the coming developments in the investigation into the FBI, DOJ, and Clinton campaign. I think the subpoenas are a continuation of the abuses of power by Trump's opponents. However, there may be no judicial remedy, and Trump may need to comply. I remind you that you seem to believe that Trump's intent in firing Comey is relevant and that his intent in considering firing Mueller is relevant, even though he has the absolute constitutional authority to fire either one of them. In contrast, congressional oversight does not give Congress unfettered authority to investigate anyone for anything. Nevertheless, if a court does consider the subpoenas, it may not be in a position to question Congress's intent.

Marc. Oh, I guess the Republicans did want to embarrass Clinton. Trump has the absolute right to fire the person investigating him, just as Congress has the absolute right to subpoena and impeach.

Marc. When Trump is voted out and says he isn't leaving the White House, you will probably back him.

Stephen. As usual, you're talking through your ass. You manage to combine lack of knowledge with poor analysis.

BACK TO TRUMP'S POLICIES

MARC. I don't know—that combination has made Trump a false idol to millions of fools.

MARC. *Fools* is the noun that defines people who have been fooled. Fooled by a moron they think is brilliant. Fooled by someone they think loves Israel who didn't contribute a dime to the country before his presidency. Fooled by someone who ran on "America first" yet thinks Russia is an honest broker in denying their nefarious behavior.

STEPHEN. Trump has shortcomings, but it is his opponents who have lied, have broken the law, and are delusional. You "knew" that Trump was guilty of collusion, except there was no collusion. But that doesn't change your mind about anything. When former FBI and intelligence officials are prosecuted for their abuses of power, will that change your mind? Similarly, your uninformed views on Trump's policies on Russia lack any factual basis. Trump might believe he can work with Putin, but he has opposed Russian interests in Syria (attacking Russian troops), Venezuela, Ukraine (sending arms), energy policy, and military buildup. The Trump administration has countered Russia much more forcefully than Obama. In fact, Obama was caught on an open mic telling Medvedev to tell Putin that he would have more flexibility after his reelection. Obama also mocked Romney for calling Russia a geopolitical foe: "The '80s are calling, and they want their foreign policy back." If you prefer to have a weak economy, weak military, open borders, legal infanticide, and the Green New Deal, vote for the Democrat in 2020. I'm sure your children will appreciate your vote when they are living in a socialist paradise.

MARC. I'm tired of people voting only for what is good for *them*. I'm not the only one who should get their head out of their ass. So should everyone who thinks that lower taxes on the rich and supporting Israel are going to save this country.

STEPHEN. Again, you continue half-assed arguments. I'm in favor, first and foremost, of individual liberty. That necessarily requires a smaller government. Second, policies that create economic growth, jobs, and higher wages should be everyone's goal. That's what Trump's policies have achieved. The United States should support Israel because it is the right thing to do. Also, historically, the fate of the Jews is a bellwether for everyone else. America is safer if Israel is safer. By the way, I paid higher taxes under Trump, not lower taxes. If it's at all possible, think before you speak.

MARC. Those aren't Trump's policies. Those are Republican policies. As every day passes, with every new inane comment and every scandal unearthed, it only proves my point that a charlatan has scammed half the country. That fact is paramount for me, and I (obviously) can't get past it.

STEPHEN. The only scandal that has been unearthed is the effort to frame Trump for a nonexistent crime. Trump's detractors have been making inane and false comments about him since he was elected. Your problem is that he is not a charlatan. He is actually doing what he promised to do, and the results have been good. Trump-Russia collusion was the scam, and those who perpetrated it continue to lie.

MARC. On your list of indignations, you won't find an attorney general who acts like the POTUS's PR man.

STEPHEN. Barr is acting like a PR man? Based on what? Because the Democrats and the media, who were lying about collusion, say so? That's a convincing argument.

APRIL 27, 2019

STEPHEN. Another area where Trump's critics have been consistently wrong: "Has the Recession Been Cancelled?"

STEPHEN. https://www.wsj.com/articles/has-the-recession-been-cancelled-.

MARC. Any progress has been made despite him or directly due to his aides. He is capable of nothing except carnival talk and conspiracy bombs.

MARC. My mistake—not his aides. His bosses.

STEPHEN. That's a stupid, if typical, response. None of it would have happened without him.

MARC. Except for everything.

MARC. Minus the increased division and toxicity he thrives on.

MARC. The fools in this country who watched *The Apprentice* should be fooled, not you.

STEPHEN. You're right. Lying about collusion is not divisive. Calling him—and everyone who supports him—racist and xenophobic is not divisive. Ignoring the results of his policies—economic growth, low unemployment, low black and Hispanic unemployment—is not divisive. Trump's critics are divisive and support policies that will set back the progress Trump has made.

BACK TO TRUMP'S SUPPORTERS

April 28, 2019

Marc. Does it feel good to share adulation for Trump with people who chant, "Jews must not replace us"?

Marc. And I'm not for Rashida Tlaib types.

Stephen. Trump was not elected by people who chant, "Jews must not replace us," nor has Trump offered support to them. In fact, he is pro-Israel and, for that matter, pro–black American. He has pursued economic growth policies that have led to the lowest black unemployment and enacted prison reform long sought by black leaders. So I don't care what a handful of irrelevant people think about Trump.

Marc. More than a handful. Now you are talking out your ass. Hundreds of other people could have instituted the policies that Trump did. He was hardly uniquely qualified. In fact, he was elected *because* of a "handful" of people.

Stephen. Really? You believe there are large numbers of neo-Nazis in the United States? You believe there is an audience for their views? Show me the data. Not only are you totally misinformed and ignorant, but you have no problem slandering millions of Americans because they don't share your angry and stupid views on Trump.

Stephen. I can characterize your last message as "It doesn't matter what Trump does, only what Marc thinks about him."

Marc. Large numbers of anti-Semites support Trump.

MARC. And if I have angry and stupid views, it's 'cause I am looking at an angry and stupid president on a daily basis.

STEPHEN. No. You make things up. The anti-Semites are in the Democratic Party. Members of Congress.

MARC. There are indeed some there. Much more around Middle America. It's a big country.

STEPHEN. Most of them are on the left. I saw them when Occupy Wall Street was camped out in Zuccotti Park.

STEPHEN. Similarly, in England, Jeremy Corbyn is the leading anti-Semite, not imaginary Nazis.

EXTREME ABORTION

MARC. The douchebag of a person you defend incessantly is going to rallies and saying that babies are born, wrapped up, held, and then killed by doctors after discussions with moms. That is another heinous example of spinning a false narrative that could get someone killed by some idiot thinking he is a zealot preventing atrocities that aren't happening the way Trump says.

STEPHEN. He's repeating what Democratic politicians are advocating. Who are the douchebags?

MARC. Nobody is advocating that.

STEPHEN. Ralph Northam explained that if the baby is born alive, it will be kept comfortable until the mother and doctor decide. The Democrats opposed the Born Alive Act. Get your head out of your ass.

MARC. Northam misspoke, and you left out that he admitted that he misspoke. Everybody knows it, and your spin is becoming disgusting.

STEPHEN. No, he didn't misspeak, and the Democrats opposed the Born Alive Act, which would require a baby born alive to receive medical care. Your lack of knowledge is embarrassing.

MARC. Oh, I guess that's the same thing as wrapping them up and then murdering them.

MARC. Infanticide is against the law, and he is telling crowds of people in the whole country that doctors are committing crimes now.

STEPHEN. The Democrats have advocated for allowing babies born alive to die. To me, that's murder.

MARC. The only embarrassing thing is that years from now, all the people who supported Trump will be using the excuse "I never loved him, but he was better than Hillary." I'll know that won't work for you, because you defended him constantly on every topic.

STEPHEN. My views on infanticide have nothing to do with Trump. You should be embarrassed for your lack of humanity.

MARC. I am proud to be prochoice.

STEPHEN. Abortion is one thing. Allowing a baby who has been born alive to die is another.

ISRAEL AND ANTI-SEMITISM AGAIN

Marc. Every Democratic politician states publicly that Israel is a strong ally, but they wish Israel could become more liberal and less hard-line. I would respect that statement. If, however, they said Israelis are killers and deniers of human rights, I would refute that statement. You consistently lack the nuance to even criticize anything Trump says that's all falsehood or even a twist on some truth.

Stephen. I don't agree with everything Trump says or does, but I don't agree that he is a racist or a Nazi because he does something I think is poorly thought out. Trump's critics, including you, lie about him every day. I defend him against baseless attacks. Regarding Israel, what do you mean by *hard-line*? Do you consider [Palestinian leader Mahmoud] Abbas a moderate? If so, compared to whom?

Stephen. https://www.congress.gov/bill/116th-congress/senate-bill/311/text.

Stephen. The Born Alive Act.

Stephen. https://thehill.com/homenews/media/440957-ny-times-opinion-apologizes-for-cartoon-depicting-anti-semitic-tropes.

Stephen. Speaking of anti-Semitism, did you see the cartoon the *New York Times* published? Talk about offensive. Hey, they're not Trump.

Marc. Bad cartoon.

BACK TO OBSTRUCTION

May 1, 2019

MARC. I actually understand the concern about the genesis and bias of the FBI and think it's worth an investigation. I also think Trump clearly obstructed justice by requesting the firing of Mueller and would have been indicted but for the guidelines of the office of legal counsel. Regardless of what he thought about the investigation, you can't fire the investigator without the fallout, and you can't ask your lawyer to change the record. McGahn has no reason to lie and is a compelling witness.

STEPHEN. Really? How did Trump obstruct Mueller? Also, obstruction of justice is a legal concept. You have to commit acts that meet the criteria. Nothing Trump did meets that criteria. The bottom line is that Mueller had more access to Trump and his staff than in any other investigation. It's part of the effort to keep the focus off the FBI. By the way, Trump is president and has the absolute legal authority to fire the investigator. However, he didn't do it. It doesn't matter if he told McGahn to do it but didn't expect him to carry it out, told him to do it and thought better of it, or never told him at all. It didn't happen. McGahn's job was to give Trump advice.

MARC. So someone under investigation is allowed to shut down the investigation if *he* believes he committed no crime? There was no conclusion about the absence of a crime at the point he acted to obstruct. Can someone commit to not tell the truth if he is under investigation, without actually having committed a crime?

MARC. Can the president not tell the full truth to investigators if he believes he didn't commit a crime?

STEPHEN. The president can shut down any investigation. He would have to deal with the political fallout or impeachment. In Trump's case, he fully cooperated, and there was no crime, yet he's accused of obstruction because people like you want to believe he's guilty of something. The liars are the investigators—Brennan, Clapper, Comey, McCabe, etc. If you want to know what real obstruction of justice is, it is deleting emails and destroying hard drives and iPhones. It also looks like Obama and Lynch directing the FBI to conduct a sham investigation.

MARC. Do you personally have a problem if a president knew the investigation was politically motivated and therefore didn't fully cooperate with it?

STEPHEN. He fully cooperated, even though he knew that he didn't collude and that the Steele dossier was a bunch of lies. In Hillary's case, she actually broke the law. She set up a private server to violate the law because she didn't want her communications to be available for disclosure. In her case, the DOJ protected her. In Trump's case, the DOJ sought to frame him.

MARC. He tried to fire the investigator! What if Bill Clinton had done that? Wow!

MARC. Consciousness of guilt. When all the evidence comes out from everything outside the Mueller report, all you will be left with is "He was framed!"

MARC. If you were introduced to Trump, you would probably kneel and say, "Yes, my king?"

STEPHEN. Bill Clinton did not have the authority to fire Ken Starr. Ken Starr was an independent counsel who reported to Congress. The independent counsel statute was allowed to lapse. Bill Clinton did everything in his power to undermine Starr and committed perjury to boot. That's why he was disbarred. There is no evidence outside of the Mueller report.

DIGRESSION TO OMAR

MAY 2, 2019

MARC. Random thought: What's so bad about Omar being anti-Semitic, when the president is anti-Muslim?

STEPHEN. I agree. There's nothing wrong with a congresswoman who opposes Israel's existence, accuses Jews of dual loyalty, and apologizes for terrorism, especially if the United States has a president who took the position that immigration from Muslim countries with active terrorist networks should be prohibited until we can verify the identity of the immigrants. Two peas in a pod.

MARC. I got a chuckle out of that.

STEPHEN. There is hope!

BACK TO COLLUSION

May 3, 2019

Marc. Please explain to me how Putin can hack our election, and Trump talks to him for an hour.

Stephen. Russia might have hacked DNC emails, which is illegal and hostile, but it did not hack the election. However, nations spy on each other and always have. It happened during the Obama administration, and Obama did nothing about it. I remind you that the Iranians, among other bad things, boarded an American ship and held American sailors captive. Did that stop the Obama administration from agreeing that the Iranians could develop nuclear weapons?

May 4, 2019

Marc. Hey, what does your "spin anything" computer say about the North Korean missile test? Trump really helped with them, it seems.

Marc. A master stroke of diplomacy.

Stephen. Maybe yes and maybe no. We will see. There is no guarantee that Trump will be successful in achieving a nonnuclear North Korea. However, the policies pursued by Clinton, Bush, and Obama were completely unsuccessful. Do you suggest we continue doing what they did, which is basically to provide aid in exchange for broken promises? Do you support war? Trump is trying to leverage threats with promises that North Korea can achieve prosperity. He has a very personal style. As long as the threat that the United States would use force is credible and Trump holds firm on sanctions, he may succeed.

SHOULD MUELLER TESTIFY?

STEPHEN. According to the Mueller report, on April 25, 2016, Joseph Mifsud (who may have been planted in the campaign by the FBI) told Papadopoulos that the Russians had dirt on Hillary in the form of emails. It's not clear from the report where the Mueller team got that information. According to the report, on May 6, 2016, Papadopoulos told an Australian diplomat that the Russians had dirt that could hurt Hillary and help Trump. It's interesting that the Australians did not relay that conversation to the US government until July 16, 2016. It's more interesting that Papadopoulos never told anyone in the Trump campaign about his conversation with Mifsud. I hope Bill Barr finds out more about Mifsud. Not only is Papadopoulos a big nothing, but it looks like he might have been set up to spread the story about Hillary's emails.

MAY 5, 2019

MARC. Maybe you can admit that if Trump was totally exonerated, then he should have no fear of Mueller.

STEPHEN. I would like Mueller to testify, because I would like to know several things: Why doesn't the report on Russian interference explore the origin of the Steele dossier, which the *NYT* has acknowledged may have been Russian disinformation? Why didn't the investigation look into the reasons foreign diplomats were approaching George Papadopoulos, a nobody? Why didn't Mueller look at Joseph Mifsud, who told Papadopoulos that the Russians had dirt on Hillary? I could go on. Trump has nothing to fear from Mueller. Mueller has made his conclusions. It's not Mueller's job to cast aspersions on any person who has not been charged with a crime, especially an imaginary crime. The question you should ask yourself is, why do the Democrats fear Barr, and why are they trying to undermine or obstruct the investigation into the origins of the investigation into Trump?

May 6, 2019

Marc. Knowing your impeccable judgment of character, I'll assume you judge Trump to be more reputable and honest than Mueller.

Stephen. If I had disputed that Mueller was a fine soldier, your response would be relevant. That's not the question. The question is the credibility of the report. It's full of holes and innuendo. The fact the Mueller displayed heroism as an Army Ranger does not change that, nor does it mean he's a good guy.

Marc. Oh, I'm sorry. I thought the report was a "full exoneration." Those were the words of the president.

Stephen. Mueller determined not only that did Trump not commit any crime related to collusion but also that no such thing as collusion occurred—a complete exoneration on that point. He also did not find that any of Trump's actions, such as firing Comey, constituted obstruction of justice, although he left it to Barr to decide. Barr, for many excellent reasons—including the facts that it is very difficult to establish obstruction when there is no underlying crime, Trump fully cooperated with the investigation and did not assert executive privilege, and a president cannot be guilty of obstruction for firing an executive branch officer, regardless of his reasons—found there was no basis for an obstruction charge. Again, that's an exoneration. Although Mueller found no collusion, the report goes on for pages about nonevents to make it seem like the FBI had a reason to investigate, but it's full of holes and, frankly, misleading.

Marc. Okay, so I am sure his testimony before the world will clarify.

Stephen. His conclusions are final. There's nothing to clarify there.

Marc. You said it's full of holes.

MARC. He will fill in those holes and complete the picture of someone who would have been indicted but for the department regulations.

STEPHEN. No. Why don't you read the report instead of talking through your tuchus? Department regulations have nothing to do with it. There was no collusion, except for the Steele dossier, which somehow isn't discussed.

MARC. Regarding obstruction, he started by talking about the limitations.

STEPHEN. He didn't make the decision; Barr did, and Barr made it without regard to DOJ policy.

ELITISM

May 7, 2019

MARC. At least you were correct about Trump being a successful businessman. An *NYT* report shows he lost $1 billion dollars in the '90s, eight out of ten years of losses. Ha-ha-ha. Genius. I call it the work of a scam artist. No excuse for scamming someone as smart as you, though.

STEPHEN. You have to have a billion to lose a billion. He rebounded. He's an entrepreneur and businessman.

MARC. Rebounded my ass. Wait till the other more recent years come out. Only *The Apprentice* bailed him out. I'm not elitist. I want to pay more in taxes and give back to other Americans.

STEPHEN. You are an elitist.

STEPHEN. By the way, if you want to give your money away, give it away. You don't need the government to be charitable.

MARC. I do give money away.

STEPHEN. So do I.

MARC. I never said you didn't.

MARC. What I have said is that Trump is a complete charlatan who has fooled many people into believing he is a brilliant person of great judgment. Other brilliant people know what he is but pretend he is something else.

MARC. There probably hasn't been a better con artist in world history.

STEPHEN. Who is stupid: a person who ignores actual events and continues to believe a story that is false and will be proven to be criminal or a person who supports reality (economic growth, rational foreign policy, and constitutional judges)? You're amazing.

MARC. The person who ignores actual events is actually smarter because he can see through the things that the simpleton cannot. All three metrics you cited would have been accomplished with any of the other Republican nominees, outside of perhaps Kasich.

STEPHEN. No other Republican would have done all of the following: stood by Kavanaugh, moved the embassy to Jerusalem, pulled out of the Paris Accord and Iran deal, imposed tariffs on China, funded the wall, and eliminated regulations. All Republicans might have supported tax reform, but they would have cut and run on most of the other issues. That's why Trump will win reelection. Ironically, because he sticks to his word.

MARC. He should have pulled Kavanaugh and put in Amy Barrett—more conservative and a woman and not an attempted rapist.

STEPHEN. If he'd pulled Kavanaugh, he would have legitimized character assassination. Luckily, Trump is not a dupe like you.

MARC. Wrong, because he assassinated Blasey Ford's character without pulling Kavanaugh, and Kavanaugh is left humiliated for the ages. Everyone will remember his crying and his gambling debts and know that he was a misogynistic, drunken teen (and no, I wasn't, nor were you).

STEPHEN. I'll remember how the Democrats attempted to destroy a good man.

May 8, 2019

Marc. A crybaby drunk.

Marc. Some public display. It is etched in the memory of millions.

Stephen. Millions of morons.

Marc. You have a trigger when I call the middle-American Trump supporters stupid, yet you do the same. Before Trump aligned himself with Republicans, if I had come to you in the '90s and asked you for your take on him, it would have been the same as my take remains today.

Stephen. It's not the same. I'm calling people morons for accepting a planned effort at character assassination based on a totally uncorroborated recollection from thirty-six years ago embellished with other uncorroborated, crazy allegations as factual. You and they accepted these ridiculous allegations, which never should have seen the light of day, because you hate Trump.

MORE SUBPOENAS

MARC. https://twitter.com/walshfreedom/status/.

MARC. I guess the Republican-controlled Senate Intelligence Committee is really out to get Donald Trump

MARC. https://twitter.com/johnwdean/status/.

MARC. Rubio calls for Barr to resign! [It was a clip of Rubio calling for Obama Attorney General Eric Holder to resign for obstructing Congress.]

STEPHEN. Aren't you tired of making statements without knowledge of the facts? I don't know the circumstances of the Senate's subpoena to Don Jr., so we will wait and see. I do know that Holder was held in contempt for refusing over a period of one year to respond to a subpoena for information on Fast and Furious. Holder truly was obstructing Congress. The subpoenas to Barr are political theater over a matter that has been resolved. It is nonsense. Barr is right. The real abuses of power and crimes are going to be exposed by Horowitz and Barr.

MARC. Rubio's words against Holder are certainly applicable.

STEPHEN. Apples and oranges.

MARC. Both delicious fruits!

MARC. Same thing.

STEPHEN. I know they don't matter to you, but the facts matter.

STEPHEN. Read "The Pseudo-Impeachment: Democrats hold show trials rather than vote to oust the President."

STEPHEN. https://www.wsj.com/articles/the-pseudo-impeachment-.

May 9, 2019

Marc. So what did you come up with as to why the Republican-led committee would subpoena Trump Jr.? I say they are fed up with being lied to and with executive branch hubris.

May 10, 2019

Marc. You never told me why the committee would call Trump Jr. in, and now there's a *WSJ* report that Trump tried to get McGahn to say there was no obstruction, and McGahn wouldn't! Ha!

Stephen. Trump-Russia collusion is over. The real wrongdoing is going to come out. I'm glad you're happy about the never-ending efforts to find Trump guilty of something. The simple truth is that he was the victim of the most egregious abuse of power in the history of the United States. Trump didn't commit any crime or engage in any conduct that could be called collusion. Nor did he obstruct the abusive investigation into that nonoccurrence. Those responsible for the bogus investigation should and will go to jail.

Marc. No way.

Stephen. You have been wrong about everything to date, and you will be wrong again. Trump will be reelected.

Marc. https://twitter.com/tribelaw/status/.

May 11, 2019

Stephen. https://www.nationalreview.com/2019/05/trump-russia-investigation-partisan-politics/.

STEPHEN. Marc, this article expresses my views on the Mueller probe very well. I hope you read it.

MARC. Okay, I just listened to an hour-long podcast on how Trump repeatedly fleeced Deutsche Bank, repeatedly defaulting on loans and asking for more. Disgusting on all levels. They got a deal by saying that the 2008 crisis was force majeure and that the bank actually owed him money, despite his huge debt.

POLITICAL HIT JOB

MARC. I read the article. So the whole point of the Dems' crusade for truth for the sake of the law was a political hit job to obstruct Trump? That would be horrible and unprecedented. It's not like Mitch McConnell would have ever tried that, nor certainly ever verbalized something like that. It's not like anyone like Donald Trump himself would ever impugn the character and legitimacy of Barack Obama. As for the pee tape, I can't say it didn't happen, because Trump surely had some Russian tail; the Russians are known for *kompromat*; and other things in the dossier were true, so it may well have been true. If someone had said Trump told him he could grab pussy because he was famous and could get away with it, absent a tape or proof of it, nobody would have believed it.

STEPHEN. A political hit job is exactly what this is. That is what Horowitz and Barr are investigating, and that is what the Democrats are afraid of. We will have the facts soon enough. There is no question Mueller could not prosecute Trump, so he smeared him. I don't know what you think Mitch McConnell has done or might do, but he has not used law enforcement and intelligence agencies to impugn the opposition party's nominee or attempted to undo an election. This is not a conspiracy theory, as has been confirmed in the Strzok and Page texts, the first Horowitz report, and testimony by FBI officials. It will be established, as well as the fact that the FBI was investigating Trump well before July 2016 without any legal justification. As for Trump's character, the fact that you think he's a lowlife for things he actually has said and done is your right. However, the people who voted for him came to a different conclusion. The fact that you and others feel he is unfit for office is an argument to be made in the political sphere. It is not a basis for charges that everything he does is a violation of law.

MARC. I don't "think" he is a lowlife. He proves it with each new reporting, and there is much more to come. He asked McGahn to lie and restate and clarify, all of which he refused to do. Why? You never, ever mention even the slightest of Trump's many legal transgressions, always playing his lawyer or mollifying Trump's action by aligning it with someone else's mistake and saying, "Everybody does it." You have zero credibility, and you are as biased as those you accuse. To you, the ends justify the means. If someone is a powerful supporter of Israel and corporate America, we will accept the immorality that the leader radiates. You are as out of touch as Jack Nicholson's character in *A Few Good Men*.

STEPHEN. What are you talking about? I never say, "Everybody does it." You have been proven wrong about everything: collusion, the Covington kids, and obstruction. Yet I have no credibility? You will be proven wrong again. I defend Trump because he is the victim of a gross violation of civil liberties, committed by people you think are so great. You are very short-sighted. Even if you don't like it, the American electorate chose Trump. It is not the FBI's or CIA's job to undo it or to favor one candidate over another. That is exactly what happened. Don't like Trump? Don't vote for him in 2020, but stop imagining that he broke any laws. He did not.

MARC. He clearly misreported his finances to get loan after loan that he defaulted on, and also, those losses he reported are bogus, as you well know. That's illegal.

STEPHEN. You have no idea what you're talking about. How many of Trump's financing transactions have you reviewed? How many of the documents have you reviewed? There is risk in business. Not every investment works out. Trump's financial difficulties were reported on extensively. Trump even wrote a book, *The Art of the Comeback*. You should become an FBI agent because you can establish wrongdoing without knowing any facts.

MARC. You are right. He is brilliant, compassionate, and upstanding and only says stupid things that are not reflective of his baseless character. You act like my views on him are singularly held by me, which is astonishing. New York businesspeople have known for years he is an ass, and someone gets that reputation for a reason.

STEPHEN. Why do you put words in my mouth instead of addressing what I actually say? Again, you talk through your ass. Your argument is that people who don't like him don't like him. That's compelling. By the way, how do you know who likes him and who doesn't?

MARC. Obstruction of justice is a crime. He will be impeached by the House. The majority in the House don't make a habit of impeaching the president. The only reason Trump didn't commit Clintonian impeachable offenses is because he didn't testify in person.

STEPHEN. Except he was not charged with obstruction of justice after a two-year investigation. Mueller didn't have a basis for charging him, so he smeared him—exactly what a prosecutor is not supposed to do. Furthermore, the idea that defending himself against charges that he was guilty of a crime that did not occur and that required him to respond to an investigation that never should have been initiated is obstruction of justice is very dangerous, especially considering the cooperation he provided. There was no obstruction of anything.

MARC. He didn't smear him. He gave evidence gleaned from the report of obstruction but said he couldn't do anything about it. Even Trump himself said there was "essentially" no obstruction, so you are incorrect.

STEPHEN. He smeared him. He did not prosecute him but suggested he really could be guilty. That's the worst smear I can imagine.

MARC. He was hired to collect information. He did, and it has been inferred by many that he was saying he would charge Trump but for the guidelines. What's wrong with that? The guidelines don't say that the president can't be reported against.

STEPHEN. He wasn't hired to collect information. He was a special prosecutor. His job was to determine whether a crime occurred and to prosecute if he believed a crime had been committed. He did not say Trump was guilty of obstruction but could not be prosecuted. He left the determination to the attorney general, presumably because he could not charge him, but chose to smear him.

MARC. Oh yeah, I forgot that part: "I leave the attorney general to make the call. It's his baby."

STEPHEN. I know you want to believe Trump is guilty of a crime—any crime—so you ignore the results of the actual investigation and fantasize that you will wake up to find that Trump is guilty. He won't be, because he isn't guilty of anything. I'll enjoy the prosecution of Comey and the others responsible for this mess. The results for them will be different because they are guilty.

MARC. If you think Comey will be indicted, let alone convicted by a jury, you have actually lost it.

STEPHEN. I know that Comey lied to the FISA court. I also know that he leaked to the press. Those acts are criminal. Based on your track record, I take comfort in your confidence that it won't happen.

CHINA TARIFFS

May 12, 2019

Marc. Trump repeatedly has said that China pays the tariffs. That's a lie that he has said repeatedly, and Kudlow confirmed that today.

May 13, 2019

Stephen. Regarding China, Trump has received grudging acknowledgments from free traders that his policy may work. China "pays" for the tariffs in the reduction of its exports to the United States. It creates an economic problem for them that may lead to fairer trade arrangements. Your ignorant focus on the fact that the tariffs raise the cost of Chinese goods for American consumers misses the point. Trump's statements about tariffs are far more accurate than most political arguments (see the Green New Deal, Medicare for All, the Iranian deal, and "If you like your doctor, you can keep your doctor"). I could go on and on.

Marc. You will see Trump capitulate to China despite his tough stance.

Stephen. Great analysis. If he does capitulate, he still will have done more than his predecessors to address abusive Chinese trade practices. My guess is that he will get something tangible in any deal. We will see.

Marc. If everything is so great under him, as he repeatedly touts, why not leave well enough alone instead of sabotaging the market?

Stephen. What is your point? We should not address any difficult problems? I'm glad you're not the president.

May 15, 2019

Marc. By the way, just so you know, I am not a liberal, have no qualms about collateral damage on the enemy in a necessary war against an aggressor, and think global warming is overblown!

Stephen. There is hope for you yet.

MORE ON ABORTION

MARC. Abortion is legal and free in Israel. Have a problem with that?

STEPHEN. I'm against abortion in the United States, Israel, and everywhere. It devalues human life.

MARC. So you're okay if a young woman is raped by her father and has to carry and deliver that baby?

STEPHEN. No. I'm not an absolutist. However, the debate is not about abortion in a sick case. It is about unfettered abortion, including the right to kill a baby born alive.

CONTINUED INVESTIGATIONS INTO TRUMP AND RUSSIA

May 21, 2019

Marc. Since you have told me repeatedly that the public should respect the process and accept Trump as POTUS, I'm sure you agree that things like the law should be respected, even by Trump.

Stephen. Trump is being harassed for political purposes. That is not an appropriate basis for continuing to investigate false allegations about something that did not occur. Doesn't that bother you? If Comey is indicted, will that change your mind?

Marc. A Comey indictment would have me as cynical of bias as you are now. I believe there is a massive story of criminality in Trump's past, and that is based on many reports that scratch the surface. I believe the FBI knows this, though can't prove it, and their initial investigation could have been started, aggressively and perhaps even unkosherly, to prevent the presidency from being held by someone who is leveraged by the Russians.

Stephen. I think the Democrats' harassment of Trump is indefensible and damaging to the country. Your belief that Trump has engaged in "massive criminality" is crazy. It's sad that someone as smart as you and generally as fair as you is willing to believe something like that. Tell me what the FBI knows. Did Comey blurt something out while you were examining him? The real criminals—Comey, McCabe, Strzok, Page, Brennan, Clapper, and more—are being exposed. The evidence against them will be overwhelming. Furthermore, the Russians have no leverage over Trump. They didn't expect him to be elected and had no ties to his campaign. They did not even know whom to call. It's in the Mueller report.

Stephen. Why Congress can't force Don McGahn to testify: https://www.wsj.com/articles/don-mcgahns-immunity-. Read this and learn something.

IT'S HARD TO SAY GOODBYE TO COLLUSION

MARC. Russians were giving Trump money through Deutsche Bank.

STEPHEN. You are ridiculous. I didn't realize you were conducting your own investigation at the same time as Mueller. When are you issuing your report?

MARC. I'm in the middle of it. It's an epistolary report in the form of texts to my brainwashed friend.

MAY 22, 2019

STEPHEN. I think you're Bruce Willis's character in *The Sixth Sense*. You're the one who is brainwashed and impervious to facts.

MAY 24, 2019

STEPHEN. All of your heroes are going down. They are the liars. They abused their power. They interfered in the election and tried to undo Trump. It can't happen soon enough.

MARC. He'll be impeached by the Senate, and his family will be indicted, before that happens.

STEPHEN. Impeached for what? You're going to have a difficult next few months, culminating in Trump's reelection.

May 29, 2019

Marc. Mueller wrote and today declared that if no crime had been committed, he would have said so. If you took a college logic course, you would infer that a crime was committed. It doesn't matter what you think a special prosecutor is supposed to say or rule. He said, "If no crime had been committed, we would have said that was the case." And another thing. While one can debate whether the crime was major or impeachable, to believe that Comey was part of a coup is more gullibility than you have ever accused me of.

Stephen. I read the Mueller report. No crime was committed.

Marc. Oh, then why didn't the author declare that, as he said he would have had no crime been committed?

Stephen. His job was to identify any crimes that were committed. He didn't identify any crimes. No prosecutor should ever say, "I haven't identified any crimes, but that doesn't mean no crimes were committed." That's a smear.

Marc. You are 100 percent wrong. For once, I am right! He said that according to policy, he could not indict a sitting president, but if there wasn't a need to indict, he would have stated that!

Marc. He didn't say what you quoted. He is essentially saying, "He committed a crime, but I can't do anything about it."

Marc. But Congress can.

Stephen. In fact, it's an outrage. Read the report. The report itself is an outrage. However, it was very clear about one point: there was no collusion of any kind.

Marc. I agree.

MARC. But there was obstruction of lots of kinds.

MARC. You should and could be upset that Mueller, along the lines of Comey when he both cleared and impugned Clinton, said too much. But he said what he said, and anyone with powers of inference and deduction can conclude that a crime was committed, based on these two sentences: (1) "If he didn't commit a crime, we would tell you," and (2) "If he committed a crime, we couldn't indict because of policy."

STEPHEN. That is not his job. Identify a crime, or shut up—that's his job.

MARC. Here is where you are wrong and won't acknowledge it. If Mueller had not added the provisos to the report and the Democrats' spin had added, "Well, he didn't say he didn't commit a crime," or "He couldn't indict because of policy," then you would be dead-on correct. But he chose to add those provisos, which communicate that Trump committed criminal acts (or else I would have told you he didn't).

MARC. By the way, my constant claims that Trump is a bad guy and crooked business guy apparently are echoed by Steve Bannon, who knows Trump a hell of a lot better.

STEPHEN. That says a lot about Mueller and nothing about Trump. Think about what you're saying.

MARC. Also, as for collusion, they concluded there was insufficient evidence of it to pursue. That's a little different from there being no collusion.

STEPHEN. No. Read the report. There was zero evidence of collusion.

MARC. The author said there was "insufficient evidence to pursue further investigation."

MARC. You might be confusing Mueller with the conclusions of Barr, Trump's "attorney."

MARC. "Charging the president with a crime was not something we could consider." Bam!

STEPHEN. What a joke. Read the letter appointing Mueller. Trump did not collude with the Russians. As there was no underlying crime—and Mueller probably knew that on day one—there was no obstruction. First, Trump did nothing to impede Mueller and, in fact, never asserted executive or any other privilege, and because there was no collusion, Trump had no reason to obstruct. You can believe whatever you want. I hope the Democrats are stupid enough to impeach for allegedly obstructing an investigation into something that did not happen and which resulted from a gross abuse of power. Trump will win in a landslide.

MARC. I thought he was already going to win in a landslide? You know, after Comey is executed for treason. A regular Dreyfus. He should be exiled to Devil's Island. I hope you don't practice criminal law in the future, because you sure wouldn't have given Martha Stewart sound advice. If Trump was so innocent of everything, Barr wouldn't have had to misrepresent everything Mueller said.

MARC. No evidence would have allowed Mueller or the DOJ to charge Trump with a crime. Nothing.

STEPHEN. Keep living in your fantasy world, but realize it is a corrupt world.

MARC. Indeed, a corrupt world with a corrupt leader whom you support.

STEPHEN. Trump is the only honest one in this story.

MARC. We are all entitled to asinine comments.

STEPHEN. You're living proof of that. You should start a blog called *Asinine Marc*.

May 30, 2019

Marc. I do have that blog. It cultivates asinine comments from other people, like "Trump is the only honest one in the whole story."

Marc. White House staff sent emails concerned about Trump's rage at seeing the USS *John McCain*. They had the ship's sailors take the day off and covered the name of the ship. Stephen Barry: "There's nothing wrong with that. McCain was not loyal to the king."

Stephen. Trump does not act like a king. I think you're thinking of Obama, who, aside from unilaterally amending laws, spying on journalists, weaponizing the IRS against ordinary citizens, and obstructing the Hillary email investigation, oversaw the biggest abuse of power in the history of the United States: spying on and attempting to frame his successor. Trump has done none of those things. Many of Obama's people, if not Obama, are going to go down—and soon.

Stephen. One more thing: Mueller did not, in his report or his press conference, say that he believes he could not prosecute Trump for obstruction of justice. Notwithstanding DOJ guidance on the constitutionality of indicting a sitting president, nothing prevented Mueller from saying a crime had been committed. He didn't say that because he could not establish it. So he smeared Trump. Also, Mueller's report is one side. The idea of prosecuting someone for obstruction of an investigation—that was not obstructed—into something that did not happen only makes sense to MSNBC anchors and certain orthopedists.

Marc. If he believed Trump didn't commit a crime but didn't say that, then he smeared him. He did say that he didn't commit conspiracy. Therefore, if he was not guilty of a crime, he would state such. But he didn't state such regarding obstruction. What can we infer from that? Boy, I really wish I could go back to your law school class.

STEPHEN. Because he didn't state that Trump committed the crime of obstruction, we can infer that he could not make a case for obstruction. If he was unable to make a case for obstruction, Trump, by definition, did not commit the crime of obstruction. As I learned in law school, and you should have learned too, you're presumed innocent in this country until proven guilty. Mueller does not even have a basis for accusing Trump of breaking the law, let alone proving it. Again, Mueller would have to prove Trump obstructed an investigation, which he acknowledges was not obstructed, into collusion that did not happen. Good luck.

MARC. Your first sentence is wrong because he said he could not make the case for conspiracy; he said no such thing for obstruction. It could have been Cellino, Barnes, and Lieberman! I'd have the prestige of a fine injury attorney!

STEPHEN. But he didn't make the case for obstruction. He did not say, "Because Trump did X, Y, and Z, he committed obstruction." He simply laid out scenarios and suggested they could constitute obstruction, but he could not say that Trump did commit obstruction. Nor did he indict anyone else for obstruction, because as he acknowledged, the investigation was not obstructed.

MARC. It's a shame that a president is cited as doing things that could even be talked about in the same breath as obstruction.

STEPHEN. No, it's a crime he was set up to be investigated based on the Obama administration's abuse of power. Fortunately, I believe there will be some, if not perfect, accountability.

MARC. Right—Comey's execution for treason.

STEPHEN. Let's speak about Comey after he's indicted. He committed real crimes.

MARC. Treasonous. Hates his country.

STEPHEN. He broke multiple laws.

MARC. Trump admitted Russia helped get him elected. That's a start.

STEPHEN. Really?

MARC. Need you any more evidence the guy is a effin' moron?

STEPHEN. If you read Trump's statements about Mueller's statement, his position is very clear. Trump should not have to defend himself against this nonsense, which should have ended with the Mueller report. It will end when the abuses of power that culminated in the Mueller report are fully exposed. Also, if Trump is an "effin' moron," I would rather have an effin' moron, sound economic policies, sound foreign policy, support for individual liberty, and support for Israel than Obama, Hillary, or any of the nonentities currently running for the Democratic nomination.

MARC. I would like all the same policies (except prochoice) and a normal, decent person. That's not asking too much. I don't want someone who tells the navy to cover up the name of a ship because he didn't like the guy.

STEPHEN. I need to check into that story. You're not a reliable source.

STEPHEN. According to the *NYT*, Trump had nothing to do with it (the USS *McCain*).

MARC. Please.

MARC. At least Trump finally confirmed that Russia helped him get elected.

STEPHEN. You're ridiculous. It was a poor decision [the USS *McCain*], but it is inconceivable that Trump knew anything about it.

STEPHEN. Mueller backtracked. He clarified today that the DOJ guidance that a sitting president cannot be indicted had no impact on his decision not to find obstruction of justice. Bam!

May 31, 2019

MARC. I missed that clarification.

MARC. But if that's the case, then he did the Democrats a favor so they won't impeach, which you believe would be a really stupid move for them, which of course means it would be a really smart move.

MARC. I think (for once, actually) you clutched on to a false story. I only see that report on certain right-wing stations. It's probably phony. Do you think he would make such a careful script and announcement and then need to clarify it but in a hidden manner? The fact that you feel the need to report that he backtracked proves what he said was damaging.

MARC. Clutched like a man falling inevitably and futilely grasping for something to stop the fall.

MARC. But I'm sure you defend him for his tariffs on Mexico. Watch the market today.

MARC. Mueller didn't backtrack on anything. You can't believe everything you read!

STEPHEN. Did you read his spokesman's statement? It is clear he did not base his decision on the OLC guidance. Not that either statement matters. The only thing that matters is that the report did not find that Trump obstructed justice, which, based on the fact that the report acknowledges that the investigation was not obstructed, is the only rational conclusion. Regarding Mexico, I'll wait for your plan to deal with Mexico for aiding and abetting illegal immigration.

MARC. The report found that there was not enough evidence to show conspiracy, but there were some actions that, at the very least, border on obstruction or could be considered obstruction. It's an important distinction because if the obstructive acts were nonexistent, then the report would have the same conclusion for both volumes.

JUNE 3, 2019

STEPHEN. The Mueller report doctored the transcript of a conversation between Trump's lawyer, John Dowd, and Flynn's lawyers to make it look like he was trying to influence Flynn. The transcript of the full conversation has been released. Mueller prosecuted Flynn for far less.

LEGAL VERSUS POLITICAL

June 4, 2019

MARC. You like to share with me improprieties committed by law enforcement but never those committed by the president. Yesterday, while on foreign soil, he called for the boycott of an American company that has been critical of him. That's about as autocrat-in-waiting as it gets.

STEPHEN. Your priorities are very backward. I don't know what Trump said, but if he said something you think is inappropriate, that's a political issue. I hope you're as concerned about Trump being criticized overseas by US leaders. You might call that traitorous. Mueller abusing his power to impact the presidency is both criminal and unconstitutional.

MARC. Trump uses his power as the president tenfold.

STEPHEN. I don't know what that means. Trump uses the power granted to him by law and the Constitution. The courts, particularly the liberal Ninth Circuit, have attempted to prevent him from exercising his powers. For example, preventing him from overturning an Obama executive order on immigration. That's the scandal: the court telling the elected president that he cannot overturn the policy supported by the losing side in the election. Try thinking with your head.

MARC. What about telling people that Amazon sucks or CNN sucks?

STEPHEN. That's political, just like Obama telling small businesses, "You didn't build that." Marc, who built your practice? You or the government? Should every orthopedist be as successful as you? Do you think it was right for Obama to say, "You didn't build that"? Did suggesting that the government built your practice make him an autocrat?

MARC. I had help. You did too. A supportive mom and grandparents and friends in school to model. And probably student loans. That's all he was saying.

MARC. Many successful people overcame crazy odds and succeeded pretty much autonomously. Many didn't yet act all haughty like they didn't benefit from breaks.

STEPHEN. That's not what he was saying. He was saying the government—by building infrastructure and providing services—made it possible for you to be successful. Of course, he had it ass-backward. It is successful businesses that fund the government and make it possible to build and provide.

MORE PROBLEMS WITH THE MUELLER REPORT

June 6, 2019

STEPHEN. Another disclosure about the Mueller report: Mueller describes Konstantin Kilimnik, who worked with Manafort, as having ties to Russian intelligence. However, Kilimnik was a US State Department intelligence source. Mueller had the information on Kilimnik's ties to the State Department but chose to describe him as tied to Russian intelligence. The Mueller report also discusses Kilimnik's efforts to present a Ukrainian peace plan to the Trump transition team, without noting that Kilimnik presented the same plan to the Obama administration. That's dishonest. The Mueller smear—which did not identify any wrongdoing but attempted to smear him anyway—is going to be completely discredited.

June 7, 2019

MARC. I love how you select occasional supportive facts to your claim of conspiracy and ignore numerous facts of Trump's obstruction.

STEPHEN. Because the investigation was not obstructed in any way, there aren't any facts of obstruction. There are facts that Mueller suggests could be considered obstruction but that neither he nor Attorney General Barr found constitute obstruction. However, you don't have a problem with a prosecutor smearing a person who is not charged with any crime by doctoring a transcript of a phone call and omitting key details about a person characterized as tied to Russian intelligence to make ordinary interactions seem improper. Mueller should indict himself for making false statements. It is such an abuse of power it should make you sick.

MARC. A hostile adversarial power offered help to win the election, and Trump's team took it and then tried to thwart the investigation into it. It's very simple.

STEPHEN. That didn't happen. That's what the investigation, notwithstanding the Mueller report's effort to smear Trump, conclusively shows. On the contrary, the Democrats paid for Russian disinformation and disseminated it through law enforcement as a pretext to spy on and investigate Trump. That's the only collusion that occurred. Some of your heroes will go to jail. It's very simple.

MARC. Even you don't believe that. Unless, of course, the country is placed under martial law under Trump.

STEPHEN. It's going to happen. The Obama administration, Hillary, Brennan, Clapper, Comey, Lynch, and more violated multiple laws, obstructed justice, and violated Trump's constitutional rights. That's what will be established in the coming weeks and months.

MARC. Obama is going to jail?

STEPHEN. I doubt that. However, I believe he was fully aware of everything that was going on: the nonprosecution of Hillary, the spying on political opponents, and the complete disregard of the Constitution.

MARC. So if the fix was in for the nonprosecution of Hillary, why didn't Comey just exonerate her instead of Muellering her with condemnation that fell short of legal wrongdoing?

STEPHEN. He didn't Mueller her. He didn't conduct midnight raids on her associates. He granted everyone close to her immunity. He did not charge her with obstruction of justice, even though she destroyed evidence and hard drives. He let her off the hook for both actually breaking national security laws and obstructing justice—a small price to pay for being publicly chastised.

IRAN

June 21, 2019

Marc. Are you hawkish on Iran? And what's with his vacillating?

Stephen. I support sanctions and pressure but not another war. Iran appears to be trying to scare the Europeans and Japanese into pressuring the United States back into the nuclear deal. We should continue the pressure.

E. JEAN CARROLL'S RAPE ALLEGATION

JUNE 24, 2019

MARC. "She's not my type," Trump said, implying, "So I couldn't have raped her." And if she had been his type, it would be more plausible? What a disgusting human being.

STEPHEN. I would not have put it the way Trump did, but I assume she is making a totally false, made-up allegation. Who is the disgusting human being? The person making a false allegation or the accused?

THE BORDER CRISIS

June 26, 2019

Stephen. Who do you think is most responsible for the border crisis?

Marc. That one I am not sure of. I am only sure of one thing: Trump is the biggest con man in history, and you are being fooled.

Stephen. How about Democrats who one month ago said that immigration was a "manufactured" crisis and now say it is a crisis caused by Trump? In other words, the same people who denied there was a crisis, oppose border enforcement, and want to make illegal immigration legal say that Trump caused the crisis. Who are the con men?

PART 7

JULY 4, 2019– SEPTEMBER 30, 2019

REVOLUTIONARY WAR AIRPORTS AND MORE ON PUTIN

July 4, 2019

STEPHEN. Trump has the upper hand with Putin. The United States is much more powerful. Putin took over Crimea and Eastern Ukraine while Obama was president. He also shot down Malaysian Airlines Flight 17 during Obama's term. Finally, Putin interfered in the US election while Obama was president. Obama did nothing. Trump has provided arms to Ukraine, confronted Russian mercenaries in Syria, and allowed the United States to become an energy exporter. By what standard is Trump kissing Putin's ass? Trump thinks he can work with Putin. If he wins reelection, he'll get the chance. No doubt he will be more effective than Obama. Regarding the reference to airports, he misspoke. So what? It was a good speech.

MARC. Trump is so tough on Putin and Russia that Putin gives him smiling handshakes.

MARC. They're defending the airports.

July 5, 2019

STEPHEN. You respond to facts with irrelevant and, frankly, stupid observations.

TRUMP SUPPORTERS CHANT, "SEND HER BACK"

July 18, 2019

MARC. You can vehemently disagree with Ilhan Omar's views. They are certainly not pro-Israel. You can have no respect for her. But does it concern you that a crowd of people are calling for her to be expelled from the country, with Trump leading the charge?

STEPHEN. She's a despicable anti-Semite and racist. She's also rude and provocative. Trump is turning it against her. This is my dilemma: Trump is provocative. He does not try to find common ground with Democrats, who may be concerned about Omar. However, I don't think the Democrats will let him find common ground. They will call him a racist no matter what he says, as they call all Republicans. In addition, I do not believe any other Republican would call out Omar's anti-Semitism and for the Democrats to make a choice. Of course, they are making the wrong choice. I'm with Trump on this.

MARC. I don't know how to phrase it, but many people with average intelligence and certainly most of those without who live in rural and impoverished white communities will hear Trump and make an inference that violence and hate are warranted.

STEPHEN. What do the sophisticated liberals who accept anti-Semitism infer? The ones, like Hillary, who look down on working-class whites? The ones who support and excuse Antifa's violence? Yes, it's all Trump. Be real.

MARC. None of them rile up the masses like a Hitler.

MARC. And Omar isn't a rabid anti-Semite. She is against the state of Israel and their politics. You know the difference. Tell me a remark she has made against a Jew that relates to religion or physical appearance.

STEPHEN. No, she's a rabid anti-Semite. I feel bad for you if you don't see it: "Israel has hypnotized the world. It's all about the Benjamins." You should read Ayaan Hirsi Ali's recent editorial in the *Wall Street Journal*. Omar was raised in a hotbed of anti-Semitism. The truth is that the left calls anyone who disagrees with leftist policies racist. Trump attacks the so-called Squad because they are foolish ideologues who are anti-American and anti-Semitic, not because of their ethnicity.

MARC. That doesn't mean she should be told to get out of the country, and do you think the people I referred to care that she hates Jews? They also hate Jews!

STEPHEN. Those are you prejudices. It's not true. Republicans are very pro-Jewish and pro-Israel.

MARC. Republicans are, not people who scream, "Lock her up!" or rally with swastikas.

STEPHEN. That's a bigoted statement.

STEPHEN. The fascists are on the left.

MARC. You had no problem with the people at the Trump rally whooping it up with mob-mentality screams of "Lock her up!" You said, "I'm with Trump." Well, he said today he didn't agree with those chants and thought they were wrong.

STEPHEN. In addition to being an anti-Semite, Omar seems to hate America and Americans. Pressley is a racist, insisting that black and brown people need to think a certain way. Ocasio-Cortez is a liar, saying immigrants were forced to drink out of toilets. Tlaib, also an anti-Semite, called Trump a motherfucker. That's why the Trump supporters take issue with them. It's not an unfair question to ask why they are in Congress. It's also not unfair for people to wonder what kind of country they would like the United States to be. I can't imagine living in a country that the Squad would approve of.

MARC. They said Obama hates this country. You know who actually hates it? The person who says America isn't great.

STEPHEN. I don't think Obama hates the country, but he certainly apologized for it often. He also had a negative view of many Americans who were "clinging to guns and religion." I prefer a president who has a more positive view of America and Americans. America is and has been the greatest force for good and human dignity.

MARC. Trump thinks we aren't great.

STEPHEN. Yes, he does think we're great. Remember Greg Brady and exact words. Trump's issue is with the political establishment.

MARC. His slogan is "Make America Great *Again*."

July 19, 2019

MARC. Just to be clear, you don't find allowing a crowd chant of "Send her home" to be despicable race-baiting?

STEPHEN. No. It's not race-baiting just because CNN says it is. As I said before, their race has nothing to do with it. It's their views.

MARC. What happened to being free to have your own views?

STEPHEN. Okay. Explain to me why it is race-baiting.

MARC. Because she is a minority naturalized from a Muslim country, and the chant is essentially to "Go home to your stinking country," which is not far from people of color being told to "Go back to your own neighborhood" or to Africa. It's not what he says verbatim; it's how people process it and act upon it, and their chant was eerie in its historical parallels.

STEPHEN. No, it is what he says. Otherwise, you can, as you have done, declare something that has nothing to do with her race as racist.

MARC. The mob boss never orders the hit verbatim.

STEPHEN. How convenient for you. No matter what Trump actually says, he means what you want him to mean. The truth is that criticism of the Squad is justified based on the positions they take and the things they say. Trump is an equal-opportunity critic. Omar's critiques of America and Americans are particularly ironic because America and Americans gave her refuge and even elected her to Congress.

MARC. Criticism is allowed, even vehement criticism. But not "Go home," which is tantamount to "Get out of our country." She doesn't hate America. Hey, why doesn't he tell neo-Nazis to "go home" to Germany?

MARC. Please answer. Why not?

STEPHEN. Please send me a list of statements you find acceptable. They [the Squad] seem to believe everyone in America is a racist, including Nancy Pelosi. There is much more evidence for my assessment that they hate America than there is that Trump's comments are racist.

STEPHEN. The argument that he didn't also ask neo-Nazis to leave the country is very weak. He is in no way sympathetic to Nazis. That is another media lie.

MARC. [*Sends an attachment in which Trump is compared to Nazis.*]

MARC. Thank you!

STEPHEN. Someone who doesn't like Trump compares him to Nazis. Compelling.

MARC. Other rabbis and Trump himself said the crowd chanting was over the line. But not you.

STEPHEN. My point is that the "Send her home" chant is not racist. It does not elevate the political discourse in this country, but neither do the constant attacks on Trump.

MARC. Stagnant political discourse pales in comparison to mobs chanting on TV to harm someone.

STEPHEN. There are violent mobs in America. Antifa wear masks and beat up people and destroy property, including an ICE detention center. Of course, they are on the left. There are no pro-Trump mobs running around doing that, and no one threatened to harm Omar or anyone else. Face reality.

MUELLER TESTIFIES

July 24, 2019

Marc. Donald Trump said the Mueller report gave him a complete exoneration. The author of the report said it didn't exonerate him.

Stephen. Trump is right. There were no charges. Mueller should be disciplined for referencing exoneration. It is a smear.

Marc. Trump said the report said it exonerated him. Mueller said it didn't.

Stephen. It did exonerate him. Prosecutors either bring charges, or they do not. If they do not, they're done. To say, "I am not bringing charges, but the individual is not exonerated," has no legal meaning and is a breach of ethics. It simply is a smear.

Marc. It's not a smear. He was saying, "We would have indicted him, except we weren't allowed to."

Stephen. That's absolutely not what he said. He said the opposite.

Stephen. Furthermore, even if he could not indict, he could have identified criminal acts. He did not.

Marc. Mueller just said that ordering to stop an investigation is obstruction. That's one of the many things Trump did. You excused it by saying it is okay because the investigation wasn't fair.

Stephen. No. Trump did not order the investigation to be stopped; otherwise, it would have been stopped. In the United States, communication between a client and a lawyer is privileged. The only reason Mueller knows what Trump and McGahn discussed is because Trump allowed him to testify. That's the opposite of obstruction.

MARC. McGahn was compelling and credible that Trump asked him to fire Mueller and then asked him to refute a report that revealed it.

STEPHEN. Again, Mueller was not fired, which is the best evidence that Trump did not order Mueller to be fired, notwithstanding his discussions about it with McGahn. Do you really believe someone should be accused of obstruction in connection with an investigation that was not obstructed in any way with respect to a crime that did not occur?

MARC. Uh, maybe better evidence would be McGahn's own words: that Trump asked him to do it, and basically, he ignored him.

STEPHEN. You don't seem to understand basic facts. Mueller wasn't fired. Even if he had been fired, it would not have been a crime.

MARC. If Trump was not president, Mueller would have indicted him for the same actions.

STEPHEN. No. He did not indict him, and he did not identify any crimes, because there were no crimes, except the crimes committed against the Trump campaign. Those will be prosecuted.

MARC. He was asked by a Republican senator to agree with her statement that there were other reasons besides the OLC opinion that he didn't indict, and he wouldn't do so!

MARC. What more do you need?

STEPHEN. It doesn't matter. He stated in a public statement that the OLC opinion had no impact on his decision not to indict. Furthermore, the OLC guidance would not prevent him from stating that a crime had been committed. The report makes no such claim. Without his having indicted or identified a crime, to suggest that Trump could have committed a crime simply is a smear.

MARC. Oh, okay. Well, today he said live that it did.

STEPHEN. He should be stripped of his law license.

MARC. Look, he probably doesn't like Trump and probably is friends with Comey and is just as biased as those who once publicly called out Trump for what he is and now are forced to ignore those comments.

STEPHEN. He would indict himself for perjury.

STEPHEN. Mueller already has corrected the statement he made to Representative Lieu this morning. He stated that he did not make a determination that the president had committed a crime.

MARC. When I told you what Mueller said, it didn't impress you, yet now you're pointing out that he corrected it.

MARC. I always out-lawyer you.

STEPHEN. I'm glad you think you out-lawyer me. I guess that's true in the court of orthopedic law but not in any other branch.

MARC. I told you something he said, and you said it meant nothing. Then you volunteered that he corrected what he said, thus giving it import.

STEPHEN. I didn't say it meant nothing. I said it was perjury. The fact that he corrected himself shows I was correct.

MARC. [*Forwards a comment by Dinesh D'Souza that Mueller looked "mentally retarded," which was retweeted by Donald Trump Jr.*] This is why I will never respect Trump. Keep defending him. He is an abhorrent piece of trash, as are his progeny.

STEPHEN. That's not nice. I do not approve. I also do not approve of Mueller's abusive investigation, which harmed many innocent people, or his cowardly effort to smear Trump after he did not find any criminal conduct. You should be as outraged by that conduct as you are by D'Souza's mean comment.

MARC. Wrong. Because while Comey, Mueller, and other Never Trumpers might have overreached, it's a tough biz on all sides, and the Republicans are not innocent choirboys. But there are mentally retarded people in the world, and there are POWs and people with cerebral palsy. If you start messing with them, you are done in my book. So no, I'm not as outraged at Roger Stone or Steve Brannon as I am at Trump.

STEPHEN. Trump didn't do anything. You're outraged at D'Souza and Trump Jr.

STEPHEN. It appears the Mueller hearing was a disaster. It is clear that Mueller was not in charge of the investigation. He did not know he had a Clinton Foundation lawyer on his staff. He was not familiar with Fusion GPS. That being said, he acknowledged that his investigation was not impeded in any way. A good day for the truth.

BALTIMORE AND ELIJAH CUMMINGS

August 2, 2019

Marc. Stephen Barry: proud to stand in allegiance with Donald Trump.

Marc. A Trump rally is a freakin' Nazi rally!

Stephen. Yes, I am proud to stand with a president who is working to make life in the United States better. It is a side benefit that he is taking on a corrupt cabal of former officials who sought to subvert our Constitution and the results of the 2016 election. A further benefit is that he is willing to point out the abject failure of the political class responsible for running Baltimore into the ground. Call Trump a Nazi all you want. He has done more to help blacks in three years than Cummings has done throughout his long, ineffective career.

Marc. There is policy, politics, and human decency. Do you simply ignore his cheering on a felony against Cummings, regardless of his statements or views? Yes or no?

Marc. And I suppose there are no white Republican centers of rural poverty he could pick on?

Stephen. I don't know what he said. I would not cheer a felony against Cummings. Trump may not elevate the discussion, but the moderators at the Democratic debate asked questions premised on Trump's "bigotry," which is outrageous. Trump is not a perfect gentleman, but it wouldn't matter if he was. He still would be savagely attacked. Look at Bush and Romney. With Trump, it's more of a fair fight. Democrats believe they can say whatever they want about Republicans, no matter how false or malicious, and the Republicans can't fight back. That's not Trump.

Furthermore, not everyone is a Reagan, who could turn attacks around with a joke and a smile.

MARC. He said, "That's really bad news. The house of Elijah Cummings was robbed. Too bad." That is unfathomable.

MARC. You make the Republicans sound like victims. They both throw verbal barbs at each other. Nothing has changed since the Pat Buchanan and Newt Gingrich era.

MARC. I think you have told me I have no right or evidence to call Trump a moron. How is this?

STEPHEN. Trump is not a moron, but he is a narcissist. I don't know why his comment about Cummings is unfathomable. It is ironic.

STEPHEN. Trump did not express hope that Cummings would be victimized. He noted the irony and made a sarcastic comment. Your subtle change is dishonest, but all is fair in love and Trump hatred.

MARC. He said, "He got robbed. Too bad." No?

[8/2/19, 2:48 p.m.] STEPHEN. That is a sarcastic comment in response to an ironic news report. It is not an expression of hope that Cummings would be robbed. You can argue that his reaction to the news was not nice, but you can't equate it with wishing harm. Trump deals with terrible, nasty comments about him and his family almost daily.

MARC. Come on. Can't you even admit when he reveals his complete lack of empathy? He should just keep his mouth shut! He is the effin' president! Of America! There are not just Jews and white people between the coasts!

MARC. Your criticisms about the things Tlaib and Omar say, as inappropriate and offensive as they are, have no merit because you deflect everything Trump says. It is also offensive and inappropriate, yet you call it "sarcastic" or say, "I wouldn't have said that." You have adopted Trump's motif of never, ever giving an inch or admitting any wrongdoing, and it's actually a horrible trait to have.

STEPHEN. Do you realize how ridiculous—and racist—you sound? Elijah Cummings is a politician. He is not above criticism or having his hypocrisy pointed out. His race has nothing to do with anything. He doesn't need Marc to defend him against the bad orange man.

MARC. If Cummings was killed, there would be similar sarcastic statements or trite replies of compassion, followed by, "But you see? This is what happens."

STEPHEN. Tlaib is an anti-Semite who takes positions that are objectively anti-Semitic, such as support for the Boycott, Divestment, and Sanctions movement. Trump says things you don't like that you think are boorish, but not based on race. Your comment on what Trump would say if Cummings were to be killed is your imagination, not real.

MARC. And furthermore, I'll state this: if you are white and not an observant Jew or lover of Israel and you love Trump, you are probably a closet racist, whether you know it or not. Now, be smart, and read that twice, because you are not in the latter category because you are a Jew who loves Israel.

MARC. Comments that are boorish but not based on race? Oh, like calling every black reporter a moron.

MARC. Or calling poor black countries "shitholes."

MARC. If I was walking on the street and saw some white MAGA-hat guy teasing some black kid and calling him names, I would jump in and get involved to my own peril. You?

MARC. You probably would think, *Too bad, but because of Black Lives Matter and Rashida Tlaib, the kid's getting what he deserves.*

STEPHEN. All who support Trump are racists, including black and Hispanic supporters? Why would you ever think that I would think it would be okay to harass someone because he is black? You would jump in if the assailant was wearing a MAGA hat, but it would be okay if the assailant was wearing a Biden hat? How about a kid wearing a MAGA hat being assaulted by Antifa? Would that be acceptable to you? Your hatred of Trump is making you stupid.

THE EL PASO AND DAYTON SHOOTINGS

August 4, 2019

Marc. You've got to admit that if a Muslim or a black person with a Black Lives Matter shirt blew away scores of white people, Trump would exploit it or at least make impassioned statements against it. Both of this weekend's shootings were whites against immigrants and blacks, and Trump gave a one-line statement.

Stephen. Okay. I'm glad you're clairvoyant.

Marc. Well, we saw what his statement was this weekend. I'm happy to show you what the previous ones were from nonwhites and the future ones I am sure he will be idiotic enough to craft. He has already cited the occasional illegal immigrant murderer as cause for tighter immigration. But these automatic shooters of white persuasion can be cause for nothing.

Stephen. You conflate different issues. Trump made an appropriate statement about El Paso. The political dispute over the border has no relevance to this tragedy. If this crime had been perpetrated by an illegal immigrant or a radical Muslim, I would expect Trump—and anyone with a brain—to recognize that that fact could be relevant to the political dispute.

Marc. Do you not agree that if a Muslim or illegal committed this kind of crime, Trump would likely exploit it and say, "This is why we need walls"?

Stephen. *Exploit* is a loaded term. Are gun control advocates going to exploit these tragedies, or are they going to argue that these tragedies highlight the need for more gun control?

MARC. I have a simple serious question: If a Muslim ISIS guy were to kill thirty whites, would you be okay if Trump tweeted, "This is why we can't let Muslims into this country"? Because if the answer is yes, one would be similarly fair in saying the shooting in El Paso represents why there cannot be anti-Muslim rhetoric.

STEPHEN. Trump would never say that. Trump has never taken the position that we can't let Muslims into the country. He has taken the position that we cannot let in people from Muslim-majority countries that are controlled by terrorists or are otherwise dysfunctional. I'll concede that he has been provocative on the issue, and that has been controversial, but his critics are provocative too.

MARC. Perhaps.

August 6, 2019

MARC. White House flags are at half-mast until 8/8. H/H.

STEPHEN. What is H/H?

MARC. Heil Hitler.

STEPHEN. What do you mean?

MARC. *H* is the eighth letter.

STEPHEN. Good point. You're very insightful.

MORE ON TLAIB AND OMAR

August 16, 2019

MARC. Here's a chance to educate me: What is the worst thing Tlaib or Omar has said about Israel? Quotes, not your own inference.

STEPHEN. They both support BDS. Omar has said that Israel has "hypnotized the world" and that support for Israel "is all about the Benjamins." Tlaib has said the following: "There's a kind of calming feeling I always tell folks when I think of the Holocaust, and the tragedy of the Holocaust, and the fact that my ancestors, Palestinians, who lost their lives, their livelihood, their human dignity, their existence in many ways, have been wiped out."

MARC. I don't understand the last quote. Is she saying that she was happy Jews were once mass-murdered because now they are in a position of power and oppressing her people?

MARC. I don't know the Israeli constitution, but as long as she didn't say anything that was a threat of murder or terror, you shouldn't be banned from entering a free country, and I am glad Israel saw it that way and again sees it that way.

STEPHEN. No. She sees the Holocaust as a tragedy for the Palestinians. Furthermore, her description of what took place is, I hope you know, not true in any way. Regarding Israel, Israel passed a law denying entry to supporters of BDS. I want Israel to let them in. I want them to be given as much coverage as possible.

MARC. If they passed that law and she is a true supporter, then I can't argue other than to say the law is questionable in a strong democratic union.

STEPHEN. The law is questionable. However, as Hillel [the Talmudic sage] asked, "If I am not for myself, who will be for me?"

[8/18/19, 10:27 a.m.] STEPHEN. Marc, I have a simple question: If Omar and Tlaib have the right to support a boycott of Israel, why doesn't the Israeli government have the right to boycott them? This is a case of "Free speech for me but not for thee."

August 18, 2019

MARC. Boycott a person? Deny them rights of freedom for their opinion? By the way, I do think Tlaib's planned visit to Israel was a ploy to make Israel look bad, and when they protested and then were allowed and then refused, the ploy was exposed, but Trump-Putin nontolerance is catching on.

STEPHEN. Yes. Most countries don't permit avowed enemies entry.

MARC. Come on. Avowed enemies?

STEPHEN. They support the destruction of Israel. What would you call them?

MARC. They are many degrees of separation away from that. They have never said anything like that.

MARC. You wouldn't have to use hyperbole if the facts were on your side.

MARC. Boycott, Divestment, and Sanctions is BDS.

STEPHEN. That's the goal of BDS and the organization that was sponsoring their trip.

MARC. Yes. Boycott. Divest. Sanction. Not destroy. I see your point, but you don't have to embellish it.

STEPHEN. I'm not embellishing my point. The people behind BDS seek Israel's isolation and ultimate destruction.

MARC. You're doing lots of connecting dots. The women are anti-Israel. You don't have to like them, but banning them from the country is Trumpian. Trump has also dealt with governments he has lauded who have connections to anti-US policy.

STEPHEN. If you think you need to connect dots to understand the goal of the BDS movement, I suggest you do a little research. Do I need to remind you that Palestinian leaders from Hamas to the Palestinian Authority call for the destruction of Israel, notwithstanding Oslo; support terror against Israel; support rocket attacks against Israel; and are vile anti-Semites? Even if you ignore the real aim of BDS, does it make sense to you that Israel, alone among nations, should be targeted for isolation for legitimate self-defense? Where is the BDS for Russia, China, Syria, Iran, or Turkey? Don't be naive.

MARC. Hamas is Hamas.

STEPHEN. If you believe that BDS exists to pressure Israel to change its policies, which policies are its proponents seeking to change? What do you think? I think it is the existence of Israel as a Jewish state.

MARC. You are admitting that you are inferring that Tlaib et al. ultimately want to actually destroy a country and its people rather than simply curtail what they erroneously see as human rights violations. Not everything is black and white. I am for personal liberty, and being banned from a country because I support an organization isn't kosher!

STEPHEN. I'm not inferring anything. I'm evaluating her positions in the context of reality. Considering the history of the State of Israel and the Jewish people, it is impossible to accept that the goal of Tlaib is to curtail human rights violations. If that were the case, Israel would not be her target. I have no obligation to accept a justification for BDS that clearly is not true.

MARC. Israel is a democratic state. Unless the people are on a terror list, they should be allowed, which is why they ultimately were. I'm right again!

MARC. You are the brains in this ongoing argument, but I am the heart!

STEPHEN. Omar was not permitted to enter. Tlaib was only permitted to visit her grandmother. A democratic state has the right to protect itself.

THE INSPECTOR GENERAL'S REPORT ON COMEY

August 30, 2019

MARC. Comey could have done things differently and made a few errors in judgment but committed no crimes. If that sort of summary is good enough for Trump, it is also for Comey.

STEPHEN. No. The inspector general found violations of FBI and DOJ policy and referred him for prosecution. That's exactly what did not happen to Trump. Furthermore, this is the tip of the iceberg. Mr. Comey and others are going down, and they should go down.

MARC. The report says, "No evidence of leaking."

MARC. And he didn't refer him for prosecution.

MARC. You wouldn't need to exaggerate if the facts were on your side.

STEPHEN. He did refer him for prosecution. The inspector general found that Comey "made public sensitive investigative information unilaterally and without authorization." Furthermore, he found that Comey's claim that the memos were his personal property was a sham. The inspector general found that Comey interacted with Trump only in his capacity as FBI director. He shared the memos with senior FBI officials. The memos contained classified information, which is never personal. The inspector general found that Comey's claim that the memos were personal is "wholly incompatible with the plain language of the statutes, regulations, and policies defining Federal records." In other words, Comey is a liar, but we knew that already. Finally, Comey disclosed the Steele dossier to Trump with the hope of obtaining evidence from Trump without his knowledge that he was being investigated. Because as we will soon definitively know, there was no basis for the investigation; Comey was simply engaged in a conspiracy against Trump. He and the other Obama officials are going down. I have been right about this since the beginning.

Marc. If he had referred him for prosecution, it would be all Trump tweeted about and make all the headlines.

Marc. I haven't seen it.

Stephen. The attorney general has, at this time, declined to prosecute. The coming cases about FISA abuse and the origins of the investigation will be much stronger and more compelling.

Stephen. All Americans should be outraged by the Obama administration's and Comey's interference in the 2016 election. They don't get to choose who may or may not be president. It should not matter that you don't like Trump. Imagine the reaction if Trump were to take similar actions.

Marc. You mean Barr decided not to prosecute?

Marc. No more outraged than by the president's actions on a daily basis.

Stephen. Barr has declined to prosecute now. The investigations are continuing, and he will have stronger, more consequential cases to bring shortly. If you are not concerned about the Obama administration interfering in the election, you will be okay with it if Trump does it in the future. Hey, how could he permit a successor he disagrees with to be elected?

August 31, 2019

Stephen. The Democrats never need to worry. The mainstream media is their propaganda arm. As for liars, focus on Comey and McCabe. They will be joined by others: Brennan and Clapper. It goes all the way to

Obama, the source of the illegal and unconstitutional investigation of Trump and the effort to frame him.

MARC. You've been saying this, and so far, nothing has happened, and Comey has been exonerated of crimes.

STEPHEN. Nothing has happened? The inspector general found that Comey violated FBI policy, lied, and leaked. He was the head of the FBI. When the investigations are completed, he will be indicted.

IRAN SHOOTS DOWN A DRONE

SEPTEMBER 18, 2019

MARC. Trump's bluster is more impotent than Obama's. "Locked and loaded"—what a fool. And Lewandowski—real smart for his political future to state that he only has to speak the truth under oath.

STEPHEN. Don't vote for them.

SEPTEMBER 19, 2019

MARC. I won't have the choice to. He's not running.

STEPHEN. A vote for the Democratic nominee will be a vote for empowering Iran, among other disastrous consequences. The Democrats have vowed to end fracking, which would make us energy dependent. They will also reenter the Iran deal. Geniuses.

KAVANAUGH REVISITED

STEPHEN. You should read this article. What do you think? The ritualistic stoning of Brett Kavanaugh shows how implausible the idea of a Democratic moderate is, per Dan Henninger.

STEPHEN. https://www.wsj.com/articles/the-democrats-ritualistic-stoning-of-brett-kavanaugh.

MARC. Here is my article: Kavanaugh was a douche—we all know that—and he lied about it under oath.

MARC. By the way, no grand jury, apparently, has been willing to issue indictments against McCabe and Comey.

STEPHEN. No. You don't know Kavanaugh and have no basis for a nasty statement. Furthermore, it is clear that his accusers, including Blasey Ford, lied under oath. McCabe and Comey will be indicted and, in all likelihood, will plead guilty or be convicted. Be patient.

MARC . Blasey Ford didn't lie. His own yearbook corroborated not her accusations but mine.

STEPHEN. Do you follow the news? Blasey Ford's friend Leland Keyser has publicly stated that Blasey Ford's story does not make sense. She has no recollection of any party like the one Blasey Ford described and has no recollection of ever meeting Kavanaugh. She also stated she was pressured by Blasey Ford's team to change her story. In addition, her lawyer made a speech in which she said that Blasey Ford was motivated to protect *Roe v. Wade*. Regarding your belief that Kavanaugh lied, I already explained to you why that is nonsense during Kavanaugh's confirmation hearing. Suffice it to say no one ever has contradicted a single statement he made about his yearbook or anything else.

MARC. Her friend, yeah. Some Republican.

MARC. Who was paid?

STEPHEN. You mean the person she identified as a witness.

MARC. People who paid off Kavanaugh's debts can certainly pay off Leland Keyser.

STEPHEN. When will you be appearing on *The Rachel Maddow Show* with this bombshell information? Have you provided your evidence to Nadler?

MARC. When Trump resigns, are you going to say he was forced out of office?

MARC. I do wonder whether Trump's high intelligence; impeccable integrity; and empathetic, caring nature, though all off-the-charts high, are collectively enough to have garnered such adoration from you.

STEPHEN. I haven't said a single thing about Trump. My disgust with the dishonest character assassination of Kavanaugh has nothing to do with Trump. It is about fairness and truth. Focus, young man.

THE DEMOCRATIC CANDIDATES

MARC. You don't have disgust for the elephant in the room?

STEPHEN. What should I be disgusted about? That you don't like him?

MARC. That such a buffoon has been empowered to lead others.

STEPHEN. Biden is only a candidate.

MARC. He hasn't been empowered to lead others.

MARC. You should have gone with a current office holder. You blew the joke.

STEPHEN. They're all buffoons—Warren, Sanders, Harris, Booker, Beto (the biggest buffoon of all).

MARC. Yet you chose Biden, who isn't in power. See? Trump is dumbing you down!

MARC. I have neither the time nor the crayons to explain this to you any further. (I stole that.)

STEPHEN. Biden is the most high-profile buffoon. Yesterday he made a comment about the impact on 750 million women. The US population is less than 350 million.

MARC. I'm not a fan of his, despite his label as the most moderate. I'm hoping for Trump to be forced out with facts and a new Republican nominee.

STEPHEN. Trump is going to be the nominee. The continuing effort to find something on him will ensure his reelection.

MARC. Perhaps.

MARC. The country is filled with morons and also with really smart, ethical, loyal people temporarily blinded by their love of money and Israel and a subconscious but paralyzing fear of being exposed as having acted like the former.

STEPHEN. Do you think the country would be better off if Biden were president? Warren? Sanders? If you do, I would say you're temporarily blinded by irrational hatred.

MARC. Hatred for people who stick to their core principles instead of re-creating themselves according to who is giving them money or blackmailing them? I think I have been very lucky in my lifetime, and I am tired of the world being less of a meritocracy than a downhill coast for offspring of the wealthy and connected. Sue me.

UKRAINE

MARC. Trump is toast.

STEPHEN. What are you talking about? You are ridiculous.

MARC. Trump told Ukraine he would withhold aid unless they dug up dirt on Biden and his son. Bye-bye, Trump.

STEPHEN. Actually, when he was vice president, Biden threatened to withhold aid from Ukraine if they investigated his son, which they were doing. Funny.

MARC. Okay, then Biden should be impeached if he is president.

STEPHEN. Not necessary. He won't be president.

MARC. Nor will Trump.

SEPTEMBER 20, 2019

MARC. The problem here is that the only reason the president would ask Ukraine to investigate "corruption" (which, by the way, it sounds as if Biden did too) was for political purposes. Otherwise, the DOJ would be handling that with Ukraine. We both know that. You may say it's okay for the Trump campaign to dig up dirt, even with a foreign power (though campaign law says it's not allowed if something is promised in return), but it's not okay for Trump to look for self-benefit while acting in a professional capacity. In Trump's own words, he is effed.

MARC. I see you have received your talking points yet from your Still Supporting Trump Club before trying to defend what Giuliani called a ridiculous allegation, which Trump denies, yet this morning, Giuliani tweeted a tacit admission that is was true. It's called "staying ahead of the story." He will resign.

STEPHEN. The Lieberman rule: any allegation of wrongdoing against Trump must be true (i.e., Trump actually did it, and it actually constituted wrongdoing). The good thing about the Lieberman rule is that it is reliably wrong.

MARC. Wrong. Trump denies everything, and then, when it is proven, he says, "So what?" Why not say, "So what?" out of the gate (e.g., with the Stormy Daniels situation or asking McGahn to fire Mueller).

MARC. I'm not sure if I need to explain his error here with this statement [an attachment]. This is the president of the United States. What a complete doofus.

STEPHEN. I'll fact-check, and I'm sure you will be proven wrong again.

MARC. The *Wall Street Journal,* Steve! Come on!

MARC. I'll foreswear Democrats. I pledge love for Israel. I'll contribute to your favorite charity. Just please tell me this is wrong!

MARC. You know you told me that although Manafort might have been guilty, it was only because he was unfairly targeted in a probe driven by political motives. So I'm sure you are equally troubled by Donald Trump's targeting of his potential political opponent.

STEPHEN. You're wrong.

MARC. I can't wait to hear your spin of how it's okay for the president to ask a foreign country that needs defense against an adversary (that has been helpful to you) to dig up dirt on Biden in order to receive the aid Congress voted on.

STEPHEN. I'm not troubled. I think Trump would be better off allowing his subordinates to do his dirty work, but that's the beauty of Trump: no pretense. It also would be well within Ukraine's rights to politely decline or to tell Trump any investigation needs to go through normal channels. However, Ukraine was investigating Biden's son until Biden, while vice president, threatened that the United States would withdraw aid. All Trump did was ask.

MARC. So lame.

MARC. Such an utter fool.

MARC. Trump is also!

STEPHEN. Everything you say is lame and wrong.

MARC. Okay, I'll say something else. The president shouldn't be withholding aid, voted on by the US Congress, to a country on the condition that they help *him*.

MARC. Is that wrong?

MARC. And now they are deploying forces. Jeez, such an obvious diversionary tactic. Hey, if Trump's actions were innocuous, they wouldn't be hiding the whistleblower report.

SEPTEMBER 21, 2019

STEPHEN. As with everything else related to Trump, this allegation will end up exposing wrongdoing but not by Trump.

MARC. No, this one will expose wrongdoing by Trump but, as with everything else related to Trump, amount to nothing. But these things aren't invented or concocted. He does them, and people have to clean up his shit.

MARC. And he lies: "The whistleblower is a partisan, but we don't know his identity." Yeah, sure you don't.

STEPHEN. Hunter Biden was making over $80,000 a month as a board member for a Ukrainian energy company. Hunter Biden had no expertise on energy or on Ukraine. Vice President Biden was the Obama administration's point person on Ukraine. What was Hunter Biden being paid for? Did Biden threaten Ukraine with a withdrawal of aid if a prosecutor was permitted to investigate? That's the real story.

STEPHEN. Unlike the Trump-Russia hoax, Biden's Ukrainian issue is real.

MARC. Of course Biden got a sweet deal, just like countless people connected to politics—both parties. You can even hear in Biden's denial yesterday his equivocation and parsing: "no evidence." You can't even make the right argument. So let me understand—is there something wrong with Biden threatening Ukraine with withdrawal of aid if there was an investigation? I think we can infer from your text that there is. But when the president does it (which might be proven), it's okay?

MARC. I'm the only one of us who isn't spewing the party line and defending every transgression.

STEPHEN. There is no evidence Trump threatened anyone.

MARC. He asked Ukraine to help dig up dirt. He held back the aid that was voted on until he was forced to release it. Connect the dots.

MARC. Your unwillingness to ever cast any doubt on or criticize anything about Trump is disappointing. It is true that many people are always looking for something to take him down, because we feel confident something is there from his own lies and words ("Putin is a great guy," etc.). That's not the same as manufacturing. Almost every story about him is true, initially denied, and then met with "So what?"

STEPHEN. There are no dots, and Hunter Biden's role in the Ukrainian energy company is a real issue, based on real evidence. You only believe in investigating fake allegations based on misinformation. I think Trump is a schmuck for raising the issue with Ukraine's president, but there is evidence of real wrongdoing [by Biden]. Nor was Trump asking anyone to break US laws, which was the premise of the phony collusion claims against Trump.

MARC. You are selective in your indignation, and you also deflect by saying that various mistakes I point out are not illegal. At least you qualify wrongdoing with "real." That's progress. That's all I hope for—that you are willing to speak negatively of him when you see fit.

STEPHEN. I'm not selective in my indignation. Trump has been unfairly and illegally targeted by the Obama administration, rogue law enforcement and intelligence officials, and Democrats and their media allies to force him out of office. They want to undo the election. He was elected because he rejects the norms of the political class. Trying to use his rejection of those norms against him will not work. You think you're fair, but you're not. You may acknowledge that the Clintons or Biden used their offices to enrich themselves, but you treat it as a minor issue. You respond to every allegation against Trump, no matter how ridiculous, as grounds for impeachment. I don't consider Trump the ideal Republican, but he is making a difference and is by far the country's best option now.

MARC. I guess your use of *you* was representative of a larger body, because I don't often talk about impeachment, besides maybe regarding actions long acknowledged, like his interference with Comey and Mueller in attempts to stop the investigation. My driving force is an urgency in trying to make you see what you can't, despite the futility of the exercise. Each new story gives me an excitement that you will finally see. When Trump pulls questionable loopholes to pay zero in taxes, it's "smart business." When Elizabeth Warren checks off "American Indian," it's not simply getting the edge. When Manafort is arrested, you think it is unfair targeting, but Trump targeting Biden's family is understandable. If Biden's son is shown to be crooked, Biden should drop out.

STEPHEN. Your analysis is wrong on all points. I'll give you a couple of quick rebuttals. Trump did not interfere with Comey and Mueller. That is a fact. Furthermore, I'll bet you Comey will be convicted or plead guilty in connection with his conduct in the Trump investigation. Trump has paid a lot of money in taxes. More importantly, there is no claim that he took advantage of "questionable loopholes," whatever that means. Manafort was charged with crimes that the government previously declined to prosecute for one reason only: to squeeze him on Trump. Nevertheless, he was guilty. Biden's son is an example of abuse of power and should be investigated on the merits, just as the Clinton Foundation should be.

MARC. The Clintons should all go to jail! Real pressing, topical issue.

MARC. Comey to plead guilty? Ha!

STEPHEN. The issue is abuse of power. Biden allegedly used his power over government policy to enrich his son. If that happened, Biden should at the least drop out. And yes, there should be consequences for the Clintons' self-dealing. It would be much more important than revisiting ten-year-old conduct by Manafort. Comey is going down.

MARC. Abuse of power—hmm, using the presidency to halt aid unless you dig up dirt on your political opponent?

STEPHEN. That didn't happen. It's another thing that will blow up on the media.

MARC. And when it is shown to have happened, you will diminish its importance.

MARC. But only after a showing that it happened, of course.

MARC. Generally, accused people don't deny allegations against them if they are certain they did nothing wrong.

MARC. I assume the new Republican leadership has influenced you so positively as to make lying acceptable unless one is under oath, and therefore, you have no problem with the countless lies Trump and his team have told. Of course, Cory Lewandowski already told everybody about this when he stated that he had no obligation to tell the truth.

STEPHEN. Be patient.

MARC. The *Wall Street Journal* says Trump asked eight times. Eight!

STEPHEN. So what?

MARC. Hmm. There probably are transcripts of him asking Ukraine to make stuff up.

September 22, 2019

MARC. I've read all morning about this situation. Regardless of what shakes out of the Biden tree, if Trump urged, as reported, Ukraine to investigate Biden while at the same time holding back aid that they desperately needed, he is done. You don't need to prove a quid pro quo. Even if he asked nicely for them to investigate while holding back their defense funding, it's indefensible.

STEPHEN. Trump is not done. This is going to blow up in the Democrats' faces, particularly Biden's. Like all previous attacks on Trump, there will be no problem with his conduct but a very big question about an intelligence official reporting Trump's conversation to the DNI. The president's conversations with foreign leaders are not properly the subject of whistleblower laws. One by one, these illegal efforts to undermine him are being exposed. There will be consequences.

MARC. Stick to this matter. You know the report is likely correct, and Trump's admitting it means there is a transcript. If so, how does he extricate from this?

STEPHEN. There will be nothing for him to extricate himself from. As I said the other day, you believe every allegation against Trump and believe it is evidence of wrongdoing. This will blow up like everything else. For argument's sake, assume that the worst, as you see it, is true (which is not going to be the case). Explain to me what Trump did that you believe should stop his reelection.

MARC. He just confirmed the report.

MARC. What could be wrong with holding up a nation's defense funding voted on by Republicans until they agree to do your dirty work? The president works for the people!

STEPHEN. This is September. The call took place at the end of July. Ukraine has received its funding. As far as I know, Ukraine hasn't done any "dirty work" for Trump. By the way, what dirty work did Trump ask them to do? Did he ask them to do anything illegal? Should Biden's alleged pressure on Ukraine to drop an investigation into his son's business be investigated or not?

MARC. Stop talking about what Biden did. It's irrelevant. It doesn't matter what they did or that the money was eventually released. It might not be a crime, but it will be impeachable, and Republicans will tell him to resign. They can't support that kind of behavior. A stupid shakedown for no reason.

STEPHEN. Why don't you identify a single thing Trump did that is problematic? This issue will hurt Biden, not Trump. I agree it will be reported to be the crime of the century, until it disappears like all the other improper conduct directed at Trump.

MARC. Biden is toast regardless. He is a bumbler, and people don't want the safe choice anymore. It will be Warren and Beto or Buttigieg.

MARC. Biden's crony financial gain is as disgusting as the Clintons' and as disgusting as Trump's.

STEPHEN. Now you allege that Trump has profited off his office? Based on what? The fact is that he is losing money by being president. In the competition to make unsubstantiated claims against Trump, I believe you're the first to accuse him of influence peddling. You'll probably be on CNN or MSNBC this week. If Warren were to be elected and followed through on her unconstitutional promise to ban fracking on day one, before even getting to her idiotic and unsupportable proposals for health care, the economy would likely take a dive, tens of thousands of good-paying jobs would disappear, and the United States would again be beholden to unstable foreign regimes for oil and gas. Beto is a buffoon; the idea that he could beat Trump is laughable. Buttigieg is not ready for prime time and is very sanctimonious. No chance.

MARC. Nikki Haley will be your 2020 president.

STEPHEN. You understand nothing. If there is an issue, it is Biden's issue. Trump will be the nominee and will be reelected. We will have four more years of texting.

SEPTEMBER 23, 2019

MARC. Here is all that matters other than Biden being toast: for his own interest, Trump held back aid that was voted on by Congress. Nobody is going to buy that his request was to combat corruption, when the transcript will show he asked them to investigate only one person: the candidate he polls worst against.

STEPHEN. No, he did not. The claims are falling apart. There are only two real issues: Biden's corruption and the exposing of conversations between the president and foreign leaders. By the way, it has been reported that the so-called whistleblower did not have firsthand knowledge. With Trump, anything goes.

MARC. The report will have meat to it. You know it; I know it. You will fight the politics of the whistleblower, of course, but there will be a transcript, and it will show Trump asking for help eight times, and that's all you need. He will be impeached and humiliated and damaged in the election.

MARC. Ha-ha-ha. He is screwed [regarding the Mulvaney press conference].

STEPHEN. How many times have you predicted that Trump is going down, only to be disappointed? I guess you like looking foolish. Assuming Trump told Mulvaney to hold back aid, this article sheds no light on the reason. However, I have no doubt it would not have been to pressure Ukraine. The Ukrainian foreign minister and Ukrainian president have stated that they were not pressured. As I said, this incident raises only two issues: Biden's corruption and the fact that Trump's private conversation became public. We'll have to wait until Comey and company are indicted for the past illegal efforts to undermine Trump before we get to this one.

MARC. Of course the Ukrainian president isn't going to say anything; they need us. You know the reason. He held the aid back, and right after, he called him and asked him eight times to help investigate Biden. You can't win this argument. You know what happened and soon will shift to "So what?"

SEPTEMBER 24, 2019

STEPHEN. You're right. Evidence only counts if it implicates Trump.

MARC. I suppose you will say, when the story proves true, the president can ask anything he wants. If you go that route, then Obama was entitled to confer such powers to Biden. Trump told Mulvaney to kill the aid and then asked eight times for Ukraine's president to speak with Giuliani, who last night said he was not working on his own. The Ukrainian president ran on an anticorruption platform, and Trump is extorting *him*? On what basis did Trump hold back $391 million from Ukraine?

MARC. The *Wall Street Journal* confirms the report! And Trump's denial was, essentially, "I didn't say the (exact) words that I would give them the aid if they did something for me."

MARC. Wait until you get your daily defend-Trump talking point. I assume it will be "Everyone is out to get him." As if Obama wasn't constantly attacked for suit color, what he drank, where he was born, and use of executive privilege. Bush was attacked as well.

Marc: By the way, he had Ukraine's president talk with Rudy, who isn't even part of the government!

STEPHEN. You're like Javert. As Jean Valjean said, "You are wrong and always have been wrong." No one has confirmed a quid pro quo because there was none. Don't you see the pattern? The Democrats do something—in this case threaten to withhold aid—and then accuse Trump of doing it. Reminds me of collusion. By the way, Rudy was appointed by the State Department to discuss this matter with Ukraine. But facts don't matter to you.

MARC. He said, "Hey, hold up that money. Hold it up! I'm talking to Zelensky this week," and then to Zelensky, "Oh, hello. Uh, we have the aid for you, but there's a little bit of a delay, and in the meantime, I'd like your help with something." Boom!

MARC. Why was he holding up the aid and telling his administration to lie about the reason? He's finished!

STEPHEN. Keep dreaming. Trump will be finished around January 20, 2025. Between now and then, you will probably find fifty reasons he allegedly won't finish his term. I look forward to the back-and-forth. It's like Alabama versus MIT in football.

MARC. Similar, but I'm a Notre Dame fan, so it's more like Notre Dame versus MIT.

MARC. Hey, I'll give you this: at least the brilliance you give Trump credit for is on full display with his energetic and captivating orations like the one this morning at the United Nations.

STEPHEN. Don't keep me in suspense. What outrage did Trump commit this morning?

MARC. He spoke like he was on Thorazine.

MARC. I love the smell of impeachment in the morning!

STEPHEN. If it makes you feel good, dream away.

STEPHEN. Trump says the "complete, fully declassified, and unredacted transcript" of his conversation with Ukraine's president will be released Wednesday.

STEPHEN. https://www.wsj.com/articles/trump-says-he-held-up-ukraine-aid-over-frustration-with-europe.

STEPHEN. We should plan for an active texting day tomorrow.

MARC. Probably a made-up one.

MARC. Let's hear the complaint!

STEPHEN. Trump: "Congratulations on your election. I look forward to working with you on areas of mutual interest. As you know, we support Ukraine's territorial integrity and will support you in your efforts to defend it." Zelensky: "Thank you, Mr. President. It truly is an honor to work with such an upstanding and brilliant leader as yourself." Trump: "You're so right. It is a tremendous honor for you." Zelensky: "It's not like working with that SOB Biden." Trump: "I have nothing bad to say about Joe. I hope he's my opponent." Zelensky: "He's corrupt, just like the Clintons." Trump: "I can't comment on that." Zelensky: "We should investigate him, the dog." Trump: "I can't get involved in internal Ukrainian legal proceedings, but it is important to root out corruption." Zelensky: "Thank you, Mr. President; you are so wise." Trump: "Thank you. Good luck."

MARC. This can't be real.

STEPHEN. It is to me.

MARC. Ha.

MARC. Mitch McConnell is pushing for the release of the whistleblower report.

SEPTEMBER 25, 2019

MARC. My office is offering you complete immunity for you to please say, "I was wrong," and that Trump is much worse than clumsy or unorthodox. He is everything I have said he was.

STEPHEN. This is going nowhere. Trump raised a real publicly disclosed issue. I agree that it is not wise, but it is not illegal or impeachable conduct. In fact, it does not compare to the Obama administration's efforts to get Ukraine to provide dirt on Trump and Manafort. You can dream of impeachment, but you're guaranteeing Trump's reelection. Go for it.

MARC. Everyone says that, but I have an intelligent (for a change) question. In the states where new Democratic congresspersons flipped seats, places that Trump won in 2016 and that rejected Trump in 2018, I wouldn't assume they will be opposed to impeachment. In fact, I think the Republicans want him out and Pence in now, and today's release was an "Emperor's New Clothes" episode.

STEPHEN. No Republican who wants to remain a Republican will oppose Trump.

MARC. I seriously think they want to take their party back, and they now have cover to explain why they are getting rid of him.

STEPHEN. No Republican will oppose Trump over this. Despite the coverage, it is nothing. It shows Trump being Trump. Trump's supporters, including me, see this: any act taken to undermine Trump, regardless of legality, is acceptable. Every act taken by Trump is presented as a high crime. It's ridiculous. That's why he will be reelected, and Republicans will not abandon him.

MARC. He said, "I would like you to do us a favor, though." Here's a little English lesson for you: *though* is a conditional modifier. There it is, my friend. And this is only what the White House allowed to be released!

MARC. (1) Ukraine is our ally, and it is in their interest and against Putin's interest for them to receive our financial support; (2) the support was voted on and then held back by Trump; and (3) Trump, while holding back the support, said, "I need a favor." As he was holding up the money! What am I missing?

MARC. Even the Republican Senate majority leader couldn't find out why that money was being held back. Trump has tried alternate bogus explanations for two days.

STEPHEN. Trump has been very supportive of Ukraine. What you refer to as "bogus" explanations are the explanations. They are not bogus just because they don't support your conspiracy.

MARC. Trump used the power of his office for his own gain and benefit at the expense of national security. He is finished.

STEPHEN. Okay. Some might say he is doing exactly what he was elected to do: expose the corruption of our political elite. How many times have you declared that he is finished? I look forward to the next time.

MARC. Okay, though we spar, I usually secretly give your points credit for intelligence. To say that Trump's singling out Biden as the one instance of corruption that lingers and should be resolved, with nothing to do with what Trump himself would gain from that investigation, is the most ridiculous contention you have ever made, and you know it!

STEPHEN. Read the transcript.

STEPHEN. https://www.scribd.com/document/427409665/Ukraine-Call-Transcript.

MARC. I read it.

STEPHEN. Good luck on impeachment.

MARC. Great job by Trump in spending time to find corruption going on in Ukraine regarding his possible opponent for the good of Ukraine and the United States.

STEPHEN. The Democrats' position: The Democrats used Ukraine in 2016 against Trump. That's okay. Trump asked the new president to look into it. That's bad. Biden got a Ukrainian prosecutor fired who was investigating a company that paid Biden's son millions. He threatened to withhold aid if they didn't fire him. That's okay. Trump asked the Ukrainians to look into it. That's bad. Yes, the Democrats' position makes perfect sense.

STEPHEN. The Ukraine story is going to take down Biden. He's finished. Whom will you support? Warren? What part of her program do you like the best? Gun confiscation? Open borders? Confiscatory taxes? The Green New Deal?

Marc. I like that she isn't Trump.

Stephen. It's hypothetical, as she will not be president.

September 26, 2009

Marc. Trump is finished.

Stephen. Only in your dreams. This idiotic push on Ukraine is a gift to Trump.

Marc. The cover-up is always worse than the crime. Recall Clinton.

Stephen. The only cover-up is by the media and Democrats. Trump has released the transcript and whistleblower complaint. The media is mischaracterizing the transcript because it doesn't say what they would have liked it to say. The "favor" Trump requested related to cooperation with the election-interference investigation being conducted by Barr, not Biden. Zelensky promised everything would be done "candidly and openly." The media claims that Biden has been investigated and that nothing was found to be improper. That will be blown up today.

Marc. We shall see. The Dems *will* impeach. Then we will see what Middle America thinks. Nobody who wasn't voting for Trump is going to vote for him now.

Marc. Tell me who is voting now for Trump who wasn't before, versus those who were voting for Trump who believe he should not have done even a percentage of the things you have acknowledged were stupid and Republicans have called inappropriate.

Stephen. He is at more than 50 percent approval in certain polls.

Marc. Rasmussen always favors the Republicans.

MARC. The transcript of the call with Ukraine was so bad that the White House pushed it away into hiding. Once the whistleblower revealed what had happened, the White House had to reveal it.

STEPHEN. It was so bad? Why? Because the whistleblower says so? I read it. As I noted earlier, the media and Democrats keep mischaracterizing it because it doesn't actually say anything. It's ridiculous, but on the positive side, it reassures Trump's reelection.

MARC. Then why was it buried until it was forced to be turned over?

STEPHEN. What does that mean? Transcripts of the president's phone calls are not public. What the complaint shows is that Trump cannot trust the intelligence staffers assigned to the White House. Somebody leaked info for the purpose of making trouble for Trump. Whoever did that should go to jail.

MARC. What about the people who leaked all the things you hear about Biden or anyone else you impugn? When they uncover an Arab terrorist plot, you won't be too worried about who leaked the plans. And you are wrong about the leaker going to jail. According to Trump, the leaker should be murdered.

MARC. Did it ever occur to any Trump lovers that despite whatever targeting you believe exists (which was never so effective against any other president since Clinton), Trump's response heightens things to the point where even his supporters are going to feel that there is just too much division since he came on the scene and become fed up with his whole act?

MARC. Polls indicate that 49 percent of Republicans support impeachment, and when the White House goons lean on people to vote in their favor, they will turn.

STEPHEN. The Democrats have been seeking to remove him from office since he was elected. People are sick of them.

Marc. Many people are sick of the Democrats, and many people are sick of Trump, so we'll see who has the larger group.

Marc. The Republicans were trying to get rid of Obama for eight years.

Marc. McConnell declared his aim to halt anything Obama wanted to do before they even knew what it was.

Marc. They claimed he was illegitimate. I forget which one of the Republicans was leading that charge—oh yeah, it was Donald Trump!

Marc. Bottom line: it's obvious to any objective person that Trump was muscling Ukraine and even more obvious now that the White House tried to cover it up.

Stephen. It's obvious to people who thought Trump should be impeached on election night.

September 27, 2019

Marc. When I remind you for years that you were a proud Trump supporter, at least you can cite that you were right that he was a sharp, smart guy.

Stephen. When I remind you for years that you were proud to support rank injustice because it was directed against someone you did not like, I hope I'm not doing it from our reeducation camp after we are found guilty of being enemies of the people because your heroes decided we must have committed crimes because we live too comfortably.

Marc. Is that from Orwell?

Marc. Trump is guilty, the evidence is there, and he has given plenty of people plenty of reason to actively look for the skeletons. Republicans will cut bait.

STEPHEN. What is Trump guilty of?

STEPHEN. You don't know, do you? He's just guilty.

MARC. He is guilty of putting himself and his reelection above the country. Clinton did nothing to harm the country. He was inappropriate, he lied, and he was impeached, and I wasn't against it, and I'm not now. Trump did the same at the very least.

STEPHEN. No, he didn't. He asked the Ukrainian president to cooperate with a pending investigation into the origins of the Russia hoax and to look into reported corruption involving Biden. Is it a crime to investigate a Democrat for corruption if he is running for president? Trump did not ask Zelensky to make anything up. Furthermore, if Trump were extorting Ukraine to do something they would not otherwise do—although there is no reason to suspect they would have a problem with cooperation— why would Trump release the aid before they actually did it? That's not how extortion works.

MARC. He held back the aid. It will be proven in the inquiry. He only released it when they feared the optics. That will be his downfall. But worse, they put the transcript in another server to hide it. Cover-up consciousness of guilt. And Trump also asked for the favor right after the guy referred to aid.

STEPHEN. They have the aid. Period.

MARC. Imagine Clinton saying, "My affair with Monica Lewinsky is over, period." Trump is dumbing you down. You don't write *period* after a period. It's redundant.

STEPHEN. This is a fake scandal created by a fake whistleblower.

MARC. It's wrongdoing revealed by one.

STEPHEN. There was wrongdoing by Biden and the individuals who leaked.

MARC. This was wrongdoing by Biden and utter, sheer stupidity by Trump and callow enabling by his staff.

MARC. It's a crime to ask a foreign government for anything of value in an election. Period. That's the law. There doesn't have to be a quid pro quo. Nothing needs to be actually received. You don't have to prove extortion. The asking is a crime.

MARC. That's not from me but from another lawyer.

STEPHEN. Nonsense. Explain to me what you mean by (1) asking for something of value and (2) "in an election." I'm glad you went into the medical field.

A DIGRESSION BACK TO RUSSIA

STEPHEN. Barack Obama was president when Russian interference occurred, and he was not concerned about it. He said so on TV. By the way, he was right. As demonstrated in the Mueller report, Russian interference was irrelevant. The much bigger concern, which will be disclosed in detail by Horowitz, Barr, and Durham, is the Obama administration's interference in the election. I look forward to the indictments.

MARC. He wasn't concerned about it?

STEPHEN. Obama was not concerned about it. He mocked concern about Russian interference. More importantly, he did nothing.

MARC. The dam has broken. The whole thing is going to come out.

MARC. Did nothing about what? Nothing?

STEPHEN. Russian interference.

STEPHEN. Nothing is going to come out. This is Russia hoax 2.0. The more I learn, the more clear that is.

BACK TO UKRAINE

September 28, 2019

Marc. Of all the stretches you have made in defending this clown, you have tried to say that asking Ukraine's president to investigate Biden had nothing to do with the fact that Biden was a potential adversary. That's ridiculous, and now it has come out that Trump went to two other countries with requests. When those countries would provide possible information, Trump would put our country in a position of owing something back, hence the already favorable treatment for MBS [the Saudi crown prince].

Stephen. It is irrelevant. It is appropriate to investigate wrongdoing. There is a pending investigation into Ukraine's role in the 2016 election. Trump requested that Zelensky cooperate. Biden is an offshoot of that. If it's improper for Trump to seek Ukraine's investigation into Biden because he's running for president, it must be wrong for the Democrats to investigate Biden's opponent: Trump. Interestingly, Representative Al Green made a comment that we need to impeach him, or he might win. That's pure election interference.

Marc. Oh, Al Green said that? I guess we should just ignore all the evidence. These reports are all proving to be true. This is what happens when you threaten to execute a CIA agent. Trump will probably resign in another week. The rats are fleeing the ship. I assume the scores of Republicans who will give word that they would impeach, if not end up voting for it, are all partisans too? I assume the Nixon impeachment was not warranted because of election interference? What about Clinton's?

Marc. Are you concerned that the whistleblower wasn't a firsthand witness?

STEPHEN. There is no evidence of anything, other than Trump asking for cooperation. Nothing illegal or improper. The evidence is that Trump continues to be spied on.

MARC. Not improper?

STEPHEN. No, it's laughable. Trump did not threaten Ukraine in any manner, certainly not for his benefit, nor did he even suggest Ukraine do anything improper. The Democrats are using the timing of the release of aid to suggest something nefarious. They manipulate the whistleblower rules to make this an issue, and the media reports as if it's a serious issue. It is serious because it is part of the never-ending assault on Trump.

MARC. I guess he wouldn't benefit from digging up dirt on Biden, the only moderate Dem with a chance (before this scandal and his ultimate resignation).

STEPHEN. All the Democrats do is try to dig up dirt on Trump based on lies. Ukraine was central to the Democrats' preelection efforts to frame Trump. It just so happens Biden also used Ukraine to enrich his son. That's not Trump's fault. You seem to think it is off-limits to investigate. Why? Because it might benefit Trump? The Democrats believe their candidates should be immune from the consequences of their illegal conduct, but there is no such rule. In that transcript, Trump did not mention foreign aid, threaten Ukraine in any manner, or suggest that Ukraine should do anything improper or make up allegations. All he did was ask for cooperation in ongoing investigations. Only people who believe something is illegal if Trump does it believe this call is an issue. It is not.

MARC. You can't dig up dirt if it doesn't exist. They would've impeached Obama if they could have. Hey, for what possible reason—please tell me—did Ben Sasse caution fellow Republicans not to attack the whistleblower and say that the facts were deeply troubling?

STEPHEN. You're such an undisciplined thinker. There were no impeachment inquiries into Obama. I can't speak for Ben Sasse, but I can evaluate the public information, and I don't find any deeply troubling facts, other than the evidence of the continuing efforts to get Trump.

MARC. Efforts to get Trump will continue to be futile if there is nothing to find. And if what they find is not compelling to the Republican Party, they won't be able to impeach him.

STEPHEN. Even if he's impeached, he won't be convicted, and more so than Clinton, he will benefit politically.

MARC. Oh, he'll be impeached for sure. I just meant that he won't be convicted unless the evidence is compelling. Fortunately for my hopes, most of the senators loathe Trump for the reasons that most intelligent, perceptive people do, and I believe they will take him out, regardless of the fallout. They should calculate that their lives will be filled with speaking appearances, appointments, and honors, rather than having to be controlled in their states by white racist idiots.

STEPHEN. Again, you're spouting nonsense. Any Republican who would support Trump's removal from office would be finished. Your belief that Trump's supporters are white racist idiots says a lot about your prejudices, not Trump's.

MARC. Yes, they would be finished with Republicans in their backwoods states but not in New York City or Los Angeles, where they would thrive with the respect of the majority of interesting people on either coast.

STEPHEN. They would be useful idiots. Once they were no longer useful, they would be forgotten.

MARC. They'd be useful on CNN. They'd be useful at Columbia University. They would be useful at the Ninety-Second Street Y.

MARC. They'd be useful in writing best-selling books.

Marc. They'd be useful in running for president in eight years.

Marc. Meanwhile, Trump supporters will be rendered into phrases like "I know, I know. How many times you gonna remind me? I know" and "I know, I know. I had terrible judgment, but I still should be able to pick the wine for all of us."

Stephen. The Democrats are playing with fire.

Marc. When you play with fire, sometimes you get burned, but sometimes you get whatever good thing comes from playing with fire.

PART 8

OCTOBER 2, 2019– DECEMBER 30, 2019

UKRAINE, CONTINUED

October 2, 2019

Marc. At least this crisis for Trump has allowed for a test that he has passed. Calm, cool leadership. Class and poise all the way. A great example. Bears out all the praise you've been heaping on him these last few years.

Stephen. I don't know what you're talking about.

Marc. [*Attaches a tweet from Trump blasting "Do Nothing Democrats."*]

Stephen. He's right. The Democrats are seeking to obstruct Bill Barr, soften the blow when the Horowitz FISA report comes out, and continue the false narrative that Trump is colluding with foreign governments. It's worse than bullshit.

Marc. Here is how I can use logic to prove Trump is a moronic idiot. He constantly mitigates what he is accused of by citing other people whom he implies are guiltier than he is. Instead of saying, "Obama did it, nobody complained about it, it's perfectly fine, and there was nothing wrong with it," he says, "Obama did it, nobody said anything, and that's who you should be investigating! Same with Biden's son. Talk about nepotism."

Stephen. His point is valid. It's not that he's acknowledging wrongdoing. He is pointing out hypocrisy. He's accused of doing something that is characterized as illegal or immoral. However, others who actually have done what he is accused of doing get a free pass. This is because Trump's accusers do not really believe that what he is accused of doing is wrong. They are making accusations to create a false narrative. Because Trump did not actually do what he is accused of doing, it makes the accusations even more reprehensible.

Marc. He did do what he is accused of. He tried to extort Ukraine for dirt on his political opponent, and that is corroborated by his efforts to dig up such dirt from other countries.

Marc. I assume you don't agree with people who don't obey the law. Unless, of course, it's because they are unfairly accused? There is a due process, and Trump and his idiots are stonewalling. Hillary complied with every subpoena. Now there's a report from a few minutes ago that State Department officials were threatened not to cooperate. Newsflash: senators are institutionalists and are going to dump this idiot. I mean Republican senators.

Stephen. He's accused of extorting Ukraine, but it is a laughably weak accusation that should never see the light of day. The evidence that Biden extorted Ukraine is far stronger and is being explained away, which is exactly Trump's point. The only "intimidation" appears to be coming from Congress. Trump hasn't stonewalled anything.

Marc. When he is impeached and you claim it was a coup, I guess it will prove that Republicans are weak wimps and that their media are impotent.

Stephen. According to the *NYT*, Adam Schiff met with the so-called whistleblower before the whistleblower filed his complaint. When the complaint was made public, Schiff stated that he had not spoken with the whistleblower. This is a setup.

Marc. So desperate.

Stephen. I always have one insurmountable advantage over you: regardless of the issue, I rely on facts. You just hate Trump. In fact, you hate Trump more than you love the truth. I'm not desperate. I'm impatient. This phony impeachment inquiry will blow up on the Democrats and ensure that Trump wins a second term.

MARC. For the last few days, you said there was nothing there. Now you say that the nothing was actually concocted?

MARC. Nobody defends Trump; they just attack the attackers. If there is nothing there, why attack the attackers?

STEPHEN. Yes. The transcript of the actual phone call establishes that Trump did absolutely nothing wrong. The controversy over this nothing call is concocted by the Democrats and the whistleblower's hearsay complaint. The Democrats have undermined our security by orchestrating the leaking of the president's private conversations. You're very credulous. This was an illegal leak of hearsay info, not a whistleblower complaint.

MARC. You sound like a guilty party defending themselves with "I was framed, I tell ya!"

STEPHEN. The Democrats have been desperate to find a basis for removing Trump from office for three years. Lo and behold, a whistleblower arrives who goes to the Democrats with a complaint about a phone call he did not hear. Even though he is an intelligence official, he needs to speak to Adam Schiff to learn that he should go to the inspector general. He also gets advice to go to an anti-Trump lawyer. When asked if he spoke to the whistleblower, Schiff lies and says he did not but would like to. Also, magically, a month before he files his complaint, the whistleblower rules were changed to permit a complaint to be made on hearsay evidence. Another coincidence—and such a good idea. Right. I sound like I'm defending a guilty party.

MARC. I agree with your first sentence.

STEPHEN. Open your eyes. These idiots will ensure Trump's reelection. They may already have done it.

MARC. They aren't making anything up. The call transcript was released, and it is backed up by similar requests of several countries to dig up dirt on Biden. Why? Why is he asking for dirt on Biden? I'll tell you why: because he can't help himself. They probably told him to shut his mouth!

MARC. If their actions are ensuring Trump's reelection, then why attack them? Let them just do it!

MARC. It's so easy to debate you when you can't refer to your notes.

STEPHEN. Can you read? Trump did not ask for dirt on Biden. He suggested that a matter of public record be investigated. There is nothing wrong with that.

MARC. Why is he making this personal appeal repeatedly? Biden is his election rival. There are laws against this.

STEPHEN. He did not make it repeatedly. He said it once. You didn't read the transcript, did you?

STEPHEN. By the way, the Lieberman rule is that Trump is the only candidate who can be investigated. It's illegal to investigate credible allegations of corruption against anyone running against Trump. That makes sense.

MARC. You leave out that Trump ordered the aid to be held up! That is where he effed up.

STEPHEN. No. Trump released the aid. The Ukrainians were not even aware that the release of the aid was delayed. Furthermore, payments are delayed all the time for different reasons. There's zero evidence that the delay in the release in the aid was connected to the ten-second reference to the Biden matter. It's so stupid.

October 3, 2019

Marc. You sound like Johnnie Cochran defending O. J.

Stephen. You never respond with arguments, only silly, irrelevant comments.

Marc. My argument is that he held up the aid for no reason that has been explained. It sure as hell wasn't to prevent corruption. Then he asked for dirt on none other than his political rival. The deduction from those two points is elementary, and when it is proven, your argument will move to "So what?"

Marc. You can keep defending him, but he is actually *trying* to get impeached!

Marc. How is this different from Biden's crony capitalism?

Stephen. You don't know what a fact is.

Marc. Do you like that China would be helping to find "the truth" about Biden?

Stephen. Fine with me. Unless, of course, Democrats should be immune from investigation.

Marc. He just reinforced the validity of everything in the whistleblower report that everyone on your side seems to have such a problem with.

Marc. Volker has texts from before this episode was public wherein he told Trump that it wasn't wise to hold back the aid for political reasons.

Marc. For two years, you debated that Trump didn't collude with Russia to help him win the election. Now it's okay, in your mind, to solicit help from other countries to help him win an election?

STEPHEN. He didn't solicit help in the election. He asked the Ukrainian president to investigate a publicly disclosed matter that Biden has acknowledged and bragged about. Why is it improper to do that? It's not. Let's compare it to the Steele dossier. The Democratic candidate paid Russian sources for misinformation, which was then passed off as intelligence to the media and used to illegally obtain a surveillance warrant. Is that the same thing? Which one do you think is a problem?

MARC. He is soliciting help today in front of the world!

MARC. "The president alone must devote time and resources and leverage his power to get to the bottom of Biden's corruption, even if it means using China, because the Biden corruption is a uniquely important problem, putting aside the fact that Biden will be the president's opponent in the next election." This is an excerpt from Stephen Barry's upcoming treatise.

MARC. I'd like you to explain what the purpose is for using China to get to the bottom of the Biden-Ukraine story.

STEPHEN. I guess the Democrats' Ukraine impeachment fantasy is falling apart. I understand that Kurt Volker, who recently resigned as envoy to Ukraine, was questioned today in the phony impeachment probe. He reportedly blew apart the impeachment theories. Don't expect Schiff to release the transcript anytime soon. Transparency works only one way. On to China. Of course, there are no facts, except that Hunter Biden was involved in another lucrative deal after flying to China on Air Force 2. Is it Trump's fault that there is evidence that Biden was involved in corruption in the two countries of which Obama put him in charge? By the way, I heard a report that in 2016, Hillary Clinton told Biden that if he entered the race, she would not go after Hunter, but she couldn't speak for her staff.

October 4, 2019

MARC. I figured texting at such an early hour might catch you in an absorbent, rather than deflective, state. The text messages show they knew that what they were doing was a quid pro quo. They wanted Ukraine to have defense, and they were planning to tell Zelensky to just tell Trump on the call that he would investigate Biden. They all played Trump for the fool he is. One of the three guys in the text was a Trump donor who was awarded an appointment, and when he was told, ostensibly just to have a text record of their wrongdoing, "Hey, this is stupid to hold up the aid in return for political favors," the Trump guy said, "Let's not text. Call me." So, my friend, today is the day it gets real. Republicans will fold and dump this clown.

STEPHEN. Facts don't matter to you. Trump's opponents called it a quid pro quo, so you believe it. It doesn't matter that there is no evidence that it was a quid pro quo or that the Ukrainians had any problem with being asked to investigate the evidence-based allegations against Biden.

MARC. They told Zelensky he had to convince Trump he would investigate Biden in order to get the money. Stop deflecting, and start absorbing. It was extortion, and it's over.

MARC. Plus, he asked, in front of the world, for China, our effin' adversary, to help him by investigating Biden!

MARC. Then he said, "We have power over China if they don't do what we want."

MARC. And the aid to Ukraine was released two days after the whistleblower complaint!

MARC. Smart move—don't reply with anything until you have legal counsel.

STEPHEN. The bottom line is that Trump did not use aid to compel the Ukrainians to investigate allegations about Biden, which, based on the evidence, should be investigated. Senator Sasse is wrong. We ask foreign governments to investigate matters all the time. That's why treaties regarding mutual legal assistance are in place. The issue here is with Biden and the Democrats who are on record threatening Ukraine with aid unless, in Biden's case, Ukraine dropped an investigation and unless, with respect to the Mueller investigation, Ukraine cooperated with Mueller. You don't have to parse words. The threats made were explicit.

MARC. We ask, meaning people in the government. Not the president and not for selfish reasons, which you know was the case if you can sit still and stop spinning.

MARC. Either Trump gets lost, or you will lose the Senate.

STEPHEN. In Lieberman's world, every allegation against Trump is presumptively true, regardless of how ridiculous. No allegation about Trump's opponents, no matter how much evidence there is, may be investigated if it might help Trump. Do I have that right?

MARC. Is it okay for Trump to ask China to dig up dirt on Elizabeth Warren, whom he has no claims against other than her exaggerating her ethnic diversity? Think before you answer, because when you say no, then you can't say, "I don't have a problem with it," when those reports bear out. Once again, you have zero credibility because you never, ever do anything but defend Trump. I say that Biden's son was reaping crony benefits, and Biden may also have used muscle and shouldn't run.

MARC. He promised Xi silence on the Hong Kong protests. I guess you don't admire the Hong Kong people protesting for freedom?

MARC. Most of the reports are true from the main newspapers. Both ways.

MARC. [*Attaches a statement by Tucker Carlson.*]

MARC. You can't ever get to here. This is Tucker Carlson! Take your medicine, and admit is was improper!

STEPHEN. I defend Trump because he is the target of an attempted coup.

MARC. He doesn't need your defense. He has other acolytes.

MARC. When Putin was running against Navalny, Putin had Navalny's brother arrested for "corruption." Do you think that was a noble attack against corruption or politically motivated?

STEPHEN. Trump is the only one in the Ukraine saga who hasn't done anything wrong. It looks like Biden might be a crook. He definitely used foreign aid to compel the Ukrainians to fire a prosecutor, and it looks like that prosecutor was investigating his son. It looks like Adam Schiff worked with a CIA employee to make a whistleblower complaint and expose privileged presidential communications. It looks like the Democrats have accused Trump of doing something that they have repeatedly done to him—use foreign sources to smear an opponent—except Trump has legitimate grounds for it, and they did not.

OCTOBER 6, 2019

STEPHEN. It's been one year since Kavanaugh was confirmed. Leland Keyser, who is a Democrat, was told that if she did not support Ford, stories would be spread about her. Today we have a different issue and the same tactics.

MARC. Here is the fact: Trump tried to leverage aid for Ukraine to get dirt on Biden. You know full well it wasn't about ending corruption. The texts back it up, and you know full well the final text wherein the guys spells out, so incriminatingly, "This is not a quid pro quo," was cover. "Call me." Now, if you want to tell me that it's not that big of a deal to ask for Ukraine's help in the election, do so now before it becomes your only remaining defense. As for bias and tactics, they exist on both sides.

MARC. Trump wants to impeach Romney for disagreeing with him and criticizing him.

MARC. The defense of the accusations with Ukraine are so paltry that now Trump says he didn't want to make the call, but Rick Perry made him! "Oh, there was nothing wrong with the call; it was perfect—but Rick Perry made me do it!"

STEPHEN. I know you're an intelligent man, so I assume your exuberant acceptance of all accusations against Trump must be the effect of drugs you're taking. Trump has been accused of using aid to compel Ukraine to find dirt on Biden. It is an accusation, not a fact. Furthermore, it is a baseless accusation. Putting aside the fact that the Democrats used Ukraine to find dirt—ultimately disinformation—to use against Trump and threatened Ukraine with the withholding of aid if they didn't cooperate with Mueller, there is no evidence that Trump demanded a quid pro quo. Nor is there anything wrong with asking the Ukrainians to investigate the allegations—based on very credible evidence—of the Bidens' corruption with Burisma. The bottom line is that you believe that Trump should be investigated over nonsense based on illegally leaked information (it is not a true whistleblower complaint), but Biden cannot be investigated. It's irrelevant that the investigation could be helpful to Trump. What will the next allegation be? Trump tricked Biden into using his office to protect Burisma?

MARC. When did I say Biden couldn't be investigated? I told you he probably used influence. Investigate him. But it insults common sense and the powers of inference that Lindsey Graham said were needed with Clinton (he isn't just going to come out and say, "Lie for me"). The facts and timing surrounding the texts and release of aid are damning, and you know it if you read them and know the players. The subsequent investigation will uncover it.

STEPHEN. Like the Mueller investigation uncovered collusion? By the way, Clinton did essentially say, "Lie for me." Also, does it bother you that the Democrats refuse to initiate a real impeachment inquiry, which would allow the Republicans to subpoena witnesses?

MARC. Just like the Republicans ran every meeting like a judicial inquiry on Benghazi? Clinton did essentially say that, just like Trump essentially said, "They aren't getting that aid until I get the dirt on Biden."

MARC. Republicans are leaving Trump. Romney will form a caucus. They don't need Trump anymore.

MARC. Your defense is starting to sound as credible as Clinton's "vast right-wing conspiracy against my husband."

STEPHEN. You never counter my arguments. Notwithstanding that Obama and Clinton were never held accountable for lying about Benghazi, Benghazi was not an impeachment inquiry. If the Democrats seriously believe that Trump committed impeachable offenses, they should put their money where their mouths are. Instead, they want to conduct a partisan smear campaign. Any Republican who joins that campaign is finished.

STEPHEN. By the way, if Benghazi had occurred during Trump's term and Trump had lied about it like Obama did, the Democrats would have been calling for impeachment.

MARC. They are both partisan and both look for openings. See? I'm the only one here who sees things in a nonpolarized way. I want Mitt Romney or Ben Sasse or any other Republican who speaks up. Any party or president is going to have mess-ups and unethical behavior, but Trump here is being true to all the fears about him. He's completely unhinged and selfish. You have to admit he is more interested in retaining power than in governing. To make such an effort just to get dirt on an opponent? We can do better than that. I want a decent, principled person running the country. I'll take Pence. I'll take Warren. I've been true to this vision, my own vision. You see that "draining the swamp" is a bunch of bullshit.

I'd rather go back to leaders who exhibit caring and humanity. Like G. W., who told America to lay off anti-Muslim rhetoric after 9/11.

STEPHEN. I don't know what Trump "being true to all the fears" means. The Democrats, not Trump, are unhinged. They have spent three years trying to remove him from office. Now they are accusing him of doing something that they have done to him—use foreign governments—except it appears that Trump did it entirely appropriately and the Democrats did not. The fact that you would accept Pence doesn't make you fair. The Democrats have abused US law and process to target Trump. It is illegal, unjust, and terribly divisive. There is an election in one year. This effort is a smear campaign.

MARC. And the effort to get info on Biden was not done to smear him at all?

MARC. Even a little bit?

STEPHEN. There's a difference between conducting never-ending investigations in which every act is presented as unprecedented and impeachable, including acts that the accusers have clearly been engaged in, and investigating credible allegations of wrongdoing—allegations that have been reported on by the *NYT* and that Biden confirmed by his bragging about getting the prosecutor fired.

MARC. That prosecutor wasn't investigating Biden or Burisma.

MARC. I have faith in the process, and we will see how it pans out. In retrospect, perhaps the lack of fallout from the Mueller report was appropriate, cast in the new light of these revelations.

MARC. You forget or never mention that the aid for Ukraine, only released after the knowledge of the whistleblower report, was a benefit to Russia.

STEPHEN. The prosecutor was investigating Burisma and was going to interview Hunter Biden before he was fired. You claim you're evenhanded, but if Trump had done what Biden did and bragged about getting the prosecutor fired, you would be all over him. We'll see how much faith you have in the process when the Horowitz and the Barr and Durham reports come out.

MARC. Uh, Trump did. Ask Don McGahn!

MARC. Multiple whistleblowers are now reported. He is so effed!

STEPHEN. The Trump administration has provided lethal aid to Ukraine, something Obama did not do. This is another example of your belief in a discredited hoax. There was no collusion with Russia, only Trump's publicly stated desire for better relations with Russia—something the Democrats claimed to want until they decided to use Russia against Trump. Of course there are multiple whistleblowers. It's the Kavanaugh playbook. The transcript is out there. We know what Trump said and did. We'll see what these people say, but what they're doing is illegal. I can't wait until the conversations of a future Democratic president are leaked as purported whistleblower complaints to support Republicans. I can assure you that the media coverage will be 180 degrees different. As a result, so will Marc's perspective.

MARC. Congress provided aid. Trump held it back.

MARC. I guess Tucker Carlson sees what I see, and you don't.

STEPHEN. I didn't say it was a good idea, but it is not inappropriate. Trump did not create the issue; Biden did. Maybe if the mainstream press did its job, this would have been investigated properly at the time. Instead, the *NYT* allegedly gave Biden a heads-up that his son was going to be questioned.

MARC. [*Attaches a report that the claims against Biden have been debunked.*]

STEPHEN. Right. I understand. There are people who suffer from Trump derangement syndrome. If Trump said that story had been debunked, would you believe him? It's probably totally false.

MARC. [*Attaches an AP report.*] Giuliani associates Lev Parnas and Igor Fruman planned to steer lucrative contracts from a Ukrainian gas deal to Trump allies.

STEPHEN. Sounds like a real scoop. Someone planned to do something, which I assume means they did not do it, for unnamed Trump "allies."

October 7, 2019

MARC. I understand that Russia didn't actually hack the DNC server, as Trump publicly requested. The DNC hacked their own server, causing the release of damaging information on their candidate only so that if they were to lose the election, they could say that Russia did the hacking and impugn Trump and cause his impeachment. Do I have that right?

WITHDRAWAL OF TROOPS FROM NORTHERN SYRIA

MARC. Do you still think Putin isn't calling the shots?

MARC. Here comes my screaming voice: Wake up!

STEPHEN. I have no idea what you are talking about.

MARC. Trump ordered the military out of northern Syria to allow Turkey to move in against the Kurds.

STEPHEN. I think we should support the Kurds. However, I would need to know more about this decision. I'm glad you're a neutral arbiter in all matters Trump. Based on the nothing that you know, you conclude that Putin is calling the shots. Amazing.

MARC. Anything that helps Putin has me suspicious. It's not just Marc who feels this way. And the theory I alluded to above—that Trump is starting to claim the DNC hacked their own sever, exonerating Putin—has me rightfully suspicious.

STEPHEN. That's because you're delusional. US policy should be based on the best interests of the United States. As bad a deal as the Iran deal was, Obama did it because he foolishly believed it to be in our best interest, not because it helped the Iranians. The DNC server is a mystery. There is no satisfactory explanation for the FBI's failure to take control of it.

STEPHEN. Based on the *Jerusalem Post* article, Trump is pulling out of Syria because he does not believe the US mission should be extended beyond the removal of ISIS. I do not agree, but this is exactly what he ran on. There is a case to be made that the US presence has not made things better and that it costs American lives.

MARC. I'm somewhat isolationist myself, but when he acts unilaterally against Congress and against Barry, you have to wonder.

STEPHEN. He is the commander in chief. It is his decision.

MARC. Nah-ah-ah.

STEPHEN. Trump's not the commander in chief?

MARC. It wasn't his decision.

STEPHEN. Why not? Was the Constitution amended?

MARC. It was Putin's decision.

STEPHEN. You do realize that Trump did not collude with Russia, notwithstanding the abusive effort to prove that he did? Based on your reasoning, Obama clearly was an Iranian stooge. We need all of his emails and transcripts.

BACK TO UKRAINE AND IMPEACHMENT

MARC. He colluded with Ukraine! It's a simple fact. Trump's invocation of the name Biden was only because of Biden's status as his opponent. Period.

STEPHEN. How did he do that? Please explain. So you can't obtain information from foreign sources on your opponent? Isn't that what the Obama administration did to Trump? Oh, I forgot—they had Russian disinformation. All Trump had was credible evidence of wrongdoing. I guess if the information Trump had on Biden had come from Christopher Steele, you would agree that his request that the Ukrainians investigate was entirely appropriate.

MARC. I don't know if Obama did it, but if he did, both he and Trump broke the law. FEC law. I didn't write it. So I guess they both should be impeached!

STEPHEN. No. It's not a violation of election laws. The DOJ already has ruled on that. You're comment about impeaching Obama is funny. Apparently, you believe that Democrats should not be held accountable for their conduct after they are out of office or while they are running for office. When is it okay to investigate misconduct by Democrats?

MARC. The DOJ? Ha!

MARC. When they have a president.

STEPHEN. You must be thinking of the Obama DOJ. Nevertheless, the idea that Trump committed a campaign finance violation only sounds plausible if you are suffering from Trump derangement syndrome.

MARC. Trump derangement syndrome deranges the crazy person into a cogent thinker.

October 8, 2019

STEPHEN. The Democrats want the leaker whom they call a whistleblower to testify from an undisclosed location and to conceal his identity. If that doesn't convince you that this is a farce, nothing will.

MARC. Uh, they don't want him to get killed after Trump's implication of "what they used to do in the old days to traitors." You have devolved into "You don't tell on people."

MARC. Sondland was supposed to testify. At the last minute, he was pulled back, and now Republicans are saying, "Too bad he didn't speak, because it would have exonerated Trump." They are also saying impeachment is not fair because an election is coming. Ha!

MORE DISCUSSIONS ON TURKEY AND THE KURDS

October 9, 2019

Marc. Turkey has been determined to be one of the largest customers, if not the largest customer, of Trump hotels, and Trump has a property in Turkey. Any concern that this is a conflict of interest on his pro-Turkey decision several days ago?

Marc. In Trump's explanation of why he turned his back on Kurds, he said they didn't help us in Normandy! Normandy! What a moron! And he didn't care that ISIS prisoners would be let free, because they would only be on the lam in Europe! How can you, Steve? Really?

Stephen. I get it. Trump makes a decision, which, by the way, is the fulfillment of a campaign promise, on an issue you know nothing about, and because the people who criticize everything Trump does criticize it, you're convinced it's because he owns hotels in Turkey. That's compelling. Right out of a *Scooby-Doo* plot. It's also interesting that you withhold judgment on Biden, whose son got paid millions for doing nothing, but immediately conclude that it's suspicious that Turkish officials use hotels that are open for all guests. You would have been better off atoning for sins today.

Marc. Lots more is at stake when it's the current president of the United States, who is so easily fooled or influenced.

Marc. I knew nothing about Turkey and Trump. Then I read facts, which I shared with you. The same way you learn facts.

Stephen. You have no idea what you're talking about. No, you know nothing about the issue. You shared irrelevant facts. What are the US troops doing in Syria? How long should our troops stay there, and for what purpose? Should we create an independent Kurdish state in Syria? In Turkey? Iraq? What's your strategy? Trump does not believe the US has any interest in having ground troops in Syria. Why is he wrong?

MARC. He is wrong to give Erdogan, another strongman autocrat, what he wants. What's so hard? Erdogan called him, and he changed the policy without consulting anyone! Is that good? It's consistent with my whole issue with Trump. You like that he makes spontaneous decisions, but do you really think he is informed?

STEPHEN. Does it bother you that you have no idea what you're talking about? Your comments have as much validity as my suggestions on an orthopedic plan would have. I can read an article in an orthopedic publication too.

MARC. Erdogan wanted the Kurds to be vulnerable so he could expand into northern Syria. Trump is allowing that. Is this wrong? Also, Trump has business interests in Turkey that could obviously be a factor in what his own party has implied was a rogue decision. Am I incorrect in these contentions?

STEPHEN. You have not answered my questions regarding the substance of Trump's decision. (1) It is consistent with his campaign promises, and (2) he does not see how it is in the United States' interest to keep troops in Syria. Although I have concerns about the decision to pull out—because I respect many of the critics—I believe Trump has put a critical question front and center about US military commitments. Frankly, I don't believe there is a good answer to the questions "Why are US ground troops in Syria, and when should they be removed?" It cannot be that we will stay there indefinitely simply to protect the Kurds.

October 10, 2019

MARC. I confess to knowing only, but importantly, that the Kurds fought ISIS on our behalf and hold all these prisoners. How can releasing those prisoners be a good thing? And to completely ignore the possibility that Trump is conflicting US interests with personal business isn't wise. If somehow he is just misunderstood and really a brilliant and altruistic fellow, you are correct and have always been so. If he really is as I and many others describe, you are not correct.

STEPHEN. There is absolutely no evidence or reason to believe Trump has ulterior motives. It is a fact that he owns real estate—hotels and resorts. It also likely is a fact that Turkish officials use those hotels. The leap to speculate that Trump made a decision regarding US troops in Syria because of it simply is baseless.

MARC. To assume he has ulterior motives without evidence is unfair. You are correct. But to be wary and investigate, given the fact that there has been no explanation for this move from Republican senators, isn't wrong either. Once again, I've given a measured, intelligent response, unlike your reflexive defenses.

STEPHEN. No. The president (or any other citizen) should not be investigated unless there is probable cause (such as Biden bragging that he got Ukraine's chief prosecutor fired or, possibly, Hunter Biden being paid millions of dollars for a no-show job) that a crime has been committed. It is not a crime that Trump owns hotels or that officials of foreign governments stay at those hotels. This is the crux of the problem. The Democrats want to keep Trump under permanent investigation for nothing and anything. It is an abuse of power and corrupt. The result will be Trump's reelection.

MARC. [*Attaches an opinion that Trump's abandonment of the Kurds demonstrates he cannot be counted on to support Israel.*]

STEPHEN. That's someone's opinion. I think it's ridiculous. It ignores the questions that I asked you. Why are we in Syria, and for what purpose? The statement is ridiculous for several reasons: Israel has never requested that US troops fight for it. Israel picks up the laboring oar for the United States. Israel has both military and intelligence capabilities that support the United States. The bottom line is that Israel and the Kurds and Israel and Syria are completely different situations that have different implications for the United States.

BACK TO UKRAINE AND IMPEACHMENT

MARC. I just got an email from Adam Schiff. I concur with you that the mantra of "The president is profiting off the presidency" is too simplistic, maybe not true, and hard to prove if it is. What *is* at hand is that there is direct and circumstantial evidence that Trump leveraged aid for political purposes on Biden (don't deny this; even his aides and supporters are giving up the BS about "ending corruption").

STEPHEN. There is no evidence of that. There is speculation. If there was evidence of it, the Democrats would not be lying about the actual transcript, as Schiff disgracefully did on the floor of the House. The actual transcript says nothing about aid, and Kurt Volker reportedly testified that the Ukrainians did not even know the aid was being held up.

MARC. How did he disgracefully lie?

STEPHEN. He read an imaginary transcript in which he quoted Trump as saying something like "I'm going to say this seven times: I want you to make up dirt, blah-blah-blah." It must be on YouTube. Needless to say, it was totally made up. Trump didn't say anything like that.

MARC. Do you understand that it is illegal to have donations from foreign nationals to a campaign?

MARC. Trump is so effed! As is your reputation as an astute political voice and impeccable judge of character!

STEPHEN. The facts don't matter to you. You simply want to believe that Trump did something wrong. All you need is an accusation. The validity of the accusation doesn't matter. You're not fair. Just admit you want Trump out no matter the cost.

MARC. Fiona Hill, Trump's Russia expert, is going to testify next week that Giuliani and Sondland were running a shadow government executing Trump's issues. Rudy may flip. And the two guys who were arrested that Trump said he doesn't know were in numerous photos and meetings. Hey, this is where perception is reality. There's just too much crap here, and it smells to America. They don't want him, and Republicans' silence at this point is deafening.

STEPHEN. Now for the real news. There is a report that the whistleblower worked for Biden when he was vice president.

MARC. So what? The whistleblower might have been biased, but his information was corroborated by the transcript and others, Bolton likely among them.

MARC. Guess who said the whistleblower complaint is about Biden's son? Trump. Think he is biased?

STEPHEN. His information was undermined by the transcript. The evidence about Biden's son is a matter of public record. It doesn't come from Trump.

MARC. Who was talking about Biden and his job? And big deal! He got paid for doing nothing because his dad was the vice president. Ivanka Trump has the same perk. What do you mean his information was undermined by the transcript? Several people heard Trump's call and reported it. That's coming out now, and they put the transcript in a deep secret server to block it because it was so inappropriate. That is the fact.

STEPHEN. Also, the whistleblower's ties to Biden matter. This is a setup. A failed setup.

MARC. A setup? Trump being an idiot and holding up the aid unless Ukraine gave him information on Biden? How was he set up?

STEPHEN. The transcript confirmed there was no quid pro quo. It confirms Trump did not ask for a favor with respect to Biden. It confirms Trump did not repeatedly raise the topic of Biden. You can believe whatever the Democrats tell you to believe, but that doesn't make it true.

MARC. It did not establish that.

MARC. "I need a favor, though."

MARC. He didn't have to ask repeatedly. He brought Biden up and the stupid CrowdStrike BS.

STEPHEN. Of course it establishes that. He used the word *favor* with respect to CrowdStrike, not Biden. The whistleblower reported that he repeatedly brought up Biden. That did not happen. Why is CrowdStrike BS? Like most comments you make, you make it without any knowledge. Open your eyes.

MARC. As for today, only Trump's lawyer is involved with Russians pumping money into Republican campaigns against the law. You know what? Regardless of what's illegal or what's proven, people are going to dump Trump.

MARC. Okay, so the whistleblower said "repeatedly," and it wasn't repeatedly. The whistleblower report isn't the evidence.

STEPHEN. Trump raised $125 million last quarter, more than twice all the Dems combined. That's real. Regarding the whistleblower, you just made my point. The whistleblower had no knowledge of anything. He didn't report anything. He worked with the Democrats to make false charges against Trump. Thankfully, it will ensure Trump's reelection.

MORE ON THE MIDDLE EAST

October 11, 2019

MARC. [*Attaches report on three thousand troops being stationed in Saudi Arabia.*]

MARC. Fulfilling a campaign promise?

STEPHEN. Is there a war in Saudi Arabia?

MARC. He claims to want fewer troops overseas, period.

STEPHEN. He wants to end the US involvement in ongoing wars. He noted yesterday that US troops in Syria and Afghanistan are not actually fighting. They are policing civil wars. He is against policing at the cost of American lives. Of course, this does not mean US troops should never be stationed overseas. If you would take even ten seconds to think, you might recognize that there are reasons for Trump's actions other than your default that Trump is a liar.

MARC. Oh, I see. Troops overseas are bad for wars and okay for presence—got it. I'll apply that formula to make sense of his moves for the next two months, until President Pence is making the calls.

MARC. I know the reason: to help Saudi Arabia. What a conflict of interest.

STEPHEN. I'm glad you're being so thoughtful. What a rational analysis.

October 13, 2019

MARC. I didn't write this but found it. A new Trumpist talking point: the only way to stop Turkey's massacre of Kurds is to go to war against Turkey. But Turkey never believed that; that's why they asked Trump's permission to invade. All he had to do was say no. He said yes. Why? All the plausible answers are corrupt.

STEPHEN. Why don't you answer the only real questions? Why are we in Syria, and how long should we keep our troops there? As I have told you, Trump, unlike the Clintons or Biden, is losing a lot of money by being in politics. How is Trump benefiting?

MARC. Remember when you said you don't agree with it? Stick to that instead of being an apologist.

STEPHEN. I don't agree. However, I recognize that Trump has a valid point. I also have not heard a good explanation of the strategy. Also, there is an article by Christine Rosen that rebuts the argument that Trump has abandoned the Kurds. I note that you don't have any answers.

MARC. I have an answer. This wasn't his initiative. He was asked, and he gave the okay. The move is not really in our interests, but he has a personal relationship with Erdogan.

STEPHEN. No, that's not an answer. That's ignorance. You have no idea why, but you know it's not in our interest. If Trump is for it, you're against it. Brilliant analysis.

MARC. All but five of the fifty-plus *Republican* senators are against it. Good enough reason?

STEPHEN. Vote for his opponent in the 2020 election. I'm sure the Democratic candidate will be as strong as Obama was.

MARC. The underlying aspect of all my protests is that I am convinced Trump, perhaps unbeknownst to even his closest advisers, is being blackmailed. It's not impossible and not even ridiculous. He has singlehandedly changed the course of our foreign policy to one that cozies up to dictators and pseudo-dictators.

MARC. Actually, to show I can make the case both ways, here is my argument for Trump's decision. Let me know if you think it's intelligent. Turkey has been fighting with the Kurds for many years—for centuries. It's like some people go to lunch. That's what they do: they fight with the Kurds. It's time for to us leave.

MARC. [*Attaches a tweet by Dan Crenshaw criticizing the withdrawal from Syria.*]

MARC. Dan Crenshaw is a Republican congressman and former vet who knows a hell of a lot more than you about this.

STEPHEN. Okay. He's not the president. Roosevelt agreed to support Lend-Lease against the opposition of his advisers, who thought that the United Kingdom would be occupied and that the Nazis would capture our equipment. Who was right? Bush supported the surge against almost universal opposition. Who was right? If you think Trump is wrong, vote for someone you think would do better. Unfortunately, there is no one.

OCTOBER 14, 2019

MARC. Here is a simple college logic problem. Trump assures everyone that Turkey won't do X, and if they do, there will be major sanctions. One week later, Trump advocates major sanctions. (1) Can we infer that Turkey did what Trump said they wouldn't do? (2) Was Trump wrong in his assumption that Turkey wouldn't do X because of the threat of sanctions?

STEPHEN. Trump does not believe US troops should police conflicts like the one between the Turks and the Kurds. The conflict predates US troops and likely will continue after US troops leave, even if they were to be pulled out in the future. Trump further believes that the parties to the conflict need to resolve it and that we can't resolve it for them. Finally, he believes we will spend hundreds of billions of dollars and will get no benefit. These are strong arguments. The critics of Trump's decision believe that by pulling out, we are putting the victory over ISIS at risk and harming our credibility—serious concerns. I believe Obama pulled out of Iraq too quickly, which resulted in the emergence of ISIS. I note that we made a much bigger commitment in Iraq and had much more ability to shape events. The Iraqis even wanted us to stay but on negotiated terms. That's why I tend to support keeping our troops there. But there needs to be an endgame. We cannot spend billions without limit with no goal. Regarding your question, both Trump and the Turks may have miscalculated. Trump may not have anticipated the opposition from supporters like Lindsey Graham, and the Turks may have assumed that with Trump's decision to pull out, the United States would not respond. The key question is not whether Trump was wrong but how he adjusts. Many decisions do not go as planned. A good leader can make the necessary policy changes.

MARC. Okay, we shall see. I happen not to disagree with a more isolationist view.

MARC. [*Attaches a tweet from Adam Kinzinger criticizing Trump for the Syria withdrawal.*] Kinzinger is a Republican and a vet. Learn something from him.

STEPHEN. Okay, that's his view. He doesn't address the larger questions. What are we going to do in Syria, and for how long? By the way, I do not know whether Kinzinger has expertise and knowledge of the facts on the ground or just has a relatively uninformed opinion. Even if Kinzinger ultimately has the better argument, there are military people who agree with Trump. What does that prove? You get excited whenever anyone criticizes Trump. That's all you need to know.

MARC. When it is a nonpartisan, correct!

STEPHEN. Think for yourself. Also, accept that the wisdom of a decision cannot be determined by adding up the number of people who agree and the number who disagree. Leaders don't become leaders by following conventional wisdom.

BACK TO UKRAINE AND IMPEACHMENT

MARC. Trump's own lawyer is so filthy with Ukraine dirt that you are going to have to find a new distraction other than "corrupt Hunter Biden." Rudy was funneling money from his "security firm" into a Trump super PAC. Oh, and Trump's kids sure don't want the scrutiny that is on the precipice of being unleashed. Maybe just go back to "They are framing Rudy!" None of the evidence is true! You don't have the whistleblower anymore either—everything he said was true.

STEPHEN. Okay, I don't know what you're talking about. However, I know that the whistleblower was wrong about every key detail about the call. I read the transcript. I know the call was not remarkable. Trump didn't do anything improper. I also know that the whistleblower worked with Biden when Biden was vice president. I know he worked with Schiff's staff prior to making the complaint. I know that Schiff does not want him to give testimony. I know that the second whistleblower seemingly has disappeared. This impeachment inquiry is a setup. It's blowing up in the Democrats' faces. I'm not worried about Rudy. Investigating credible allegations that Biden abused his office is not "Ukraine dirt." It is official misconduct. Passing off Russian disinformation as intelligence is dirt.

STEPHEN. In addition, the Democrats' impeachment inquiry is a kangaroo court. Why? Open your eyes.

MARC. The whistleblower could be wrong about all the details, and it would be irrelevant because the details are revealed now with surrounding transcripts and texts.

STEPHEN. That's right, and the transcript establishes that there was nothing improper. This has been confirmed by the Ukrainians. Please enlighten me on what Trump said during the call that forms the basis for an impeachment inquiry.

MARC. The call is part of the evidence, combined with facts before and after it.

STEPHEN. What facts? More importantly, why is Trump being investigated? The call, which was leaked illegally, offers no basis for an investigation. It's a setup.

MARC. Holding back the aid—don't bother with the BS reason.

STEPHEN. You're not serious, are you? The president can be investigated because he delayed the release of aid? Should that standard apply to you? There is no evidence of any wrongdoing and no basis for an investigation. The only ones who threatened Ukraine were Joe Biden and Democratic senators.

MORE DISCUSSIONS ON TURKEY

October 15, 2019

Stephen. I am not a fan of Erdogan. He is an Islamist and an anti-Semite. I do not trust him. Nevertheless, it is important to understand his point of view. "Syria's refugee flows, violence and instability have pushed us to the limit of our tolerance," writes Turkish President Erdogan.

Stephen. https://www.wsj.com/articles/turkey-is-stepping-up-where-others-fail-to-act-.

Marc. Trump shouldn't be doing anything that an anti-Semite asks. Fortunately, we won't have to worry about that for too much longer; he is done. He probably will be impeached by Senate in a few months.

Stephen. Trump will be done in 2025.

Stephen. https://www.nationalreview.com/2019/10/turkey-and-the-kurds-its-more-complicated-than-you-think.

Stephen. This is a good article on the actual situation in Syria. If you're interested in having a deeper understanding that goes beyond accusing Trump of incompetence or corruption, you should read it.

BACK TO UKRAINE AND IMPEACHMENT

MARC. John Bolton, respected by many Republican senators, said Rudy was involved in illegal activity, and that will be linked to Trump. Trump is done!

STEPHEN. Right. What exactly did he say? What did he actually know? You probably don't know. So what? Bolton said something bad about Rudy. How many times has Trump been done, according to you?

MARC. You are fighting an uphill battle. Just come to grips with the most likely scenario based on all the testimony and text messages, which is that Caesar Trump let power go to his head and tried to shake down Ukraine. Possible?

MARC. They asked Lindsey Graham today about Rudy not honoring the subpoena (in 1998, he said it was impeachable to ignore one). He brusquely said, "Nothing has changed." Republican senators like the rule of law!

STEPHEN. In fiction, anything is possible. I'm glad the Democrats' decision to question witnesses in private and leak select comments out of context can't fool someone as perceptive as you.

STEPHEN. Also, not every situation is analogous. For example, in 1998, the House voted to hold an impeachment inquiry and afforded the Democrats and President Clinton due process. Not these clowns.

MARC. I see you are advocating for transparency. Ah. When Trump shows his taxes, we can talk!

STEPHEN. That's relevant. If it's important to you to see a candidate's tax returns, only vote for candidates who release them.

October 16, 2019

Marc. Good thing Trump "wants to get out of the Middle East." I'm sure he will be a real loyal backer of Israel if and when needed. I mean, it's not like he ever turns his back on a supposed ally.

Stephen. Israel doesn't need and has never requested US troops to fight its battles. Obama turned his back on Israel in the United Nations. Try to maintain contact with reality.

Marc. [*Attaches a copy of Trump's letter to Erdogan.*] I apologize for telling you repeatedly that Trump is a moron. I was wrong. He is brilliant. This was a very impressive letter he sent Turkey. And by the way, it's the real letter.

Stephen. What's wrong with the letter? Did he forget to use the magic word? Or is it not legalistic enough for you?

Marc. Aside from being the work of a sixth grader, it was supposed to impact Turkey?

Marc. "I'll call you later"?

Stephen. Isn't that what you say when you're going to call someone? I write a lot. I always try to make my points as simply and clearly as possible. Trump probably has someone draft a letter for him, which he probably edited. It didn't sound like a sixth grader to me. He was making a very clear point.

October 17, 2019

Marc. [*Attaches a story on Sondland testifying that he was disappointed Rudy Giuliani was involved in Ukraine.*] Is this the whistleblower's fault? Trump is done!

STEPHEN. You're foolish. The Democrats are investigating a nonevent and leaking select statements to make it seem like Trump did something wrong. Trump is president, not Gordon Sondland. His opinion may be worth considering, but it's his opinion. However, without having access to his full testimony, the leaked snippets are likely very misleading. There certainly is much more (however irrelevant) being discussed. If it makes you happy that Adam Schiff thinks Trump is a bad guy and wants to impeach him for any reason or no reason, enjoy the inquiry. Like every other attempt to subvert the 2016 election (and the 2020 election), it will fail spectacularly. Until it does, have fun.

MARC. [*Attaches a report on Mick Mulvaney's press conference.*] Every single time Trump or his team is accused of something, they deny it and eventually are forced to say, "Okay, yeah, we did it. So what?"

MARC. I guess there *was* a quid pro quo.

MARC. Ha!

STEPHEN. We are getting selected leaks and do not know if there was a quid pro quo. The aid was released. I also note that the Democrats threatened Ukraine unless they cooperated with Mueller. Same thing?

MARC. He is finished. You only admit something like that when you know you've been beaten.

MARC. His requesting Giuliani to do this work secretly is the consciousness of guilt you need.

STEPHEN. Keep dreaming. By the way, Giuliani's work was anything but secret. Trump asked everyone to work with him.

MARC. We shall see.

STEPHEN. Here's a question for you: If any prior president had requested that a foreign leader investigate that country's involvement in interference in the prior presidential election, would there have been an impeachment inquiry? You know the answer.

Marc. Easy answer. If the Republicans controlled the House and the president was a Democrat, absolutely.

Stephen. Never. This would never happen. Otherwise, Obama would have been subject to impeachment for various matters.

Marc. The reason he wasn't was because there was nothing impeachable. They could only muster up garbage on Benghazi.

Stephen. You're a caricature. Imagine if Trump sent his national security adviser to go to Sunday talk shows to tell a bald-faced lie.

Stephen. Imagine what would have happened if Trump had publicly stated that his secretary of state did nothing wrong by having a private server that he knew she had?

Marc. And what was the result of the investigation?

HOSTING THE G7 AT THE DORAL

October 20, 2019

Marc. Good morning! As always, you continue to be right about President Trump's deft touch with decisions and leadership, undaunted by his use of phrases like "cleaning out" the ethnic minority in Syria with the ultimate solution and, of course, his choosing his own club to enrich himself. His own chief of staff said he knew he would face criticism for the decision, but he did so anyway and then reversed, citing criticism.

Stephen. It's very easy to criticize Trump when you're starting point is that everything Trump does is wrong. All you need to know is that Trump did something. The Doral is a great example. The United States will pay more to host the event somewhere else. What an achievement.

Marc. Oh, so you think Doral was the right call?

Stephen. I have no problem with it. It's a resort that has the necessary facilities. The government would have paid the cost. A great deal.

Marc. Paid the cost to him, which, as you know, is against the law.

Stephen. It's not against the law or the Constitution. It's not a gift or a bribe. It's a business transaction that would have benefited the US Treasury. Opposing it is evidence of Trump derangement syndrome.

October 21, 2019

Marc. Stephen Barry holds the president in high regard.

STEPHEN. What a joke. The party that defends Hunter Biden accuses Trump of scoffing at the emoluments clause. In Trump's case, the government is entering into a beneficial transaction at Trump's expense. In the other, it is a real emolument. Biden's family was making millions off Biden's office. You may say, "Burisma is not the Ukrainian government." I would say the emoluments clause does not apply to ordinary business transactions. Marc doesn't know or care what is right or wrong.

MARC. Biden should have been impeached! I agree totally.

MARC. Biden was guilty of violating the clause! But he can't be impeached at this time. But Trump can! I believe in the Constitution!

MARC. I agree totally with you. I understand your outrage at Biden for breaking the emoluments clause.

STEPHEN. You miss the point. Biden did something dishonest; Trump did not. However, you are willing to accept the Democrats' cockamamie argument that Trump would be violating the Constitution.

MARC. You didn't write the Constitution, nor did I. It says the president cannot receive something of value while in office. Am I wrong? You even defended Manafort's crimes by saying, "They wouldn't have found them if they weren't looking." *You* are the selective one and blind not to see what a money-hungry criminal Trump is. What anyone sees is that he is a self-centered ass.

STEPHEN. I think for myself. You agree with any allegation against Trump. There is constitutional scholarship that the emoluments clause is not intended to cover ordinary business transactions, which makes perfect sense.

MARC. There is constitutional scholarship that says he is violating the clause. By the way, I don't care about emoluments; I care about holding up aid for an investigation, which Mick Mulvaney confirmed along with the texts. The DOJ knows, or no investigation into Ukraine.

THE ELECTION

MARC. Clinton was cleared of serious breaches!

STEPHEN. You don't know what you're talking about. This impeachment is a farce. The Democrats are conducting it in secret because if they did it in public, it would be dead. Nevertheless, they may never even bring it to a vote, but I hope they do. Once they vote on it, they will lose control of the process. Then the fun will begin. The farce will be fully exposed.

MARC. Trump threatened to go to war against Turkey after stating we shouldn't be in Turkey.

STEPHEN. Obama and Biden gave billions of dollars to the Iranians. Biden also is corrupt. Prove your decency. Vote for Biden.

MARC. I'm leaning toward voting for a woman because women are a hell of a lot more decent and caring than men.

STEPHEN. Vote for Warren, a serial liar.

MARC. Yeah, a rotten person who just wants poor people to have a little easier time. I think rich people should just worry about staying rich.

STEPHEN. If Warren becomes president, the poor will have a terrible time. Recession or depression won't help them. What do you think of young people who support Bernie Sanders because they don't want to repay their student loans?

MARC. I like Buttigieg!

MARC. Is he too stupid for you? Or maybe too selfish?

STEPHEN. I don't know what you mean.

MARC. Pete Buttigieg.

STEPHEN. What do you mean by too stupid and too selfish?

MARC. You will probably tell me that he is stupid and selfish. (He's a genius and went into the military.)

STEPHEN. He hasn't impressed me.

IMPEACHMENT DISCUSSIONS RESUME

OCTOBER 22, 2019

MARC. You'll soon have a new president to defend or attack. This was the sworn testimony of Ambassador Bill Taylor. Unless you want to accuse him of lying too.

MARC. [*Attaches article on Taylor's testimony, in which he says Sondland told him the president wanted Zelensky to publicly announce investigations.*]

STEPHEN. Enjoy it now. I'll remind you when Trump is reelected.

MARC. And in thirty years when we are at a group function and you try to order pizza with a specific topping, I'll remind you to ignore that choice because you were a defender of Donald Trump.

STEPHEN. I'm eating dinner. If I have time, I'll explain to you the lack of relevance.

MARC. Put the waiter on the phone now!

STEPHEN. Very funny.

OCTOBER 23, 2019

MARC. Nobody is going to question Taylor, who has impeccable credentials. His testimony added more that Sondland had, unintentionally or intentionally, left out. He had a conversation with Sondland, documented with impeccable notes, regarding what specifically the Ukrainians needed to do to receive the congressionally approved funds. So what is the strategy you will choose this morning from your daily email of talking points? (1) Taylor is part of the smear, or (2) there's nothing wrong with Trump demanding reciprocation for the aid in order to "root out corruption" in the interest of only our country.

MARC. If you want to go with "He fucked up and made a mistake, but it's not an impeachable offense," Judge Lieberman will allow it! I bet Republicans will make him apologize like Reagan did.

STEPHEN. There is nothing that even should rise to the level of a possible impeachable offense. Furthermore, Taylor's testimony is hearsay as to whether or not there was a quid pro quo. It also is undercut by Sondland, who confirmed to him that there was no quid pro quo. Taylor also confirmed that the Ukrainians did not know aid was being held up. More importantly, Taylor may not agree with how Trump conducts foreign policy or whether or not Giuliani should be involved, but it is not his business. Trump is the president, not Taylor or his State Department colleagues.

MARC. Sondland didn't confirm that. He wrote a line of text after calling Trump for advice and after texts and conversations delineating why the aid was being held up. It's a stupid thing for you to be stubborn about. We all know what happened, and Mick Mulvaney said it happens all the time!

STEPHEN. I'm not being stubborn. I have no doubt Trump wanted the Ukrainians to cooperate with the Barr investigation and to reopen the Burisma-Biden investigation. I also know there was no quid pro quo. It was not necessary. Both requests are totally legitimate. If the Ukrainians do not cooperate, Trump will have every right in the future to take into account Ukraine's cooperation or lack thereof when deciding whether to support the current Ukrainian government. However, at present, the aid was released. The real story of inappropriate interference by foreign governments will be the use of foreign disinformation against Trump by Obama and the Clinton campaign and the use of foreign intelligence services by Obama to spy on Trump. The difference between 2016 and today is that Trump has legitimate reasons to investigate both Ukraine's role in 2016 and the Burisma-Biden situation. The Democrats had nothing except disinformation.

MARC. The real story is that Trump tried to extort Ukraine to help him gain information that could be useful. Everyone knows this, except for the 35 percent of the country who are in the Trump caucus (95 percent of whom are ignorant white Christian men).

STEPHEN. Trump didn't do anything improper. Your belief that this nonissue is extortion (it can't be) or otherwise impeachable is evidence of your ignorance about the law and the conduct of foreign policy. Before Trump, Congress never would have considered impeachment over this matter. The real issue is the constant bureaucratic spying on Trump. That should be investigated. Regardless, if Trump was pulled over for speeding but did not get a ticket, you would support Democratic calls for impeachment.

MARC. How did you do in law school oral arguments? You wrote above that (1) he didn't do anything improper but then that (2) Congress wouldn't have considered impeachment over this matter before Trump. Now, since you probably don't see the error in your logic, I'll point it out. If he did nothing improper, you wouldn't have to write the following sentence. Sentence two implies that he did something wrong but that it would never have been mentioned had it not been for Trump. Almost all the *Republican* senators have actually stated, or tacitly stated in their lack of defense, that what he did was wrong!

STEPHEN. Thank you for your scintillating logic. However, did it occur to you, Dr. Supergenius, that no Congress would have considered impeachment because it is so obviously not improper?

MARC. Stephen Barry did not mug that woman, and furthermore, the police would never have found him guilty of the mugging. Does your law school have an honorary law degree they can give me?

STEPHEN. That's logical. As I did not mug the woman, it is logical that I would not be found guilty. By the way, the police don't make findings of guilt.

October 24, 2019

MARC. You never mention that Ukraine was, is, and should be a US ally! Yet Trump would hold back aid because of an instance of Ukrainian corruption wherein they gave a nothing job and payment to Hunter Biden? That's his reason to hold up aid needed to save lives and fight off Russian aggression? Or is it more likely that someone who has demonstrated himself over three years to be petty and vindictive was myopic and selfish about getting personally helpful dirt on Biden?

STEPHEN. Your knowledge of world events covers only the events that the Democrats say are important. You have no knowledge of context. My guess is that there are no Ukrainians who would prefer Obama to Trump. During Obama's presidency, the Russians annexed Crimea and invaded Eastern Ukraine. Obama refused military aid, which Trump agreed to provide. Furthermore, Ukraine, during Obama's presidency, interfered in the 2016 election to help Hillary (not something for an ally to be proud of). Finally, Biden, who was supposedly leading the charge to help Ukraine eradicate corruption, was using Ukraine to enrich his family. I recognize that it is more satisfying to you to find ways to accuse Trump of wrongdoing than to actually know what you're talking about, but seek the truth, and it shall set you free!

MARC. Uh, Congress passed (which they don't usually do) the aid to Ukraine. Stop right there for a second. Anything wrong with that? Why would they aid Ukraine? Is that a Democratic talking point?

MARC. Trump unilaterally blocked the aid. It's not in dispute. His reasoning for it is hollow and ridiculous, and you know it but just cannot admit. You can't do it. You say, "He didn't like the corruption over there."

The only problem is that he cited only Biden as evidence of corruption, along with a crazy theory that would exonerate Russia from guilt in hacking the DNC server.

STEPHEN. He is the president and is in charge of foreign policy. He did not block aid. The aid was released. By the way, he cited interference in the 2016 election and CrowdStrike. Ukraine's interference in 2016 was the subject of a January 2017 Politico article (Politico is on the left) and is being investigated by Barr as part of the investigation into the truly corrupt origins of the Russia probe. Trump asked for Ukraine to cooperate with Barr, which they are obligated to do by treaty.

MARC. He blocked the aid, clearly. It was released eventually—I believe after reports of the whistleblower. He is screwed.

TRUMP-HATING REPUBLICAN

MARC. I'm a Trump-hating Republican.

STEPHEN. I think you mean a truth-hating Republican or a fairness-hating Republican. Republicans made the mistake of nominating a candidate you don't like, and the electorate elected that candidate. Since Trump was elected without your permission, you want him removed from office. Maybe you should produce an ad in which you explain that you hate Trump, and as a result, he should be removed from office. Include a *Brady Bunch*–like warning to America that it should never elect anyone you don't like ever again, and say, "If you do, I'll call him or her names and accuse him of crimes."

OCTOBER 25, 2019

MARC. The strength of my argument and opinion lies in your previous text, which is probably the dumbest thing you have ever written. I wanted Romney in 2012 but didn't seek to remove Obama from office. (You probably did, though there will be no written proof.) I also wanted Dole and Bush Sr. and didn't seek to remove Clinton until he was shown to have lied. So I am an equal-opportunity opponent to liars.

MARC. And I take you back to this: "Trump didn't do anything improper. Before Trump, Congress never would have considered impeachment over this matter." This is damning evidence of the weakness of your argument. If Trump did nothing at all improper, your argument would start and stop with the first sentence. But since you know your contention is shaky at best and wrong at worst, you modify with a tacit "and even if he did" to imply that the action would never be considered for impeachment. Considering him for impeachment over nothing goes unsaid. Lastly, if I believe that Trump is a bad guy, am hoping he is impeached, and can't look at things objectively, does that make me "scum"?

STEPHEN. Trump has been called every name under the sun. He has been the target of a three-year smear campaign based on lies. The efforts to undermine him and to remove him from office are fundamentally dishonest, as evidenced by Schiff's secret impeachment inquiry. So in this context, I'm not upset that Trump used a bad word to describe his critics. When they respect him, I'll reconsider. Did you see the news that the Barr-Durham probe is now a criminal investigation? The efforts to thwart the 2016 election—the real crimes—will be exposed.

MARC. No, they won't, and the same targeting you claim he has been victimized by is now being returned. "It's not right; it's not fair. Oh, did you see the new investigation against *them*?" I wish you could see things as they really are.

STEPHEN. No. This investigation is based on evidence of wrongdoing, not "opposition research" passed off as intelligence. That's why people will go to jail.

MARC. Yeah, you've been saying that.

A PHILOSOPHICAL DISCUSSION

October 26, 2019

Marc. I have a non-Trump question—not rhetorical. How would the world change if individuals were prohibited from being worth more than $100 million? If all innovators, young entrepreneurs and aspiring athletes were told this going in? If Bill Gates had been told this in 1980?

Stephen. I would point you to the Talmud. The goal should be to apply the law and the rules fairly to everyone, rich or poor. You should not take away something that someone acquires fairly. However, the rich should not receive special favors. The government should not give them advantages. I recognize that the world is not perfect and that certain people will be treated differently, either favorably or unfavorably, but I think it would be dangerous to enact a rule that permits the majority to take something away from people they deem should have enough. It would legitimize a bad concept. What if the majority decides that certain disfavored people have had enough health care or education or any other scarce resource? Let's say a political party comes to power who decides Jews should not live.

Marc. What about change?

Stephen. What do you mean?

Marc. I just feel fortunate and don't take things for granted or leave life unexamined. Taxation is always going to be subjective and hasn't been flat in a long time. Those who have more than $100 million being asked to pay more is not the same as being told you have to die because of your religion.

MARC. You are outraged by the Biden story. Do you think that kind of thing goes on all the time with rich, connected people of all political persuasions?

STEPHEN. I think it's a terrible idea based on envy, a mortal sin. It has nothing to do with revenue. It is targeting a small group of people. If it's okay to target one unpopular small group, why not another? I'm outraged by the Biden story for many reasons, including the hypocrisy. The idea that Biden shouldn't be investigated is ridiculous. I'm disgusted by the abuse of power.

MARC. There are reports that Trump's brother benefited from some government contract and that he screwed Amazon. Where does it start and stop for anyone who has influence?

MARC. [*Attaches a criticism of former chief of staff John Kelly as not being "equipped to handle the genius of our great President."*]

MARC. This is the kind of thing you would see in a dictatorship. It's an innocent comment but revelatory as far as I'm concerned.

OCTOBER 27, 2019

STEPHEN. Your position on Trump is clear. You don't like him. It's nothing like Chris Matthews saying he feels a thrill up his leg when he hears Obama speak or dozens of other sycophantic statements. Or it's nothing like Obama saying he was a better speechwriter than his speechwriters, knew more about policy than his policy directors, and was a better political director than his political director.

MARC. On this, perhaps you are right. I can't always be.

Killing of Al-Baghdadi

STEPHEN. I think US troops killed the leader of ISIS last night. Trump is scheduled to make an announcement at 9:00 a.m. We'll see whom he gives credit to.

MARC. He tweeted last night impulsively like a child who couldn't wait until the morning. Just act like a president for once!

STEPHEN. You never will understand his appeal.

MARC. That is an understatement. You would rather have his policies and most decisions delivered in a conventional, respectful, secure, measured fashion, I hope.

MARC. I guess we can just have all forces come back to the United States, true to Trump's promises and strategy! And I guess the intelligence agencies are all corrupt and useless—you know, the ones that located this guy.

STEPHEN. Once again, scintillating analysis based on absolutely no knowledge of the situation.

MARC. By the way, as I watch him—and I'm being serious here—he always has had a genuine reassuring quality that should have long ago been harnessed. I actually don't dislike him. I dislike how he repeatedly acts. This guy on the podium now would have 60 percent approval.

STEPHEN. The difference between Trump and many others is that he does his dirty work directly, not through surrogates.

MARC. Correct. It's just a question of how dirty it is.

October 28, 2019

Marc. Army Colonel Vindman, a Jew who fled the USSR in the 1970s, is the Ukraine expert for the White House who heard the Trump call and reported it. He said that you cannot urge a foreign power to investigate a US citizen and that Ukraine investigating the likely Dem favorite would threaten the bipartisan support Ukraine had at the time. Nobody of intelligence will believe that Trump's insistence on the Biden investigation had to do with national security.

Marc. [*Attaches a report questioning Trump's description of Al-Baghdadi's "whimpering and crying and screaming" when he was captured and killed.*]

Marc. Un-effin'-believable.

Stephen. Nobody seriously believes that Trump's call should be the subject of an impeachment inquiry. There is no chance any other president would have been investigated for asking a foreign government to investigate real events involving corruption and former US officials. As we shall soon find out, the Obama administration worked with foreign governments not to investigate actual events, such as Ukraine's interference in the 2016 election or Biden's role in pressuring Ukraine to fire its top prosecutor, but to provide disinformation to use against Trump. That's "un-effin'-believable." Your concern that Trump might have embellished the circumstances of Al-Baghdadi's death is precious. Maybe you would have preferred Trump report that he died a hero spitting in the eyes of the Great Satan. Then the media could have started a recruitment campaign for his replacement. Anyone who criticizes Trump for his description of Al-Baghdadi's death is a moron.

October 29, 2019

Marc. You already called me scum, so I'll take *moron*!

Stephen. Nevertheless, you are very high-functioning!

BACK TO IMPEACHMENT

MARC. Please resist your innate, reflexive urges and speak out against the nascent attacks against Vindman due to his "former Soviet" status, which is really cloaked anti-Semitism. The significance of what he heard is debatable, but he didn't make anything up.

MARC. A Republican congressman this morning said that he questioned whether Vindman, a decorated US war vet, is loyal to United States less than his homeland and that Vindman seemed "awfully concerned about Ukrainian defense," despite the fact that the United States favors Ukrainian defense against Russia.

STEPHEN. I don't know anything about Vindman. However, I know that his opinion on the propriety of Trump's comments is irrelevant. The fact that his opinion is touted as evidence shows how political this charade is. Do you believe Trump should be impeached based on Vindman's opinion? You probably do.

MARC. I agree on Vindman's opinion not being more than supportive of other evidence.

STEPHEN. It's more than supportive of nothing but other people's opinions.

MARC. He is going to make Sondland change his mind. You should change your argument to say that the quid pro quo is not a problem, not that it never happened.

STEPHEN. I don't think there was a quid pro quo, because that would require a personal benefit to Trump. Asking for Ukraine to investigate Burisma and Biden is not a personal benefit to Trump, even if he would benefit politically. However, I agree that Trump's request that Ukraine look into Biden, however you characterize it, is not a problem.

MARC. [*Attaches a report about Sondland's testimony that there was a quid pro quo.*]

MARC. I think he knows more about this than you. And the reason he changed his mind? It's called fear of perjury.

STEPHEN. I look forward to seeing the full picture. I agree no one should lie to Congress. However, this remains nonsense.

MARC. You can't be selectively indignant. If something is wrong, it's wrong. Both ways.

STEPHEN. I meant that Trump's dealings with Ukraine are normal and within his powers as president. Any other president who did what Trump clearly did—request that the Ukrainians (1) cooperate in the investigation into Ukraine's role in the 2016 election and (2) look into the circumstances of the firing of the prosecutor and Biden's role—would not be the subject of an impeachment inquiry. It would not be an issue at all, and anyone who leaked the president's phone call would be prosecuted. They were both matters of public record. In light of the Obama administration's, Hillary's, and the DNC's use of foreign governments to seek to frame Trump for collusion (which I believe the Barr-Durham investigation will expose), the rationale for this nonsensical impeachment is laughable. The only people who take it seriously are people like you who are simply looking for a pretext to undo the 2016 election. It is not going to work.

MARC. You can say the same thing over and over again, and when Republicans say, as some have already, that what Trump did was wrong, your words will be meaningless. The president does not have the power to hold back money voted on by Congress. The reasons given for the delay—that it was held until corruption was cleared up or because Europe wasn't paying their fair share—were concocted after the fact. My thoughts are shared by hundreds of lawmakers who are as ethical as Republican lawmakers or Trump.

STEPHEN. You never know what you're talking about. Never. At least you're consistent.

MARC. We'll see.

STEPHEN. Presidents hold back money all the time. Presidents hold up foreign aid all the time as leverage. That's simply a fact. In addition, Trump repeatedly expressed that Europe should contribute to Ukraine with respect to the appropriation. However, even if Trump was primarily interested in getting Ukraine to investigate, that's not an impeachable offense or any offense at all.

MARC. How come nothing you write here has been uttered by the White House or defense attorneys?

STEPHEN. Maybe I should go to work at the White House.

MARC. Yes! They need you.

OCTOBER 30, 2019

MARC. [Attaches an opinion by Jonah Goldberg.]

MARC. I guess I am just as crazy as Jonah Goldberg.

STEPHEN. I read the article and disagree. Who apologized to Trump for the Steele dossier and the resulting Mueller probe? No one. That was disinformation. In the case of Trump's phone call, the transcript speaks for itself. Trump asked Ukraine's president to look into the Biden-Burisma situation. Unlike with the Steele dossier, there is real evidence of potential corruption. Why should Trump apologize for raising it?

STEPHEN. By the way, Jonah Goldberg is a Never Trumper.

NOVEMBER 1, 2019

MARC. [In a Yiddish accent] "It's okay; he's good for Israel."

BACK TO IMPEACHMENT AND TRUMP'S INQUISITORS

STEPHEN. It's okay. He's more honest than the clowns investigating him.

MARC. I think Schiff is a really decent person—I entirely disagree. They probably all do hate Trump, just as Clinton and Obama were hated.

STEPHEN. Trump has been subjected to spying, false accusations, leaks, and nonstop efforts to prevent him from doing his job. Impeachment has been a goal from day one. Members of his administration have been hounded in public. None of these things happened to Clinton or Obama, who also were protected by the media.

MARC. Schiff exaggerated one Trump quote, stretching "what we used to do to traitors" into "kill," which was a stupid thing to do. Otherwise, to claim his mendacity exceeds Trump's would be incorrect.

STEPHEN. Schiff repeatedly claimed he had evidence of Trump's collusion with Russia. Schiff read a made-up version of Trump's call with Zelensky in which he claimed Trump said, "I want you to make up dirt on my opponent—lots of it," among other things Trump did not say. Schiff's office worked with the whistleblower prior to the complaint. Schiff's conduct of the inquiry is patently unfair.

MARC. [*Attaches a report regarding the maintenance of the transcript of Trump's call with Zelensky on a secret server and Vindman's testimony that a White House lawyer told him not to tell anyone about the call.*]

MARC. Are you familiar with the concept of consciousness of guilt? If there was no problem with the "perfect" call, then why?

STEPHEN. I don't know, but I know that Vindman testified to the effect that he did not agree with Trump's views on Ukraine and Russia. Taylor gave similar testimony. Vindman and Taylor appear to be very pro-Ukraine and to disagree with Trump's concerns about Ukrainian corruption (which, in 2016, was used against him). They also allegedly want the United States to provide Ukraine military support against Russia (which, ironically, Trump has provided). The crux of this nonsense is that Trump does not need Vindman's or Taylor's approval for his policy decisions.

November 4, 2019

Marc. Please stop saying, "Ukraine got the aid," when defending Trump's extortion.

Stephen. The only extortion that occurred was committed by Biden.

Stephen. There is no question that Trump sought Ukrainian cooperation with the DOJ investigation into the basis for the Trump-Russia investigation. That was totally legitimate. He also raised the Biden-Burisma matter. However, he didn't extort anything.

Marc. Of all the debates we have had, with conjectures and rumors and theories, here is the fact of what happened. It's pretty clear. Trump acted totally true to his form and wanted dirt on Biden. When I say "his form," I'm talking about the person who declared in front of the world that he wanted Russia to dig up dirt on Hillary. He couldn't control himself. And the master plan was that his request of Ukraine in order for them to receive the aid was seeking a twofold benefit: to harm Biden and also to try to make it look as if Ukraine, not Russia, was the country that hacked the DNC. Manafort was a party to this, as well as Giuliani. And Putin was the one who brainwashed Trump against the horrible people of Ukraine.

Stephen. He didn't want dirt on Biden. He asked him to investigate the circumstances around the ending of the Burisma investigation. If that is a problem for Biden, it is because he abused his power for money. Similarly, Trump never asked Russia for dirt on Hillary. He made a sarcastic comment about Hillary's destruction of thirty-three thousand emails that were under subpoena. Hillary's destruction of evidence was the problem, not Trump's reference to it. If Trump has reservations about Ukraine, he is justified. They actually provided dirt to the Democrats in 2016. Nevertheless, Trump has provided Ukraine military aid that Obama refused to provide. How is it possible that you manage not only to get everything wrong but also to get it exactly backward?

MARC. "Russia, if you are listening" was sarcastic? Regarding every asinine thing he says or does, his defenders say he was kidding.

MARC. Now for some conjecture and unsupported rumor. When they find out that Kushner gave the okay to have Khashoggi taken out and then Trump is blackmailed on that knowledge, Trump will be on par with the John Wilkes Booths of history.

STEPHEN. Yes. Hillary destroyed evidence. The sarcasm is that if Hillary wouldn't turn over the emails, maybe the Russians would. Regarding Khashoggi, take your medication.

MARC. [*Attaches an excerpt from an article stating that "Trump used congressionally appropriated aid to Ukraine, as well as the promise of a White House visit, to try to extort Ukraine's president to announce investigations that would benefit Trump politically."*]

STEPHEN. Nonsense. Trump did not extort Ukraine, and neither Ukraine's interference in the 2016 election nor Biden's abuse of his power to protect Burisma and his son's $50,000 monthly payoff is a conspiracy theory.

MARC. Giuliani and his goons took out the ambassador for no reason just to clear away opposition.

STEPHEN. The ambassador serves at the pleasure of the president. He doesn't need a reason to replace an ambassador appointed by his predecessor. Putting in his own person is his prerogative. In fact, every president puts in his own people.

MARC. Pleasure of the president? Come on. He isn't a king.

MARC. We know why he wanted his own person.

STEPHEN. That's the rule. Go back to high school. The president runs the executive branch. He gets to pick his ambassadors. It is sad that you don't know this.

STEPHEN. Read: "Ambassadors of the United States are persons nominated as ambassadors by the President to serve as United States diplomats to individual nations of the world, to international organizations, and as ambassadors-at-large. Their appointment needs to be confirmed by the United States Senate.[1] An ambassador can be appointed during a recess, but he or she can only serve as ambassador until the end of the next session of Congress unless subsequently confirmed.[2] Ambassadors serve "at the pleasure of the President," meaning they can be dismissed at any time. Appointments change regularly for various reasons, such as reassignment or retirement."

MARC. It's sad that you continually defend such a criminal. Once again, I will take Mike Pence as president, and unlike you, who never admits you are wrong about anything in this realm, I do—like being part of a party filled with racists, misogynists, ant-Semites, and, yes, Orthodox Jews (who deny or don't realize they share support for the same person as those who can't stand their guts). If you are now going to tell me that most non-college-educated flyover-state white men are anti-Semites, I will reply yes. The sad part is that even the leaders of your own party are already saying that what Trump did was wrong, but you can never bring yourself to admit it.

MARC. The whistleblower's identity is protected by law. Why should he or she be revealed, and what errors in fact were there in his or her statement?

STEPHEN. I will agree that Trump did something wrong if I see evidence that Trump did something wrong. All I see is an effort to remove Trump based on nonsense. Regarding the whistleblower, he is not actually a whistleblower, so the law does not protect him. He is a leaker making accusations against the president in coordination with Schiff. His complaint alleged that Trump demanded a quid pro quo. That's not true. He accused Trump of repeating his request for information on Biden several times. He did not. There probably is more, but I don't have time to go through it now.

MARC. You don't even say he ever says something wrong when he does so—no evidence required. You say things like "He used a poor choice of words" or "I probably would not have said it."

STEPHEN. I don't think Trump is infallible. However, he is the target of a series of lies—Russian collusion, Ukraine, and other matters—with the goal of forcing him out of office. The efforts to remove him are outrageous violations of our rights. The media supports the attacks on Trump and us. I'm not going to quibble with Trump over nonsense until there is accountability for the efforts to undo the 2016 election.

NOVEMBER 5, 2019

MARC. Sondland, the Trump guy who Trump kept saying proved there was no quid pro quo based on his text, admits now that there was.

MARC. This is the *NY Post*. This is Trump's guy. He changed his testimony.

MARC. And here is the kicker: the condition wasn't that Ukraine investigate; the condition was to simply announce that they were investigating.

MARC. Since you are such a Trumper, I thought you might have evolved into enjoying New Testament scriptures: "Beware of false prophets, who come to you in sheep's clothing, but are inwardly ravenous wolves."

STEPHEN. Your heroes are the false prophets. If the situation in Ukraine was reversed and Trump was Biden, you would be demanding an investigation. By the way, the evidence that Biden ran interference for Burisma is getting stronger. I guess it's okay if Biden makes money off his office. He's sacrificed so much for us.

MARC. Bribery!

MARC. It's an impeachable offense.

MARC. That snake was going to have Ukraine make a press conference and then still deny them the aid, because that's what he does.

STEPHEN. Okay. Trump was bribed? Please explain.

MARC. "If you don't make a public announcement of opening an investigation, you aren't getting the aid."

MARC. [*Attaches a legal definition of bribery: "Proof of bribery requires demonstrating a 'quid pro quo' relationship in which the recipient directly alters behavior in exchange for the gift."*]

MARC. Do I have to out-lawyer you again?

STEPHEN. The Ukrainians bribed Trump to get aid? I thought Trump abused his office by withholding aid. Both are wrong and, in context, laughable, but let's stick with bribery. The Ukrainians offered to investigate corruption committed by Biden (which looks like a real crime) for the release of aid? I'm laughing. If you were in sixth grade, I would give you a high mark for creativity.

MARC. Funny, Trump wanted Ukrainian corruption to end so badly that instead of letting his law enforcement department or Congress handle it, he had to get Rudy to back-channel and pave the way. Or maybe he was put up to this shit by Putin, who told him Ukraine is bad, and he has a vested interest in Ukraine getting screwed.

STEPHEN. Of course it must be Putin.

MARC. No, it's Trump, a buffoon whom Stephen Barry defends and loves.

MARC. Are you proud of that? To be so aligned with him?

STEPHEN. Say, "Hey, Schiff, I've got a great idea: it's bribery," and he'll say, "Lieberman, you're a genius. Bribery it is."

MARC. Career prosecutors who devoted their careers, long before Trump, to taking down criminals—people you would have called criminals before your head went into your ass backward—call it that. People who gave up their chance at the money you and I have. And you probably think Joyce Vance, Glenn Kirschner, and others are vile liars.

STEPHEN. That's great. When is Trump going to be removed? I'll mark it on my calendar.

MARC. (1) When the vote in the Senate happens (they aren't telegraphing their vote) and (2) when they tell him not to seek reelection (because they will vote against him).

STEPHEN. Do you want tickets to Trump's second-term inauguration? I'll see what I can do.

MARC. "You do this for me, and I'll give you this." Bribe!

STEPHEN. Trump never said that, unlike Biden.

MARC. Mob bosses don't say things straight out. If you were on the jury and there were transcripts and testimony from a lackey who said, "He wanted me to kill that guy when he told me that it would be a shame if something happened to him," you would convict. Because you are so outraged about Hunter Biden reaping the usual spoils of the swamp.

STEPHEN. I guess Biden is a bad mob boss. In Trump's case, it's hard to prove a quid pro quo when no one involved knows if there was a quid pro quo. I accept that Trump wanted Ukraine to investigate Biden's criminal conduct. That's the only fact. Good luck, Prosecutor Lieberman.

MARC. Please tell me why Trump would want Ukraine to investigate Biden and hold up millions in aid to make it happen. It's a simple question.

STEPHEN. Because he knows that Biden had the prosecutor fired because the prosecutor was investigating the company paying Biden's son $80,000 a month.

MARC. Do you think he has any special interest in Joe Biden perchance? Please explain how that activity is worth holding back the aid they need to save lives and fight Russia, all the while keeping it secret? Why insist they make a public announcement that they will investigate? I submit to you that rather than a national security issue, it was more about the 2020 election. Crazy? Bonkers? Neither I nor millions of other people think so.

STEPHEN. Trump asked Ukraine to cooperate in the DOJ's investigation into Ukraine's 2016 election interference. That is very important. Biden demanded a quid pro quo. He sold out the United States for money in Ukraine and China. That's worthy of investigation. Could it help Trump? Possibly. However, I don't think Biden is going to be the nominee. He's a terrible candidate. Does Trump oppose foreign aid to corrupt governments? Yes. Is Ukraine corrupt? Yes, very corrupt. Was that corruption used against him in 2016? It looks that way. So is it crazy that Trump wants to know that the new government will investigate corruption? Of course not. He'd be an idiot not to raise the 2016 interference or the Biden corruption.

MARC. Ukrainian election interference? Try Russia.

NOVEMBER 6, 2019

STEPHEN. When faced with reality, just say, "Russia."

MARC. The Kentucky governor was up five points until that idiot held a rally for him and lost it.

MARC. Numerous Republicans and cabinet members acknowledged that Russia hacked the DNC. Trump, in public, asked the Russians to do it.

SELF-ABSORPTION

MARC. [*Attaches a tweet mocking Trump for appealing for votes for Kentucky Governor Matt Bevin by saying "You can't let this"—a Bevin loss—"happen to me."*]

MARC. Read the last word. Leadership Stephen Barry style? Me, me, me, me.

STEPHEN. Okay. Bevin was very unpopular. He had 56 percent disapproval. Trump is very popular in Kentucky. He tried to push Bevin over the top based solely on his endorsement. What's wrong with that? No president talked about himself more than Obama. It's only a problem if Trump does it. In your case, it is a problem if Trump does it and you read an article in which someone says it's a problem.

MARC. "Me, me, me" isn't a problem; it's indicative of all I have ever said. No, Obama didn't refer to himself *nearly* as much.

STEPHEN. You're wrong about Obama. I'll find stories on how much Mr. I'm A Better Speechwriter Than My Speechwriters credited himself. You don't know about it because you apply a different standard to Trump.

STEPHEN. https://apnews.com/fae [Obama mentions himself 467 times in one speech].

STEPHEN. Here's one article.

STEPHEN. https://www.mrc.org/commentary/obama-speeches-have-it-nearly-1200-times.

STEPHEN. Another article.

MARC. On a friendly, nostalgic note, I just heard a song from our best days that I hadn't heard in a while: "I'm the Man" by Joe Jackson.

STEPHEN. Good song. So are "Look Sharp" and "Is She Really Going Out with Him?"

QUID PRO QUOS

November 7, 2019

Marc. Did you think it was improper when Bill Clinton was seen talking on a plane with Loretta Lynch, especially if you got wind that he was asking for Lynch to make a statement about the innocence of Hillary?

Stephen. Those aren't the facts. I don't know what Bill discussed with Lynch, but there is no doubt the US government chose not to really investigate or prosecute Hillary for actual crimes while at the same time conducting a scorched-earth investigation into her opponent based on disinformation she provided. That's a problem. With Biden, there is evidence of wrongdoing. Biden threatened to withdraw US aid if the Ukrainians did not fire the prosecutor. He bragged about it. That prosecutor may or may not have been investigating Burisma. Burisma thought it was being investigated and, before the prosecutor was fired, had been lobbying the US State Department to help. In their communications with the State Department, they advised that Hunter Biden and other prominent Americans are on their board. As Biden might say, "Son of a b, the prosecutor was fired." So in your example, Lynch made a crooked deal to give Hillary a pass. In this case, Trump raised a real issue that our government, at the time, ignored. In one case, the meeting was criminal; in the other, the request was appropriate.

November 8, 2019

Marc. I have a simple question: If Trump wanted to hold back the aid until corruption in Ukraine was investigated or Europe helped more, why was the aid released two days after the whistleblower report that revealed he was holding it back?

STEPHEN. I don't know. This is the real world, and there are many considerations. However, I know that the delay in the release of the aid, the request to look into Biden's real corruption, and the request that Ukraine cooperate with the DOJ are in no way inappropriate and, even if you think these acts are more examples of Trump's boorishness, do not come close to conduct that should be the subject of impeachment. Impeachment would not have been raised if any other president had done exactly what Trump did. If Obama had done it, the press would have congratulated him.

A FARCE

MARC. Putting aside your belief that facts are conspiracy theories when they are unfavorable and that conspiracy theories are facts when they are favorable, the facts are these: there clearly were conditions of some sort on the release of the aid, and the conditions were not met, yet the aid was released two days after the unilateral executive branch holdback was discovered. That's pretty damning of consciousness of guilt. Try to stem your reflexive combativeness. I make a strong point.

STEPHEN. Politics always plays a role in political decisions. However, the fact that the Democrats frame the decision to delay the release of aid as an impeachable offense doesn't make it one. Therefore, even if the aid was released solely or partially because of the concern over the political fallout from the illegal leak of the Ukraine phone call, it doesn't turn Trump's actions into impeachable offenses. If Trump double-parked in front of the White House, Schiff would say double-parking is a crime and an affront to the Constitution, and Marc would agree.

MARC. You move pretty quickly off of your prior stances into "Even if (it's true) ..." You know what he did, and we can have a more level discussion on whether it's impeachable. Lying about it, covering it up, moving things to secret servers, and only behaving properly when you are caught doesn't serve anyone.

STEPHEN. I haven't moved off my stance, which is simple: this whole thing is a farce. The only crime is that Schiff worked with the whistleblower to leak a confidential conversation as a pretext for these proceedings. I guess the efforts to sweep Biden's abuse of his office under the rug also could be crimes. Ironically, Trump is the only person who has been victimized by the US government's pressuring foreign governments to cooperate in the violation of US laws. Your ignorance about secret servers should be embarrassing.

MARC. Your ignorance about improper, self-serving conduct by a president is embarrassing.

MARC. The only reason Trump didn't lie under oath was because his lawyers were smart enough to keep him away, unlike Clinton's.

MARC. And I'm you sure you now say, in retrospect, that Clinton's impeachment was a farce.

STEPHEN. You don't agree with my conclusions. The difference between me and you is that I understand the facts, and you do not. Your facts fit your conclusions. Trump hasn't lied under oath because he hasn't lied under oath. There is no scenario in which he lied under oath. The Clinton impeachment was based on the independent counsel's findings that he committed multiple felonies. That's not a farce.

NOVEMBER 9, 2019

STEPHEN. This is an excellent editorial: https://www.wsj.com/articles/why-impeachment-will-stay-partisan. "Mr. Trump's Ukraine actions are not illegal, and I doubt the sacredness of Ukraine policy matters to many Americans," writes Holman Jenkins.

MARC. Is the editorial about how Trump made a stupid mistake that all his defenders excuse completely instead of holding him accountable for?

MARC. Every single article you cite is from the *WSJ* or a Republican, and those I cite are the opposite. I'm the only one who thinks for himself—a lifelong Republican with the clarity to evaluate a person and his character and history above his policy.

STEPHEN. Read it, and maybe (I'm not holding my breath) you will see things more fairly. You never think for yourself. You never bother to know the facts. You just get excited when you read something negative about Trump.

CHARACTER

MARC. I knew he was an ass and a complete fraud the minute he started making fun of the disabled and mocking war heroes. I knew it then, and I know it now.

MARC. Now, if you want to say that he earned the presidency and that his stature should continue to be channeled by smart people like many of his advisers, I can respect that.

STEPHEN. Like everything else you uncritically accept about Trump, the claim that he mocked the reporter's disability is not true. The reporter, Serge Kovaleski, does not make the arm motions that Trump made when he was criticizing him for changing a story and getting caught. However, there are multiple examples of Trump making similar gestures to describe other people, including himself, who are in the position of being flustered. Trump is not a fraud. He has been dedicated to keeping his promises. The frauds are the ones who make false allegation after false allegation against Trump, even though they know those allegations are false. The frauds also are the Clintons and the Bidens of the world, who make money off their elected offices. You don't care because your mind is made up. Be careful what you wish for.

MARC. Trump was never a respected member of the New York business community, just a shameless self-promoter who borrowed and borrowed and lost and lost, all of which is documented.

STEPHEN. Is that based on your annual survey of the New York business community? Regarding his ups and downs, the real estate development and casino businesses are not risk free. Not all projects succeed, and projects that succeed at first may ultimately fail. Trump is a successful developer, real estate manager, and TV show host. That's documented.

MARC. Are you now going to tell me he was a pillar Republican conservative and a generous philanthropist toward Israel?

STEPHEN. He was not a Republican or conservative, but generally, he is now. He certainly is standing up for capitalism, sound economic policies, an originalist Supreme Court and judiciary, sane immigration policies, and Israel. He also is standing up to China, which no one has done, and attempting to make progress with North Korea and not to be the world's policeman. Most Republicans support most of his agenda, even if some prefer a more internationalist foreign policy. Regarding his personal financial support for Israel, I have no idea what he has done. However, the issue is what he does as president.

NOVEMBER 10, 2019

MARC. https://twitter.com/jessecharleslee/status/ [a clip in which the commentator argues that Trump's conduct was inappropriate but not impeachable].

MARC. Try this argument. At least it's honest and accurate.

MARC. Not one person has testified—and none will be called to testify—nor has anyone stated publicly, nor has any testimony leaked that Trump expressed any concern with "corruption" in Ukraine other than Biden and debunking the bipartisan-accepted research that Russia hacked the election. It's that simple and that damning.

STEPHEN. That's not true.

MARC. The whole Trump administration's policy toward Ukraine was written by Putin-employed or -connected people.

MARC. [*Sends an attachment that states, "Donald Trump is a stupid man's idea of a smart person, a poor man's idea of a rich man, and a weak man's idea of a strong man."*]

MARC. I reached out to the author to add, "Except Stephen Barry."

STEPHEN. Ask yourself this question: What does Trump do that triggers these comments? Is it his policies? In many objective ways, his policies are working. Is it corruption? The Clintons and Bidens became wealthy off their offices. Is it alleged lying? What is it?

MARC. It's the sort of helpless frustration you would have if someone from your past whom you knew to be unethical or harmful was successfully influencing someone you loved. I have been consistent on this from the beginning. You never heard me say anything positive about Obama before 2015. I don't care how arrogant I sound. Is there anything in this world that you just know? Did you ever feel certain about a conviction without proof? If Pence took Trump's place (though I believe now in gay rights), we would agree on everything. You can tell me all you want about Trump's policies, but the ones you find unique to him as compared to other current Republican are not Trump-born initiatives. He is an empty vessel that his advisers channel through.

STEPHEN. The truth is that you don't know anything about Trump. All you know is negative coverage.

MARC. I know what is in the public record. Long before 2015, he was involved with numerous lawsuits for unpaid bills, a phony charity, a phony university, and sexual harassment.

MARC. And I have seen him inexplicably kiss Putin's ass.

MARC. *Inexplicably* as in nobody ever explained.

STEPHEN. Trump gets sued—and sues—because he does things. Many companies are the subject of lawsuits that have no basis in fact. Trump is a deep-pocketed target. That doesn't mean he's right, but it doesn't mean he's wrong. Trump thinks it is in our interest to work with Putin. So did Obama and Hillary. Remember the reset button? Putin might be a bad guy, but so are the Chinese. They are a much bigger issue. Trump is taking them on. Biden wants to kiss their asses. Any idea why?

MARC. Obama and Hillary don't owe Putin millions.

STEPHEN. Let it go. Trump has no ties to Putin, no matter how much you want to believe it.

RICK PERRY UKRAINIAN GAS DEAL

November 11, 2019

Marc. [*Attaches a report that associates of Rick Perry "got a huge Ukraine gas deal" after Perry's meeting with the new president.*]

Marc. Does this upset you even a fraction of the Hunter Biden situation?

Stephen. I don't know. I don't know any of the details. Why do you assume it's inappropriate? Also, why would it have any bearing on Joe Biden running interference for Burisma for his son's benefit?

Marc. The swamp is the swamp. Why do I assume that people connected to Perry got favors right after Perry met with Zelensky? I think it's a fair assumption that there was some connection. I'm just saying you are always indignant about things that Democrats do from a standpoint of political privilege, but you always have a shifting defense when a Republican is nailed. It takes smarts to pull that off, and you definitely have that. You'd make a good criminal defense attorney.

Stephen. Perry was nailed? Based on that clip you shared with me? Why don't you wait until you have facts? You jump to conclusions based on nothing. This is why everything blows up in your face.

Marc. My marriage didn't.

Stephen. Everyone deserves to get lucky at least once.

BACK TO IMPEACHMENT

NOVEMBER 13, 2019

MARC. For the sake of argument, assume Biden was taking money from a company he didn't deserve. (1) Why wasn't he investigated in 2016 and 2017? (2) Why was Giuliani involved in back channels to influence the government to pursue the investigation instead of the DOJ investigating, especially when Sessions was beholden to Trump after pissing him off? (3) Why do several of the witnesses tell us that Trump wanted an announcement of the investigation rather than just starting the investigation? Usually, investigations aren't announced unless it's for political reasons. For all these obvious reasons, Trump was nailed for doing something ridiculously stupid.

MARC. https://twitter.com/cspan/status [*attaches a clip from Deputy Assistant Secretary George Kent's testimony, in which he testified that he did not think that what Biden did and what Trump did were "the same thing"*].

MARC. I assume you know more than George Kent.

STEPHEN. Why not?

MARC. The prosecutor whom Biden bragged about canning was part of the corrupt prior government that was more aligned with Russia. That's a fact. Kent and Taylor painted a compelling picture with historical perspective. Ukraine, with a new young regime, needed US support! It's in US interest to have a strong Ukraine!

STEPHEN. That's their view. As far as I know, neither one of them was elected president. And remember, Ukraine interfered in the 2016 election on behalf of Hillary.

MARC. That hasn't been brought up by Republicans.

STEPHEN. It will be.

MARC. Today would have been the day. Objectively, would you say it would be in the United States' favor to have a strong Ukraine that could fight back against Russian aggression?

STEPHEN. I don't agree with Trump about Putin. However, Trump has provided more military support to Ukraine than Obama did.

NOVEMBER 15, 2019

[11/15/19, 6:56 a.m.] MARC. I'm finally seeing things your way in this impeachment debate. I've been influenced by some Fox News people. A few things: (1) the witnesses were nerds, (2) George Kent had a very big water bottle, and (3) Adam Schiff has a long neck. You finally got me!

STEPHEN. What should get you is the fact that the Democrats do not have a single witness who can testify that Trump demanded an investigation or a meeting as a condition for the release of the aid. Putting aside that Trump would be within his authority to put conditions on the release of the aid, it didn't happen. Yesterday the Ukrainian foreign minister stated that no one from the Trump administration ever told the Ukrainians there were conditions on the release of aid. Of course, the aid was released. This idiotic case boils down to a group of officials—who never spoke to Trump, didn't agree with Trump on policy, and didn't like that Trump relied on Giuliani—speculating that Trump might be putting on conditions. As Trump might say, sad!

MARC. "Putting aside"? If your "putting aside" arguments were strong, that's all you would need.

STEPHEN. As usual, you're wrong. This isn't just a legal matter. It's a political matter. The Democrats again have made false allegations against Trump. It is important to expose them.

MARC. Sondland will clarify that Trump wanted the aid held back for the specific reason of extorting Ukraine to provide two political favors: investigations into two isolated corruptions that just happened to benefit him politically. The day after his "perfect" phone call, Trump spoke with Sondland, and Trump wanted to know one thing: "Will they do the investigation?" (meaning "Did they take the deal?"). Once again, unlike you, who cedes nothing, just like Trump—not a good quality, by the way—I will allow that the talking point "Ukrainians were dying" is a bit hollow. What you should be saying is that Trump shouldn't have gone down this path; it is improper behavior; and at the very least, censure or an apology from Trump is in order, but the Democrats are trying to exploit the situation.

MARC. By the way, your idiot of a president was moronic enough to tweet disparaging comments against Yovanovitch rather than let your ironclad facts tell the story, and they are now, during the hearings, reading his comments to her for her response. Keep defending his bearing and his judgment.

MARC. It's called witness intimidation, by the way. Or is that another principle you don't give two shits about?

STEPHEN. It's not worth responding to your nonsense. Nothing happened.

MARC. You are right. A perfect call and a perfect president who can do no wrong.

STEPHEN. I would call it a call in the ordinary course of business. There's nothing remarkable about it other than its being illegally leaked as a whistleblower claim.

STEPHEN. Trump had another conversation with Zelensky in which he did not discuss aid or investigations. That won't fool you.

MARC. Oh, I see. So the call in which he didn't try to extort Ukraine absolves the other in which he did? Why not reconsider Nixon's impeachment by playing some of the tapes in which he was talking with Haldeman about increasing efforts to reduce crime and lower taxes?

MARC. The State Department should be crafting foreign policy and standing behind people who spent a career in good standing working for bipartisan governments. Yovanovitch was canned only to pave the way for the shadow policy.

STEPHEN. I respect you and am proud of our lifelong friendship. However, your analysis is idiotic. The president makes policy. The State Department is supposed to carry it out, whether they agree or disagree. They are advisers. Yovanovitch was canned because Trump decided he wanted someone else. His policy is US policy. By the way, she said nothing when Ukraine took sides in the 2016 election. Is that bipartisan?

MARC. I respect you and am proud of our lifelong friendship, and that's why it concerns me that you have been made unable to separate political views from obsequious defense for someone so entirely reprehensible.

STEPHEN. The reprehensible ones are the ones who are trying to remove Trump from office through nonstop harassment and false allegations.

MARC. It's not nonstop harassment. He gives them reasons. Impeachment was a dead issue until this.

STEPHEN. He gave them reasons to investigate collusion with Russia based on disinformation created by Hillary Clinton?

STEPHEN. By the way, "this" is nothing. It is just as fake as the allegations of collusion.

MARC. You haven't been capable of giving a simple answer, but I'll go back to the well. Did Trump not hold back approved aid until two investigations would be announced, both of which would potentially benefit Trump personally? A yes won't condemn you.

STEPHEN. Although there is no question that Trump wanted Ukraine to investigate, there is zero evidence that Trump directed anyone to hold back aid. Furthermore, the fact that one of the investigations could have highlighted one of his opponents' corruption is irrelevant. It is an issue for Biden, not Trump.

MARC. Actually, there is evidence on that from Sondland, who repeatedly texted that the White House needed certain actions before aid would be delivered.

STEPHEN. No one says Trump ever directed anyone to withhold aid.

MARC. "Trump wants the deliverables."

MARC. Sondland will be testifying.

STEPHEN. No one has testified that Donald Trump directed them that the aid should not be released until the Ukrainians announced an investigation or anything like that. In fact, Sondland testified the opposite—that Trump told him, "No quid pro quo." As I said earlier, he could have done it, and it would not be impeachable, but he didn't do it.

MARC. Is it logical to infer that by your saying he could have done it and it would not be impeachable, you are hedging for the possibility that it is revealed that he in fact did do it?

MARC. You underestimate my powers of logic, inference, and intuition.

MARC. If your company is accused of doing something improper or unethical, I suppose your denials would be strong and not "We didn't do it, but even if we did, it would be okay."

MARC. That's how we know you're playing a very weak hand.

STEPHEN. I don't think that's a possibility. If that were the case, we would know it. My point is that we are investigating something that has no consequence. That's the weak hand.

MARC. [*Attaches a report that Ken Starr said Trump's tweet about Maria Yovanovitch during her testimony demonstrated "extraordinarily poor judgment."*]

MARC. Why are you incapable of saying things like this? Kenneth Starr has been staunchly pro-Trump and anti-impeachment, and look at what he says. You have a mind of decency that should be able to call out shit like this. He attacked this career diplomat for answering questions and leaving her post when she was asked.

STEPHEN. If Trump asked for advice, he would have been advised not to say anything. I would advise him not to say anything. I don't see how it helps him. Nevertheless, I believe it is outrageous that Trump has to defend his decision to fire an ambassador. It also is outrageous that people serving in the executive branch are called to testify about their views of the president's conduct. I'm confident you are very fair to your patients and do not do anything simply because it benefits you. How would you feel if your staff were asked to testify about their views about procedures you performed, even if you never had discussed anything with them?

MARC. You know, this misogynist didn't attack either of the males yesterday.

STEPHEN. He doesn't attack males? Do you watch the news?

NOVEMBER 19, 2019

MARC. So whom do have more respect for: an entitled son of a billionaire who attacks people who serve the military with unimpeachable honor and dedication or the son of a Russian Jewish refugee who gives up his entire life to his young sons, who then return the privilege by dedicating their lives to our country?

STEPHEN. That's irrelevant.

NOVEMBER 20, 2019

MARC. Not one witness has said anything other than that, in their opinion, what Trump did was wrong, and you won't allow for that. You have always said he can do foreign policy wrong. The Republicans wanted to call the whistleblower and were stopped, but they couldn't call anyone to defend what Trump did. Nobody. The aid was released only after he was caught with his stupid scheme.

STEPHEN. What diplomats who disagree with Trump and do not approve of how Trump conducts foreign policy think about Trump's phone call is irrelevant. Not one of them has any authority or responsibility to opine on it. I can evaluate the facts myself. This farce is a setup orchestrated by Schiff's office and anti-Trump officials. The idea that it should have been off-limits for Trump to ask about Burisma and Biden doesn't pass the laugh test. The argument that there was a quid pro quo—assuming that would be a problem—is not consistent with the undisputed fact that the aid was released. The fact that the impeachment arguments are being made by people who have supported illegal leaks, use of foreign disinformation, and false affidavits to investigate Trump is mind-boggling.

MARC. The argument that murder was attempted is not consistent with the undisputed fact that murder didn't occur.

MARC. "How dare they leak information of my crime? Who told on me? Who is the rat?"

MARC. Perhaps a quid pro quo is not a problem, as Mulvaney said, but then why, after he said it, did he change what he had said and take it back?

MARC. Sondland spilled the beans. Case closed!

STEPHEN. Remind me when Trump is reelected.

MARC. Elected as what—the most hated person of the decade? The only question is, which decade?

STEPHEN. Funny man.

MARC. [*Attaches a tweet commenting on Sondland's testimony that to receive the aid, Zelensky did not have to do the investigations but only announce them.*]

STEPHEN. That's exactly the point of this impeachment. The Democrats are not going to remove Trump months before an election. They simply want to say he did something that should result in his removal. Biden's conduct as vice president is relevant. If the press did its job, Biden would be investigated by the press.

MARC. Do you agree that Trump was wrong for doing this and that he was not genuinely interested in illuminating corruption and Ukraine and was more concerned about the political implications?

MARC. Let's find some common ground. Obviously, the Democrats want to get Trump out of office, and obviously, they've been obsessed with impeachment, but Trump handed them the goods on a silver platter.

STEPHEN. I don't agree that Trump is not interested in corruption. In the case of Ukraine, he believes he was victimized by Ukrainian corruption in 2016. I also believe he feels aggrieved that while the Ukrainians worked against him, leading in part to the Mueller investigation, Biden has gotten a pass on what looks like corruption that certainly is worthy of investigation. Generally, Trump does not believe we should give taxpayer dollars to corrupt and, in many cases, anti-American governments. To answer your question, nothing Trump did should be the subject of an impeachment investigation. If you want to argue that he should not have requested that the Ukrainians investigate or announce an investigation, make that case. I'll make the case that Biden should be investigated and that asking foreign governments for help in investigating candidates for president was not a problem when Trump was the illegitimate target of such an investigation.

MARC. Let me just break this down. For my own sanity (which is as capricious as yours), given all the information unearthed, can you agree now beyond your parenthetical "And even if it was ..." that the aid for Ukraine was held up until the investigations into Burisma and the DNC server issue were announced? A simple yes would be accurate and appreciated.

STEPHEN. I don't know that.

STEPHEN. https://www.wsj.com/articles/sondlands-unimpeachable-offenses.

STEPHEN. Witnesses in the impeachment hearings are providing more detail about what we already know.

MARC. They [the *WSJ*] acknowledge that the condition of an announcement of an investigation is improper but term it as the result of his personal impulse and merely not impeachable. Some ringing endorsement.

STEPHEN. They also point out that Trump did not release the aid because of the whistleblower.

MARC. Yeah, he did. Because he told Ron Johnson he didn't?

STEPHEN. It is evidence.

MARC. Hey, if Trump had held back the aid until corruption was investigated in Ukraine, given that he didn't want to irresponsibly give away taxpayer money, his demand and condition would have been quite reasonable. Why did he ask for "a favor"? Why not insist on the investigation with authority?

STEPHEN. Because he was having a congratulatory phone call. He was not insisting on anything. Impeachment had a bad day today. Sondland testified that no one ever told him there was a quid pro quo. No one.

MARC. He didn't have to know there was a plan. Trump just told him what to do.

STEPHEN. You don't need facts. You don't care what happened. You don't care that this is a farce. You just want Trump out. So believe what you want to believe. As I have said many times, vote for his opponent next year.

MARC. "I need a favor, though."

MARC. A personal favor. "*I* need a favor." *He* needed a favor. Favors are personal.

STEPHEN. If you were capable of being embarrassed by your Trump derangement, you would be embarrassing yourself. Trump was having a conversation, not arguing in court. As Greg Brady taught, you can't rely on exact words. By the way, the favor was to cooperate with Barr, not to investigate Biden.

MARC. If he wanted Barr involved, if he was entitled to this request, if it was entirely legitimate, why the hell was Rudy Giuliani needed? Why this mission? Just hold back the money because it's okay and his prerogative!

MARC. And why did they give up the aid without the needed investigation?

MARC. Why not wait for the announcement that was booked on CNN for two days later?

STEPHEN. Giuliani learned of Ukrainian involvement in the 2016 election and Biden's interference in the Burisma investigation because he was investigating the phony Russian collusion story, in which some of the sources were Ukrainians. Trump relies on Giuliani because he trusts him. Based on this farce, it's clear there are a lot of people in the government who are against him. Finally, he gave up the aid without an investigation because he wasn't holding it up for an investigation. This is a joke.

MARC. He gave up the aid without an investigation because he wasn't holding it up for an investigation? He wasn't? Why was he then?

NOVEMBER 21, 2019

STEPHEN. He is not a fan of foreign aid to corrupt governments, particularly governments that worked with the Democrats to smear him. He was lobbied by others, like Senator Ron Johnson, who supported aid to Ukraine and believed the new government was serious about fighting corruption and deserved our support.

MARC. And he gave in as soon as he was caught, and he sure "aided" Turkey.

MARC. Your talking points are all a cover. There was a dirty conspiracy against Joe Biden. Period.

MARC. The most obvious indicator is that most of the actual diplomats on the ground were in the dark of the shadow diplomacy that Rudy was running along with Sondland and Mulvaney, and Trump was so transparent in his sudden acquiescence as soon as the plot was revealed.

MARC. "I want no quid pro quo"? He would never say that unless he was advised to use that term to place it into the record through a potential transcript.

STEPHEN. Quite the opposite. There is significant credible evidence that Biden intervened to quash Ukraine's investigation into Burisma. It is not surprising. That's why Hunter Biden was paid millions. The travesty is that Trump is being investigated for asking the new anticorruption president to look into why the investigation was not pursued. As for your views on what Trump would or would not have said, Sondland testified that Trump, in response to Sondland's question of whether Trump wanted something from Zelensky for a meeting, said, "I want nothing—no quid pro quo. I want him to do the right thing." This is the only testimony about what Trump said. It is corroborated by what actually happened.

MARC. You keep citing that quote from Trump, but every objective person knows the context and the timing of his saying that. So if there is a case wherein there's evidence of a conspiracy, the investigators have a hidden wire, and the mob boss says, "I told you: don't commit conspiracy," that is somehow exculpatory?

NETANYAHU'S INDICTMENT AND ADAM SCHIFF

MARC. Is there a witch hunt against Netanyahu also?

MARC. He's been indicted.

MARC. I guess US aid to Israel might be curtailed now that Israel is a hotbed of corruption.

MARC. Is Adam Schiff "human scum"? Yes or no?

STEPHEN. Does it ever occur to you that it might be helpful to know what you're talking about? Netanyahu is a hero. Although I haven't closely followed the story, I believe the charges are very weak. The left in Israel, as in America, seeks to achieve in court what they cannot achieve at the ballot box. Regarding Schiff, he is a proven liar and man of no integrity.

MARC. Human scum?

MARC. Trump's a proven liar.

STEPHEN. Not on any issue that's consequential.

MARC. It's okay. You can say that *scum* is probably too strong a term. Give it a shot. Try yielding a teeny bit.

STEPHEN. That's not how I speak. Schiff is an embarrassment to Congress, but on the positive side, he's going to ensure Trump's reelection. Maybe he's secretly working for Trump.

November 22, 2019

Marc. When you wake from your stupor, or perhaps torpor, it will dawn on you that there are some people who devoted themselves to law enforcement and others who devoted themselves to skirting the law. How you could have ever thought James Comey and Andrew McCabe were more corrupt than Trump is beyond me. Your guarantee of their being arrested seems to be a failure.

Marc. And as for your reminders that I should think for myself, you are being hoodwinked by a person almost half the people in this country think is God, untouchable, and always right, despite his history of depravity. I, on the other hand, *actually* think for myself, am open to ideas, and am respectful of a whole range of politicians and leaders with diverse views—people with impeccable reputations. As someone with an impeccable reputation, I would think you would not want to be idolizing someone like Trump

Stephen. I'll wait for the Durham report.

NAVY SEAL GALLAGHER

November 24, 2019

MARC. Do you have any explanation or defense for Trump's not accepting the military's discipline of a soldier for breaking the rules?

STEPHEN. Do you know anything about the Gallagher case? If not, it's not worth debating this with you. The decision to restore Gallagher's rank and to allow him to retire as a SEAL is based on the specific facts of his case. It is not about whether Trump should or should not generally accept military discipline decisions.

MARC. I don't know it; I am trying to learn it, but he sure sounds like he did a disgusting thing, and people in his group reported him at their own peril. In an era when institutions and corporations often fail to enforce wrongdoing, I can't imagine the military was wrong or unfair. I'll read up on it. And no, I don't think this would be impeachable, but I believe that Trump is being guided to gain control over as many elements as possible of the distribution of power that makes us great. It's not an irrational fear to have.

STEPHEN. Trump is the commander in chief. He has the power. Every president has had the power.

MARC. I don't like a president who thinks he is more important than the coequal branches. Yes, I know Obama had lots of executive orders, and I didn't like that or him either.

STEPHEN. The military is not a coequal branch. It is a fundamental precept of the United States that the military is subject to civilian control and that the president is the ultimate authority. He is commander in chief. It's in the Constitution.

MARC. It's not about whether he has the right, and I didn't say he didn't have the right. It's about the decisions and their rationale. If he were to reverse course and order an attack against Israel, do you think you'd say, "It's his right"? This is where I think you have no credibility. When he makes decisions you like, it's easy to defend his decisions by saying it's his right to make them. If I or anyone else raises a concern about an action he takes or a statement he makes, "It's his right as CIC" is weak. On this story, I'll read more. I can't wait to see when you defend his actual decision rather than his right to make it.

STEPHEN. So who governs the United States? The elected leaders or faceless bureaucrats? Who is the final word in your office? You or your staff? Are you allowed to overrule them?

MARC. If the staff decided they were going to be more effusive with patients and made a new initiative to be friendlier and more attentive to patients, would I be allowed to tell them, "Stop being nice. Just tell them to sit down and wait for the doctor"? Is it within my right to do so? Yes! Would most people who learn of that response question the nature of that edict? Yes!

MARC. And if I fired them for continuing to be nice and attentive, would the public judge me as an asshole? Yes!

MARC. How would you like it if you fired a junior lawyer, and your CEO reinstated that person just because? Because it's his or her call?

MARC. By the way, Rick Perry says Trump is "the chosen one." Nice.

STEPHEN. The point is that if you disagree, you make the decision. In your case, I agree that you should not overrule your staff. I have been overruled but accepted it, even though I did not agree. I saw the Perry interview. Your comment is out of context. Perry said that everything is part of

God's plan and that Trump, like Obama, was chosen to be president. Religious Jews would agree.

November 25, 2019

Marc. Perry didn't say Obama was the chosen one. Ed Henry said after the clip that he "pointed out to me" (off camera) that Obama was also. If there is a clip of him saying that, you are right, and I am wrong. But he did say, "I know you said that you are the chosen one. You are." That's not out of context. And as for the military, as I suspected, Gallagher's lawyers are Giuliani and another presidential lawyer.

Stephen. I watched Ed Henry's interview of Rick Perry. Perry explained what he meant by Trump being chosen and pointed out that he believes that God is active in this world and that Obama also was chosen. Regarding Gallagher, I don't know all the details, but he had been accused of murder and was acquitted after another SEAL confessed to having killed the enemy fighter. Gallagher was demoted because he took a picture with the corpse, but other men also were in the picture, and they were not demoted. After Trump restored his rank, the navy considered taking away his trident, which appears to have been a bit vindictive. Gallagher very well may have deserved to be disciplined in some manner. The allegation is that the navy went too far to try to convict him.

November 28, 2019

Stephen. Happy Thanksgiving.

Marc. You too.

November 29, 2018

STEPHEN. Protesters in Hong Kong were holding up the Trump-as-Rocky picture. Why do you think that is?

November 30, 2019

MARC. I don't know.

DERANGED

December 3, 2019

Marc. Please put your gloves down and tell me if you think this is an accurate perception [*attaches a clip of Trump calling Schiff a maniac and deranged*].

Stephen. Schiff is a liar.

Marc. If by that you mean someone who has told a lie or lies, so is Trump. Do you actually think he is a deranged human being and a very sick man?

Marc. I thought you would agree. Trump is the highest-profile person on the planet. In this tweet, he is claiming that Schiff is literally mentally ill and implying that he is so ugly that his ugliness gave him a complex. Schiff prosecuted criminals for years and went to Harvard. There are facts here that he is pursuing, just like those many other politicians of both parties pursue. His lies were really minimal—that he doesn't know the whistleblower. Yeah, he probably does. Just like Devin Nunes lies, and others do as well. My outrage against Trump is specifically about his saying such perverted things. Lisa Page is a woman, and even though she didn't like Trump, you can't show me any evidence that she personally did anything corrupt, yet this bully shamed her, imitating her having an orgasm, in front of millions of people. Does that amuse you? There is no "What about ..." here, unless you can "What about ..." Lisa Page doing anything close to this kind of intentional humiliation.

Stephen. Schiff is obsessed with Trump. He's abusing the impeachment process. He has been working to manufacture a basis for impeachment. He lied about having evidence of collusion. He lied about the whistleblower. He is a threat to our democracy. If you read the transcript of the July 25 phone call, you know that Trump was interested in an investigation of

Biden. Biden should be investigated. If the Trump standard were applied to him, there would be wall-to-wall coverage of Biden's corruption.

MARC. Is he "a deranged human being and a very sick man"?

STEPHEN. He clearly suffers from Trump derangement syndrome, so yes.

MARC. You know, you can say no without taking away from your criticism of him.

MARC. A civil and humane person should not be saying things like that. It's an insult to those with deranged relatives or the victims of crimes committed by insane, evil people.

STEPHEN. Many of Schiff's comments about Trump, whom sixty-three million Americans voted for, are not "civil" or "humane." Who does Schiff think he is?

MARC. Oh, and Trump and Giuliani cooked up this scheme. It's all true. It's also true that Dems were looking for the goods on Trump. They got the evidence. Republicans looked for it on Obama and didn't get it and looked for it on Clinton and got it. You cannot be credible if you only attack Democrats. I could count five or six who routinely do yet always defend Trump other than his using bad words.

UKRAINE CLEARED?

MARC. The inspector general has no charges against the people you said would be arrested, and the senators cleared Ukraine of any involvement. Even Lindsey Graham shot that down. So your track record on this topic is weak.

December 4, 2019

STEPHEN. When did senators clear Ukraine? It's not over. There will be accountability. The inspector general's report will be out next week. We can see what he says when it's out. The Durham investigation is not finished but will be soon enough.

MARC. In 2017, the Senate Intelligence Committee concluded that Russia and Russia alone was involved in affecting or attempting to affect the election and hacking the servers, not Ukraine, and Lindsey Graham made the statement definitively yesterday.

MARC. So you agree that despite all the mendacity on the part of Schiff, he is probably not a deranged human being and a very sick man?

MARC. Why is the president's personal lawyer making repeated calls to the budget office?

STEPHEN. A Ukrainian court determined that Ukrainian officials interfered in the 2016 election. I haven't heard or read Graham's comments, but *hacking* is not synonymous with *interference*. Schiff is a dangerous man who seems to believe he has the right to undo the last election and interfere in the next election. He is very unprincipled and obsessed with Trump. I know you want to believe that Trump committed a terrible abuse of his office. He did not, and he is not going anywhere. Schiff has made his reelection more likely. It is Schiff who is abusing his office and the impeachment process.

MARC. Many besides Schiff are obsessed with Trump and are trying to undo him, myself included, because we cannot believe that someone this corrupt (don't make me go down the list of shadiness pre-2016) was able to fool so many people. Had this story of obvious impropriety not arisen and had this idiot acted like a unifying force, people would have just focused on 2020.

STEPHEN. You have no knowledge about corruption. However, I know that everyone arrayed against him is corrupt and afraid of being exposed.

MARC. I don't have knowledge of corruption because I am an honest person.

STEPHEN. You're not honest enough. You're willing to accuse Trump of corruption with absolutely no evidence. It is bearing false witness.

MARC. Trump University. Ruling against him, including perjury.

MARC. Is that evidence?

STEPHEN. No. Trump settled the Trump University lawsuits. There was no ruling and no perjury.

MARC. Trump has never erred, according to you. He's a perfect specimen, a golden boy who just uses a little harsh talk. He never lies and never does anything shady or slimy.

STEPHEN. I never have said Trump is perfect. I simply point out that you don't know what you're talking about. I evaluate Trump by the same standards that apply to other public figures. He comes out looking pretty good. However, if you don't like him, don't vote for him.

MARC. I have a simple question. I would appreciate a simple response. When Trump held back the aid to Ukraine until, as you say, he made sure there was no corruption, do you believe there was even a small degree of his wanting to gain personally advantageous information on Biden? Or no?

STEPHEN. https://www.wsj.com/articles/schiffs-surveillance-state.

STEPHEN. Adam Schiff demands and then discloses the call logs of his opponents. As I said, Schiff is a dangerous man.

DECEMBER 5, 2019

MARC. The inspector general report found nothing, and neither did Durham.

MARC. So your track record on assessing decent, law-enforcing civil servants as bad people is weak. Maybe the bad people are the ones that are bad in plain sight?

STEPHEN. Have you lost all connection to reality? Did Horowitz send you an advanced copy of his report, or did he give you a private briefing? Were you and Durham college roommates? You have been consistently wrong on Trump. You have predicted that he's finished for three years. Meanwhile, the good law enforcement people already have been fired, demoted, and criticized by the inspector general. It will get worse for them before it's over.

SELECTIVE OUTRAGE: SHOOTING AT FLORIDA MILITARY BASE

December 7, 2019

Marc. If a Mexican shot you at a military base, do you think Trump would have said, "This shooting does not represent the feelings of the Mexican people"? And what happened to Muslim outrage, given this shooter was from Saudi Arabia? Oh, right—Trump and his family do business with Saudi Arabia, so it's all good.

Stephen. You're criticizing Trump for something that you speculate would happen (but would not—Trump has been very complimentary of Mexico since the Mexican military has been policing the border). Regarding Saudi Arabia, I must have missed something. Every US leader in my lifetime has been pro–Saudi Arabia. Many of them take money from Saudi Arabia in various ways.

Marc. Is it a Muslim country? Were the 9/11 perpetrators from Saudi Arabia?

Marc. Trump is always selectively outraged.

Stephen. So is everyone else, including you.

Marc. Good point!

THE INSPECTOR GENERAL'S FISA ABUSE REPORT

December 9, 2019

STEPHEN. Apparently, Horowitz found only seventeen significant errors in the FISA application, which sounds reasonable to me. I'll have to read the report myself.

MARC. Errors. So when is Comey going to jail? I suppose Trump never makes any errors?

STEPHEN. Barr and Durham are investigating the origins of the investigation. They have much broader authority than Horowitz. We'll see what they say. They can bring criminal charges. Also, I want to see the bases for Horowitz's conclusions. I want to see if he looked at the "insurance policy."

MARC. The report blows all of Trump's lies—ones you believed—out of the water. The report is quite clear!

STEPHEN. I know you haven't read it. It appears to be a devastating report for the FBI. It's the facts that matter. Durham will take care of the indictments.

MARC. You told me the investigation into Trump was illegal.

MARC. No grand jury is going to return an indictment, 'cause they won't find (forget how many) people who love Israel, have millions they don't want taxed, or are racists (the latter is not you).

MARC. Trump told the world countless lies about the FBI that are unsupported—such a gross abuse of power.

MARC. Treason? Planting informants in the Trump campaign? Spying?

MARC. Oh, Christopher Steele is a friend of Ivanka Trump, who used him in the past. Ha-ha-ha!

STEPHEN. Horowitz reported that Christopher Steele used a single source and that the FBI interviewed the source in January 2017, after the first FISA application and before the second. The source told the FBI that the information the source provided to Steele was hearsay, said in jest, and not meant to be reported. Yet the FISA renewals claimed the allegations were true. There is so much more. Most importantly, Barr and Durham put out statements saying that Horowitz—who, as the DOJ inspector general, is limited to the DOJ—does not have all the information and that they disagree with his conclusion there was a sufficient predicate to commence the investigation in July 2016. You have no reason to be laughing now, but it is clear Barr and Durham have concluded there was a conspiracy against Trump. Even if you accept Horowitz's position that there was a sufficient predicate to start an investigation, there was no basis for continuing it past January 2017. As I have said from the beginning, your heroes are going down.

STEPHEN. "The Inspector General's report now makes clear that the FBI launched an intrusive investigation of a U.S. presidential campaign on the thinnest of suspicions that, in my view, were insufficient to justify the steps taken," Barr said in a statement. US Attorney John Durham, who is leading a wider investigation into the FBI's Trump-campaign probe, said in a statement that his office did not concur with Inspector General Horowitz's conclusions. "Based on the evidence collected to date, and while our investigation is ongoing, last month we advised the Inspector General that we do not agree with some of the report's conclusions as to predication and how the FBI case was opened," Durham wrote.

MARC. Did you think it proper when Comey commented on an ongoing investigation?

STEPHEN. Durham and Barr commented on the inspector general's report, not the investigation.

MARC. Based on the evidence collected *to date*.

STEPHEN. He didn't discuss the evidence, the subjects of the investigation, or the timing—nothing. What is improper is to suggest that someone who may not be charged is being investigated or to tell someone he is not under investigation when he is. Do you ever think before you speak?

DECEMBER 10, 2019

MARC. Here is where you lose credibility. The Mueller report listed numerous serious issues and errors and questions, and you dismissed them all as "not crimes," yet now you cite the errors in the inspector general's report but leave out the fact that no actual crimes were found.

MARC. The Durham report is planned to be a sham because Barr knew the inspector general was turning up nothing, and it will be filled with BS if it ever sees the light of day.

MARC. [*Attaches remarks by Russia's foreign minister, Sergey Lavrov, denying that Russia interfered in the 2016 election.*]

MARC. This is absurd, and people like you—that's right, you—enable it. The FBI has clear and incontrovertible evidence of GRU hacking us, and this is confirmed by many Trump backers. Forget whether Ukraine might have been also involved. Lavrov is denying Russian involvement. What say you?

STEPHEN. The inspector general report has found significant failures in the FBI's conduct of the FISA process. The inspector general's role, as set out in the report, was to determine whether decisions made by the FBI complied with or were authorized by department rules, policies, or procedures. Furthermore, the report states, "If the explanations we were given for a particular decision were consistent with legal requirements, policies and procedures, and not unreasonable, we did not conclude that the decision was based on improper considerations in the absence of documentary or testimonial evidence to the contrary." In other words, unlike with Mueller, there was no requirement that the FBI exonerate itself. Nevertheless, the misconduct described should be unacceptable under any circumstance, let alone when directed at a presidential campaign. If Mueller had found one-tenth of the wrongdoing that Horowitz found, Trump would have been removed. Finally, it's not over; Barr and Durham dispute Horowitz's findings on predication. The investigation into Trump didn't start in July 2016, as reported by Horowitz; it was going on for months. Your friends are going down. Regarding Lavrov, I don't care what the Russians say. I have no doubt they sought to interfere, and through the Steele dossier, if in no other way, they succeeded beyond their wildest dreams.

EXECUTIVE ORDER DEFINING JUDAISM AS A NATIONALITY

December 11, 2019

MARC. Trump is pushing for a recategorization that being Jewish is a nationality.

STEPHEN. What is the purpose of classifying "Jewish" as a nationality? Do you know? I don't, but I don't assume it's nefarious. Your default position, without any knowledge, is that there is some evil intent. Just stop it. *Am Yisroel Chai* (the nation of Israel lives).

MARC. I do know. It will allow anti-Jewish crime to be prosecuted more harshly, though I don't think I get that.

MARC. Soon Trumpers (except the small group of New York Jews) will be telling Jews to go home back from where they came.

STEPHEN. Trump is the most pro-Israel president we have had. Evangelicals are very pro-Israel and pro-Jewish. Which Trumpers are you talking about? You must be thinking about the Squad or Bernie Sanders.

MARC. Racist white male David Duke people.

STEPHEN. You're absolutely right. The sixty-three million voters who voted for Trump are all white male racists, except for the Jews, blacks, Latinos, women, and others who are included in the total. After the exceptions, the total must be at least seven white male racists, but they're obviously controlling the agenda: prison reform, Jerusalem and settlements, and so on. They also must be pushing the policies that have resulted in record black and Latino employment. What can I say? Sometimes you make very strong arguments.

UKRAINE: MEETING WITH ZELENSKY

MARC. Ukraine was thoroughly vetted before the aid was supposed to be released. And eventually, it was released, so I guess it's all good, right? Then why hasn't Trump had his meeting with Zelensky, his ally?

STEPHEN. He has met with him.

MORE ON THE FISA ABUSE REPORT

STEPHEN. The inspector general's report directly contradicts multiple statements made by Comey and Schiff regarding the FISA application, including the Democrats' report on the FISA application. It directly contradicts congressional testimony by Brennan regarding the intelligence assessment that found the Russians sought to help Trump. Horowitz called the FISA application inexplicable. It also establishes that the FBI interviewed the single Russian source for the dossier, who told them it was hearsay—discussions told in jest in a bar—prior to Mueller's appointment. Your heroes will be prosecuted. Furthermore, Durham is going to report on the true origins of the surveillance of Trump. It didn't start in July 2016. As I have been saying, this is the biggest political crime in American history.

DECEMBER 12, 2019

MARC. You classify anything the Democrats say or write as partisan, not credible, and a continued attempt to get Trump. Yet you never consider what Trump and Barr say as equally partisan to save themselves and attack back. By the way, please tell me the rationale for Durham, other than that they knew the report would not be as strong as they wanted and found someone who would say what they wanted to be said. Trump said Mueller's report would be clouded because Mueller wasn't allowed in Trump's club!

STEPHEN. I read the Mueller report cover to cover. Based on the evidence presented in the report, he found that people associated with Trump had occasional, random, unremarkable contacts with Russian individuals, with no connection to collusion. Even the findings about the Russians' use of Facebook were not compelling and amounted to nothing. Mueller's discussion of obstruction boils down to Trump objecting to an investigation into something that did not happen, which was conducted in a very heavy-handed manner, completely unlike the kid-gloves investigation the FBI conducted against Hillary Clinton about something that absolutely did happen: mishandling of classified information. The Horowitz report is a completely different story. It outlines significant abuse of the FISA process, which he described as "inexplicable" and "pretty bad." He identifies seventeen significant errors and omissions. He declined to attribute these inexplicable errors and omissions to political bias because there is no email that said, "Get Trump" (but there are the Strzok and Page texts and common sense). Every significant error and omission was against Trump. He also confirms that the FBI knew prior to Mueller's appointment that the Steele dossier, which was the sole basis for the FISA warrants, was based on a single Russian source who heard the things Steele reported in a bar. Therefore, there was no basis for Mueller's appointment. Finally, Horowitz concludes that the opening of the Trump investigation in July 2016 met the low threshold required because the FBI received a tip from Alexander Downer about his conversation with Papadopoulos. Barr disagrees that that was sufficient. More importantly, why did Downer, a high-ranking Australian official, even seek out Papadopoulos? That's what Barr and Durham are looking into. Also, why did Brennan lie under oath about the dossier? Why did Comey repeatedly lie about the dossier? They said it wasn't the basis for the FISA warrants or the intelligence assessment, when it was the sole basis. Open your eyes.

MARC. You excuse Trump's improper behavior as a defense against what he felt was unjust treatment. I submit that the FBI can also act improperly if it seems dangerous behavior is taking place.

MARC. That text exhibits why I am one of the area's foremost legal minds.

STEPHEN. The Mueller report does not find that Trump did anything improper. It characterizes Trump's objections to the investigation and exercise of his rights as potential obstruction. It was not. The FBI has absolutely no right to investigate a presidential campaign, conduct surveillance on a candidate or his campaign staff, or continue to conduct surveillance on a president-elect and then a president because they think he shouldn't be president. If someone as smart as you is okay with antidemocratic police-state tactics like that, it shows how easily we could end up in a police state. God help us!

MARC. You lost me at sentence one. How can you say that and still have credibility? There were many, but I will start with this: Trump asked both Don McGahn and Corey Lewandowski to fire Mueller.

STEPHEN. That's not improper. And it didn't happen.

MARC. You mean that Mueller wasn't fired? Or Trump didn't tell McGahn to (in so many words) get Mueller out? Because he sure did talk to both those guys about it, and neither has refuted it.

MARC. How about lying (doesn't matter if under oath or not) that he had nothing to do with Russia while he had a letter of intent to build Trump Tower Moscow?

STEPHEN. You're grasping. The Trump Tower Moscow project is totally irrelevant to anything. It was what is known as a busted deal. It didn't go forward and had nothing to do with collusion. The FBI, the CIA, and Adam Schiff repeatedly lied about their basis for investigating the opposition party's presidential candidate because they had none.

MARC. And his request to have his investigator fired?

STEPHEN. He had the right to fire him. That is not obstruction. Obstruction is destroying evidence (like Hillary Clinton did) or suborning perjury (like Bill Clinton did). Based on the inspector general's report, there was no basis for Mueller's appointment. So Trump was right to oppose the investigation.

COMMENTS ON GRETA THUNBERG AND PUTIN

MARC. [*Attaches a Trump tweet saying, in part, "Greta [Thunberg] must work on her Anger Management problem ..."*]

MARC. Think before you answer. This girl is on the spectrum. Isn't this regrettable behavior on Trump's part, whatever she said about him?

STEPHEN. If that offends you, I'll find a safe space for successful middle-aged men where you can compose yourself. The child abusers are the ones who use this young woman as a prop, not Trump.

MARC. That's an unfortunate reply. You're better than that. Hey, you think Putin is corrupt?

DECEMBER 13, 2019

STEPHEN. There was nothing wrong with calling out Greta Thunberg. She is uninformed and nasty. She is used as a prop by climate activists. If you are concerned about her, that is where you should look. They put her in the spotlight. Trump's comments, other than the fact that they came from Trump, were not vicious or demeaning. Putin is a thug, but he's also the leader of Russia. That's why Hillary Clinton provided his foreign minister a "reset button." That's why Obama told Medvedev on a hot mic, "Tell Vladimir I'll have more flexibility after the election," and mocked Romney for saying Russia was our geopolitical foe. There are arguments for and against if it is in the United States' interest to work with Putin. Trump, by allowing the United States to become the world's leading energy producer, has given us a lot of leverage over Putin, who relies primarily on energy exports. In your little mind, the only criterion you look at is Trump's position. If Trump supports it, it is bad. If Trump comments, the comment is bad. Try your little thought experiment on yourself.

MARC. Do you think Vladimir Putin is corrupt?

MARC. It's a simple question: Do you think Vladimir Putin is corrupt?

STEPHEN. I told you what I thought.

MARC. Putin is corrupt, yet Trump has met with him sixteen times without concern about corruption. Same with North Korea. The holding back of the aid was done for self-interest. Everyone one knows it.

MARC. If you had a close relative with burns all over her face or perhaps who was bald from alopecia and chose to go without a wig and she was making anti-Trump statements about his policies, and he said, "Shut that ugly, bald burns-all-over-the-face woman up," you would probably be as incensed as I am. Maybe not. Maybe you would calmly say she deserved it.

STEPHEN. Obama gave Iranian terrorists hundreds of millions of dollars. If I had an autistic relative giving speeches at the United Nations and being named Person of the Year, I wouldn't be surprised if he or she was criticized, especially if he or she made ignorant statements and was nasty. I also would resent the people who were using my relative to further their political agenda. I want to be very clear. Your ignorant and hateful views about Trump do not give you any moral superiority.

JUDGMENT

MARC. Let me ask you something. I never voted for a Democrat in any election before 2016. I am in favor of a strong military and low taxes (but will pay higher taxes if I have to) and am against big government. So why would I all of a sudden "hate" someone? My judgment is pretty good in life. I'm not a religious or social zealot. I don't have a cause I am so passionate about that it would make me ignore Trump's faults as necessary evils. So why? I just have an irrational, incorrect hatred for Donald Trump? Or I am blessed with a clarity of vision that you apparently aren't? I am not morally superior.

STEPHEN. Time and time again, you make snap judgments before you know the facts.

MARC. Perhaps, yes.

MARC. You won't ever get a "Perhaps, yes" from Barry. He's always right about everything, right?

STEPHEN. That's because I think before I text.

MARC. Aren't your thoughts ever wrong?

STEPHEN. Yes. But I reduce the opportunity for glaring mistakes by trying to get the facts. Trump has his flaws, but the caricature of Trump that you buy into has no basis in reality. Furthermore, the only fact that is relevant to you in any situation in which Trump is involved is what Trump said or did. If he says something or does something, you conclude it was wrong.

BACK TO IMPEACHMENT

December 14, 2019

MARC. The aid to Ukraine was released the day or days after the whistleblower report became known within the administration. If you think the release of the aid was not tied to this and was merely coincidental, please tell me why it was released, when none of the conditions and favors Trump asked for were met.

STEPHEN. Because Trump never imposed any conditions on them. There is no testimony from anyone, including hearsay testimony from anti-Trump bureaucrats, like Vindman or Fiona Hill, that anyone acting on behalf of the Trump administration told any Ukrainian officials that the release of aid was dependent on an investigation. The Ukrainians have repeatedly denied that any such demand was made. Furthermore, the OMB released a report going over the time line for the release of the aid, which shows it was within guidelines. Nothing happened. That's why the whistleblower was so important to this fake story. Before Trump released the transcript, Schiff planned to make the claim that Trump demanded an investigation for the release of aid during the phone call. After the transcript was released, he had to scramble to find what is now described as "an abuse of power." However, no demands were ever made of the Ukrainians, and the aid was released in accordance with applicable guidelines. This impeachment is an abuse of power. Furthermore, if you want to know what real abuses of power are, read the Horowitz report.

MARC. You always try to bury your lame answer under your stronger facts. The collective testimony was clear that the aid was being held up. I don't think you deny that the aid was held up, so what is your explanation for the reason for the holdup and then release? It had already been vetted by Congress. You are too smart to join the chorus of "He cared about corruption." And if he did, why release it? Answer, please.

STEPHEN. The aid was held up, but aid is often held up for various reasons. Even the Democrats aren't willing to say holding up aid is impeachable. They are saying that he held up aid to compel the Ukrainians to commence investigations for his personal benefit. I'll put aside the personal benefit nonsense and focus on the only relevant fact: If Trump or Trump administration officials never communicated to Ukrainian officials that the release of aid was contingent on the commencement of an investigation, how exactly was he abusing his power? Again, the game plan prior to release of the transcript was to accuse Trump of demanding an investigation as a condition for the release of the aid. However, it was a lie, and Trump exposed it by releasing the transcript. If you want examples of real abuse of power, read the Horowitz report. No one who excuses the FBI (and the Obama administration) or ignores the report can be taken seriously on this nonsense. To answer your irrelevant question, there were various considerations for holding up the aid and various considerations in releasing the aid, including pressure from Trump allies, like Senator Ron Johnson. More importantly, there was, according to the OMB time line, nothing unusual. Finally, Trump is on record as opposing foreign aid to corrupt governments.

MARC. Then why did he approve the same aid in 2017 and 2018?

BACK TO CHARACTER

MARC. Why does Trump praise corrupt leaders, like Putin and Netanyahu? (Oh, I suppose Netanyahu's indictment is baseless as well.) And the text messages of those diplomats clearly illustrate that the president would only meet and release the aid to Ukraine if an announcement was made about an investigation. Who announces investigations that are meant to be effective? Come on, Steve. Just stick with "He overstepped his bounds, but that is not enough for impeachment."

MARC. You love to accuse people before they are even indicted when it serves your narrative, but people like Netanyahu, who's been indicted with serious documentation, is innocent because he is a champion for your agenda. I think you probably would prefer to have an emperor or king who is strong and doesn't have to answer.

MARC. [*Attaches a quote from the Access Hollywood video.*]

MARC. Stephen Barry's guy!

STEPHEN. This exposes you. The truth about Ukraine doesn't matter. You think he's crude and want him out.

MARC. Worse than crude. Evil. Yes. And if he was George Bush and did the same thing, he would be wrong but probably censured. Few of my texts to you try to make the case for impeachment. They are trying to make the point that Trump is just bad, bad, bad.

STEPHEN. How is he evil? You think that because you don't make any effort to go beyond biased reporting and false allegations. For example, he didn't mock the disabled reporter's disability. He mocked the reporter's change in positions in exactly the same way he mocked others. The *Access Hollywood* tape was crude and does not reflect well on him, but unlike Bill Clinton, he did not pal around with Jeffrey Epstein and has not been credibly accused of rape. Unlike Hillary and many other Democrats, he was not an enabler and defender of Harvey Weinstein. He made his money in business, and as an entrepreneur, he has not always succeeded, but he has far more often than not. Notwithstanding his high profile, which makes him a target for litigation, and the claims made against him over the years, nothing of consequence has ever emerged. The Clintons and the Bidens became rich by selling access to the government. Who is more honorable? I respect your personal dislike of Trump. I object to your belief that your personal dislike of him is based on anything more than that. He didn't collude with Russia. He didn't strong-arm Ukraine. He's not a racist. He's not a corrupt businessman. He's not a liar. In fact, he's the most transparent president in US history. He has been the target of unprecedented efforts to remove him from office based on lies.

MARC. He *did* pal around with Epstein, and he has been accused of rape on two occasions, one from Ivana. And there is evidence in plain sight from his own statements that he has been influenced to be pro-Russia.

MARC. And he is a liar—too many to mention.

MARC. Nothing emerges on all his crap because he settled things with hush money and catch-and-kill techniques.

MARC. Of course he wouldn't mock a disabled person. Like he wouldn't attack a sixteen-year-old with Asperger's, a Gold Star parent of someone killed in combat, or someone who was a POW and elected to stay with his squad in captivity.

STEPHEN. Again, you don't know what you're talking about. You believe anything that confirms your bias.

MARC. As do you. It's called confirmation bias. It's pretty common these days.

STEPHEN. No. I have a bias, but I try to get the facts. I don't accept something just because it makes me feel good to hear it.

MARC. Oh, like the FBI being out to get the president? You accepted that?

STEPHEN. The Horowitz report concludes that the investigation into Trump met the low bar for opening an investigation. Horowitz accepts that the investigation was initiated based on a phone call from the Australian government regarding Alexander Downer's conversation with Papadopoulos in April. He does not inquire into why Downer, the former head of Australian intelligence, met with Papadopoulos. Durham is investigating that. I expect to learn that our government was spying on Trump prior to opening Crossfire Hurricane. Furthermore, the FBI has absolutely no basis for continuing the investigation. They lied about Steele and the Steele dossier. It was the only basis for the FISA warrants, and they knew it was bullshit. They knew Steele had one Russian source. They interviewed that source in January 2017. The source told them that the information in the Dossier was bullshit, but the investigation continued, culminating in Mueller's appointment. Furthermore, the FBI did not give Trump defensive briefings prior to the election and, following the election, briefed Trump for the purpose of gathering intelligence. There were seventeen significant errors and omissions in the FISA applications, including use of a doctored email. Finally, both Barr and Durham disagreed with Horowitz. The FBI wasn't out to get Trump? That's another example of your confirmation bias, not mine.

BACK TO IMPEACHMENT

MARC. [*Attaches a clip of Lindsey Graham supporting the impeachment of Bill Clinton.*]

MARC. Laughable.

STEPHEN. There is a little hypocrisy. Look at Nadler's and Schiff's contemporaneous statements about Clinton's impeachment. That being said, Clinton committed perjury and suborned perjury. He also got blow jobs in the Oval Office while on the phone with world leaders. If it was a mistake to impeach Clinton, who actually broke laws, what does it say for this nonsense impeachment for "abuse of power"?

MARC. You have to admit it is possible to have something be impeachment worthy without the committing of a crime. This may not be it in your view. Likewise, there could be crimes that are not impeachment worthy.

THE WHITE-POWER HAND GESTURE

STEPHEN. Nothing that Trump is accused of is impeachment worthy. It is simply the best the Democrats could come up with.

MARC. [*Attaches photos of cadets at the Army-Navy game allegedly making a white-power hand sign.*]

STEPHEN. The black cadet is making a white-power symbol? Are you trying to prove my point?

MARC. No, it's the white cadet. By the way, I just saw *Uncut Gems*—what a brutal but excellent movie filled with Long Island Jewish stuff and basketball.

STEPHEN. They are making the same gesture.

NANCY PELOSI'S TEETH

December 15, 2019

MARC. [*Attaches a Trump tweet that says, "Because Nancy's teeth were falling out of her mouth, and she didn't have time to think."*]

MARC. "I'm Stephen Barry, and I support this tweet. It's funny, like so many of Trump's other insults, but people around the country are smart enough not to take his example and let their childish impulses, uncivil discourse, and baser nature unleash. People should have a thicker skin and insult each other more based on things like age, looks, and height with impunity!"

STEPHEN. The Democrats are proven liars. They lied about Russian collusion. They lied about the FISA applications. They read the applications and lied about what was in them. They lied about the Ukraine phone call. Pelosi has lied—all roads lead to Putin. She is trying to remove Trump from office. She deserves everything she gets.

BACK TO IMPEACHMENT

December 16, 2019

MARC. An interesting topic on a mistake Republicans in the Senate might have made. We know how they are voting, of course, but their statements about already having decided could lead the House to have rationale not to send the impeachment for their ruling, letting it hang over Trump's case and allowing Dems the narrative of saying he was not exonerated of impeachment.

STEPHEN. If the House doesn't send the impeachment to the Senate, it is only to avoid the consequences of their abuse of the process.

MARC. Right!

STEPHEN. I'm glad you agree.

MARC. I don't.

STEPHEN. Of course not. That would require an understanding of what actually is happening.

MARC. Here is what is happening: Trump effed up, and the Democrats are exploiting the fuckup.

MARC. If the Republicans came clean by agreeing that Trump was wrong and supported reprimanding him, the Dems probably would have got what they wanted.

STEPHEN. No. The Democrats have been looking for a reason to impeach Trump. Because their opposition to Trump is based on lies, they keep coming up empty. Mueller came up empty. Schiff came up empty—he planned to claim that Trump threatened to withhold aid in exchange for an investigation for his personal benefit when he spoke to Zelensky in July. However, Trump released the transcript and blew that lie out of the water. The Democrats are going down. Comey is going down. Trump will be reelected.

MARC. You might be right in the last sentence, and you are right on the second sentence. Trump will be down long before Comey.

MORE ABOUT LIES AND LIARS

STEPHEN. Comey is a proven liar. Read the inspector general's report. He also was previously referred for prosecution for leaking. Comey has zero credibility left.

MARC. That's how I feel about Trump, who lies on a daily basis.

STEPHEN. No. Trump is actually truthful. It is Comey, Brennan, and Schiff who have told demonstrable and consequential lies. Tell me what lies Trump has told.

MARC. Are you serious? I'll have twenty of them by tomorrow morning. Maybe you are trying to ask me what significant ones has he told. Yesterday he claimed that *Time* magazine asked him to be Man of the Year, but he turned them down

MARC. He said he didn't have a relationship with Stormy Daniels. How's that one?

STEPHEN. I am serious. Schiff lied about having evidence that Trump worked with Putin to subvert the election. Obama lied about the terms of the Iran deal and said, "If you like your doctor, you can keep your doctor." But you think Trump lied about being offered to be Man of the Year. I see your point. Trump denied having a one-night stand ten years before running for president. Assuming he is lying, it may be consequential to Melania but no one else.

MARC. He said, "I'll release my tax returns once my audit is over."

MARC. He said he had no business dealings with Russia.

STEPHEN. He never said he had no dealings with Russia. You can't come up with anything that is a lie. Schiff had access to the FISA applications and falsely claimed that they weren't based on the Steele dossier, that the Steele dossier checked out, and that the FISA warrants produced important information. Those were outright lies.

MARC. Why is denying Stormy not a significant lie, when Clinton's lie was impeachment worthy?

MARC. He had dealings. He had a letter of intent to build Trump Tower Moscow.

STEPHEN. Clinton committed perjury while he was president. He had a twenty-one-year-old intern giving him blow jobs in the Oval Office. He asked his staff to lie to the independent counsel's investigators. Those are slight differences. As I said, Trump did not deny he had a potential deal for a Trump Tower in Moscow. Nor did he provide any testimony on the timing of that project; I believe Cohen did. Furthermore, the project had nothing to do with collusion.

CHILDREN

MARC. I have a simple question. Why should China investigate the Bidens, as Trump asked? China should investigate Hunter Biden and his issues in Ukraine?

STEPHEN. Hunter Biden's private equity firm partnered with a Chinese firm to take over or invest in a Chinese business. It was a transaction the Chinese declined to do with Goldman Sachs and other big banks. But they did it with Hunter Biden at the same time that, coincidentally, Joe Biden was the Obama administration's point person on China. I believe Hunter is estimated to have a $20 million equity position in the subject company.

MARC. I suppose Ivanka and the other kids never benefit from any other type of beneficial alliance.

STEPHEN. You think the Trump kids are profiting off of Trump's office? What are you smoking or vaping?

CORRUPTION AND UKRAINE

December 17, 2019

MARC. The president wants to have whomever he wants in the State Department. Rudy said on the record he canned Yovanovitch because he needed her out of the way, and last night on TV, he added, "Because she is corrupt." There is zero evidence of that, and this is the kind of thing that drives me crazy! She was a longtime respected career diplomat.

STEPHEN. What do you know about Yovanovitch? Nothing. What do you know about her tenure as ambassador to Ukraine? Nothing. What do you know about evidence of wrongdoing? Nothing. What do I know? At the very least, she was briefed on Hunter Biden's position at Burisma and Biden's apparent conflict of interest. I also know that the FBI and Democratic Party have told multiple lies about Trump. The fact that you talk through your ass drives me crazy.

MARC. Everyone is corrupt, except Donald Trump. Is that it?

STEPHEN. Trump is the most investigated man to ever hold the presidency. Where is the evidence of corruption?

MARC. Trump University.

MARC. Did you help Trump with his professionally written, cogent letter he sent today?

STEPHEN. Trump's letter has the benefit of being true. Your Trump hatred is based on Trump University? Wow!

MARC. Don't twist my words. I am pissed now.

MARC. You asked me for an example of corruption, and I have one.

MARC. I don't hate him because he is corrupt. I hate him because he is a rotten individual.

STEPHEN. Okay. Don't get pissed. I'm trying to follow your logic. You think he is a rotten individual because you think he is corrupt, has allegedly treated women badly, hurls insults at people who attack him, and tells lies. That is your right, but based on facts, he measures up very well against his opponents.

MARC. I reference his being corrupt as significant because it's a ridiculous premise that he wanted "corruption" in Ukraine cleared up before releasing approved and vetted congressional aid, yet in asking Zelensky to clear up that corruption, he never used the word *corruption* and only cited two issues: Biden and the unproven claim that Ukraine was hacking and not Russia. Despite your lawyerly advocacy, you know what he was doing, and you've tacitly admitted it by saying, "Even if he did …" It might indeed be within his power. The chief of staff thought it was. Certainly it was not illegal. Yet it has been raised by people of both parties as an impeachable offense, and an impeachment in the House is akin to a grand jury indictment.

STEPHEN. You're wrong about his concerns about corruption. However, as part of that, he wanted Ukraine to investigate "what happened with that whole situation with Ukraine." Then he mentioned CrowdStrike but added, "There are a lot of things that went on—the whole situation." He wanted Ukraine to cooperate with Barr in the broader investigation into 2016. So you're wrong; it wasn't just CrowdStrike. Later on in the conversation, Zelensky brought up Giuliani and said he hoped Giuliani would see him in Ukraine. Trump encouraged that, noted Giuliani is a very capable guy, and added, "The other thing, there's a lot of talk about Biden's son—that Biden stopped the prosecution—and a lot of people want to find out about that, so whatever you can do with the attorney general would be great. Biden went around bragging that he stopped the prosecution, so if you can look into it, it sounds horrible to me." This is not improper. It is actually a valid request. It is nothing like what the FBI did to Trump in 2016: using phony Russian disinformation as a pretext for spying on him. I think they tried to frame him. People will go to jail for that. One last thing: there is no evidence that Trump or anyone acting on his behalf demanded that Ukraine investigate Biden as a condition for the release of the aid. There is no one who testified, "I was in the room when Zelensky [or the foreign minister or anyone else] was told they would not get the aid." Zelensky and the Ukrainians deny such a demand was made. Without that, there is nothing, just a legitimate request for Ukraine's cooperation.

December 18, 2019

Marc. There was nobody testifying, "I saw O. J. Simpson kill Ron Goldman and Nicole Simpson." Why are you even stating that there was no evidence that Zelensky was told he wouldn't get the aid? I thought it was okay to hold it back?

Marc. Trump is a disgrace. His reputation is tainted; his brand is ruined. When you look up Andrew Johnson, what's the first thing you see?

Stephen. Because there is no evidence, other than Sondland's testimony that Trump told him, "I want nothing." There was overwhelming evidence of O. J.'s guilt. The Democrats, particularly Pelosi, Schiff, and Nadler, are disgraced, not Trump. Comey too. More to follow.

Marc. Trump's letter will memorialize his weak grievance victimhood. At the core of my antipathy for him is his hubris that he is never wrong. His racist letter that the Central Park Five (who I actually think were guilty and not innocent heroes) set the stage. He never apologized for that. He never apologizes for anything.

IMPEACHMENT

MARC. [*Attaches a statement: "Conservatives will someday face the horrible truth that the Republican Party fought so hard to justify and excuse an amoral and self-serving president, and what he gave them in return was bigger government and erosion of the principles and values they once claimed to cherish."*]

STEPHEN. This is ridiculous. Republicans defended Trump against false charges of Russian collusion and the nonsense that raising Joe Biden's corruption with the Ukrainian president is an impeachable offense. The Democrats are fighting to justify the Obama administration's efforts to frame Trump for Russian collusion in the 2016 election and to interfere in the 2020 election. I hope they and we will not look back on their police-state tactics as the point at which we lost control of our government.

MARC. A police-state tactic is ignoring lawful subpoenas.

STEPHEN. Once again, you're talking through the wrong orifice. The subpoena may or may not be lawful. Even if it is lawful, it may be subject to privilege or other defenses. Resisting and testing the validity of subpoenas is part of the process. Eric Holder was the king of ignoring congressional subpoenas. I don't recall Congress initiating impeachment proceedings against him or Obama.

MARC. Today Trump has learned that actions have consequences. He has been punished.

STEPHEN. The Democrats will learn that lesson on November 3, 2020.

MARC. I'll concede one thing: Trump is a phenomenon and is Teflon. Neither his kids nor any associate will enjoy his success. If he wins in 2020 (no doubt with chicanery, if not pure tampering), he'll be impeached again, or the Republican Party will be extinct.

JOHN DINGELL

MARC. John Dingell was a World War II vet and served in Congress for fifty years. He died this year, and he was given a nice federal funeral. Debbie Dingell called Trump some months ago to thank him for the funeral. Trump said at his rally, "John must be looking down now or perhaps looking up." The crowd booed him. So, Steve, this is an example of why I hate him and anyone else who would desecrate another's memory.

MARC. He's buried in Arlington. Would you like to concede that this a revolting thing to say?

STEPHEN. I'm not going to respond to every statement Trump makes. It sounds like it was a joke.

BACK TO COLLUSION

December 21, 2019

MARC. Trump says that he believes Ukraine was hacking because Putin told him.

STEPHEN. I'm not a fan of Putin, but I know the January 2017 Obama administration intelligence assessment that found Putin was seeking to elect Trump was false. I know that the FBI misled the FISA court. I know that the FBI knew there was no collusion prior to Mueller's appointment. Therefore, Putin has as much credibility as those clowns.

MARC. They found a report that Brezhnev said Nixon wasn't guilty, and now they've reversed Nixon's resignation.

STEPHEN. Why do the Democrats lie about everything related to Trump?

MARC. [*Sends tweet stating that VA Choice was signed into law by Obama, not Trump, despite Trump's taking credit for it.*]

MARC. The same reason Trump lies every day.

STEPHEN. Trump is the most honest man in DC.

MARC. I'll let you slide on that one. It's too idiotic to counter. Okay, he's maybe the second-most-honest man behind Justice Brett Kavanaugh.

STEPHEN. Compared to the Democrats, it's not even close. One day you will remove your head from whatever dark canal you have placed it in and will see the light.

MORE ON NAVY SEAL EDDIE GALLAGHER AND THE ARMY-NAVY GAME

December 22, 2019

MARC. [*Attaches a photo of Trump welcoming Navy SEAL Eddie Gallagher.*]

MARC. I won't even try to make my case anymore. I will now only send photos that show what a backward person he is. Yes, I know the story of Gallagher, and even if he was not deserving of such a severe punishment, he had an unbiased review and was by no means a completely innocent person and certainly not a hero to be trotted out by Trump.

STEPHEN. By the way, the Naval Academy reviewed the slanderous lie that the midshipmen and cadets were making white supremacist gestures. As the Naval Academy concluded, of course they weren't. As for Eddie Gallagher, when you volunteer to do what he did for the United States, I'll reconsider your comments.

MARC. Like Trump volunteered when he was of draft age? I can't assess a veteran's conduct? As for the cadets, yeah, sure, they were playing a game: "Whenever you are on TV, you make this sign to get points!"

STEPHEN. You could assess his conduct if you knew anything about him. You know very little—that he took a picture with a dead terrorist. That is inappropriate, but it is one incident in what I believe is a long career. Regarding the cadets, you immediately accepted a false allegation. Whatever they were doing, they weren't making white supremacist gestures. You can't let it go.

December 23, 2019

MARC. You can continue to spin things. I read the details of Gallagher, and he does not deserve to be treated like a hero. This all went down long before Trump got involved. I trust the soldiers who spoke out against him, just like you trust the so-called circle game. You can't have it both ways or have the Trump mantra that there is never culpability, only victims.

STEPHEN. I didn't say that Gallagher did not bear responsibility for breaking the rules regarding the photo. My point is that that transgression does not mean Gallagher is a terrible guy or that he has not served his country honorably. Compare to Bowe Bergdahl, who deserted and caused the death of fellow soldiers who were searching for him. He was referred to as serving honorably.

MARC. Thus, he does not merit being welcomed to Mar-a-Lago, correct?

STEPHEN. That's a political decision. There probably are more people who are grateful to Gallagher for his service as a Navy SEAL than people who believed he should be punished for taking a picture with a corpse. If the navy had not overreached and charged him with murder, he would not have become a cause célèbre. Based on what I know, he is more deserving of being honored than Bergdahl was. Bergdahl, if you recall, got a press conference. Finally, even if you feel it is inappropriate to honor Gallagher, that doesn't support your thesis that every act by Trump is evil.

December 29, 2019

MARC. Wishing you a 2020 filled with health and happiness and an awakening that Trump is the worst thing to happen to this country. He has tweeted all morning—nothing about the Monsey victims. There wasn't this level of anti-Semitic hate before him. Just because his advisers were bold in favor of Israel, his daughter converted, and his grandkids are

Jewish doesn't, in my opinion, mean he is a fan of the Jews. He is disloyal and will be close to any Jew who can help him.

STEPHEN. Thank you for your New Year's wishes. I wish the best for you and the entire family. I look forward to your recognition that whether you support Trump or not, he is far from the worst thing that ever has happened to our country.

MARC. (1) The Civil War, (2) the Vietnam War, (3) the Butt Fumble [another infamous moment in the sad saga of the New York Jets], and (4) Trump.

STEPHEN. I can't argue about the first three.

MORE SPECULATION ABOUT TRUMP'S TIES TO PUTIN

MARC. Here is what happened. It's not hard to connect the dots. Putin wanted Trump not to get close with Ukraine and have a relationship with them. He convinced Trump to stop the aid. All Trump's aides told him not to. Only once the whistleblower came along did he agree to release it. This isn't about Trump's conversation with Zelensky. This is about why he unilaterally stopped the aid in the first place

DECEMBER 30, 2019

STEPHEN. There are no dots. Trump does not believe it is in the United States' interest to be adverse to Putin. He knows the Ukrainians worked against him in 2016. Nevertheless, he has provided Ukraine with lethal military aid, which the Obama administration did not. He wants a Ukrainian commitment to address corruption, particularly the type of corruption that evidence suggests Biden engaged in.

MARC. To say he provided them with aid is ridiculous because he obviously, according to many witness testimonies and reports, held back the aid against everyone's advice and only released it when he had to. I will concede would be an interesting dilemma for Trump if Ukraine actually harmed him personally [in 2016], but is actually a country with which the United States should be strongly allied.

STEPHEN. He provided aid and sold weapons prior to the subject of aid being held up, so it's not ridiculous. Furthermore, I agree it is important to stand up for the territorial integrity of all nations. I further agree that Russia's justification for seizing Crimea and invading Eastern Ukraine—the presence of ethnic Russians—is bull and dangerous. I agree we should support Ukraine, and Trump has provided support. However, I also agree it is not in our interest to alienate Russia, which has more nuclear weapons than any other country. We should be able to work with them to achieve common interests. That may mean being evenhanded with respect to Ukraine.

PART 9
DECEMBER 31, 2019–
APRIL 12, 2020

THE US EMBASSY IN IRAQ

MARC. Our embassy was attacked Benghazi style, and your loser is still on the freaking golf course.

STEPHEN. In this case, the United States is defending the embassy and placing blame where it likely belongs, not on a hapless video maker.

THE KILLING OF SOLEIMANI

January 2, 2020

MARC. If you're in political trouble, with reports surfacing that you were told by the Pentagon that holding back the aid was illegal, start a war to divert attention.

January 3, 2020

STEPHEN. The United States killed one of the worst people in the world. The Iranians are the ones looking for a diversion from the effects of sanctions.

MARC. I have a serious apolitical question. For all the Soleimanis and Bin Ladens who are killed, aren't there replacements waiting to continue their cause with increased zeal for revenge?

STEPHEN. Is your point that it is futile to kill terrorist leaders? Or is it that killing the leaders is not enough, and we need to target hundreds who might take their place? Or, most likely, if Trump takes an action, you believe it was wrong? I believe the economic pressure Trump has placed on Iran is causing Iran significant problems. I further believe the killing of Soleimani and the Hezbollah leader removed an effective military leader and emboldened enemies of the regime. Iran will be in more disarray. Our goal should be to take steps, like killing Soleimani, that will hasten the inevitable collapse of this horrible regime.

MARC. Trump didn't kill Bin Laden. That's why I called it an apolitical question. You are the one who makes everything about Trump.

STEPHEN. Unless, at the time Bin Laden was killed, you expressed concern that killing Bin Laden would result in his replacements continuing their cause with increased zeal, your question was about Trump.

MARC. When my question is about Trump, you'll know it's about Trump.

STEPHEN. Okay. I apologize for putting words in your mouth.

A DIGRESSION TO COLLUSION

MARC. Ha-ha!

MARC. [*Attaches a report that a Deutsche Bank whistleblower told the FBI that a Russian state-owned bank underwrote Trump loans.*]

MARC. I wonder if this has anything to do with Trump being complimentary about Putin.

BACK TO SOLEIMANI

STEPHEN. So you believe that Trump took out Soleimani to distract from impeachment? Not because of the recent Iranian role in attacking the US embassy in Iraq? Not because of the attack that killed the US contractor? You think it is totally contrived? Also, you think Trump wants to distract from impeachment? Why would he do that? It's a disaster for the Democrats. It's 2020. It's time to think before you make mindless attacks on Trump.

MARC. That contractor was meaningless. I like people who weren't killed.

MARC. Saudi Arabia loves that we are on the verge of taking out Iran.

MARC. What happened to de-escalation?

STEPHEN. I don't think we're on the verge of taking out Iran. I believe the Iranians will talk a big game but will act much more cautiously. I believe the Iranian government will eventually fall at the hands of the Iranian people. Trump's economic pressure and the killing of Soleimani will hasten the eventual end of the Islamic republic.

MARC. Hope you are right!

BACK TO IMPEACHMENT

January 14, 2020

Marc. Damning news today. Serious. Keep an open mind. Yovanovitch was a successful and honest diplomat; there's no evidence to the contrary, despite her possibly not intervening with the Hunter Biden issue. Trump was entitled to fire her. Many believe the plan was to remove her to pave the way for influencing Zelensky. But today the text messages from Parnas show they were spying on her and confirming that she was alone one night. Per the evidence, it was said, "Some things are going to happen to her." In addition, Trump lawyers Sekulow and Giuliani both sent letters acknowledging that Trump wanted to communicate with Zelensky privately. Why privately?

Stephen. Dreams, dreams, dreams. Trump didn't need to get her out of the way. All he had to do was fire her. As for the significance of Trump wanting to speak with Zelensky privately, I have no idea what you're talking about, but whatever it is, it will blow up like all the other things that supposedly were going to take Trump down. By the way, the media was certain the killing of Soleimani fortified support for the Iranian regime. How long did that idiocy take to blow up?

January 16, 2020

Stephen. Robert H. Jackson, who was a Supreme Court justice from 1941 through 1954 (appointed by FDR) and the chief prosecutor for the Nuremberg war crimes trials, in a speech he made to federal prosecutors, explained why the current impeachment farce is an abuse of power. He noted that a prosecutor could likely find reasons to prosecute anyone and that "it is not a question of discovering the commission of a crime and then looking for the man who committed it, it is a question of picking the man and then searching the law books, or putting investigators to work, to pin some offense on him … It is in this realm—in which the prosecutor picks some person whom he dislikes or desires to embarrass … and then looks for an offense—that the greatest danger of abuse of prosecuting power lies. It is here that law enforcement becomes personal, and the real crime becomes that of being unpopular with the predominant or governing group, being attached to the wrong political views, or being personally obnoxious."

MARC. Interesting. Someone once wrote, "Trump is a lying schmuck with henchmen and sycophants, and his days as POTUS are numbered." That was Marc on January 16, 2020.

STEPHEN. You're right; this statement will also be quoted in the future in psychological studies trying to explain the irrational opposition to the Trump presidency (2017–2025), notwithstanding the longstanding economic and foreign policy successes achieved.

MARC. You should be in my sister and brother-in-law's camp. They say he is an ass and a moron but better than any of the Democratic candidates. All I can say, being true to myself, is "I want what I want," and I want anyone but Trump. It's not irrational. Some people have a better detector for evil.

STEPHEN. Did you see the Project Veritas interview with a Bernie Sanders campaign worker who believes that reeducation camps should be established for billionaires (and highly successful orthopedists)? I think your evil detector needs recalibration.

MARC. Perhaps.

JANUARY 17, 2020

MARC. Alan Dershowitz defended Trump this evening by stating that abuse of power is not impeachable, and the founders wanted it that way. Well, at least we can agree that he abused his power!

MARC. Because you don't make an argument that something somebody did "isn't illegal" if he didn't do the thing in the first place. Your argument would be "He didn't do the thing."

MARC. [*Attaches a tweet showing messages to and from Devin Nunes's staff regarding Ukraine.*]

MARC. This is Devin Nunes's assistant coordinating with Lev Parnas to dig up dirt on Biden, yet Devin Nunes was the ranking member who denied even knowing who Parnas was and claimed the coordination to get dirt on Biden was ridiculous.

STEPHEN. Trump wanted Ukraine to investigate Biden. He asked them to do it. That's not an abuse of power, but even if you accept for the sake of argument that it is an abuse of power, it's not impeachable. Similarly, delaying the aid was not an abuse of power, but even if you accept for the sake of argument that it is an abuse of power, it is not impeachable. I don't know what these tweets prove, except that it appears they were looking for information related to actual allegations.

JANUARY 18, 2020

MARC. If Donald Trump went to Moscow next week and signed an agreement with Putin to cede Alaska to Russia, would that be an impeachable offense? A simple yes or no, please. You know the answer.

STEPHEN. Does Adam Schiff claim that Trump sold Alaska to Russia?

MARC. Answer my question, please.

STEPHEN. I do not know all the reasons why a president could not sell a state, but I have no doubt it would be illegal, unconstitutional, an abuse of power, and, ultimately, a nullity. In fact, I doubt it would be possible to sell a state. I note that we fought a civil war over the principle that a state, once admitted to the Union, could not secede. As I'm not able to imagine the context for this stupid hypothetical, it doesn't deserve a response. However, if Trump took an action that was outside of his power (he has no power to sell a state) and, in doing so, violated the rights of millions of Americans, among other issues, that would be impeachable. However, this has nothing to do with Trump's conduct of foreign policy within his constitutional authority.

MARC. Dershowitz today said that Trump could do so; it would be an abuse of power but not impeachable.

STEPHEN. If that's what Dershowitz said, I disagree. I don't think Dershowitz has thought that hypothetical through.

STEPHEN. I would have to read it for myself.

STEPHEN. I also note that Ukraine did not sell Crimea. Russia took it by force. However, I believe if Russia invaded Alaska, the US Congress would declare war. If the president, in such a situation, allowed Russia's occupation to stand, it would likely be treason.

MARC. Fair response. Sometimes you make sense.

MARC. As I think about it more, Trump's actions with Zelensky, as I see them, might indeed lower the bar for future impeachments, but to me, that doesn't exonerate Trump for ridiculously bad judgment, and hardly any of his backers will even cede that, except and unless more and more evidence surfaces.

STEPHEN. There are two reasons why Trump supporters should not give credence to the Democrats' case for impeachment: (1) The Democrats have been talking about impeachment from the moment Trump was elected. The Mueller report didn't do it. Then Schiff raised the issue of Ukraine after his staff met with the whistleblower, and he claimed, falsely, that Trump repeatedly demanded that Zelensky "dig up dirt on [his] opponent—lots of it." (2) The Democrats have had no interest in Obama's and Clinton's use of US intelligence and foreign intelligence to surveil Trump's campaign and to create the false Russian collusion narrative.

January 20, 2020

MARC. [*Attaches a tweet with a 1998 quote from Dershowitz stating that impeachment doesn't require a crime "if you have somebody who completely corrupts the office of the president and who abuses trust and who poses great danger to our liberty."*]

STEPHEN. None of that is true about Trump, but it is true of the Democrats.

MARC. I'm glad he clarified that a noncrime can be impeachable.

STEPHEN. In this case, there is no crime, there is no abuse of power, and there is no corruption of the office—there is nothing.

MARC. Well, Alan Dershowitz explained all weekend that abuse of power is not impeachable, so since he would only be making pertinent comments, we can infer there was a nonimpeachable abuse of power. And one of the Republican senators declared that Trump is human and made some mistakes. Yes, so is Clinton.

STEPHEN. The problem with this impeachment is that the Democrats were looking for a basis for impeaching Trump from the day he was elected. Mueller disappointed them. They were determined to act prior to the election. Schiff clearly was working to find something. He worked with the whistleblower to concoct this nonsense. However, there is no impeachable conduct; therefore, they have to convince useful idiots like you that a nonevent like this Ukraine story justifies removing the president from office by claiming he abused his power. Thankfully, most Americans, even many who don't support Trump, understand what's going on.

MARC. If there had been no whistleblower, how would they have succeeded in achieving that goal?

STEPHEN. There would have been something else. According to Pelosi and Schiff, every act he takes is impeachable, even killing one of the most dangerous terrorists in the world. The press would give credence to virtually any charges against Trump.

MARC. That's ridiculous. Your comments usually aren't. This is.

STEPHEN. Why is it ridiculous? It's absolutely true.

MARC. Before the whistleblower, impeachment was dead.

STEPHEN. That's why they were looking for something. You don't really believe that the Democrats believe the Ukraine allegations are impeachable, do you? They could not even figure out how to characterize it. And these are the same people who oppose Durham's investigation into real wrongdoing—working with foreign governments to entrap Trump campaign aides—and ignore the FISA abuse findings. The Democrats know it's bullshit, but they have cheerleaders like you who don't care.

MARC. I concur they were looking for something. And you should concur that the Republicans were looking for stuff on Obama.

STEPHEN. The Republicans did not impeach Obama, nor was it ever realistically considered. This is true, although Obama spent money that was not authorized by Congress, weaponized the IRS to go after conservatives, made changes to Obamacare without going to Congress, and more. All these acts were abuses of power and had much more significant consequences than the Ukraine situation. Finally, Obama permitted the government to surveil the opposition party's candidate in 2016.

MARC. Yet despite those transgressions, the Republicans were so ethical that they decided not to pursue impeachment of O? It was the wrong thing to do, huh?

MARC. Trump's actions indeed have zero consequences. Because he was caught.

STEPHEN. The only fact is that the administration released the aid within the scheduled time frame. It doesn't matter why he did it. Nor is there evidence that he did anything for his personal benefit. Nor is there evidence that Ukraine was pressured in an unusual way. Obama violated the rights of Americans.

MARC. Yeah, there's evidence.

STEPHEN. There are allegations, not evidence. Trump asked Ukraine for a favor for "us" based on what our country just went through (Trump spoke to Zelensky the day after Mueller testified). The Ukrainians have stated that they were not pressured (but even if they had been pressured, it would mean nothing), and there were several meetings following the call in which aid was not mentioned. The picture is accurate.

JANUARY 25, 2020

MARC. Trump is on tape with Parnas, a guy he previously said he didn't know. Parnas has tapes. Today the newly released tape shows Trump asking in 2018 how long Ukraine could last without our help against Russia, and he was told, "Thirty seconds." Yet he held aid back. As I will tell you tomorrow, wake up! He is a thug.

STEPHEN. Ignorance is bliss. Putting aside whether the United States has an interest in supporting Ukraine against Russia, Trump has provided military aid to Ukraine. The Obama administration did not. The aid package that is the subject of this idiocy was released on time. Tell me—what did Trump do wrong?

January 26, 2020

MARC. [*Attaches a Trump tweet in which he says, "Shifty Adam Schiff is a CORRUPT POLITICIAN, and probably a very sick man. He has not paid the price, yet for what he has done to our country."*]

MARC. This is a threat that will spark some people to enact violence.

STEPHEN. First, it is demonstrably true. Schiff is a proven liar. He lied about the FISA application. He lied about the whistleblower. Second, political violence is much more prevalent from Antifa and BLM.

MARC. If Adam Schiff were to be assassinated, would you look at this tweet in a new light?

STEPHEN. The only congressmen targeted for assassination have been Steve Scalise and Republican colleagues. Schiff is Trump's ace in the hole.

MARC. [*Attaches a tweet alleging that according to the* New York Times, *John Bolton wrote in the manuscript of his upcoming book that "Trump told Bolton in August he wanted freezing of Ukraine aid until officials there would help investigate Democrats."*]

STEPHEN. Is Bolton quoted? This is the playbook. They're trying to keep the story alive. However, it doesn't change the fact that Trump did not seek a quid pro quo, the Ukrainians never felt threatened in any way, the Ukrainians did not announce an investigation, and the aid was released.

MARC. They felt threatened. They just couldn't speak up about it.

STEPHEN. Next time you have drinks with Zelensky in New York, invite me to join you. I assume you must be good friends. He hasn't confided in anyone else.

January 27, 2020

MARC. [*Attaches a tweet with attached clips of Fox anchor Steve Doocy saying, in December 2019, it would be a big deal if Trump had told Zelensky, "I'll give you the money, but you have to investigate Joe Biden," and, on January 27, 2020, questioning whether the* New York Times *report on the Bolton manuscript offered anything new.*]

STEPHEN. Putting aside the fact that Steve Doocy's legal opinion has no relevance, I do not believe Bolton is alleged to have stated that Trump made a demand on the Ukrainians. The allegation is that Bolton has stated that Trump told him that was his reason for delaying the release of the aid. Regardless of what Trump discussed with Bolton, which, by the way, is and should be privileged, the aid was released without any strings attached. There is no question that Trump wanted the Ukrainians to investigate Biden's role in Ukrainian investigations into Burisma. There is also no question, as stated above, that the aid was released. It also is clear that Trump did not personally raise the question of aid with Zelensky and that there were several meetings between administration and Ukrainian officials after the July 25 call, in which aid was not mentioned. The Ukrainians have publicly stated that they were not pressured. Finally, a privileged discussion between Trump and Bolton (assuming it is what is being reported, which I do not believe) is not the same as making a demand on the Ukrainians.

MARC. The aid was released—from Trump holding it up—because of the whistleblower. There isn't the evidence to show that, but the time line is crystal clear on it, and evidence can be inferred if it's circumstantial. You know I'm right about this, and you should even admit it, because it doesn't hurt your case that he can do whatever he wants to do. Why didn't Republicans investigate Biden when he was vice president and they had the majority in both houses?

STEPHEN. It doesn't matter why Trump held up the aid, and it doesn't matter why he released it. He's entitled to consider his options, even options he later rejects. The bottom line is that the Ukrainians received the aid with no strings attached. That's the only fact that matters. Furthermore, it is ridiculous to argue that Biden's conduct does not raise legitimate questions. Are you arguing that the Republicans should have convened an impeachment inquiry into Biden, or do you now believe all presidents and vice presidents should be under constant investigation? There would have been no political benefit to raising an issue in Obama's second term that would have been (as it has been) dismissed by the press.

MARC. Oh, it does matter. Let's say he held it up because he was trying to siphon it to his kids. Would that matter? You are making unforced errors in your usually effective game!

MARC. If they found Palestinians plotting to bomb the Kotel [the Western Wall in Jerusalem] on a Tuesday, and then Tuesday came, and the Palestinians decided to hold off the bombing, none of that matters? "The bottom line is that they never bombed anything."

MARC. Biden's conduct was probably shady and irrelevant to Trump, who should have turned it over to the Department of Justice if he wanted something done, not some shady back channel.

STEPHEN. It's your position that Trump should be impeached and removed from office (1) because he asked the Ukrainians to investigate the circumstances surrounding a Ukrainian corruption investigation and the role the Bidens played in that investigation and (2) because Trump might have considered holding up aid to Ukraine to pressure them to do it, even though the aid was released with no strings attached. Really? Do you know any doctors who thought of filing an embellished claim for reimbursement for a medical procedure? If the doctor considers it but doesn't do it, should the doctor be kicked out of the network? If a doctor friend came to you and told you, "I'm going to file a false claim," and you responded, "That's not a good idea," would you write to the insurance company to have your friend kicked out of the network?

January 28, 2020

MARC. Here is what happened. Trump, or one of his goons, said, "Let's hold back this aid to get Ukraine to besmirch Biden by announcing an investigation," thinking, *It's perfect because we will be helping Putin too!* That's what happened. He announced to the world that China should investigate Biden. Why the hell would he ask China to do that?

STEPHEN. Biden is corrupt. Unlike Trump, he and his family have profited off his positions.

MARC. Biden has been in government his whole life and probably is as guilty as any other member of Congress in terms of favors. I'm sure there is absolutely nothing to Bibi's indictment, right? It's a witch hunt, right? Haven't you told me that nobody is guilty of anything until proven guilty?

STEPHEN. Yes. You're right. No one has proven that Biden is corrupt, but his brothers, his son, and his son-in-law all have made money in ventures that have government connections. Hunter may not even be the most egregious. His family's government-funded ventures and businesses are documented. These benefits and sweetheart deals are paid for with our money or, as in the case of Hunter, at the expense of legitimate US interests. Bibi's case, as I understand it, is a stretch. One of the things he is accused of is doing favors for media in exchange for better coverage. I don't remember the details, but it was not compelling. However, I think Bibi has been a great prime minister, but he's been in power a long time. For that reason alone, it may be time to give someone new a chance.

January 29, 2020

MARC. If release of the aid to Ukraine was not conditioned on the investigations, then what was required to have the aid released?

STEPHEN. Apparently, nothing. The aid was released with no strings attached.

MARC. But like the day after the whistleblower report, it was released. Let's see if you agree with this. Republicans could make the argument, "Bolton probably is correct, and Trump held the aid for questionable reasons, but it's not impeachable, so we don't need Bolton to testify." Instead, they argue, "The Dems had their chance to procure evidence, so it's too late," which is ridiculous since the Dems couldn't get Bolton.

STEPHEN. That's irrelevant. In the United States, considering doing a criminal act is not a criminal act. In this case, delaying release of the aid, whatever the reason, is not criminal. However, Trump indicated to Senator Ron Johnson at the end of August that the aid would be released. Therefore, your premise is wrong.

MARC. Conspiracy.

MARC. If the release was held back because of corruption, why was it released soon after?

STEPHEN. In all likelihood, the aid was held back while Trump considered his options. He wanted to ensure the money would not be wasted through corruption, and as part of that, he wanted them to do the investigations. However, no one ever told Ukraine that release of the aid was conditional, and Trump decided or was persuaded by his advisers to release the aid.

MARC. Excuse me. He has already stated that he was concerned about corruption. So what was resolved in that sphere that allowed for the release? I guess the Biden situation was already sorted out?

MARC. Just admit what the whole world knows and stick to it not being impeachable, because this defense undercuts your own intelligence.

MARC. We know why he held it up, and we know why he released it. Everyone knows.

MARC. That's who he is.

STEPHEN. It doesn't matter if he did it, because it was a nonevent. Why don't you admit that it should not have been the subject of an impeachment inquiry? This was concocted by Schiff, who worked with the whistleblower to undermine Trump in the 2020 election. They (Schiff and the whistleblower) planned to claim that Trump asked Ukraine to make up dirt on Biden (which is what the Democrats did to Trump), but Trump released the transcript. If you want to know who the Democrats are, wait for the Durham investigation. The Durham report will detail real election interference.

MARC. I'm still waiting for Comey to be in jail.

STEPHEN. The inspector general's report on FISA abuse, which outlines the FBI's abuse of power, was not enough for you? There is more coming.

MARC. [*Attaches a tweet from Hillary Clinton adviser Philippe Reines commenting on Trump tripping over his words during a rally in Wildwood, New Jersey.*]

MARC. This idiot made fun of Biden for stuttering.

STEPHEN. But it's okay for government officials to discuss invoking the Twenty-Fifth Amendment or for CNN anchors to mock Trump and Trump voters? Trump is treated disrespectfully, and Biden is protected.

MARC. Play that video back and forth. This is the man you think is fit to be president. Neurologically, psychologically, and every other *-ically*, he is deficient.

STEPHEN. Your point is ridiculous. Trump speaks at these rallies for over an hour without notes. He is entertaining. None of his lifeless Democratic opponents can do it, and they would be boring. Bernie is the only one who might approach Trump in the ability to hold a crowd. However, he'd be a total disaster as president. The economy would tank, and the United States would stand with the world's dictators and anti-Semites.

MARC. [*Attaches a tweet showing a clip of Alan Dershowitz arguing about the standards for establishing a quid pro quo, which the tweeter summarizes as "Trump can't be impeached because he believed his reelection is in the national interest."*]

MARC. Congrats. You are no longer the lawyer with the stupidest defense of Trump!

MARC. If Zelensky called Trump and said, "Hey, I have info on Biden. If you give me millions in aid, I'll give you the dirt," and Trump agreed, would that be okay?

STEPHEN. First, thank you for comparing me to Dershowitz. That's a real compliment. Regarding your example, a circumstance completely different from this situation, that's also impossible, because aid has to be authorized by Congress. Also, Trump didn't ask for dirt. He asked for an investigation into credible allegations. Finally, if Ukraine has information on wrongdoing, Ukraine is obligated by a treaty to cooperate with the United States. However, if your question is whether Trump could be impeached if he engaged in conduct that met the requirements for impeachment, the answer is yes. Unfortunately for people like you suffering from Trump derangement syndrome, Trump hasn't engaged in any such conduct.

MARC. By the way, I conceded that it is actually persuading me that this is split on party lines. I do believe Republicans would be forced to convict if it was clear. It's just that the hubris of Trump's "perfect call" is intolerable.

MARC. [*Attaches a tweet from Andy McCarthy in which he opines that Dershowitz's argument on a quid pro quo went too far.*]

MARC. I'm right!

STEPHEN. Why? You're okay with the Democrats fishing for a reason to impeach Trump for three years? That's tolerable? How about launching the Mueller probe with full knowledge that Trump did not collude? That's tolerable? Did you see the interview Bolton gave to Radio Free Europe in August? He praised Trump's "warm and cordial" call with Zelensky. Yes, a perfect call.

January 31, 2020

Marc. I'm glad several Republican senators and countless more have come to agree with my assessment that Trump's actions were wrong. Feel free to read their statements. I don't necessarily disagree that he doesn't deserve to be impeached if the Senate votes as such, and I actually believe if something was more blatantly wrong, the Republicans would vote for impeachment. This is the thought process of someone who assesses facts and has an improved mind, not bragging about a "perfect call" or saying, "Schiff is sick in the head," as you have said.

Stephen. Explain to me what was wrong.

Marc. It is idiotic and, frankly, given that you represent a highly intelligent part of the population, disturbing that you stick to the party line that Trump cared about corruption as the reason to request the investigation. Tell me that politics is dirty, tell me the Democrats probably do stuff like this all the time, and we can discuss it, but everyone knows what Trump was trying to do long before his call with Zelensky, and now there is reporting—and you know the reporting is almost always accurate—that Bolton was told to start the investigation into Biden with Zelensky.

Stephen. You make statements that reflect your belief that Trump is a bad guy but have no factual basis. I don't know what "Everyone knows what Trump was trying to do" means. There is plenty of evidence that Trump was concerned about corruption. When he learned there was evidence that Biden was involved in potential corruption, I'm sure that got his attention. But why is that wrong? The bottom line is that Trump raised Biden's name because he was presented with evidence of corruption. Notwithstanding the Democrats' claims, Biden has not been cleared by anyone at any time. Compare that to what was done to Trump in 2016: the government used the Steele dossier, a document based on false stories fed to the Clinton campaign by Russian operatives, to investigate and spy on Trump.

FEBRUARY 2, 2020

MARC. Do you think Melania Trump's "Be Best" initiative to combat cyberbullying is a worthwhile endeavor? I'm expecting a simple yes as a response. I happen to think it is.

STEPHEN. I'm sure it is. What's your angle? Are you going to accuse Trump of cyberbullying?

MARC. [*Attaches a Trump tweet mocking "Mini Mike" Bloomberg and his need to stand on boxes on the debate stage.*]

MARC. "That's different," you'll say. It's not like the husband of the leader of the cyberbullying project, who happens to be the most visible person on earth, could do or say anything to undermine her plan.

STEPHEN. That's not cyberbullying; that's politics. If Bloomberg can't take it, he should drop out of the race. Trump and Trump supporters are mocked on a daily basis, but Trump's way of handling it will be to win reelection.

FEBRUARY 4, 2020

MARC. [*Attaches a clip of Trump making hand gestures, as if encouraging people to sing along, during the playing of the national anthem.*]

MARC. I rest my case. Phony, hypocrite, moron, and senile.

STEPHEN. Are you serious?

MARC. Do you see anyone else in the room doing anything that a child would do? Stand still and wait? What a moron he is.

STEPHEN. If you think Trump's gestures are worth outrage, Trump is not the moron.

MARC. I think you just called me a moron.

STEPHEN. I would never call you a moron.

FEBRUARY 5, 2020

MARC. Even a Republican senator thinks Trump is guilty!

STEPHEN. He's going to be acquitted. So he's not guilty. Mitt Romney is wrong.

MARC. Trump was impeached. The sting of history.

MARC. The humiliation!

STEPHEN. Not exactly. If he's reelected, which I believe he will be, the Democrats will suffer the sting of history.

MARC. The vote for conviction was bipartisan.

STEPHEN. The vote for conviction did not pass. Also, there were more votes for Clinton's conviction.

STEPHEN. Romney is wrong. Trump did not corrupt the election in any way. He didn't do anything wrong. That's why he was acquitted. One day we will find out the truth about the whistleblower.

THE STATE OF THE UNION AND IMPEACHMENT AFTERMATH

STEPHEN. What did you think of Pelosi's behavior at the State of the Union?

FEBRUARY 6, 2020

MARC. [*Attaches a video of Adam Schiff's summation in the impeachment trial.*]

MARC. I think Republicans play dirty and, in Trump's case, so childishly that Dems can no longer take the high road.

MARC. [*Attaches a statement by Senator Rob Portman: "I have consistently said that Mr. Trump's request for an investigation of Joe Biden and any effort to tie the release of military aid to investigations were improper and shouldn't have happened."*]

MARC. This opinion is echoed by many Republicans.

STEPHEN. It's over. Of course you blame Trump for Pelosi's behavior. Trump is all-powerful.

MARC. Tearing a piece of paper has you and everyone else all hot and bothered.

STEPHEN. I find her ridiculous. She and her compadres never tire of making fools of themselves.

MARC. They are making fools of themselves in the eyes of many people, and Republicans are doing the same thing in the eyes of many other people. Everybody plays the fool sometimes.

STEPHEN. Americans will render their verdict on Election Day. We will see if there is a majority for nonstop harassment of Trump, lying, and spying on opposition party candidates or for economic growth, among other achievements.

MARC. We won't know because the Republicans already may have rigged voting machines purchased from China.

STEPHEN. Based on Iowa [the delay in counting the votes], I would keep my eye on the Democrats.

MARC. Oh, really. What do you think the Dems did? Make Sanders tie for first with a gay man whom blacks don't find appealing? Learn your material.

MARC. Let me stick to the Dem candidate analysis.

MARC. The Dems, my adopted children …

STEPHEN. I don't know what the Iowa Democratic party did, but I do know that the best you can say about them is that they're incompetent.

MARC. In 2012, it took three weeks to declare Rick Santorum the winner, so maybe it's an Iowa thing.

MARC. You're losing your touch. You're starting to act like me, talking shit without even knowing the facts.

STEPHEN. How is that? Does *Morning Joe* or Don Lemon claim the voting in Iowa went off without a hitch?

February 8, 2020

Marc. [*Attaches a tweet from* New York Times *columnist Frank Rich in which he states, "Trump loves 'the Jewish people' so much we can assume it's coincidence that he is prioritizing attacks against Vindman, Sondland—both from Jewish immigrant families."*]

Stephen. I'll answer after I finish laughing.

February 9, 2020

Marc. [*Attaches a tweet that states, "Republicans actually are proponents of impeaching a President for no reason. What they object to is impeaching a President for a good reason."*]

Marc. Good point here. Regardless of who the Democratic president would be, one day he must be impeached!

Stephen. Really? What is the basis for this statement?

Marc. Mark Levin. That's who.

Stephen. It will not happen, even if there would be a basis for it.

February 11, 2020

Marc. I don't think you have to worry about me being a lefty, as I'm bothered by watching how they are trying to paint Bloomberg, through stop-and-frisk, as supremely racist.

Marc. And unlike you, who's had a polarized view of everything, I am thrilled that Jussie Smollett was reindicted.

STEPHEN. I have an informed view, but I'm glad you recognize that Bloomberg is being treated unfairly. Just take that thought a little further. I haven't read about Smollett, but he deserves to be punished.

MARC. Your view has few, if any, objective departures from your side—the side that has many bad, bad people. People who think slavery had its merits. People who think the Holocaust was made up. People who wear swastikas. Don't give me your "BLM is worse" argument. They are a fringe, extreme group born to fight against legitimate discrimination. Did you have a problem with Haganah terror in the nascent state of 1930s–1940s Israel?

STEPHEN. I don't think any of those things and don't support anyone who does. If you want to understand "terror" committed by the Irgun (not the Haganah), read *The Revolt* by Begin. You'll be very proud.

THE ROGER STONE SENTENCE

February 12, 2020

MARC. I assume you are fine with Trump trying to disparage the judge in the Roger Stone case?

STEPHEN. I don't know what Trump said, but the proposed sentence for Stone was outrageous.

MARC. Do you still have zero concerns that Trump views himself as an autocrat dictator?

MARC. That he is someone who thinks the law doesn't apply to him?

MARC. [*Attaches a tweet displaying a statement by Senator Lisa Murkowski criticizing Trump's comments on the Stone sentence.*]

STEPHEN. No. Stone was tried for lying to Congress and obstruction of an investigation that should never have taken place. The FBI knew there was no collusion before Mueller was appointed. It was an investigation in search of a crime.

MARC. So you can selectively lie under oath to police if you believe the charges to be unfair or incorrect?

MARC. This a new thing in the law?

STEPHEN. No, that's not the point. The point is that Stone was a subject of an investigation that was not investigating an actual crime but looking for a crime. The Mueller probe had no business in questioning Stone. Even though Stone's conviction for lying and witness tampering might be based on facts, he was being harassed because of his association with

Trump. His sentence should reflect that he was put in a terrible and very costly position for illegitimate purposes.

MARC. What would your sentence be?

STEPHEN. Probation. He should be pardoned. What was done to Stone is sickening.

MARC. That's crazy.

STEPHEN. Comey lied to Congress about consequential matters. How many years should he get?

MARC. I don't know. He wasn't indicted.

FEBRUARY 13, 2020

STEPHEN. Stone is accused of inconsequential crimes related to an illegitimate investigation. He's sixty-seven years old and has never been in trouble. When your heroes are indicted for consequential crimes—violations of civil rights and interference in the 2016 election—I expect you will demand long sentences if they are convicted (which they should be), but I won't hold my breath.

MARC. *Inconsequential felony* is an oxymoron. You are a lawyer. You cannot break the law with the rationalization that you believe an investigation was unjust. Investigations are investigations. That's how our system works. We aren't fascist just yet. Vindman heard those calls with Trump and Zelensky, which many Republicans currently in power already have stated were improper, and he reported them. I completely understand why he would now be dismissed. But investigated for crimes? Steve, would *that* be a legitimate investigation? Yes or no? If they went into computers and found that he was a pedophile, would that be a legitimate discovery because "they were looking for a crime," as you say? When I think about how easy it is to win debates with you, I temper my excitement, knowing you are playing a losing hand very well.

STEPHEN. Your analysis is based on your feelings about Trump. The average sentence for a person convicted of rape is four years. Stone was arrested by a SWAT team, prosecuted, and sentenced not because anything he did justifies it but because he supports Trump. Vindman very possibly committed crimes. He leaked information.

MARC. He leaked information? You don't think Stone has actually been pulling stuff like that for years?

STEPHEN. No. He's not a member of the National Security Council. He wasn't accused of leaking.

MARC. He was not only accused but convicted of things, including perjury, which you felt was enough to impeach Clinton.

STEPHEN. I wasn't in favor of removing Clinton, but the case for removal of Clinton was much better than the noncase against Trump. As far as Stone is concerned, he's not a president.

GIULIANI AND NEW YORK STATE

MARC. [*Attaches a tweet accusing Trump of contradicting himself on whether he directed Giuliani to go to Ukraine.*]

MARC. Can I get an "Okay, so I guess he lied one time" from you?

STEPHEN. First, Rudy represented Trump in the Mueller probe. He went to Ukraine to investigate the phony Russian collusion allegations, some of which originated with Ukrainians. Rudy went to Ukraine to do his job. Therefore, Trump likely did not direct him to go to Ukraine. Because the question is not specific, it is impossible to determine whether Trump lied. If you ask bad questions, you get bad answers. Also, who cares?

FEBRUARY 14, 2020

MARC. Trump tweeted, "New York must stop all of its unnecessary lawsuits & harassment."

MARC. The lawsuits he wants dropped are against him!

STEPHEN. You're right. There's nothing political in New York State's suing the president.

MARC. He writes that they should stay away from politics and, in the next sentence, politics!

STEPHEN. Relax.

MARC. That is actually an apt and comforting reply. I'll try to. If he was just a buffoon, I could deal. Reagan and GWB were a bit of that. But they were also a bit self-deprecating. And altruistic.

STEPHEN. Reagan was the best president in my lifetime. He is a giant.

MARC. I agree, but he was losing it in the end. That's well known.

STEPHEN. Not true.

DOJ DECLINES TO PURSUE CHARGES AGAINST ANDREW MCCABE

MARC. [*Attaches a copy of the DOJ's letter to McCabe advising him that he is not being charged.*]

MARC. What happened to McCabe going to jail? Or is Barr corrupt?

STEPHEN. I don't know the details, but I know he was referred for prosecution by the inspector general. However, I'm waiting for Durham. If no one is indicted for Crossfire Hurricane and FISA abuse, etc., I will accept that I overstated the wrongdoing. However, based on the inspector general's report, there was serious and consequential misconduct. I will be surprised if there are no indictments. Also, it's disturbing that a guy like Stone is prosecuted and convicted over nothing, and those identified by the inspector general for leaking and lying have not been prosecuted.

TRUMP RALLIES

February 21, 2020

MARC. [*Attaches a clip of Trump criticizing CNN, Comcast, and MSNBC at a rally.*]

MARC. At least he is presidential. You know, at one of these rallies, he is going to say, "Those black people—terrible." He already said, "They ought to bring back movies like *Gone with the Wind*!" Steve, do you know the terrain that movie covers?

STEPHEN. Please rejoin the real world. Trump has made inroads with the black community because he takes their concerns seriously. He is going to receive at least double the black vote that he received in 2016. I read *Gone with the Wind* and saw the movie. Did you know the actress who played Scarlett's lifelong servant was the first black woman to receive an Academy Award?

MARC. The president of United States gets up and spews hate for two hours. A rant with people clapping because they think they are part of the show.

MARC. He doesn't inspire, doesn't educate, and doesn't talk about the world; he just mocks people based on their looks and their height.

STEPHEN. He does make fun of his antagonists, but he doesn't spew hate.

MARC. Oh, okay. That's fine then.

STEPHEN. You seem to think it is okay to make false claims about Trump; investigate him and everyone associated with him, looking for crimes; and, after coming up empty, continue to accuse him of collusion, racism, and more. But if he mocks them, he's spewing hate.

WHO ARE THE BAD GUYS?

MARC. It's pointless to convince you. It saddens me that you can't recognize that Trump is a bad person, and Schiff and Comey are good people. Look at their whole lives. There is a reason they were trying, within the bounds of the law (as neither has been charged, despite your promises), and maybe even skirting propriety, like Trump has done his whole life, to take Trump out. The reason is as likely to surface as are your promises that Comey and Schiff will be imprisoned. I cite yesterday's story that Russia is meddling again, which resulted in the firing of the messenger.

STEPHEN. Comey and Schiff are terrible and dangerous people. You have very bad judgment. You think making false allegations and dragging people through the mud is okay? Russian meddling occurred during the Obama administration. It was ignored but for good reason: it was inconsequential.

MARC. [Attaches a clip of Trump at a rally in which he jokingly stated, "Who likes Jake Tapper?" and then discussed a report by Jake Tapper that he thought was fair.]

MARC. So he insults the guy and commends and respects his posts while saying that he is being told what to say and not say. I see why you respect Trump so much!

STEPHEN. In your view, anyone can make any statement about Trump, including outright lies or plain idiotic comments, such as the dictator meme, but Trump is a terrible person for responding. The media's treatment of Trump and its rooting for impeachment are nauseating.

MARC. All accusations against Trump are based on facts and evidence, as flimsy as you think them to be, and are not about his looks! I have an issue with that—sorry! And the impeachment is over—he was "exonerated," in his words—so why continue with this daily diatribe? And why refer to any political opponent (e.g., Little Marco, Little Bob Corker) as short? If you are tall and you refer to someone small as *little* or *shorty*, you are an effin' asshole. Agree?

MARC. I can't stand that my president is an asshole. It's that simple. And you know it too.

STEPHEN. No. The allegations against Trump are based on outright lies (Russian collusion) or political disagreements (unelected bureaucrats who think they make policy). The only thing that is likely true about Ukraine is that Biden profited off his office.

MORE ON RACISM

February 22, 2020

MARC. [*Attaches a tweet posted by Donald Trump Jr. captioned "Pocahontas taking some scalps here," regarding Elizabeth Warren's dismantling of Mike Bloomberg during a Democratic primary debate.*]

MARC. I'm curious what your definition of *racism* is and how this could not fit within it. And I caution, or perhaps educate, you: something can be both racist and funny to some who hear the "joke."

STEPHEN. Trump Jr.'s comment has nothing to do with race. He refers to Warren as Pocahontas because it highlights her decades-long lie about being part Cherokee. Native Americans scalped their enemies (look it up). By describing Warren's beatdown of Bloomberg as Pocahontas "taking scalps," he mocks both of them—her for her false claims and Bloomberg for his weak performance. The comment in no way suggests Trump Jr. is expressing any views about Native Americans, mocking Native Americans, or characterizing the behavior of Native Americans. My guess is that the only ones who find the tweet racist are white liberals. It is similar to the effort to force the Redskins to change their name. We found out that most Native Americans liked the name. However, I'm glad you have the ability to find racism wherever it may lurk.

MARC. I supposed you, as of 2016, support the rights of Confederates to brandish the Union Jack?

MARC. Also, please tell this rookie, since you are such a Donald Trump devotee, how one deciphers when he says things but is "only joking." Like "I'm going to be president after 2024." Wait! I know your response: "He is only joking, but if he did want to do that, he could, but he doesn't mean it."

STEPHEN. I agree that state governments in the South should not include the Confederate battle flag (the Stars and Bars) in their state flags. I agree because that flag represented the fight to keep slaves. However, I'm against erasing it from history. As for individuals who wave the flag, it is problematic.

STEPHEN. If you're concerned that Trump does not plan to leave after his term is over, take your meds.

MORE ON ROGER STONE'S SENTENCE

MARC. You are talking about a guy whose goons asked for the judge to step down after the jury found Stone guilty, because the judge complimented the jury.

STEPHEN. Does it occur to you that the judge arguably acted very inappropriately? Or is that impossible? The forewoman of the jury was an anti-Trump Democrat who had commented on Roger Stone. Also, the judge made a false statement that the Stone case was about covering up for Trump. It was not. In your mind, anyone who attacks Trump is a good person. It's almost always the opposite.

MATT GAETZ

March 9, 2020

Marc. At least Trump is great for the stock market. At least he is a steady leader who inspires calm assurance. I can deal with his being an asshole, knowing how effective he is and how substantial.

Stephen. Trump is responsible for the coronavirus? The Democrats can't even run their nomination process. Imagine how they would handle the coronavirus.

Marc. All I can do is listen to our president, who told us repeatedly that any president who let the market tank or let a pandemic affect us was culpable and should resign.

Stephen. It ain't over till it's over.

Marc. [*Attaches a tweet from Matt Gaetz in which he includes a picture of himself wearing a gas mask in Congress.*]

Marc. Let's take baby steps with you. Would you concede that this tweet from Matt Gaetz was irresponsible from a public official, particularly given that he is now under quarantine?

Stephen. Why is it irresponsible? What did he actually do?

Marc. He took a photograph wearing a gas mask in the Congress to mock the excessive precautions people are taking. Then it turned out he has to go into quarantine.

March 10, 2020

STEPHEN. I have no idea what Matt Gaetz was doing, but I'm pretty sure he wasn't mocking people.

MARC. Please! Not mocking?

STEPHEN. I have no idea. I don't know the context. Do I need to remind you about Nicholas Sandmann from Covington High School? Why do you make the same mistake over and over again?

MARC. Oh, right. Because people were wrong to judge Sandmann as a punk, Gaetz must therefore have had a valid reason for wearing a gas mask while he signed a document and while the other party wasn't wearing one? Can we agree, upon your further consideration, that he might have been mocking the precautions?

STEPHEN. You have no idea what Gaetz was doing. All you know is that you don't like him. Then you make up a story. Regarding Sandmann, he was a sixteen-year-old boy whom a political activist tried to take advantage of. He was then attacked by the media based on a lie. That's why he's probably wealthy and will be wealthier.

MARC. Just like the Duke lacrosse players. Rush to judgment, and then rush to make them heroes and overcompensate with ludicrous money. You know what Gaetz was doing and can't even admit it; you never cede an inch. It's the hallmark of the Trump culture.

STEPHEN. I don't know what point Gaetz was trying to make, but I'm confident he wasn't mocking people's fears. It's not like he referred to 50 percent of the population as a basket of deplorables or threatened Supreme Court justices Gorsuch and Kavanaugh by name.

CORONAVIRUS

MARC. With the market in free fall, this is what the president chooses to update the nation on [*attaches a Trump tweet in which he reports that the* Fox and Friends *morning show blew away CNN and MSNBC*].

MARC. By the way, I am totally on the side that the media is dramatizing the coronavirus situation, but the other extreme that denies it as "nothing" is wrong too.

STEPHEN. No one has said it is nothing. Furthermore, Vice President Pence is coordinating the federal response.

STEPHEN. By "no one," I mean no government official.

MARCH 11, 2020

MARC. Trump sure knew how to control the panic!

STEPHEN. Explain to me why Trump is at fault. What do you think he should do differently? I note that the Democrats want panic. I further note that Trump's presumptive Democratic opponent doesn't always know his own name.

MARC. He should have had a healthy respect for the epidemic, for a start. He should stop lying that anybody who wants to get a test can have a test. But his call for normalcy has largely fallen on deaf ears, and even if the call was wise, his lack of credibility has been long established, and now he is figuratively impotent.

MARC. Who knows more about disease: you or Dr. Anthony Fauci? Because Dr. Fauci said that without aggressive containment, the number of cases could be in the millions.

MARC. Let me understand. Were you impugning Biden's cognition? Your hero is acting like he had a lobotomy.

MARC. Trump told Hannity in an interview that people with coronavirus could go to work. So there is an example of something he should have said differently. Correct?

MARC. Trump said yesterday this would go away. Ten days ago, he called it a hoax. He said he has such a good feel for this.

STEPHEN. I know that Trump never called the coronavirus a hoax. I do not know what Trump said or did not say to Hannity or whether or not he said the virus will go away. You have a very bad habit of repeating anti-Trump nonsense that turns out to be false, such as the claim that he called the coronavirus a hoax. Trump took early and effective action by suspending travel from China. The United States appears to be faring better than Europe, which did not take such action. He's working with the private sector on a vaccine and treatments. He has done a lot to make tests available. The travel ban for Europe that he announced tonight is a big step. I haven't heard anyone offer an alternative approach. It's pathetic.

MARC. You never know what he says that is bad.

MARC. I'm sorry. Yesterday he said it would disappear. Did it?

STEPHEN. Why don't you send me a link to what he actually said? That way, I can respond. If you believe Trump thought the virus would disappear today, that says more about you than about Trump.

STEPHEN. President Trump's main opponent isn't Joe Biden. It's the coronavirus. Here is an intelligent assessment of Trump's handling of the coronavirus: https://www.wsj.com/articles/the-virus-and-leadershipthe-virus-and-leadership.

March 12, 2020

MARC. Trump's plan certainly reassured investors.

MARC. The market is holding strong under Trump's leadership.

STEPHEN. I don't know what to say. We are taking aggressive steps to stop the spread of the virus. Unfortunately, there is an economic consequence. The economy is fundamentally strong, and the quicker we are able to contain the virus, the quicker the economy will rebound. If the Democrats were in charge now, we probably would be in another Great Depression.

MARC. Would you like to concede that the Fox News culture and the president himself were a little slow to take this seriously?

MARC. That the president saying it's okay to shake hands and shaking hands on video is probably a stupid move?

STEPHEN. Again, I haven't seen that reported.

March 13, 2020

MARC. For my own sanity, to know that you still have some common sense and fairness. Two nights ago, Trump announced that unity was important and said it was time to put politics and partisanship aside [*attaches a Trump tweet calling Joe Biden's handling of the Obama administration's response to the swine flu epidemic "one of the worst on record"*].

STEPHEN. You're right. Only Trump should put politics aside.

MARC. What is your problem? He just told the world to put politics aside, and the next day, he started with his crap! Explain! He sat at the desk in the Oval Office; asked for a certain behavior; and then, the very next day, reacted to something someone said. That's leadership?

STEPHEN. The Democrats did not put politics aside and are accusing Trump of incompetence and more. Not one Democratic leader took up Trump's call. So you want him to unilaterally put politics aside? Not going to happen.

MARC. Yes, that's what I want. He is the president, albeit a laughingstock of one.

MARC. He is such a loser, such a fool. His name will probably become an adjective years later—probably a synonym for *crap*.

STEPHEN. Trump and his team were very impressive today. The cooperation with the private sector is the most impressive aspect of it. A lot of the work has been underway for a while. Dr. Fauci explained that the "failing" he talked about referred to the system, which was not developed for the current situation. He noted that it has been revamped in a short time. It was very reassuring, and the markets responded.

MARC. I hope so! I didn't see it.

STEPHEN. The market closed up 1,985.

MARC. Even a broken clock is correct twice a day!

MARCH 15, 2020

MARC. Trump said tonight, "We have tremendous control of the virus."

STEPHEN. That was your takeaway from the press conference?

MARC. My consistent stance, as you know, has been that he is a uniquely moronic person. Last week, after the market was down on a daily basis for understandable reasons, when it finally reversed course, he said, "They tell me that after I was done speaking, the market had its biggest day." Yo, idiot, you were also speaking every day, all week, while it tanked. So my takeaway is that he continues to have no ability to lead or to inspire hope. He makes De Blasio look like Ronald Reagan.

STEPHEN. I agree that Trump did not do a great job in setting the right tone through Friday. He did a better job on Friday. I also agree that it is not helpful that he talks about his impact on the stock market or points out that the Europeans failed to ban travelers from China. However, he also has spearheaded a major effort that looks like it will bear fruit and mitigate the virus. That is much more important.

MARC. We shall see. These challenges can face any president, and they are often in a no-win situation (e.g., Bush and Katrina).

MARCH 18, 2020

MARC. [*Attaches two Trump tweets, one from March 9 downplaying the coronavirus and one from March 18 touting how seriously he has taken the coronavirus.*]

STEPHEN. This shows me that Trump's critics are not too smart. Both of Trump's statements are true. We're taking drastic measures to try to prevent too many people from getting sick at one time over the concern that if that number is too large, it will overwhelm the hospitals and healthcare services. However, a large number of Americans ultimately will get coronavirus. Trump's point that, as with the flu, vulnerable individuals will die, but life will go on as normal is undeniably true. We will have to evaluate whether the economic havoc we are causing was worth it. In addition, Trump's point that he took this seriously also is true. He was the first Western leader to ban airline flights from China. He declared a public health emergency in January and set up the task force. It is worth pointing out that he was called xenophobic for the China travel ban. In other words, none of the Democrats would have done it.

MARC. He hardly took it seriously, and there's tons of video evidence of that.

MARC. According to Trump, a loser president lets the stock market fall apart. Look at the market under Obama!

MARC. Trump will have the worst legacy of any president, highlighted by his "What about me?" mentality. "Me, me, me."

MARC. I will give him a pass, by the way, on calling it the "China virus."

STEPHEN. You can only say that if you ignore everything he did. Thank God Obama is not president now. The pandemic would be raging out of control because identity politics would trump safety. The economy would be even worse.

MARC. Do you believe in accountability for leaders, even if it is symbolic? Or "It's not my fault. I'm a ten out of ten! I accept no responsibility"?

MARC. What kind of "leader" says things like that?

STEPHEN. I agree. It is not helpful. Although he would be better off not saying things like that, it would be nice if he wasn't falsely attacked on a daily basis—for example, the *NYT* editor who tweeted that Trump told the governors they are on their own. He never said that or anything like that.

MARC. Yes, there is a lot of that, I'm sure. Hey, he sets a low bar. Dana Bash on CNN praised him quite demonstrably the other day.

MARC. For just being a normal, sober, reassuring, accountable truth teller.

STEPHEN. He's more honest than his critics. They attack him for the China flight ban (he's doing too much); they attack him for comparing the coronavirus to the flu (he's doing too little). They accuse him of being a dictator but complain that he hasn't nationalized the response, as if the same policies should be applied in Maine and Manhattan.

MARC. I watch the critics several hours a day. I am one of them. Nobody knocks him for the China flight ban. His flu analogy was ignorant and an attempt by him and his backers to downplay. He is a wannabe dictator because he soaks in all the sycophantic language thrown at him.

STEPHEN. Everyone knocked him for the China flight ban. They called him xenophobic, racist, hysterical, and more. Why is the flu analogy ignorant? Thousands of people die from the flu each year, but we don't shut down society. Coronavirus may be worse than the flu, but it is not clear to me that the cure has not been worse than the disease.

MARC. You may be right. I mean, what happens the next time there is a cluster?

MARC. Shut the whole world down.

MARC. [*Attaches a short clip of Trump in which he is speaking and appears tired.*]

MARC. Please, Steve. Can we call this game, set, and match? What is this?

STEPHEN. Don't you ever tire of taking clips out of context?

MARC. Do you ever tire of defending a charlatan who is in way over his head?

STEPHEN. He has proven he is not in over his head. You never address facts, except the fact that you don't like him.

MARC. He said on tape, memorialized for as long as time, a series of idiotic statements about the severity of the threat of this virus, and his tone was mimicked by the losers on the Republican side and Fox: "Go to restaurants! Anyone who wants a test gets a test. This is the new hoax." He said it, plain and simple, despite the spin. "It's like the flu." The press conferences are all viewable.

STEPHEN. We're dealing with an unprecedented situation. Trump has been more effective than the idiots who couldn't build the Obamacare website despite having several years to prepare, couldn't count the votes in Iowa, gave guns to Mexican cartels, and allowed ISIS to take control of parts of Syria and Iraq. Trump is results-oriented. If one thing doesn't work, he moves on.

STEPHEN. Oh, I forgot the Iran deal.

MARC. Trump has done nothing except build hope and then crush it, and he tweeted repeatedly about leadership and accountability and knocked prior presidents for their uselessness when they faced unforeseen challenges.

STEPHEN. That's your hateful and, frankly, ignorant view.

MARC. Has the virus "magically disappeared"?

STEPHEN. Is a parent who loses a child to cancer a bad parent? Is a parent at fault for allowing a child to get cancer?

MARC. A friend who told a parent whose child had cancer, "It will magically go away; it's like the flu," would be an apt comparison.

MARC. *Apt.* That's a good word there!

MARC. Pithy. Packs a punch.

MARC. I'm now recalling your fourth-grade essay: "Andrew Johnson, America's Best President."

STEPHEN. There is going to be an announcement tomorrow morning about antiviral drugs that may work on coronavirus. I do like *apt.* Andrew Johnson was the second-best Johnson and the second-best Andrew. I never said he was the best.

BACK TO MUELLER

March 20, 2020

Marc. I will say that it's a good thing Republicans in Congress have kept us safe from the corruption at Burisma.

Stephen. Did you know the DOJ dropped the charges against the Russians Mueller indicted? That's because the charges were bullshit, and the Russian defendants called their bluff by appearing in court.

Marc. No, it's because Barr is working for Trump.

Marc. His characterization of the Mueller report was chastised by many career officials in the judicial and legal world.

Marc. Good news: the border was just closed, so no more corona will be coming from Mexico, that hotbed of corona. Talk about exploiting corona for your own agenda.

Stephen. I'm glad you repeat nonsense about Barr. He had nothing to do with dropping the case.

CORONAVIRUS PRESS CONFERENCES

MARC. Your president just imploded on national TV. Peter Alexander of NBC asked him what he would tell Americans who are scared (and, Stephen, legitimately so), and he said, "Here is what I would tell them: you are a nasty reporter, and that is a nasty question."

MARC. Add "Can't keep his shit together" to the list of support for Marc's many concerns that Trump is a charlatan who is an entirely inadequate president.

STEPHEN. He's doing a great job. Even Cuomo and Newsom have acknowledged it. The reporters do a terrible job. They try to score points. Trump gives it right back to them. You find that distasteful. However, I shudder to think where we would be if that politically correct nincompoop Biden were in charge. Even Marc would see the light.

MARC. When the reporter from OAN "asked him" why everyone was so unfair toward him, he should have said, "That is irrelevant now. What matters is …," but instead, he said, "Yeah, you are right." You can't have it both ways. How is it a terrible job for Peter Alexander to ask him to give a message to the people?

MARC. [*Attaches a picture from a coronavirus press conference in which Dr. Fauci appears to be grimacing.*]

MARC. Fauci risks his life with a gesture that furtively suggests, "What an idiot."

STEPHEN. I agree that Trump shouldn't have to deal with biased shitheads who know nothing, especially in the middle of a crisis.

MARC. If you are asking for people to lay off a dead fool walking, I can respect that point. His failings are self-evident. For *weeks*, he downplayed this.

MARC. "Anybody who wants a test will get a test." Do you remember that quote and who it was from more than a week ago? Is that spin on my part?

[STEPHEN. The reporters are the fools. Trump is working and answering questions, even stupid and nasty questions. He's doing it every day at great length. Trump is doing a great job on making testing available. The pre-Trump system could not do it. He put in place a public-private partnership that is doing it. This would not be happening under Biden. Biden can't speak for more than five minutes.

BACK TO CORONAVIRUS

MARC. He said whoever wants a test will get one. That remains untrue. He said there would only be dozens of cases. He says things he knows nothing about, just that it's a "feeling" and that he is smart guy (a lie). He says he is ten out of ten (what leader says that, even if he thinks he is?). He accepts no responsibility (what leader says that, even if he thinks he bears no responsibility?).

STEPHEN. You're like Captain Queeg. His ship was in jeopardy, but he was worried about identifying the sailor who stole his strawberries. You want an example of an untrue statement? "If you like your doctor, you can keep your doctor." Or, if you prefer, any number of lies told about Trump. In Trump's case, he is dealing with an unprecedented crisis in real time. He's getting things done, and he's answering questions at length every day. If you want to focus on one or two comments, go ahead. It makes you petty and small-minded.

MARC. I'm glad you state that my comments pointing out things that are accurate but perhaps not ideally timed make me small-minded. You are saying that my comments, my utterances (in writing), make me look petty and small-minded. Therefore, you agree that anyone who makes accurate comments that are selective or not all that relevant given the big picture looks small and petty. Therefore, I assume that inaccurate, asinine, insulting, racist comments make those who utter them much worse than petty and small.

MARC. It's simple college logic.

STEPHEN. Not at all. Nonsense.

MARC. I'm going to send this with my application to Yale Law School.

STEPHEN. Good luck. You will be a great addition to the profession. It's great to find your calling, no matter your age.

STEPHEN. You seem to think that Trump is responsible for the coronavirus and that is the reason people are sick and at risk. The reason the economy has come to almost a complete stop is because Trump and the governors are seeking to stop the virus. Should they not do that? I believe the effort may be overboard, but I understand the rationale. But you? Do you want him to do something or do nothing? All you want to do is blame Trump for whatever happens.

MARC. What specifically did I write that said or implied he was responsible for the virus? He didn't first have it, he didn't spread it around, and he didn't create it in a lab.

MARC. Once again, the ruling is in my favor. I could sue for slander!

STEPHEN. You seem to think he's responsible for the number of victims, the economic damage, or both. How is that possible unless he is responsible for the virus?

MARC. How could I think he is responsible for the number of victims yet is not the cause of the virus? You got me there.

MARC. How could I think he is responsible for the amount of victims but is not the cause of what actually caused there to be victims? Give me a few days.

MARC. [*Attaches a tweet from Anthony Scaramucci posting a video of Trump's statements downplaying the coronavirus.*]

MARC. Here is a suggestion. Watch this, and then, before your apology, give me five hundred words on "How Donald Trump Blew It on Corona."

MARC. [*Attaches a report that Trump received intelligence reports in January and February that provided warnings about the coronavirus.*]

March 21, 2020

STEPHEN. This is rewriting history. Trump declared a public health emergency on January 31. He banned travel from China on January 31. Biden called him hysterical and xenophobic. Furthermore, the Democrats were focused on impeachment. But for Trump, the situation here would be worse than in Italy.

MARC. He probably won't even run for reelection, or he will try to cancel the election. He is an abysmal failure in every way. His Peter Alexander answer will haunt him, as will his many recorded statements that the virus would amount to nothing.

STEPHEN. Where do you get this stuff? His approval ratings have been going up during this crisis. He'll be reelected easily.

MARC. I can't wait to hear your positive spin on the wisdom of the Trump administration firing the pandemic response team in 2018.

STEPHEN. Tell me whom he fired and why. Tell me what the plan was. As usual, you talk with absolutely no knowledge. By the way, Trump and the coronavirus task force have been very visible for the last month.

MARC. My team will have the answer for you in a little bit.

MARC. [*Attaches a Trump tweet stating, "HYDROXYCHLOROQUINE & AZITHROMYCIN, taken together, have a real chance to be one of the biggest game changers in the history of medicine."*]

MARC. [*Attaches an excerpt from a coronavirus press conference in which Dr. Fauci agrees there is no evidence that hydroxychloroquine might be used as a prophylaxis against the coronavirus.*]

STEPHEN. Trump derangement syndrome must cause brain damage. You're right; Trump is wrong to push for the use of a drug that may treat coronavirus. Fauci is not contradicting Trump. He is being precise. It is the reporters who are causing the confusion.

MARC. A lot of things *may* help. Fauci has to temper things with precision.

STEPHEN. Trump is dealing with the situation. The press and people like you spend their time trying to find evidence that Trump has done something wrong. Trump's statements about hydroxychloroquine are accurate based on the testing that is ongoing.

MARC. [*Attaches a Trump tweet from mid-January expressing the United States' appreciation to China for their efforts and transparency with respect to the coronavirus.*]

MARCH 22, 2020

STEPHEN. Trump said that in mid-January. He has been very direct that China should have disclosed information about the virus weeks earlier and that China is responsible for the scale of the pandemic. He also made the decision, against pressure from the Chinese government, to ban travel from China on January 31. China's US apologists, including Biden, called him hysterical, xenophobic, and racist. You want to invert what actually happened.

MITT ROMNEY

MARC. Trump said in a clearly mocking tone, "Romney is in quarantine? That's too bad." How can you defend that?

STEPHEN. Unlike Romney, Trump is not a phony.

MARC. Wait. Are you saying it is proper, during a national press conference, to gloat that a senator who opposed Trump might be sick? Is that what you are saying?

STEPHEN. No. I'm saying Trump is not a phony, as Romney is.

MARC. Okay. Romney is a phony like most politicians. We both know that. Glad we agree. And I would take four years more of Trump if the economy can bounce back by the election.

MARC. That's how an adult should think, not wishing ill on anyone.

STEPHEN. By the way, Trump didn't sound like he was gloating. That's your hateful spin.

MARC. Come on! It was sarcastic. He said it hesitantly because he knew it was stupid to say. About Rand Paul, he said, "He has always had my back, always been there. I wish him well."

MARC. He cannot control himself; he never can. He is like a fifteen-year-old Marc!

STEPHEN. Trump was gloating just like Nicholas Sandmann was mocking the Native American activist.

MARC. You know, you really can see how sycophantic you are toward Trump or just plain obstinate, because no matter what the tone is, the words "Gee, that is too bad" are never said by anyone with sincerity, unless you are Ward Cleaver. Your standard answer should be "Marc, I agree he is a dick, not a nice person, and a jerk, but I like his views and what he stands for." Try that!

REOPENING THE ECONOMY

March 23, 2020

Marc. Trump is on the verge of a big move—one that takes balls—and I'm not sure where I stand. The move is basically "Let's get back to work and let people die," and when the governors go against him, he will have a scapegoat. What should he do?

Stephen. There is a play by Henrik Ibsen called *An Enemy of the People* about two brothers, the mayor and the doctor in a town that depends on hot springs for its economy. The doctor comes to believe the hot springs are poisonous. The mayor is not sure and has to consider the consequences of the doctor's position. I don't remember the details, but at first, you think the doctor is a hero, and then you learn he might be wrong. The economy can't stay shut down until we are certain no one else will get sick.

Marc. I agree.

BACK TO CORONAVIRUS PRESS CONFERENCES

March 24, 2020

Marc. [*Attaches a clip from one of the coronavirus press conferences, in which Trump asks Dr. Birx if there will come a time when the "very angry media" will be permitted to fill the seats that are empty because of social distancing.*]

Marc. How would you assess this moment? After hundreds have died, do you admire his focus on the matters at hand and important things, like how well he is liked?

Stephen. I watched a lot of that press conference. What struck me is the total disrespect the reporters show Trump, despite his willingness to answer questions for two hours. All they do is try to show he is not following the advice of Fauci or Birx. They are idiots. What someone as otherwise intelligent as you should see is that each day, Trump brings several members of the team to answer questions. You are blind. On another note, Pelosi is trying to blow up the economic package by adding Green New Deal requirements (airlines need to be carbon neutral in five years, for example), diversity (racial mandates for corporate boards), and more. The Democrats want small business and Americans to suffer because they think it will hurt Trump. They're wrong and pathetic.

Marc. While I agree both sides play politics and the Dems want Trump to look bad, it's irresponsible to say they want Americans to suffer. You realize that among their constituents are thousands of small businesses, right? Trump has no business answering questions for two hours; he offers nothing. He is doing it to remain visible because he is an egomaniac who can't get his usual nourishment from hate rallies. Before you know it, he will be doing his Peter and Lisa orgasm bit during the briefing. And the press and TV are starting to tune him out because he says idiotic things. My cousin is a staunch Republican who has told me repeatedly he will vote for Trump because he votes for policy and not the person, and he tells me Trump is a buffoon (I can screenshot his texts).

STEPHEN. Do you really believe what you're saying?

MARC. What part? Sometimes I don't believe things I say, but this time, I do. Which part is incredulous?

STEPHEN. "Trump has no business answering questions for two hours." It's not just Trump; it's members of his team. More importantly, he and they are fully transparent.

MARC. He went from mendacious to opaque to, now, starkly transparent. Fauci isn't up there anymore because he was too responsible and knowledgeable.

STEPHEN. He's been transparent throughout his presidency. Fauci wasn't there yesterday, but he will be back. In the meantime, Fauci has done many news spots. Most importantly, Fauci is a smart man, but he is an adviser. He's not the president.

MARC. You are missing qualities needed in a president in times of crisis: being able to look like you care, being articulate and upbeat, not mumbling and bumbling, and most definitely not being self-centered. Every president in the last sixty to seventy years, except probably LBJ, could muster this quality.

STEPHEN. That's your biased opinion. Trump is open, not bumbling. If you want to see bumbling, watch Biden's cringe-worthy videos.

MARC. Perhaps.

MARC. The market is up 1,500. Let's see what happens after Trump speaks for two hours.

STEPHEN. It went up.

MARC. Okay! I'm on his side, and I actually agree we should get back to work sooner rather than later.

POLITICS

MARC. If Trump told Cuomo he would give coronavirus economic relief if Cuomo investigated the New York Democratic Office's corruption, would that be acceptable?

STEPHEN. I don't understand your question.

MARC. Say Trump is going to hold back aid to New York until they commit to an investigation into political corruption in the state. Now do you get it?

STEPHEN. I get it. You think federal government assistance to a US state is equivalent to foreign aid. They're completely different. There is a much steeper price to pay for not providing aid to US citizens. Do you remember "Ford to City: Drop Dead"? What about the Democrats impeding financial relief to businesses and workers hurt by the economic shutdown to try to impose unrelated and unpopular Democratic positions as a price for assistance? Are they patriots?

MARC. You make it seem as if partisanship is unilateral.

STEPHEN. Show me the equally partisan actions the Republicans have taken.

MARC. Not allowing Merrick Garland's nomination to the Supreme Court to be voted on.

MARC. Defending Trump's personal behavior while impugning Clinton.

MARC. Dismissing his behavior, I should say.

STEPHEN. I'm talking about something comparable. The Garland move was political, but the Republicans did not hold the public hostage during a crisis. Nor have they promoted a lie to try to remove a president.

MARC. They held it hostage for a day, and the day after, the market had its biggest gain ever.

MARC. Point for Marc! He now leads 1,235 to 7!

STEPHEN. Against whom?

STEPHEN. "Current estimates of the coronavirus fatality rate may be too high by orders of magnitude," write Professors Eran Bendavid and Jay Bhattacharya from Stanford Medicine: https://www.wsj.com/articles/is-the-coronavirus-as-deadly-as-they-say-. This article supports getting back to work, notwithstanding Dr. Fauci.

BACK TO REOPENING THE ECONOMY

March 24, 2020

Marc. I am not against it. Many things are not adding up in this whole story. Nobody is explaining what seems to be a crazy transferability—like a floating through the air—or why some people have a malaise for a week, and others die. It's not just about old versus young, although most nonelderly people afflicted seem to be less compromised.

Marc. If ten thousand people die in option A and eight thousand die in B, do you stop the world to save two thousand people? It's an easy answer whichever option you choose, which means it's an impossible question. But I fear Trump is just saying this because when the states shut down and further harm happens to people's lives, he will blame them.

Stephen. This is the problem. An elderly person who dies from "natural causes" dies from a virus or some other medical event. If a person who dies from coronavirus in March would otherwise have died in September from another cause, is the effort to ensure that the person dies from any cause other than coronavirus worth a Great Depression? I don't think so. Of course, we should take care of every one who gets sick. If the drugs work, this is less of a dilemma.

March 25, 2020

Marc. Good news: Trump chose Easter Sunday to open the country because it's a special day for *him*, and all the churches will be filled!

Stephen. More psychotic nastiness.

Marc. Yes, it was! I don't know why he doesn't stop it! "We will resume on the day that celebrates Christ's resurrection, because it is an important day for *me*."

Marc. I don't know how you don't see his autocratic tendencies! He just picked a date that every scientist thinks is premature. I happen to think he may be correct, but this is not a country in which the leader throws down edicts.

Marc. I know there was Obamacare, but that was approved by the Supreme Court.

Stephen. Easter is an important day for tens of millions of Americans, as well as a target that is sufficiently far in the future to take steps to make it happen. Furthermore, you simply don't understand how our government works. There is no dictatorship of scientists. The scientists are advisers. The president, not his staff, makes executive decisions. For example, Roosevelt approved Lend-Lease against the advice of his military advisers. Truman recognized Israel against the advice of the State Department. The president gets the advice and makes a decision. Trump is being criticized for not "throwing down edicts." Cuomo wants him to order private businesses to do things they are doing voluntarily. Trump critics, make up your minds: Is he too much of a dictator or not enough of a dictator?

Marc. It's amazing that given your clear advantage over me in terms of knowledge, I still win most arguments. I guess it's just sheer guts and gamesmanship and street smarts!

Stephen. You win these arguments the same way the Mets won last year's World Series, the Jets won this past Super Bowl, and the Nets won the last NBA Championship: in your mind. The reality is quite different.

FURTHER DISCUSSION ON MITT ROMNEY

MARC. [*Attaches a report on Trump's response to learning that Mitt Romney tested negative for coronavirus, which was "I'm so happy I can barely speak."*]

MARC. Can you now concede that he was indeed sarcastic when I told you he was?

STEPHEN. Thank you for following up on this important issue.

MARC. You don't like when I am correct even once.

STEPHEN. You're not correct. Okay, you're correct once. His comment that he's so happy that he can barely speak is sarcastic. His first comment about Romney going into isolation was not.

TRUMP'S SUPPORT FOR NEW YORK AND CALIFORNIA

MARC. [*Attaches a tweet commenting on Trump's questioning opposition to reopening the economy on Easter.*]

MARCH 26, 2020

MARC. Okay, I have a calm question for you. Do you sense how the stage is set for the new epic divisive battle? Middle America Fox TV is saying we need to get back to work ASAP, and who cares about New York and California and minorities and liberals? You know it's coming, and as a New Yorker, you cannot like how Trump (who you know is a petty baby) will not give New York its commensurate aid.

STEPHEN. The federal government has provided a massive amount of aid to New York, including, to date, a giant hospital ship with a thousand beds, mobile hospitals, and at least four thousand ventilators. It is interesting that Trump is accused of disbanding the White House pandemic response, which is not true, but the press does not question Cuomo on his decision not to purchase ventilators in 2015. In any event, it would make sense to loosen restrictions in states that have a small problem before states that have a large problem. It does not need to be one-size-fits-all.

MARC. I have a simple, elegant question for you that I request a yes or a no to, and it really is a yes-or-no question. If a governor or a state has been harshly critical of the president and even made personal attacks against him and then the state is in trouble and needs the aid of the federal government for the people of the state (which I assume is populated by millions of people who love the president), should the president hold back the aid because of the things the governor has said in the past?

STEPHEN. Yes, but only for residents of the state who voted for the governor.

MARC. Ha.

THE CORONAVIRUS RESPONSE

March 27, 2020

Marc. [*Attaches a tweet from John Cusack asserting that Trump refused to take the threat of the coronavirus seriously and refuses to take responsibility.*]

Marc. Would you concede he had no clue early on?

Stephen. No. Trump took it much more seriously than the media, who accused him of scaremongering.

Marc. Trump's quotes in that clip are not taken out of context and will haunt him for years.

Marc. As the canary in the coal mine of Trump supporters, please, do you believe that Andrew Cuomo, our governor, whom you don't have to like and can vote out but must accept, is being wasteful or irresponsible in his request for X ventilators that Dr. Trump says are not needed?

Stephen. I could not open the John Cusack tweet. I know that Trump took the position early on that the virus would not be disruptive, as he is advocating for relaxing the current lockdown restrictions as early as possible. The key is that Trump took very effective steps to address the virus, including the China travel ban, the task force, the revamping of the testing process, the private sector support, FEMA, the provision of naval hospital ships, the building of temporary hospitals, and more. His critics downplayed the virus and the actions Trump took well into February and the beginning of March. They look frivolous, not Trump. Regarding Cuomo, he is in his third term. It is his responsibility, not Trump's, to ensure that New York has what it needs. If New York, one of the highest-taxed states, does not, whose fault is that? Nevertheless, there is no shortage. The shortage would only exist in a worst-case scenario. In the meantime, the federal government has provided New York with six thousand ventilators, and more will come online. Furthermore, each ventilator can be set up to serve multiple patients at one time.

MARC. Yesterday he said New York didn't need any more ventilators. Today he put out a call for more ventilators. You said Trump's critics downplayed the virus? Really?

STEPHEN. The reports I have heard and read indicate that, at present, the hospitals have enough ventilators. The situation is fluid, and Cuomo does not want to get caught short. But Cuomo is playing politics. He runs a government that is built on fantasy. A leopard doesn't change its spots. If you want to know what I'm talking about, read about the Buffalo Billion.

MARC. Can't find it.

STEPHEN. Google "Buffalo Billion."

STEPHEN. It was a huge waste of money. A program to transform Buffalo.

MARCH 28, 2020

MARC. If Trump is successful in influencing groupthink and even loosening regulations to get us back to work and there isn't an Italy-type catastrophe, I will say that it was one hell of a gutsy call. If he is wrong, though, it would be a horrendous error. Also, did you hear him talking about the "woman governor" in Michigan and actually stating that if the governors aren't nice to him, he won't help them? Are you in favor of that? I know you aren't, though you will spin it, as usual.

STEPHEN. That's not what he said. Just like that John Cusack tweet consisted of spliced comments out of context.

MARC. So if he had said that, you would think it improper? (This is where you say, "He didn't say it, but if he did, it wouldn't be a big deal [or he was joking], but he didn't say it!")

STEPHEN. It's an irrelevant question. The federal government is providing assistance to Michigan and every other state, regardless of what a governor says about Trump.

MARC. You mean to say Trump's comments are irrelevant, right?

STEPHEN. I mean your scenario is baseless. The federal government is not providing assistance based on a governor's comments about Trump. In your world, it never matters when someone makes ridiculous or untrue comments about Trump, only what Trump says. Nor does it matter that Trump has been effective. The country can survive with Trump's bragging, streams of consciousness, and reflexive attacks on his critics. However, it could not abide incompetence. By any measure, including taking into account mistakes that have been made, Trump has been competent. In fact, he has pushed the government to be creative. He has cut red tape to speed up testing and to roll out better tests. He has sped up drug testing. He has pushed the private sector to help. Most importantly, he is not intimidated by so-called experts. Keep in mind that no one has experience in dealing with this problem.

MARC. And in your world, it never matters when Trump says something that is off base by any normal, decent modern standard. It only matters when one of his critics says something. His words are insignificant, but his critics' words are not. I read what you wrote a second time, and I'm glad you now cede that he says what I will paraphrase as "idiotic things," and the ends might justify those mean means (you see what I did there?). The problem is that while the fight against sexism and racism has made some progress in the last fifty years, he is wiping it away. According to him, every black reporter asks "stupid" questions. He is unwittingly, or by design, shaping the thought of countless millions.

STEPHEN. If Trump was treated evenhandedly, it would be easier to criticize him for things he actually says and does. For example, your comment that Trump is "wiping away" progress on sexism and racism has no basis in fact. Nor does your comment that he is "shaping the thought of countless millions." I assume the countless millions are those people of low intelligence who don't agree with you. It's very sad that you spout this nonsense.

STEPHEN. Here's information from the CDC that's interesting: this flu season, there have been thirty-nine million infections, four hundred thousand hospitalizations, and twenty-four thousand deaths over a twelve-week period. Granted that coronavirus has spread over a shorter time frame, this information does raise questions, doesn't it?

MARC. It does. Something is not adding up. The key is that nobody dies from flu who is otherwise younger or healthy.

STEPHEN. The CDC reports 155 children have died from the flu this season.

STEPHEN. [*Attaches a clip of Governor Cuomo acknowledging that New York had a stockpile of ventilators not needed at the time but that thirty thousand would be needed when the state hit the apex.*]

STEPHEN. Exactly what I've been telling you.

MARC. What do you think they wanted to do with having an excess of ventilators? Sell them on the black market?

STEPHEN. No. Cuomo wants to have enough ventilators in the event that the worst-case scenarios are realized. However, the point is that New York currently has more than it needs and more than probably will ever be needed. The complaints that Trump isn't doing enough are political and bullshit.

MARC. Oh, I've got it. Jeez. So Cuomo actually, as you wrote, wants to have enough ventilators in the event that the worst case is realized? What! Can you believe that guy?

MARC. Your text was poorly worded to leave me the opening!

MARC. You meant to say, "New York has enough for now, and they are trying to make Trump look deficient because they don't yet have a crazy excess."

STEPHEN. Your point is stupid. Cuomo complained that New York did not have enough ventilators *now*. That's not true. The federal government has provided them enough ventilators that New York has a current stockpile and will continue to make additional ventilators available as production ramps up. Cuomo had nothing to complain about.

MARC. You wrote that Cuomo wanted to have enough ventilators in anticipation of a precipitous decline and sudden need. It's called being prepared.

STEPHEN. If Cuomo had wanted to be prepared, he would have purchased more ventilators during his three terms in office. He made the decision in 2015 not to purchase fifteen thousand ventilators. This is New York, one of the highest-taxed states, which wasted hundreds of millions on Cuomo's Buffalo Billion. Trump has provided New York with at least eight thousand ventilators and has put a process in place to ramp up US production of ventilators over the next month. More will be available, but New York does not need them now and hopefully never will. The charge that there is a shortage of ventilators is false.

[3/28/20, 9:40 p.m.] MARC. So if Cuomo had told people year after year, "We don't need any ventilators—none ever," and then this happened and the ventilators were, in fact, needed, a president should say, "Sorry, but we can't help the people in your state. You should have bought them when you had the chance"?

STEPHEN. Are you taking your medicine? Your question assumes the federal government has refused to help New York, which simply is not true. The federal government has provided New York with at least eight thousand ventilators. New York currently has more than it needs, and more will be available, although they are not likely to be needed. Until this conversation, you seemed to believe New York did not have enough ventilators now. You also seemed to believe that Trump refused to help. Both are false. Posing stupid, irrelevant questions will not change that.

MARC. "Cuomo wants to have enough ventilators in the event the worst-case scenario idea is realized" (Stephen Barry).

STEPHEN. He does not have a shortage. He'll be getting more, which he is not likely to need. Why is that so difficult for you to understand?

STEPHEN. He complained about a problem that does not exist.

MARC. I think the key here—and I think you would agree—is that Cuomo just wanted to have enough ventilators in the event the worst-case scenario was reached.

STEPHEN. That's true, but he complained that New York needed ventilators *now*. Why would he complain if he has a surplus now and a commitment that he will receive more? You know why.

MARC. New York State can survive with Cuomo's grandstanding.

MARC. Trump was not taken out of context. He said, "I told Mike (Pence), why would you return a call from that woman governor from Michigan, when she isn't nice to you?"

MARC. [*Attaches a tweet from Ari Fleischer mildly criticizing Trump's statement about Michigan's Governor Whitmer.*]

MARC. Read and learn.

MARCH 29, 2020

STEPHEN. Good advice from Fleischer. The difference between you and Fleischer is that he is giving advice. He's not trying to prove that Trump is an abject failure. As for Gretchen Whitmer, there is nothing inappropriate about Trump's comment, other than the fact that, as Fleischer points out, you don't need to publicly air every thought. For example, if you were governor and you told Trump, "I need ventilators, you buffoon," would you expect him to continue talking to you?

MARC. I have some advice for Trump: "Stop being such a self-absorbed, egocentric asshole."

STEPHEN. That's why he told Pence not to bother speaking to you.

MARC. [New York City mayor Mike] Bloomberg was advised to close the schools with H1N1 and refused. The federal government did not act because it was deemed that the economy couldn't take the hit. Lots of people died, but it was largely ignored by the media.

MARC. Someone sent that to me [referring to the prior text].

MARC. You really should be ashamed [referring to the attachment described below].

MARC. [*Attaches Trump tweets that the ratings for his coronavirus press conferences are so high that "the Lamestream Media is going CRAZY."*]

STEPHEN. Why should I be ashamed? I'm not the one who is always talking through his ass.

MARC. People are scared and dying, and he is talking about his ratings and other TV shows. Is that normal?

MARC. As always, he's obsessed with himself.

STEPHEN. Stop. This year, thirty-nine million have been infected with the flu, four hundred thousand have been hospitalized with the flu, and twenty-four thousand have died (including 155 children). These are CDC stats. I hope we don't get there with the coronavirus. However, life as we know it is not going to stop. The important thing about Trump is that he has organized an effective effort to address the coronavirus, not your obsession with everything he says, which you apply only to him.

MARC. Trump is doing well in the presser. When a guy stupidly asked, "What about your Easter?" he just said that was aspirational.

MARC. He was doing well until he attacked two black reporters.

STEPHEN. Your belief that Trump is a racist is a fantasy.

MARC. I think that the federal government is holding back masks and selling them for profit to other countries and that someone should investigate. Do you agree?

STEPHEN. Based on what?

MARC. No basis. I just think that's the case. Is that responsible of me?

STEPHEN. It looks like you have a new reason to be outraged. Please enlighten me.

MARC. Trump suggested in the press conference after I turned it off that New York City was doing that with ventilators.

STEPHEN. I don't know what he said. If he did say it, I don't know if he had a basis for it. I know I can't rely on your version of events.

MARC. [*Attaches an AP report on Trump's comments that hospital workers in New York could be illegally selling face masks and other equipment.*]

STEPHEN. He asked a different question than you asked. He asked for an accounting of the tens of thousands of masks that have been delivered. It's not a crazy question. If the media would look for corruption by anyone other than Trump, they might be useful.

March 30, 2020

MARC. He repeated his assertion that medical workers are stealing and selling supplies. He also had the MyPillow guy offer a prayer. And you are aligned with this guy.

STEPHEN. In your zeal to prove that Trump is evil, you blind yourself to reality. Trump is a New York real estate developer. He knows that supplies and materials at work sites often disappear unless appropriate efforts are made to secure them. He is asking why the federal government has delivered more supplies than New York appears to have. Because Trump raises the issue, you're not willing to consider it. He may be wrong, but he may be right. This is an area where his experience as a New York businessman informs him that there might be a problem.

MARC. Here is where you are showing a rare inconsistency. Anytime I share with you an allegation from someone, you ask for the proof. But when Trump makes a statement that no evidence bears out, you say, "He may be right, and he may be wrong." But he is broadcasting to the world and made an allegation with no evidence. Just like his birther comments.

STEPHEN. You're wrong. There is evidence. More supplies have been delivered than New York appears to have. There may be an innocent explanation. However, under the circumstances, you would think it's a concern that would be investigated.

MARC. Maybe it would be prudent to investigate the matter, given that Barr already warned against it, and not just throw out allegations—serious ones—before the whole world. You admitted Trump should shut up and stop announcing every little thing in his head, and it's a serious and repeat problem. That alone doesn't make him an evil monster. Hey, I believe he is being blackmailed overtly or tacitly by Putin. Just because Marc says it, you dismiss it. "It may be wrong, but it may be right," as you wrote.

STEPHEN. You're ridiculous. You weren't upset when false allegations were made against Trump to force him out of office. The day of reckoning for that crime is on its way. Your belief that Putin is blackmailing Trump is based on proven lies. Trump didn't falsely accuse anyone of committing a crime. He simply suggested there is a discrepancy between supplies being delivered and the supplies on hand. If he's right, that's a huge problem.

MARC. You are no judge of the veracity of allegations. You couldn't even determine that the Stormy Daniels story was exactly as it was reported; you thought they were bogus allegations. Regarding many allegations, you've said, "He didn't do it, and even if he did …," which nobody ever says if they really believe the "He didn't do it" part.

MARC. I agree that if people are selling stuff out of hospitals, that's ridiculous, worse than a huge problem. But the significance of the potential crime doesn't give the accusation a shred of merit. The significance of my accusation of Trump and Putin is colossal.

STEPHEN. I never commented on whether or not Trump slept with Stormy Daniels ten years before he ran for office. I took issue with the bullshit accusation that his payment to settle her claim was a campaign finance violation.

MARCH 31, 2020

MARC. [*Attaches a tweet mocking Mike Lindell, the MyPillow guy, whom Trump invited to speak at a coronavirus briefing as a business leader who had repurposed his factory to make medical equipment, for comments he made about God having a hand in Trump's election in 2016.*]

MARC. If you have any increasing anxiety about the virus, maybe you will find this comforting.

STEPHEN. I love MyPillow. I have one. Are you mocking him because he's religious? Would you mock an Orthodox Jew for saying to trust Hashem (God)?

MARC. He isn't a man of the cloth. I'm mocking that this is another con artist. This is the person Trump calls up to speak to the nation? Would Ron Popeil be an appropriate person to speak for the White House?

STEPHEN. This says more about you. He's not a man of the cloth. He's a religious person who committed to making fifty thousand face masks a month. Can you believe that asshole?

MARC. I forgot to remind you: Trump reassured Americans that there were only fifteen cases in the country and that the virus would just disappear.

MARC. He also called it the Dems' new hoax.

STEPHEN. Again, you have the story wrong, but it makes you feel good. Trump called the Democrats' criticism of Trump's response to coronavirus the new hoax. Trump has led a very effective response. He initially tried to keep the virus out of the country. When that proved insufficient, he took steps to modernize the structures in place. He cut through red tape, brought in the private sector, and established a top-notch task force. He has created the template for dealing with a pandemic, which will become the standard. If Obama, Hillary, or Biden were running a woke, politically correct, antibusiness response, the pandemic and the economy would be much worse.

MARC. He hasn't done anything. People in the government did anything that is positive. I know this because he talks only about himself, his ratings, TV shows, who likes him, and who praises him, and he laughs when his enemies get COVID-19. He does nothing. He also said, "It will disappear," and "If only a hundred thousand die, I will have done a great job." Also, he said, "I accept no responsibility" (what every idiot says when in a difficult fight)!

MARC. If terrorists held a hundred thousand people in a stadium and said they would blow the place up unless Americans stopped going to work for a month, what would happen?

STEPHEN. The terrorists would be killed by US or Israeli commandos. As for Trump, he gets credit for what his administration does. Look it up.

MARC. Trump today said his decisions were distracted and affected by impeachment. Do you know what that means? He is admitting that he made bad decisions! Because if they were good decisions, he wasn't affected. He is making excuses.

STEPHEN. He's right. The entire US political system was distracted by the Democrats' attempted coup. Nevertheless, Trump has been way more effective than his detractors would have been if they were in charge.

MARC. You always tell me to deal in facts and not conjecture. How do you know how they would do?

MARC. "It's their new hoax. It will disappear. It's like the flu. I want the restrictions to end by Easter because I like Easter." Nobody could match that idiocy.

STEPHEN. Based on how they handled the Obamacare rollout, Benghazi, Fast and Furious, the Iowa caucus, shovel-ready projects, and more, the Democrats can more than match any idiocy. They spend money, waste money, accomplish nothing, and lie about it.

MARC. [*Attaches a tweet listing the dates of Trump rallies in January and February and dates on which Trump played golf in January, February, and March.*]

MARC. [*Attaches a tweet commenting on Trump's statement that he was distracted by the impeachment trial.*]

MARC. Now I see why he made such bad decisions.

APRIL 1, 2020

STEPHEN. We're very lucky he won the election. Otherwise, I believe we would be facing millions of deaths as the media praised Hillary. Trump is right. The sham impeachment hurt the country. His response still has been excellent.

MARC. The impeachment vote ended long before the virus. Trump said the virus would disappear, was a hoax, and was like the flu and tried to change the narrative against scientific advice because he liked Easter and wanted to dismiss the science.

STEPHEN. You start with an irrational belief—a belief impervious to facts—that Trump is incompetent or purposefully malicious or both and then try to fit reality into your preconceived fantasy world. The impeachment trial ended in February. Trump recognized the threat of the virus and attempted to address it by keeping potential carriers from China out of the country. For that, he was condemned as a racist. When it was clear that would not be enough, he ramped up the federal response. At first, he relied on the CDC, which proved incapable of testing. He changed the whole system and brought in the private sector. More importantly, he established an effective task force to ensure we can test millions, produce and distribute ventilators and PPE, and get drugs approved quickly. The stupidity of comments like he "wanted to dismiss the science" is not worthy of a third grader. Anthony Fauci is not the president. Nevertheless, Trump, based on the data, has continued the lockdown. Apparently, you would prefer a passive president who doesn't push back, one who is afraid to make decisions. Clearly, Joe Biden is your candidate.

MARC. He wasn't condemned for stopping access from China.

STEPHEN. Yes, he was. Look it up.

MARC. Maybe by some, but there was no collective outrage. Everyone thought it was smart and logical.

MARC. My evidence for Trump's unique uselessness is that when you watch any governor on TV, they speak very well off the cuff and dispense good information. Trump reads off cards and says things like "It's a bad virus—very bad."

STEPHEN. No. He was called xenophobic, hysterical, and a racist. Democratic politicians and the media mocked the threat and encouraged people to go on with their lives, all while the Democrats were trying to remove Trump from office. This isn't ancient history. This happened in February and March. It's willful ignorance on your part. Furthermore, you give Cuomo credit. He has done a reasonable job this past month, but he is directly responsible for New York's lack of preparation. He actually ignored a recommendation to purchase sixteen thousand ventilators in 2015. If you want to believe that Trump isn't doing what it is obvious he's doing—leading an effective response—that's your choice. That's why you're always surprised he has support.

MARC. [*Attaches a statement by Trump: "So last year 37,000 Americans died from the common Flu. It averages between 27,000 and 70,000 per year. Nothing is shut down, life & the economy go on."*]

MARC. That quote was in early March.

MARC. You say the response from someone else would be worse. How much worse could things be? The market is ready for another tank. If a Democrat were in office under these circumstances, you would be tearing them apart.

MARC. By the way, "would have been much worse with someone else" is some ringing endorsement. He is the leader. Do something! The market is collapsing, and people are dying. Fix it!

MARC. [*Attaches a report that Senator Kelly Loeffler of Georgia sold $18.7 million in stock after being briefed on the coronavirus, while telling her constituents not to worry.*]

MARC. (1) This story sounds detailed and accurate, and if it is, it's abhorrent. (2) She is a Republican, so it's just the fake media going after her, right? (3) I'll wait until I hear all the facts; there might be a logical explanation.

STEPHEN. Do you accuse the pilot of the Ukrainian passenger jet shot down by Iran for not doing something? Should Trump go back in time and prevent the outbreak? He's dealing with the situation. If you believe he's not doing anything, you must believe Trump is an agent of Russia. Wait. You do believe that, even though it is conclusively not true. As for Kelly Loeffler, Tucker Carlson has gone after her and Burr. Matt Gaetz has called for Burr to resign. Loeffler is toast. She was appointed by the governor just a few months ago and is facing a primary this year. She will be ousted.

MARC. Good! There is hope for you! Trump is doing nothing. Maybe someone else would do worse. Probably someone else would do better. The idiot had numerous rallies while this was all out in the open. He completely denied and ignored it. He said it would disappear. You can't put that toothpaste back into the tube. I like presidents who don't let viruses ruin us (McCain reference).

STEPHEN. The real embarrassing statements on coronavirus come from the media and Democrats, like Pelosi and De Blasio. Trump acts. They criticize.

STEPHEN. [*Attaches a copy of Theodore Roosevelt's "Man in the Arena" speech, in which Roosevelt said, "It is not the critic who counts; not the man who points out how the strong man stumbles, or where the doer of deeds could have done better. The credit belongs to the man who is actually in the arena, whose face is marred by dust and sweat and blood; who strives valiantly; who errs and comes short again and again because there is not effort without error or shortcoming; but who does actually strive to do the deeds."*]

STEPHEN. Read this.

MARC. You are finally saluting Obama?

MARC. It doesn't say anything about if the leader is a jackass.

STEPHEN. No. But I wouldn't call Obama a jackass, just naive and incompetent.

MARC. At the end of the day, you know that Trump is a jackass and a moron.

STEPHEN. Trump is definitely not a moron. Whether he is a jackass is in the eye of the beholder.

MARC. Okay, I'll take back the *moron* and double down on the *jackass*.

STEPHEN. Do you remember the movie *A Miracle on Thirty-Fourth Street*? The judge ruled that the court could not rule on whether or not Santa Claus exists, because some people believe in him, and some do not. He was a wise judge. We cannot settle the question of whether Trump is a jackass, except through the election. If he wins, it will prove there are more people who believe he's not a jackass.

STEPHEN. I know you don't believe in facts, but here are few: (1) This was Trump's statement about coronavirus in his State of the Union address on February 4: "Protecting Americans' health also means fighting infectious diseases. We are coordinating with the Chinese government and working closely together on the coronavirus outbreak in China. My administration will take all necessary steps to safeguard our citizens from this threat." (2) This is what Pelosi said on February 24, three weeks later: "That's what we're trying to do today is to say everything is fine here. Come because precautions have been taken. The city is on top of the situation." (3) This is from a CNN story on March 4: "Half the people in America do not get a flu shot and the flu, right now, is far deadlier," Anderson Cooper said. "So if you're freaked out at all about the coronavirus, you should be more concerned about the flu." These statements speak for themselves. (4) In addition, Trump was criticized for the actions he took to ban travel from China on January 31. Regarding the travel ban, Biden said on February 2, "We are in the midst of a crisis with the coronavirus. We need to lead the way with science—not Donald Trump's record of hysteria, xenophobia, and fearmongering." (5) On February 5, the *New York Times* published an editorial criticizing the China travel ban, titled "Who Says It's Not Safe to Travel to China?" (6) In mid-March, Biden said, "A wall will not stop the coronavirus. Banning all travel from Europe—or any other part of the world—will not stop it. This disease could impact every nation and any person on the planet—and we need a plan to combat it." (7) Here is Dr. Fauci on the travel ban: "One of the things we did right was very early cut off travel from China to the United States," he said. "Outside of China, where it originated, the countries in the world who have it are through travel."

MARC. He said, "This thing is going to disappear. Everyone who wants a test will be able to get a test," and he had numerous rallies after the word was out.

APRIL 2, 2020

STEPHEN. The only facts that matter to you are ones you think portray Trump negatively. You pick one statement out of context—"This thing is going to disappear"—to prove Trump did not take the coronavirus seriously. As set forth about, that's demonstrably false. In February and

March, he was accused of overreacting by the same people who now accuse him of underreacting. It's not Trump's fault the CDC testing process initially was inadequate. It would be his fault if he had done nothing about it, but he did. He did not continue to have rallies once the guidance against large gatherings came out. He was no different from the Democrats, except that people actually attend his rallies.

MARC. I told you about his horrible insinuation that hospitals are selling supplies away from the hospital. You are missing a huge thing. Most of the New Yorkers who are dying are inner-city minorities, and Trump and his people will let them eat cake.

MARC. We've got Robert Kraft doing more for New York than the feds are.

STEPHEN. You're willfully ignorant. You know one thing, and it's wrong. Why would anyone give credence to your opinion on anything? You ignore facts and take positions that always end up being demonstrably false.

MARC. Are you a New Yorker?

MARC. The National Guard should be in here, staffing every hospital.

STEPHEN. The federal government has sent New York a hospital ship, built four hospitals, and provided supplies and ventilators. The question is, why was New York so unprepared? Why was De Blasio encouraging people to celebrate Chinese New Year? Everything you believe is the opposite of the truth. Trump is not perfect, but he acts.

MARC. [*Attaches a tweet that asks, "Why is it remotely acceptable to the country that the president's unaccountable son-in-law address the nation in a decision making role in a generational crisis of historic magnitude for which he has no requisite qualifications, preparation or experience?"*]

April 3, 2020

STEPHEN. People who are wrong about virtually everything criticize Trump. It's ridiculous.

MARC. Kushner wasn't criticizing Trump.

STEPHEN. For example, Trump's arrogant know-nothing critics were wrong about the China travel ban, which they called racist and ineffective, and hydroxychloroquine, which they called snake oil.

MARC. It's all you have to clutch on to. I know the Trump critics better than you, and the complaints against the China ban were few and fleeting. What is your thought about how the Republican states completely ignored common sense and let kids party in masses? All Trump had to do was tell DeSantis, who rode Trump's coattails to get elected, to put a stop to it. A perfect example of Trump's inconsistent and tepid overall response.

STEPHEN. You're repeating Democratic strategist talking points. You have been wrong about everything Trump and Trump-related. It's quite remarkable.

MARC. I have never been wrong about Trump. I have often been wrong about the country's response to him. "It will disappear. It's a hoax." He said that on tape. Some disappearing. New Yorkers are disappearing, and the Trump world doesn't care.

STEPHEN. You're impervious to facts. You have been wrong about everything. If you had been right, Trump would be in jail for selling out the United States to Russia or Ukraine, the economy would not have been humming on all cylinders, we would be at war with Iran, and we wouldn't be the world's leading energy producer. I could go on. You believe liars. I accept your legitimate criticism of Trump. He is an egomaniac, more than other egomaniacal politicians. You don't think he speaks in a way that honors his office. There are times when I agree he could do better, but his opponents lie about what he actually says and does. You base your position on the lies. For all his flaws, he is the most transparent president we ever have had. He's not perfect, but he makes decision and tells you why. If something doesn't work, he changes course. He gets things done.

MARC. I can respect that view.

MARC. Today was the day to apply for the Paycheck Protection Plan. All the banks told us. Nothing happened. Some rollout. Like Obamacare.

STEPHEN. Right. They had years to prepare for Obamacare. Today banks received millions of applications with a week to prepare. It's going to take a heroic effort. However, the government expanded the number of lenders that can participate. It will happen.

MARC. Uh-huh. Iowa caucus, Obamacare—couldn't get them up and running.

STEPHEN. It's not the same thing. You're impervious to facts.

MARC. It's a little bit the same thing. Maybe Obamacare was flooded with more than they anticipated.

MARC. Your own words turned against you!

STEPHEN. It's nothing like the same thing.

MARC. "The federal government needs the ventilators, not just the states. The states are part of the country." Trump said that just seconds ago. What a moron [regarding Trump responding to statements made by Jared Kushner that the ventilators in the federal stockpile should not be sent to the states only to be put into a state stockpile].

MARC. Trump said, "We need them for the federal government of the United States! Not for the states!"

MARC. This is whom you defend.

MARC. We are a federation of states!

STEPHEN. He says a lot. He has plenty of opportunities to misspeak.

MARC. [Attaches a tweet from Elizabeth Warren regarding Kushner's comment about the ventilator stockpile: "That is, in fact, exactly what it's there for. Get the states the resources they need, or get out of the way."]

MARC. [Attaches a Daily Show piece, "Heroes of the Pandumic," mocking the Trump administration's coronavirus response by attaching video clips of White House officials, Fox News hosts, and other conservative figures.]

MARC. You said CNN is filled with garbage.

STEPHEN. The new playbook is to keep repeating that Trump isn't handling this crisis. It's a lie, but it makes you feel good. You have believed every slanderous lie about Trump, which the Democrats and the media repeat endlessly.

MARC. Did you watch that clip? The entire Trump network [Fox] downplayed COVID-19. How stupid. How do you explain that other than ignorance? And Trump explaining that the federal government needs the stockpile, not the states? It's not a playbook. It wasn't a playbook when you criticized Obamacare and Iowa.

STEPHEN. I've been following this every day since the first news reports. I know, because I was paying attention, that the "expert opinion" on which our political leaders based their public statements evolved dramatically over February and early March. I know that Trump did more than his critics would have done. I also know that Trump, no different from Pelosi, didn't want to panic people while he was being advised that the virus could be contained. He has followed the expert opinion, and he has moved quickly to modernize the response. He can't just snap his fingers and overcome the complete lack of preparation at the state level in New

York and other places, but he has done a good job. If you want to watch a silly compilation of snippets, go ahead. It would look worse if you put together a clip of Democrats and media quotes.

MARC. Why were the quotes silly?

STEPHEN. Because no one has gotten coronavirus right. However, Trump, regardless of particular comments, actually has taken effective steps—from the beginning—to deal with it. At this moment, I believe there is a good chance we are overreacting now. For example, today there are thirteen thousand coronavirus hospitalizations in New York. According to the models our political leaders relied on to shut the economy down, there should be thirty-six thousand hospitalizations in New York. That's a big difference.

MARC. Hope so. The people who got it right were the people who have advocated and implemented strong measures for residents of this country, such as California's and New York's governors. They're smart and convincing. Not "If the president suggests it, that would carry a lot of weight." Trump and DeSantis fought for weeks to avoid the lockdown. Why, all of a sudden, two days ago, did DeSantis finally give in?

STEPHEN. Cuomo? You're kidding.

STEPHEN. Without Trump's support, Cuomo would be paying a much higher political price for New York's complete lack of preparation.

STEPHEN. He's in his third term!

MARC. Trump's lack of preparation was fifty times worse—as in New York times fifty.

STEPHEN. Good response. It's based on nothing, but it must be true.

MARC. Without Trump's support? You think a president could ever conceivably not support citizens of New York by saying, "Too bad. I could help, but I shouldn't have to"? Please, a direct response to that would be appreciated.

MARC. If Trump has the stockpile and New York needs it, even if it's because of Cuomo's errors, he would be praised for offering help to the people of New York, who, I remind you, in case you forgot civics, are US citizens.

STEPHEN. Of course he had to help. That's not the issue. The issue is that New York, which Cuomo has led for ten years and which is highest-taxed state (except maybe California), was not prepared. That's the governor's job. You would always help your children, but you wouldn't congratulate them for not taking care of themselves.

APRIL 4, 2020

MARC. [*Attaches a tweet posting Trump's response to a question from Jonathan Karl, in which he said he could not ensure they would have more ventilators. Trump added, "They should have had more ventilators. We have a lot of states that need to be taken care of."*]

MARC. And you don't think this is targeting New York because it's a state that hates Trump? You told me "of course" they should help New York.

STEPHEN. The federal government has done more for New York than any other state. Cuomo should listen to Gavin Newsom, a governor who has filed hundreds of lawsuits against the Trump administration. He refused to be baited into criticizing Trump when he appeared on *The View*. He acknowledged that Trump has taken all of his phone calls and immediately responded to California's requests, including sending a hospital ship.

MARC. [*Attaches the "Heroes of the Pandumic" clips.*]

MARC. There really is no excuse for this. It's so shameful and so ignorant and captured for all time.

MARC. The CDC recommends wearing masks, and the president said he won't. WTF?

MARC. My view is shared—and, yes, shaped—by hundreds of established journalists. If Trump was acting the part; not talking about ratings; being consistent; and not reading from a script, people would have nothing to challenge him on, and they wouldn't try. He is that bad.

STEPHEN. There are three issues: (1) Trump's (and everyone else's) knowledge about and expectations for the impact of the virus, (2) actions taken to respond to the virus, and (3) media coverage of the response to the virus. It appears you believe that Trump's (and only Trump's) public statements should be judged by an omniscience standard. That's ridiculous. His earlier public statements were based on the advice he received at the time. Even Dr. Fauci was slow to recognize the extent to which the virus would spread. Also, Trump, like Pelosi in San Francisco's Chinatown, wanted to reassure people that they were not in danger, at a time when they believed people were not in danger. He also is rightly concerned about unnecessarily shutting down the economy. Nevertheless, Trump took many actions to respond, even before the infectious disease specialists recognized that the virus was going to be a problem. He instituted the travel bans, he raised the topic in the State of the Union, he allocated $1.5 billion, and more. He also quickly made changes when government agencies, like the CDC, were not performing. He has undeniably provided hard-hit areas, like New York and California, with massive amounts of support. Anyone who questions that simply doesn't want to accept reality. The media and the Democrats decided early on to make the coronavirus Trump's fault. That's why they criticized his early actions and then turned on a dime and criticized him for not taking action. Fox News is not immune. People like Hannity are very strident in defending Trump from media attacks. However, based on reports I read, the Democrats' and media's position is based on a strategy produced by Democratic K Street political consultants, who advise Pelosi and Schumer. In an unprecedented situation like this, no one is omniscient. As I have said to you many times, Trump makes decisions and get things done. After it is over, we will be able to evaluate what we did, could have done, and should have done. For example, was shutting down the economy a mistake? But at this moment, Trump is Teddy Roosevelt's man in the arena. He is leading (though maybe not perfectly). His critics offer nothing but efforts to discredit him.

MARC. [*Attaches a tweet from Stephen Hayes criticizing Trump's daily coronavirus briefings generally and Trump's touting of hydroxychloroquine specifically.*]

MARC. This is a conservative writer. Wake up.

STEPHEN. Hayes was wrong about the "unproven" drug. Maybe that's why Trump is president and Hayes is not.

MARC. I guess he is right about everything else that you didn't say he was wrong about. Very troubling.

STEPHEN. As with most Trump critics, being wrong about every verifiable fact doesn't seem to result in any self-reflection for you.

THE CASE AGAINST TRUMP

MARC. If you are implying that we have thought long and hard or just simply stated off the cuff that we know Trump is substantially dumb and also completely devoid of decency, are frustrated by not understanding how smart and decent people like yourself somehow don't know this, and get excited when we are given an opportunity to prove our point, as futile as it always turns out, then you are correct.

STEPHEN. I just mean that every allegation you make is false.

MARC. Like that he told Don McGahn to fire Mueller?

MARC. Like that he fired James Comey to end the investigation into him? Oh, wait—Trump admitted that last month.

STEPHEN. Yes, including that irrelevant allegation.

STEPHEN. Trump was the target of an illegal conspiracy. You will see. Mueller furthered that conspiracy. He will be discredited even more than he discredited himself at his embarrassing testimony.

MARC. Mueller might be losing it a bit.

BACK TO THE CORONAVIRUS RESPONSE

April 5, 2020

Marc. [Attaches a tweet by Benjamin Dreyer, an editor at Random House, that says, "oh my god I just can't anymore," in response to a Trump's statement "We are learning much about the Invisible Enemy. It is tough and smart, but we are tougher and smarter!"]

Marc. Good news, Steve!

Stephen. Benjamin Dreyer couldn't take it the day Trump was elected. It's not like he was giving Trump a chance. However, who cares? He's probably a hateful ignoramus.

Marc. Okay, since you say I'm always wrong and, I assume, you believe you are right, explain this: Fauci today said the evidence about hydroxychloroquine is inconclusive, yet Trump told people they should take it if they so choose. How do you explain that dichotomy?

Stephen. Doctors all over the world are using it because it helps patients. Dr. Fauci is a research scientist.

Marc. [Attaches a tweet accusing Trump of providing medical misinformation when he said the FDA had approved hydroxychloroquine for use against COVID-19 (the FDA gave an emergency-use authorization).]

Marc. Trump just made a mistake that only an idiot makes.

Stephen. An emergency-use authorization permits doctors to prescribe a drug for a use that it has not yet been approved for through the normal clinical trial process. In other words, doctors can prescribe hydroxychloroquine for COVID-19 because there is evidence that it works and is known to be safe, even though there is no current protocol for treating the virus. What's your point?

MARC. I know what it means. Trump told the world that the FDA *approved* the drug.

MARC. Details matter, or he should shut up.

STEPHEN. Okay. He should have said the FDA authorized use of the drug. It's a distinction that means nothing to anyone but arrogant Trump haters.

MARC. And what about people who take the drug who are not sick, supported by the "approval" and by Trump's saying, "I might take it myself," despite his not being sick, as some sort of preventative? You did hear that, didn't you? Why don't you take the drug now?

STEPHEN. The drug has to be prescribed by a doctor.

MARC. [*Attaches a report on Trump's suggestion that health-care workers take hydroxychloroquine as a coronavirus prophylaxis, to which he added, "What do I know? I'm not a doctor."*]

MARC. He said this moments ago.

STEPHEN. A lot of doctors agree.

MARC. If the drug is pivotal in helping the epidemic, I will praise Trump's team for their aggressive push. Not everything his people do is wrong.

April 7, 2020

MARC. I tell you Trump lies all the time, and you ask for specifics. Several weeks ago, he said, "Anyone who wants a test can get a test. The tests are beautiful." Today hospitals still struggle with having few tests, and when that was brought to Trump's attention, he said, "The states can get their own tests."

STEPHEN. For Trump, you have an extremely broad definition of *lie*. It's so broad that virtually everything Cuomo has said about New York's preparations and the federal government's assistance would be a lie. In fact, Cuomo makes definitive assertions that clearly are false—for example, understating the federal government's assistance by billions and claiming to need ventilators immediately, when he had thousands of ventilators in a warehouse. Trump might overstate the availability of tests, but tests are available—hundreds of thousands are being administered daily, and more are on the way. Regarding important factual issues, did Trump collude with Russia? His critics and your heroes said he did, but they knew he didn't. Kavanaugh is another glaring example. Trump very transparently tells you what he's doing and why. He's more honest than any previous president.

MARC. Some of Trump's cronies own investments in companies that make hydroxychloroquine. Jeez.

STEPHEN. That's total bullshit. Do you enjoy embarrassing yourself?

MARC. Nobody will be more embarrassed several years from now than sycophants of Trump.

STEPHEN. Why? You live in a fantasy world. You believe people who report actual lies—statements with no basis in fact—over and over again. You ignore actual reality—in this case, the medical community's support for hydroxychloroquine.

MARC. [*Attaches a clip of Wisconsin Assembly Speaker Robin Vos dressed in a mask, gloves, and protective gear while telling voters in the Wisconsin primaries, "You are incredibly safe to go out."*]

MARC. This guy is as convincing as you when you make points that defend Trump.

STEPHEN. My guess is that that is not a compliment.

QUESTIONING DR. FAUCI

MARC. [*Attaches a tweet from Fox News anchor Laura Ingraham's brother criticizing her for questioning Dr. Fauci's advice.*]

MARC. She is ridiculing an expert and scientist. And you call CNN ridiculous?

STEPHEN. She didn't ridicule Fauci. She mocked the idea that the decision to open churches is solely a medical decision. If supermarkets are, by necessity, allowed to remain open, there is an argument that churches should be permitted to stay open. It is a constitutional right to worship. In order to curtail a constitutional right, the state must have a compelling interest. If it has a compelling interest, it must use the most narrowly tailored means available to address that interest to avoid impeding a constitutional right. Therefore, if accommodations can be made to permit supermarkets to open, there is a strong argument that accommodations can be made for religious services. Of course, Laura Ingraham is one of the few people in the media who respect the constitutional right to freely exercise your religion. It appears you prefer to make Dr. Fauci absolute dictator and imprison anyone who questions his judgment.

MARC. Where is our perception gap that "until Anthony Fauci allows us after Christmas" is not specifically derisive?

MARC. There's a big difference between staying in the same place for two hours while sitting still and close and moving around a store and then leaving.

APRIL 8, 2020

STEPHEN. The perception gap is that you believe that any suggestion that the government should make a decision not endorsed by Dr. Fauci is beyond the pale, and I don't believe that. He clearly is a good man and an expert, but he is not the president, and he is not infallible.

MARC. I'm not saying you have to take his suggestions necessarily, though one would think you would if he is your expert, but for Ingraham to mock him or invoke his name in a sarcastic fashion undermines the authority of experts in general and is part of the corrosive effect of the whole Trump regime, along with Fox. It's mean and disrespectful, and Fauci doesn't deserve it.

CORONAVIRUS AND RACE

MARC. Now that scientists suggest that black people seem to be physiologically disproportionately affected, watch how that emboldens Trump country.

STEPHEN. Regarding Ingraham, that's your opinion. Based on your glee in any published material that attacks Trump, it's impossible to take your concern seriously. As for your baseless comment about the coronavirus's impact on black Americans emboldening "Trump country," it simply advertises your ignorance, prejudice, and hate.

MARC. No, it advertises my recognition of prejudice and hate in people who have already demonstrated it and others who haven't yet. Anyone should be able to see that she was being sarcastic and denigrating to a guy who is just trying to help, a guy with zero political agenda.

MARC. When has Fauci projected anything other than a couple- or several-month period? She was pitting science against religion—a good old trope that appeals to God-fearing folk.

STEPHEN. Who are those people? All Trump supporters? Most Trump supporters? A handful of Trump supporters? Are there more haters supporting Trump than opposing Trump? What about blatant anti-Semites in the Democratic Party? All you're doing is making an elitist and bigoted statement about people you don't agree with. That speaks so highly of you. If you think Ingraham was pitting science against religion, you really don't understand the issue. If you think God-fearing folk are antiscience, that is another ignorant, elitist, and bigoted smear.

MARC. Have you heard of the Scopes Monkey Trial and Clarence Darrow?

MARC. Every single virologist says people should be apart, so to say that church should be an exception is exactly pitting religion again science.

STEPHEN. No, that's absolutely wrong. No one is saying that if you go to church, you can ignore social distancing. All she is saying is that free people who want church services should be able to practice their religion and that appropriate social-distancing accommodations can be made.

MARC. And that Fauci is being given too much credibility, which means, to less intelligent people, he has no credibility. See? They throw out chum to the sharks. Racists will grasp the black-people angle and think they are safe: "Ain't no black people [they won't use that term] around heeyuh."

STEPHEN. Unfortunately, not everyone is as smart as you and able to properly evaluate what it means to say, "Fauci is being given too much credibility." I'm glad you have demonstrated that all of those stupid Trump supporters will draw the wrong conclusion. Until you made that point, I mistakenly thought they might draw appropriate and nuanced conclusions. I'm also glad you demonstrated that a large percentage of Trump supporters are racists (why else would they support him?) and that they will incorrectly conclude they are safe because black Americans with coronavirus tend to have worse outcomes than others. You should be embarrassed.

MARC. I'm only embarrassed that my very good friend could be so duped.

STEPHEN. Really? Stereotyping people because you don't agree with them? Accusing them of being stupid and racist because they don't share your political views? That's embarrassing.

MARC. Do you believe there are racists among Democratic voters? Ah yes, you do, so you therefore believe there are also racists among the Republican voters, and I am saying that Trump is masterful or just innately talented at working them. Don't twist my words; I didn't quantify that sector, but I believe they are plentiful. It's not even their fault; they were raised in a cycle of ignorance.

STEPHEN. The United States is not a racist country. Trump has embraced the African American community in many ways. He has done more than his predecessor to address major concerns of the African American community, including the First Step Act. African Americans have prospered during his administration. Furthermore, Trump does nothing to work up the insignificant number of racists who actually exist. Nothing. Your view of the United States is very sad and ignorant.

HYDROXYCHLOROQUINE

MARC. [*Attaches a report that Swedish hospitals abandoned trials of hydroxychloroquine for coronavirus patients because it caused blinding headaches, vision loss, and cramps.*]

MARC. "What do you have to lose?"

April 9, 2020

STEPHEN. We have friends, a husband and wife around our age, who were hospitalized for COVID-19. The wife has underlying medical issues. They were treated with hydroxychloroquine and quickly recovered. As for the safety of the drug, look up Dr. Daniel Wallace, a rheumatologist who has been prescribing hydroxychloroquine for years. What do you have to lose? Nothing.

MARC. I'm reading a lot about this, and there may be something to it, just as heart organizations are advising against it. You never know who would respond well without it or who will have a bad reaction to it. Not everything that is reported on the negative effect of the antimalaria drugs is politically driven. But what I read yesterday explains that this virus affects blood cells and their ability to bind to oxygen, which can explain the systemic shutdown from hypoxia, and that ventilators might be useless (other than keeping people breathing). I'm not sure of the implications on the treatment, but it further explains why older people and less healthy people are dying fast.

STEPHEN. The media's effort to discredit use of hydroxychloroquine is primarily, if not exclusively, related to Trump.

MARC. You see everything that way. You may be right in terms of dissemination of reports, but heart associations don't go by Trump.

STEPHEN. I would hope not.

STEPHEN. However, the American Bar Association, which should be a trade organization, is a left-wing political organization.

DEMOCRATS

MARC. By the way, I like De Blasio now too!

STEPHEN. He is the most incompetent buffoon to ever serve as mayor.

MARC. Name a Democrat you respect and think is smart and decent.

STEPHEN. There are several. Without giving it too much thought, I would say Gina Raimondo, governor of Rhode Island; Joe Manchin, senator from West Virginia; Tulsi Gabbard; and Steve Bellone, Suffolk County executive, whom I have met. Chris Coons, senator from Delaware, seems like a reasonable guy, and Klobuchar also appears reasonable. I would not expect to support any of them, because I oppose identity politics; illegal immigration; demonization of capitalism and the private sector; environmental zealotry; support for America's enemies, including, now most prominently, China; and the Democrats' side on virtually every significant political issue. However, the people above, from what I know about them, live in the real world.

THE PANDEMIC OFFICE

April 10, 2020

MARC. Trump was caught in another lie. `When asked about his closing of the pandemic office in 2018, he said he didn't know anything about it, after he said, "It wasn't me, when you say me." And at a different press conference, he said he fired those people to save money: "I'm a businessman; we can always get these people back."

STEPHEN. The responsibilities handled by the pandemic office were reassigned. The work handled by that office continued to be handled. The Daily Signal reported on March 24 that "As part of a larger reorganization, Bolton in 2018 merged the Directorate for Global Health Security and Biodefense with two other functions into a new Directorate of Counterproliferation and Biodefense. The move was based on what Bolton believed would be a natural overlap. Not a single staffer lost his position, according to Morrison, now a senior fellow specializing in Asia-Pacific security at the Hudson Institute." It's not another lie but another example of your eagerness to smear Trump.

MARC. When the Trump administration fails, as all administrations do, it's "The people were reassigned." When it succeeds, it's Trump accomplishment. And when Obama's rollout of the ACA was horrendous, it was on Obama.

STEPHEN. This has nothing to do with whether the Trump administration did or did not respond effectively. It simply was an effort to suggest that Trump disbanded a critical office, which impeded the government's ability to respond. Whatever legitimate criticisms of the administration's actions can be made, the false claim that he disbanded the pandemic office is not one of them. The ACA failure is completely different. The Obama administration had years to prepare, they hired Democratic cronies without the right experience, and it crashed. That's not his fault?

MORE ON REOPENING THE ECONOMY

MARC. Since you are a master at covering for Trump after the fact, let's have you go on the record before he decides: Should he or will he follow through on his incessant hints at "opening up really soon"? Will he be so narrow-minded to open up in the quiet places that haven't yet hit their peak?

STEPHEN. I believe there has been a significant and destructive overreaction. I hope we open up the economy no later than early May (it won't be sooner), even if it is not opened all at once and with certain precautions, like more spacing in restaurants. The models, which significantly overestimated the number of deaths, purportedly built in social distancing, so the argument that the numbers are down because we have done a good job are wrong. The models simply overestimated the consequences. We need to get back to work. We need to deal with any related coronavirus cases, but we should, at this point, be prepared. It is very easy for Trump opponents, like Zeke Emanuel (Rahm's brother and a doctor serving as an adviser to Biden), to say the economy should be shut down for twelve to eighteen months. He knows that won't happen, but saying it gives him the opportunity to blame Trump if the virus continues to cause people to die after the economy reopens, which is likely. It is nauseatingly cynical. So yes, Trump will and should begin to open the economy. More than enough damage has been done by overreacting.

MARC. I'm tending to agree with you on this.

STEPHEN. Will you consider rooting for the Yankees this year too?

MARC. You mean in 2021?

HAPPY GOOD FRIDAY TO ALL!

MARC. [*Attaches a Trump tweet wishing a "HAPPY GOOD FRIDAY TO ALL!"*]

MARC. When I tell you that Trump is a moron, please listen to me.

MARC. Further proof that he is an imposter, unless you have a better explanation.

STEPHEN. He is a moron because he wished a happy Good Friday to all? Do you think about what you say? Have you wished anyone a happy Passover or happy Easter? I have. My guess is that Christians who find joy and comfort in celebrating the death and resurrection of Christ will put the pandemic in perspective.

MARC. That is your lamest spin ever. How does "Happy Yom Kippur" grab you? He is a charlatan.

MARC. He does not know even the basics about the religion he claims to care about.

[MARC. Hey, at least everything is all back to normal by Easter Sunday! He had a good hunch on that one.

MARC. Happy D-Day!

THE LATEST ON FBI MISCONDUCT AGAINST TRUMP

April 11, 2020

STEPHEN. The attached document is the transcript of Stefan Halper's secretly recorded conversation with George Papadopoulos as part of the Crossfire Hurricane investigation. Halper was a CHS (confidential human source) for the FBI. Read pages 157 to the end.

MARC. Why would I want to open up something and find the page to read something that proves your point?

MARC. [*Attaches a tweet posting a Rasmussen poll showing current approval for Trump: 43 percent approve, and 56 percent disapprove.*]

MARC. Rasmussen.

STEPHEN. Hope springs eternal.

MARC. Underwater.

STEPHEN. Read the transcript. The truth shall set you free.

MARC. What does he say? Cut to the chase.

STEPHEN. Papadopoulos is asked if the Trump campaign has any connection to Russia. He says no. He is definitive.

MARC. [*Attaches a tweet posting a comment by Alec Baldwin that only the "mentally ill" will vote for Trump.*]

MARC. Your Halper-Papadopoulos quote was underwhelming.

STEPHEN. I don't think you understand the significance. That's very sad. The FBI claimed they began the Trump-Russia investigation because the former Australian foreign minister reported a conversation he'd had with Papadopoulos, which he thought indicated that Papadopoulos had knowledge that the Russians hacked the DNC. However, when asked by a confidential human source (a spy) who was secretly recording his conversation, Papadopoulos stated unequivocally that the Trump campaign had nothing to do with it. That's it. There was no basis for the investigation in the first place, but this should have been the nail in the coffin. The FBI knew Trump did not collude with Russia but investigated Trump anyway. As Barr has noted, this was not sloppiness or a mistake. There will be prosecutions.

MARC. Papadopoulos was lying.

STEPHEN. Oh, right. He knew that Halper was working for the FBI, so he was playing along. Mueller proved that. That's why the FBI didn't advise the FISA court, as Horowitz established. Mueller also proved conclusively that the Trump campaign worked with Russia to hack the DNC servers. At least that must be how you remember it.

MARC. My official response to this is "Trump is an asshole and moron!" Succinct and effective.

BACK TO REOPENING THE ECONOMY

April 12, 2020

MARC. [Attaches a CNN report that Dr. Fauci stated that calls to implement social-distancing measures faced pushback early in the coronavirus outbreak.]

MARC. [Attaches a tweet reporting that Trump privately proposed letting coronavirus "wash over" America, killing hundreds of thousands or millions of Americans but keeping the economy moving.]

MARC. Shameful.

STEPHEN. Really? The claim that coronavirus would have killed millions of Americans is simply speculation. Thank God Trump is willing to question the medical experts. As it stands today, it is possible the number of deaths from all causes in 2020 won't be significantly different from the number of deaths in other years. So go ahead—blame Trump for something that didn't happen and likely never would have happened.

STEPHEN. In 2018, 2,839,205 people died in the United States, an average of 7,800 per day. To fairly evaluate the toll of the coronavirus, we need to know whether the coronavirus is impacting the daily average. This may seem callous, but death is an inescapable fact of life.

MARC. I happen to agree.

MARC. But Trump can't commit.

STEPHEN. Trump will commit, and he will be ridiculed by the media for ignoring experts and blamed for every death.

MARC. Which way will he commit? New York and California lock down, and the rest don't?

STEPHEN. He cannot override state orders, but I expect he will change the guidelines and will work with states to open the economy. It probably will take longer in New York and New Jersey.

Conclusion

Our debate takes a pause as the United States is dealing with the coronavirus pandemic and the unprecedented economic hardship it is causing, the investigation into the Russian collusion investigation is bearing fruit, and the 2020 election is on the horizon. Marc and I continue to text each other and probably will continue to text each other as long as Donald J. Trump is president.

Index

A

Abedin, Huma, 213
abortion, 312, 382–383, 404
ACA. *See* Obamacare/ACA
Access Hollywood tape, 10, 140, 160, 349, 593
Acosta, Jim, 247
Afghanistan, US troops in, 506
Al-Baghdadi, killing of, 530–531
Alexander, Peter, 666
allegations, fake/false. *See* fake allegations/false allegations
Allred, Gloria, 56
altruism, 261–262
Amazon, 163, 415
ambassadors, 537–538, 560
animals, Trump's comment about, 158, 162, 183, 363
Antifa, 4, 10, 15, 23, 75, 158, 159, 227, 426, 430, 438, 629
anti-Semitism, 4, 23, 41, 49–50, 75, 244, 264, 298, 312, 330–331, 333, 335, 342, 380, 381, 384, 387, 426–427, 437, 532, 538, 611
The Apprentice (TV show), 104, 379, 392
Arpaio, Joe, 6
The Art of the Comeback (Trump), 399
Assange, 142
autocracy, 37, 88, 89, 107, 121, 131, 132, 415, 500, 643, 681
Avenatti affidavit, 228–229

B

Baker, James, 273
Baldwin, Alec, 726
Bannon, Steve, 41, 47, 51, 98, 408
Barr, Roseanne, 167
Barr, William (Bill), 361, 366, 367, 368, 369, 378, 390, 391, 395, 398, 408, 417, 446, 468, 473, 481, 493, 522, 525, 526, 564, 579, 580, 581, 582, 585, 595, 605, 665, 693, 727
Barrett, Amy, 393
Bash, Dana, 662
BDS (Boycott, Divestment, and Sanction), 441, 442–443
"Be Best" initiative, 637
Bellone, Steve, 722
Bendavid, Eran, 679
Benghazi, 42, 215, 217, 317, 338, 372, 491, 516, 617, 696
Bergdahl, Bowe, 611
Bevin, Matt, 544
Bezos, Jeff, 163
Bharara, Preet, 169
Bhattacharya, Jay, 679

Biden, Hunter, 456, 457, 467, 475, 486, 488, 492, 501, 510, 518, 524, 541, 546, 554, 566, 603, 604, 622, 632
Biden, Joe
    as Democratic presidential candidate 2020, 451, 452, 475
    and emoluments clause, 518
    as point person on China, 603
    and swine flu epidemic, 659
    Trump's request to investigate, 474, 486, 630, 639
    and Ukraine, 453, 455, 457, 458–462, 467, 468, 471, 472, 482, 484, 489, 490, 492, 493, 501, 510, 511, 522–523, 524, 536, 537, 540, 541, 542, 546, 554, 555, 559, 562, 563, 565, 566, 604, 605, 607, 624, 631, 632, 636–637
birther movement/birtherism, 10, 149, 154, 253, 470, 693
Birx, Deborah, 675
Black Israelites, 301, 302, 303, 306
Black Lives Matter (BLM), 4, 23, 160, 227, 241, 437, 439
Blagojevich, Rod, 169
Bloom, Lisa, 56
Bloomberg, Michael, 637, 641, 642, 652, 691
Bolton, John, 215, 504, 513, 629, 630, 633, 636, 723
bomb threats, 240
Booker, Cory, 240, 451
Boot, Max, 236
border crisis, 421
border security, 129
border wall, 14, 69, 78, 87, 129, 275, 294, 302, 316, 393, 439
borders, open, 188–189, 317, 377, 467
Born Alive Act, 382, 384
Bossie, David, 186

Boycott, Divestment, and Sanction (BDS), 441, 442–443
Brady, Greg, 564
Breitbart, 318
Brennan, John, 116, 139, 164, 179, 201, 366, 386, 405, 418, 446, 585, 586, 601
Broderick, Juanita, 349
Burisma, 490, 492, 522, 523, 536, 537, 546, 563, 565, 566, 604, 630
Burr, Brooke, 699
Bush, George, 47, 154, 187, 197, 314, 388, 463, 508, 526, 593, 647, 661
Bush, George W., 154, 174, 283
Bush, Jeb, 8, 29, 61, 62, 226, 232, 241, 435
Buttigieg, Pete, 461, 519
Buzzfeed, 289, 291

C

California, aid to, 683–684, 708
campaign finance, violations of, 135–136, 141, 152, 209, 268, 271–272, 273, 326, 497, 694
Carlson, Tucker, 488–489, 493, 699
Carroll, E. Jean, 420
Cavuto, Neil, 199
CDC
    flu season statistics, 688, 691
    testing by, 697, 702
    on wearing masks, 708
Central Park Five, 10, 25, 75, 305, 606
character, 12, 226, 324, 353, 390, 393, 394, 398, 399, 450, 503, 549, 550–553, 593–595
Charlottesville, Virginia, 4–5, 75, 158, 333–334
China
    Biden as point person on, 603
    and Biden investigation, 486, 487
    economic warfare, 282

tariffs on, 393, 402–403
trade with, 325, 402–403
travel ban from, 661, 685, 701, 703
Trump's position on, 551
Christians, 49, 155–156, 245, 523, 725
civil liberties, 195, 205, 225, 261, 310, 378, 399
civil rights, 14, 80, 84, 97, 121, 141, 185, 222, 226, 644
Clapper, James, 139, 164, 179, 366, 386, 405, 418, 446
climate. *See also* Paris Climate Accord; Thunberg, Greta
   climate change, 14, 318
   toxic environments, 128
Clinton, Bill
   as centrist, 61
   disbarring of, 52
   impeachment of, 367, 474, 549, 596, 602
   as lying under oath, 52, 196, 266, 322
   meeting with Lynch, 92
   sexual misconduct of, 13, 19, 23, 132, 217, 349
   as Trump opponent, 1
   Trump versus, 12
   and Whitewater, 338, 350
Clinton, Chelsea, 342
Clinton, Hillary
   as centrist, 61
   competency of, 217
   donations by Russians to, 59
   email investigation of, 32, 33, 35–36, 38–39, 42–43, 44, 46, 51, 58, 73, 84, 85, 92, 94, 99, 135, 136, 154, 179, 386, 586
   and Fusion GPS, 22, 219
   intellect of, 13–14
   opposition research of, 150
   as part of political class, 8, 9
   and Steele dossier, 34

support for, 15
   as Trump opponent, 1
   Trump versus, 12
   on Uranium One deal, 19
Clinton Foundation, 19, 138
CNN, 21, 46, 69, 415, 634, 649, 657, 662, 701, 705, 728
Cohen, Michael, 133–134, 147, 153, 165–166, 204, 209, 210, 213, 225, 226, 268, 271, 273, 275, 289, 291, 295, 326, 336, 602
college admissions scandal, 340
Collins, Chris, 211, 222
Collins, Susan, 233
Comcast, 649
Comey, James (Jim), 16, 32–33, 38, 39, 42, 43, 44, 45, 51, 53, 80, 84, 116, 117, 133, 138, 139, 143, 144, 145, 171, 179, 261, 270, 271, 273, 290, 331, 366, 367, 372, 373, 376, 386, 390, 401, 405, 411–412, 418, 445–447, 449, 458, 568, 585, 586, 601, 606, 644, 650, 710
congressional subpoenas. *See* subpoenas
conspiracy theories, 59, 249, 289, 303, 346, 548
Coons, Chris, 722
Cooper, Anderson, 701
Corbyn, Jeremy, 381
Cordray, Richard, 82
Corker, Bob, 16, 19, 24, 100, 102, 182, 214
coronavirus, 655, 657–664, 666–671, 674–682, 685–709, 711–721, 724, 728–729
corruption, 113, 137, 453, 461–462, 465, 467, 471, 484, 485, 486, 489, 490, 503, 522, 524–525, 531, 533, 534, 536, 540, 542, 546, 547, 551, 557, 559, 562, 563, 565, 567, 574, 576, 589, 591, 604, 605, 607, 613, 631, 633, 636, 665, 678, 692

Corsi, Jerome, 354–355
Cotton, Tom, 76, 77
COVID-19. *See* coronavirus
Covington High School students (Kentucky), 294–307, 323, 399, 656
Crenshaw, Dan, 508
Crimea, 425, 613, 625
Crossfire Hurricane, 648, 726
CrowdStrike, 505, 525, 605
Cruz, Nikolas, 107
Cruz, Ted, 5, 10, 352
Cummings, Elijah, 435–438
Cuomo, Andrew, 20, 312, 666, 685, 686, 688–690, 698, 706, 707
Cuomo, Chris, 329
Cusack, John, 685, 686

D

DACA/Dreamers, 9–10, 66, 78, 82, 87, 89, 113, 114, 147
Daily Show, 705
Daily Signal, 723
Daniels, Stormy, 115, 117, 133, 135, 136, 143, 160, 209, 220, 228, 268, 271, 326, 371, 601, 602, 694
Dayton shooting, 439–440
de Blasio, Bill, 20, 722
death tax exemption, 28
Democratic National Committee (DNC), 7, 8, 9, 22, 34, 92, 99, 106, 166, 195, 260, 388, 494, 495, 525, 533, 536, 543, 563, 727
denuclearization, 163, 175, 176, 177, 330, 331, 388
"deplorables," 1, 14, 74, 301, 656
deregulation, 60, 62, 63, 113, 114, 276, 281, 393
Dershowitz, Alan, 51–52, 122, 623, 625, 626, 635
DeSantis, Ron, 706

Deutsche Bank, 397, 406, 620
dictatorship, 9, 50, 65–68, 103, 104, 148, 177, 178, 179, 201, 202, 213, 226, 277, 316, 342–343, 345, 348, 507, 529, 643, 650, 662–663, 681, 715
Dingell, Debbie, 608
Dingell, John, 608
DNC (Democratic National Committee). *See* Democratic National Committee (DNC)
Dobbs, Lou, 199
DOJ
  abuse of power by, 97
  on bringing charges prior to elections, 222–223
  Comey and, 445
  connection of with Fusion GPS and Christopher Steele, 97
  as declining to prosecute Mills and Abedin, 213
  as declining to pursue charges against McCabe, 648
  as dropping charges against Russians Mueller indicted, 665
  evidence of malfeasance at, 92
  exoneration of H. Clinton by, 68, 84, 210, 290, 339, 341, 375, 386
  firing of officials at, 254
  interference in election by, 324
  investigation into Ukraine by, 536, 542, 547, 555
  misconduct of, 194, 264, 269, 292
  Obama and, 140, 158, 226, 318, 329, 350, 497
  role of, 65
  and Steele dossier, 208, 289, 291
  Trump and, 369, 386, 409, 410, 413
Dolphin, Renate, 233, 234, 236, 237
Doocy, Steve, 630
Doral, hosting G7 at, 517–518

Dowd, John, 414
Downer, Alexander, 586, 595
Dreamers/Daca, 9–10, 66, 78, 82, 87, 89, 113, 114, 147
Dreyer, Benjamin, 711
Drudge, Matt, 318
D'Souza, Dinesh, 169, 433, 434
due process, 14, 151, 188, 189, 356, 482, 513
Duke, David, 10, 13, 135, 158, 159, 160, 301, 334, 335, 336, 371, 583
Duke University lacrosse players, 302, 656
duplicity, 80, 121, 263, 320
Durbin, Dick, 76, 78
Durham, John, 473, 526, 577, 579, 580, 582, 585, 595, 627
Durham investigation, 533, 575, 634
Durham report, 493, 568, 581, 634

E

economic growth, 60, 61, 358, 378, 379, 380, 393, 640
economy, reopening of, 674, 680–681, 683, 724, 728–729
Edwards, John, 135
El Paso shooting, 439–440
elections. *See also* Obama, Barack, and US election 2016; Russia, and US election 2016; Ukraine, and US election 2016
 Comey and, 331, 446
 DOJ on bringing charges prior to, 222
 interference in, 8, 48, 94, 140, 144, 197, 198, 201, 257, 259, 270, 324, 331, 343, 406, 446, 468, 473, 474, 524, 525, 531, 542, 555, 575, 644
 seeking to influence, 26, 45, 70, 80, 164, 165–166, 472
 undoing 2016 election, 147–148
 US presidential election 2016, 57, 194, 197, 286, 435, 515, 519–520, 525, 527, 533, 537, 539, 542, 555, 558, 565, 575, 607, 644, 694
 US presidential election 2020, 451–452, 515, 519–520, 542, 607, 634
electoral fraud/election fraud, 127, 221, 268, 326
electoral integrity, 127
electoral process, 127, 292
elitism, 392–394
Emanuel, Zeke, 724
emergency declaration, 316–319
emoluments clause, 518
An Enemy of the People (Ibsen), 674
Epstein, Jeffrey, 593, 594
Erdogan, 500, 512, 514
executive orders, 67, 82, 183, 188, 316–319, 415, 569, 583
executive privilege, 206, 367, 370, 373, 390, 409, 463

F

fake ads, 70
fake allegations/false allegations, 141, 152, 252, 286, 373, 405, 457, 550, 556, 558, 593, 610, 650, 694, 710
fake issues, 271
fake media, 699
"fake" media reports, 368
fake narrative/fake story/false narrative, 52, 290, 346, 382, 481, 591
fake news, 29, 291
fake scandal, 471
family separation, 181–182, 246
Fast and Furious, 42, 54, 317, 395, 696
Fauci, Anthony, 657, 660, 666, 670, 701, 708, 711, 715–716, 718, 728

FBI
  abuse of power by, 38, 61, 97, 271, 634
  and college admissions scandal, 340
  Comey and, 405, 447
  conduct of, 292–293
  discussion of insurance against Trump victory by, 53, 54
  firing of officials at, 254
  and FISA warrants/process, 93–94, 107, 108, 225, 580, 581, 609, 634
  Flynn and, 270, 273, 274–275
  and Fusion GPS, 58
  genesis and bias of, 385
  on hacking by GRU, 581
  interference in election by, 324
  investigation into Clinton Foundation, 138
  investigation into Hillary's emails by, 32, 33, 35–36, 38–39, 42–43, 44, 46, 51, 58, 73, 84, 85, 92, 94, 99, 135, 136, 154, 179, 386, 586
  investigation of Trump's campaign by, 99, 100–101, 102, 135, 164, 179, 194, 264, 308, 318, 339, 398, 580, 586–587, 595, 605–606, 643, 726–727
  leadership conspiracy in, 116
  and Michael Cohen, 133
  misconduct by/malfeasance at, 57–58, 83–84, 92, 194, 264, 587, 726–727
  Mueller investigation. *See* Mueller investigation
  Obama and, 84, 94, 226, 258, 290, 329, 350, 386
  role of, 84, 93, 94, 144, 399
  and Steele dossier, 43, 289, 585, 586, 595

  and Strzok and Page text messages, 80
  Trump's firing of chief, 51
First Step Act, 719
FISA. *See* Foreign Intelligence Surveillance Act (FISA), abuse/application/investigation
Flake, Jeff, 19, 24, 100, 182
Fleischer, Ari, 690
Flynn, Michael, 31, 32, 35–36, 37, 44, 46, 80, 84, 93, 132, 145, 265, 267, 271, 273, 274, 275, 278, 279–280, 315, 354, 355, 414
Ford, Blasey, 228, 232–233, 237, 393, 449, 489
Foreign Intelligence Surveillance Act (FISA), abuse/application/investigation, 44, 88, 92, 93–94, 95, 98, 101, 103, 107, 195, 213, 225, 290, 291, 371, 373, 401, 446, 481, 579–582, 585–587, 595, 598, 601–602, 609, 627, 629, 634, 648, 727
foreign policy, 91, 107, 113, 130, 199, 276, 290, 295, 377, 393, 412, 507, 522, 523, 525, 551, 558, 561, 623, 625
Fox, 21, 29, 89, 104, 108, 117, 144, 153, 154, 175, 197, 199, 278, 318, 321, 336, 366, 556, 630, 657, 659, 663, 705, 708, 715
free speech, 5, 17, 18, 227, 342, 348
Friedman, David, 129, 130
Fruman, Igor, 494
Fuhrman, Mark, 39, 43, 53, 57, 83
Fusion GPS, 22, 58, 97, 213, 219, 220, 264

G

G7, 174, 517–518
Gabbard, Tulsi, 722

Gaetz, Matt, 655–656, 699
Gallagher, Eddie, 569–572, 610–612
Garland, Merrick, 229, 230, 678
Gessen, Masha, 84, 166
Gillibrand, Kirsten, 47
Giuliani, Rudy, 171, 275, 276, 293, 295, 303, 326, 337, 453–454, 463, 494, 504, 510, 513, 514, 515, 536, 537, 540, 556, 564, 565, 571, 574, 604, 605, 622, 646
Goldberg, Jonah, 534
Gorsuch, Neil, 228, 232, 243
Gotti, John, 337
Gowdy, Trey, 102, 116
Graham, Lindsey, 76, 264, 352, 490, 513, 575, 596
Green, Al, 474
Green New Deal, 315, 316, 317, 377, 402, 467, 675
Greitens, Eric, 136
Griffin, Kathy, 128, 167
gun control, 110, 439

H

Haley, Nikki, 60, 114, 130, 214, 215, 461
Halper, Stefan, 164, 726, 727
Hannity, Sean, 26, 121, 261, 658, 708
Harris, Kamala, 251, 451
Hatch, Orrin, 5
hate speech, 183–185
hatred, 144, 159, 160, 184, 186–187, 261, 342, 436, 438, 452, 590, 604
Hayes, Stephen, 709
Helsinki press conference, 198–200, 264
Henninger, Dan, 449
Henry, Ed, 571
Hill, Fiona, 504, 591
Hillel, 442
Hirsi Ali, Ayaan, 427
hit jobs, political, 398–401

Hitler, Adolph, 48, 49, 50, 118, 183–185, 244, 343, 426
Holder, Eric, 395, 607
Horowitz, Michael, 111, 395, 473, 481, 493, 577, 579, 582, 585, 586, 595, 727
Horowitz report, 398, 580, 586, 591, 592, 595
Huffman, Felicity, 340
Hunter, Duncan, 211, 222
hydroxychloroquine, 670, 671, 703, 709, 711–712, 713, 720–721

I

Icahn, Carl, 113
immigration
  border crisis, 421
  border security, 129
  border wall, 14, 69, 78, 87, 129, 275, 294, 302, 316, 393, 439
  caravans, 239
  DACA. *See* DACA/Dreamers
  family separation, 181–182, 246
  illegal immigration, 6, 25, 34, 158, 183, 184, 187, 188–189, 245, 246, 301, 304, 413, 421, 722
  open borders, 188–189, 317, 377, 467
  Stipulated Removal, 189
  Trump's stand on, 281
impeachment
  of Clinton, 367, 474, 549, 596, 602
  of Nixon, 361, 474, 557–558
  of Trump, 180, 202, 209, 214, 350, 352, 385, 457, 465, 469, 482, 486, 494, 497–498, 503–505, 510–511, 513–516, 519, 521–525, 526, 527, 532–543, 547, 555–566, 573, 575, 591–592, 596, 597, 599–600,

605, 607, 622–638, 639, 650,
    670, 696, 697
inaugural committee, 269
income tax fraud, 151. *See also* tax fraud
Indians, 146, 296, 299, 301, 303–304
influence peddling, 461
Ingraham, Laura, 715, 717
inspector general's report, 179–180,
    445–447, 575, 577, 579, 582, 585,
    587, 601, 634, 648
insults, 172, 207, 490, 574, 598, 605,
    650, 668
intolerance, 294, 295, 342–346
investigations. *See also* FBI
    Durham investigation. *See* Durham
        investigation
    FISA investigation. *See* Foreign
        Intelligence Surveillance Act
        (FISA), abuse/application/
        investigation
    Mueller investigation. *See* Mueller
        investigation
    permanent investigations of
        presidency, 218
Iran
    attack of on US embassy in
        Iraq, 621
    Democrats and, 448
    and Europe and Japan, 419
    H. Clinton and, 73
    and killing of Soleimani, 621, 622
    Obama and, 2, 73, 77, 89, 95, 109,
        147, 150, 154, 199, 203, 330,
        388, 402, 495, 496, 519, 589,
        601, 664
    Trump and, 14, 43, 153, 163, 282,
        317, 319, 393, 618, 703
IRS
    abuse of power by, 61, 66, 67
    and conservatives, 51, 121, 147, 154
    Obama and, 2, 65, 317, 338,
        344, 627

targeting by, 51, 54, 121, 147, 154
and Tea Party, 37, 42, 319
Trump and, 148, 410
ISIS, 114, 162, 245, 282, 440, 495, 499,
    501, 508–509, 530, 664
Israel. *See also* Jerusalem
    as ally, 14
    election in, 46
    support for, 60, 114, 129, 378
    Tlaib's planned visit to, 442

J

Jackson, Robert H., 622
Jacobs, Ben, 241
James, LeBron, 207
Jeffress, Robert, 155–157
Jenkins, Holman, 549
Jerusalem
    move of US embassy to, 63–64,
        153, 155–157, 393
    recognition of, 40, 41, 49, 60, 82,
        129, 130, 188, 281, 282
Jerusalem Post, 495
Jews, 15, 23, 49, 63, 77, 146, 155, 162,
    183, 243, 244, 245, 251, 259, 264,
    300, 331, 333–334, 348, 363,
    378, 380, 387, 427, 436, 441, 528,
    538, 571, 583, 612
Johnson, Ron, 100, 563, 565, 592, 633
Judaism, as nationality, 583
Judge, Mark, 237
justice, obstruction of, 33, 42, 65, 83,
    117, 171, 257, 266–267, 290, 291,
    344, 350, 354, 355, 361, 367, 368,
    385–386, 390, 391, 399, 400,
    408, 410, 411, 414, 417, 418, 431,
    585, 586, 587, 643

K

Kaepernick, Colin, 100
Kagan, Elena, 146

Karl, Jonathan, 707
Kasich, John, 98, 393
Kasparov, Garry, 332
Kavanaugh, Brett, 226–227, 228–229, 230–234, 236–238, 243, 393, 449–450, 489, 493
Kelly, John, 529
Kelly, Megyn, 47, 336
Kent, George, 555, 556
Kerry, John, 150
Keyser, Leland, 233, 237–238, 449, 450, 489
Khashoggi, Jamal, 537
Kilimnik, Konstantin, 417
Kim Jong Un, 176, 177, 281, 282, 330, 331, 347
King, Peter, 28
King, Steve, 15
Kinzinger, Adam, 509
Kirschner, Glenn, 541
Kislyak, Sergey, 280
Klobuchar, Amy, 722
Kovaleski, Serge, 550
Kraft, Robert, 67, 323, 324, 702
Kramer, David, 344
Ku Klux Klan (KKK), 158, 159, 251
Kudlow, Larry, 402
Kurds, 495, 499–502, 506, 507, 508
Kushner, Jared, 31, 32, 70, 111, 130, 327–328, 343, 353, 355, 537, 704, 705

L

Las Vegas shooter, 27
Lavrov, Sergey, 581, 582
law, rule of. *See* rule of law
legal, versus political, 415–416
Lemon, Don, 207
Levin, Mark, 318, 641
Lewandowski, Corey, 367, 448, 459, 587
Lewinsky, Monica, 266

liars, 7, 10, 13, 26, 31, 39, 133, 138–139, 226, 232, 243, 256, 261, 312, 315, 320–321, 343, 352, 353, 354, 365, 366, 371, 372, 377, 386, 406, 427, 445, 446, 506, 519, 526, 541, 567, 573, 594, 598, 601, 629
Lieu, Ted, 433
Limbaugh, Rush, 318
Lindell, Mike, 694–695
Loeffler, Kelly, 699
Loughlin, Lori, 340
Lowell, Abbe, 328
Lowry, Rich, 220, 258
Lynch, Loretta, 1, 42, 80, 92, 139, 179, 344, 386, 418, 546

M

MAGA hats, 96, 217, 296, 302, 303, 304, 305, 306, 307, 437, 438
MAGA high school students, 295
Maher, Bill, 20
"Make America Great Again" slogan, 428
"Man in the Arena" (Roosevelt), 700
Manafort, Paul, 44, 46, 93, 179, 210–211, 213, 214, 215, 217, 220, 221, 225, 226, 273, 335–338, 341, 354, 417, 454, 457–458, 518, 536
Manchin, Joe, 98, 722
Maples, Marla, 115
MBS, 266, 474
McCabe, Andrew, 63, 88, 98, 100, 116, 132, 138, 139, 261, 270, 273, 320–321, 386, 405, 446, 449, 568, 648
McCain, John, 10, 100, 131, 140, 163, 221, 254, 344, 345, 347, 351, 410
McCarthy, Andrew, 32
McCarthy, Andy, 635
McConnell, Mitch, 398, 465, 470

McGahn, Don, 289, 365, 367, 370, 385, 396, 398, 405, 432, 493, 587, 710
media
   anonymous op-ed piece, 224
   Bergdahl press conference, 611
   Buzzfeed, 289, 291
   CNN, 21, 46, 69, 415, 634, 649, 657, 662, 701, 705, 728
   Comcast, 649
   coronavirus press conferences, 660, 663, 666–667, 670, 672, 675–677, 691, 692, 709
   Daily Show, 705
   Daily Signal, 723
   fake ads, 70
   fake media, 699
   "fake" media reports, 368
   fake news, 29, 291
   Fox, 21, 29, 89, 104, 108, 117, 144, 153, 154, 175, 197, 199, 278, 318, 321, 336, 366, 556, 630, 657, 659, 663, 705, 708, 715
   Helsinki press conference, 198–200, 264
   Jerusalem Post, 495
   MSNBC, 649, 657
   Mulvaney press conference, 462, 515
   National Review, 258
   NBC, 666
   New York Post, 197, 539
   New York Times, 143, 224, 384, 389, 392, 412, 482, 492, 493, 629, 630, 641, 662, 701
   OAN, 666
   other Trump press conferences, 201, 231, 248, 372, 723
   Politico, 525
   reporting of on Trump, 17, 197, 201, 202–203, 317, 321, 329
   Trump as fighting with, 148
   USA Today, 47
   The View, 707

Vox, 305
Wall Street Journal, 21, 41, 82, 96, 143, 197, 269, 326, 396, 427, 454, 459, 463, 549, 563
Washington Post, 21, 69, 177
Mein Kampf, 183
Mexicans, 23, 158, 159, 184, 245, 299, 301, 304, 342
Mexico, tariffs on, 413
Michigan, aid to, 687
Middle East, 506–510, 514. *See also specific countries*
Mifsud, Joseph, 389
military, transgender persons and, 123
Miller, Jason, 17, 18
Mills, Cheryl, 46, 92, 136, 213
Moore, Roy, 29–30, 105
Morrison, Tim, 723
MS-13, 158–159, 187, 363
MSNBC, 649, 657
Mueller, Robert (Bob), 26, 38, 39, 42–46, 58, 84, 96, 99, 102, 105, 141, 210, 213, 215, 254, 259, 270, 273, 274, 280, 285, 291, 316, 321, 335, 344, 351–352, 365, 366, 367, 376, 385, 389–391, 400, 407–411, 413, 417, 431, 432, 433, 434, 458, 587, 599, 710, 727
Mueller investigation, 83–86, 92–95, 102, 109, 120, 141–143, 248, 264–265, 320, 341, 350, 365–370, 431, 488, 562
Mueller report, 7–11, 26, 92, 353–356, 361–362, 366, 370, 373–375, 386, 389, 405, 407, 412, 414, 417–418, 431–434, 473, 492, 581, 585–586, 625, 665
Mulvaney, Mick, 215, 462, 463, 515, 518, 522, 561, 565
Murkowski, Lisa, 643
Muslims, 5, 23, 24, 27, 146, 158, 159, 184, 245, 342, 440

N

Nadler, Jerry, 596, 606
Napolitano, Andrew, 370
National Review, 258
NATO, 193, 194, 281
Nazis, 4, 5, 12, 48, 49, 131, 147, 159, 162, 172, 187, 242, 384, 429–430, 435, 508
NBC, 666
neo-Nazis, 4, 5, 7, 245–246, 380, 429
Netanyahu, Benjamin, 154, 567, 593, 632
Never Trumpers, 279, 434, 534
New York City terrorist, 27
New York Post, 197, 539
New York State
    aid to, 683–684, 685–686, 689–690, 702, 707, 708
    Giuliani and, 646–647
New York Times, 143, 224, 384, 389, 392, 412, 482, 492, 493, 629, 630, 641, 662, 701
Newsom, Gavin, 666, 707
NFL players, Trump comment about, 75, 172–173
Ninth Circuit Court, 415
Nixon, Richard, 99, 175, 278, 361, 474, 557–558, 609
North Korea
    denuclearization of, 163
    H. Clinton and, 73
    missile test, 388
    Obama and, 73
    release of hostages by, 153
    sanctions on, 43
    summit in Vietnam, 330–331
    Trump and, 43, 60, 175–177, 193, 194, 347, 388, 551, 589
Northam, Ralph, 312–313, 382
nuclear option, 79
nuclear programs. *See* denuclearization
nuclear-freeze movement, 131
Nunes, Devin, 92, 144, 361, 573, 624
Nunes memo, 96–99, 102

O

OAN, 666
Obama, Barack
    administration of, 1, 2, 9, 14, 19, 41, 42–44, 50, 60, 61, 65–68, 418, 470, 473
    Fox criticism of, 154
    and Israel, 46
    and Russia, 37, 118
    and Syria, 118
    and US election 2016, 132, 140, 141, 201, 320, 446, 473
Obamacare/ACA, 2, 66, 95, 147, 319, 352, 627, 664, 681, 696, 704, 705, 723
Ocasio-Cortez, Alexandria, 427
Occupy Wall Street, 4, 15, 23, 49, 381
Ohr, Bruce, 273, 289, 291
OLC, 367, 413, 432
Omar, Ilhan, 333, 335, 341, 342, 364, 387, 426–430, 436, 441–444
O'Rourke, Beto, 451, 461

P

Page, Carter, 97
Page, Lisa, 80, 92, 100, 179, 225, 273, 339, 341, 405, 573
Palestinians, 64, 82, 86, 105, 205, 210, 310, 384, 441, 443
pandemic office, 723
Papadopoulos, George, 26, 70, 93, 98, 261, 271, 274, 315, 354, 355, 389, 586, 595, 726, 727
pardons, 6, 158, 169–170, 341, 644
Paris Climate Accord, 281, 282, 316, 393
Parkland shooting, 107–108
Parnas, Lev, 494, 622, 624, 628

Paul, Rand, 672
Paycheck Protection Plan, 704
pee tape, 59, 179, 398
Pelosi, Nancy, 100, 187, 312, 598, 606, 627, 639, 675, 701, 708
Pence, Mike
  as coordinating federal response to coronavirus, 657
  as decent person, 47
  and Governor Whitmer, 690, 691
  Marc's support for, 29, 128, 130, 135, 215, 233, 242, 243, 293, 313, 353, 358, 466, 491, 506, 538, 552
  as not a billionaire, 129
  as possible author of anonymous op-ed, 224
  speech at Knesset, 82
Penn, Mark, 259
Penske file, 99
Perry, Rick, 130, 490, 554, 570–571
personal attacks, 1–3, 66, 285, 342–346, 683
personnel, 215–216
Peters, Ralph, 122
Phillips, Nathan, 300, 301, 302, 305, 307
Pirro, Jeanine, 121, 341
Pittsburgh synagogue massacre, 241–244
political, versus legal, 415–416
political hit jobs, 398–401
Politico, 525
Pompeo, Mike, 215, 310
Porter, Rob, 105
Portman, Rob, 639
power, abuse of, 38, 55, 61, 196, 210, 217, 226, 276, 317, 354, 396, 406, 409, 410, 411, 417, 458, 501, 529, 579, 591, 592, 596, 622, 623, 624, 625, 626, 634
press. *See* media

press conferences. *See* media
Pressley, Ayanna, 427
privilege, 357–358. *See also* executive privilege
Project Veritas, 623
propriety, 47–48, 94, 532, 650
prosecution, selective, 221–223
prosecutorial abuse, 274–275
prosecutorial misconduct, 158, 213–215, 274
Putin, Vladimir, 37, 39, 41, 59, 62, 84, 89, 118–119, 142, 166, 177, 197, 199, 202, 257, 276, 277, 293, 296, 308, 309, 366, 388, 425, 495, 536, 552–553, 588–589, 593, 613, 693, 694

Q

quid pro quo, 41, 179, 208, 261, 292, 293, 459, 463, 472, 487, 490, 515, 522, 532, 533, 539, 540, 542, 546–547, 559, 561, 564, 565, 629, 635

R

race, coronavirus and, 717–719
racism, 12, 23–25, 27, 34, 83, 100–101, 158, 167, 172–173, 183, 186–187, 235, 244, 247, 300, 301, 304, 305, 313, 606, 649, 652–653, 687
Raimondo, Gina, 722
rallies, 4, 5, 251, 294, 296, 304, 331, 382, 427, 435, 543, 608, 634, 649, 650, 675, 696, 699, 701, 702
rape, 230, 231, 233, 302, 306, 348, 349, 420, 593, 594, 645
Rasmussen poll, 468, 726
Reagan, Ronald, 24, 31, 281, 436, 522, 647, 661
regulatory reform, 31–34, 82. *See also* deregulation

Reid, Harry, 79
Reines, Philippe, 634
The Revolt (Begin), 642
Rich, Frank, 641
Rogen, Seth, 186
Romney, Mitt, 8, 73, 491, 638, 672–673, 682
Roosevelt, Theodore, 700
Rosen, Christine, 507
Rosen, James, 66
Rosenstein, Rod, 96, 248, 320, 321, 367, 368, 369
Rubashkin, Sholom, 158
Rubio, Marco, 130, 395
rule of law, 38, 49, 50, 51–54, 80, 84, 121, 178, 195, 198, 279, 513
Russia. *See also* Putin, Vladimir
    collusion with, 26, 31–34, 37–39, 41–46, 141, 142, 144–145, 166, 208, 225, 252, 257–258, 263, 278–279, 286, 293, 343, 378, 399, 408
    conspiracy theories about banks in, 59
    and the G7, 174
    interference by, 473
    Moscow Trump Tower, 258, 259, 263, 276, 289, 290, 292, 294–307, 308–309, 587, 602
    sanctions on, 88–91
    Trump's position on, 199, 201, 202, 377
    Trump's Russia crimes, 257–260
    and US election 2016, 48, 94, 106, 107, 118, 165–166, 200, 201, 248, 259, 270, 292, 320, 388, 418, 425, 485, 551, 575, 581, 607
Ryan, Paul, 130, 186

S

Sanders, Bernie, 29, 61, 286, 451, 452, 519, 634
Sanders, Sarah Huckabee, 186, 247, 372
Sandmann, Nicholas, 294–307, 656, 672
Santorum, Rick, 47
Sasse, Ben, 475, 488, 491
Saturday Night Live (*SNL*), 277, 318
Saudi Arabia
    US relationship with, 578, 621
    US troops in, 506
Scalise, Steve, 629
Scaramucci, Anthony, 669
Schiff, Adam
    on Clinton impeachment, 596
    and FISA application, 585, 601–602, 629
    Michael Cohen and, 336
    Netanyahu's indictment and, 567–568
    and Russia collusion, 252–253, 371, 535, 587, 601, 650
    on Trump impeachment, 515, 527, 573–574, 575, 626, 627, 639
    and Ukraine, 503, 561, 577, 591, 599–600, 625
    and whistleblower, 482, 483, 489, 510, 535, 539, 548, 634
Schumer, Chuck, 100
Scott, Tim, 76
Sekulow, Jay, 43, 622
Sessions, Jeff, 111, 214, 248
sexual misconduct, 19–21, 23–25, 31, 56, 121, 132
Shapiro, Ben, 247, 250, 290
shithole countries, Trump's comment about, 74–78, 437
shootings
    Dayton shooting, 439–440
    El Paso shooting, 439–440
    Parkland shooting, 107–108

Simpson, Glenn, 220
Simpson, O. J., 39, 43, 53, 57, 83, 120, 219, 250, 485, 606
Smerconish, Michael, 366
Smollett, Jussie, 323–324, 356, 357, 641, 642
Soleimani, killing of, 618–619, 621, 622
Sondland, Gordon, 498, 504, 514, 515, 521, 532, 533, 539, 557, 559, 562, 564, 565, 566, 606
Soviet Union. *See* Russia
speech
    free speech, 5, 17, 18, 227, 342, 348
    hate speech, 183–185
Starr, Kenneth, 266, 269, 367, 369, 386, 560
State of the Union, 90, 639, 700, 708
Steele, Christopher, 97, 105, 106, 109, 144, 166, 219, 291, 580, 595
Steele dossier, 34, 37, 38, 39, 43, 44, 46, 85, 93, 98, 142, 144, 208, 213, 289, 291, 371, 386, 389, 391, 486, 582, 586, 595, 601–602
Stein, Andrew, 259
Stephens, Bret, 250, 261
Stewart, Martha, 169
Stipulated Removal, 189
Stone, Roger, 142, 193, 310–311, 643–645, 654
Strzok, Peter, 51, 53, 58, 63, 80–81, 92, 100, 179, 194–196, 198, 209, 261, 273, 405
subpoenas, 73, 92, 94, 337, 376, 395–397, 482, 513, 537, 607
Sullivan, Emmet, 278
swamp, draining of, 113–114, 275, 491
Syria
    Obama and, 118
    Trump and, 377, 425
    US troops in, 506
    US troops withdrawal from, 279, 280, 283–284, 314, 495–496, 500, 501, 508, 509

T

Tapper, Jake, 650
tariffs, 111, 113, 177–178, 393, 402–403, 413
tax cuts, 28, 275, 276, 281
tax exemption, death, 28
tax fraud, 151, 268
tax liens, 151
tax reform, 28, 60, 63, 69, 114, 393
tax returns, 59, 73, 151, 513, 601
Taylor, Bill, 521–522, 535–536, 555
Thor, Brad, 363
Thunberg, Greta, 588
Tillerson, Rex, 46
Tlaib, Rashida, 380, 427, 436, 437, 441–444
totalitarianism, 316
toxic environments, 128
transgender bathrooms, 14, 286
transgender persons, and military, 123
travel bans, 146, 658, 661, 685, 701, 703, 708
Truman, Harry, 63
Trump, Donald
    accomplishments of, 276–277
    business ventures of, 137
    critics of, 102, 199, 247, 250, 253, 276, 281–282, 285–286, 378, 379, 384, 440, 500, 508, 527, 661, 662, 663, 681, 685, 686, 687, 703, 705, 709, 713
    evaluating, 16–18
    experience of, 104
    fitness of for office, 152, 204
    harassment of, 405
    health of, 149

as king, 121, 172, 277, 316, 386, 410, 538
meltdown stage, 116–117
at midterm, 250–251
as Moscow's man, 122
support for, 17, 74, 111–112, 167, 184, 295, 323, 329, 394, 426–430, 477, 625, 637, 718
Trump, Donald, Jr., 45, 142, 193, 220, 395, 396, 433, 434, 652
Trump, Eric, 221
Trump, Fred, 305
Trump, Ivana, 115, 594
Trump, Ivanka, 255–256
Trump, Melania, 128, 637
Trump Foundation, 278
Trump University, 12, 137, 215, 322, 345, 576, 604
Turkey
　Erdogan on Syria's refugees to, 512
　and the Kurds, 499–502, 506, 508
Trump's letter to, 514
Turley, Jonathan, 373
tweets/Twitter, 109, 131, 285, 292, 433, 453–454, 481, 530, 588, 598, 624, 626, 629, 630, 634, 635, 637, 641, 643, 646, 652, 655, 657, 659, 661, 669, 670, 671, 683, 685, 690, 691, 694, 696, 697, 702, 705, 707, 709, 711, 715, 725, 726

U

Ukraine. *See also* Biden, Joe, and Ukraine; Zelensky, Vlodoymyr
　aid to, 471, 481–494, 497–498, 503–505, 510–511, 513–516, 521–523, 524–525, 533–541, 546–547, 548, 556–557, 559, 562, 563, 565, 576–577, 584, 591–592, 605–606, 613, 628, 630–633

Obama and, 257, 425
Trump and, 118, 273, 377, 453–472
and US election 2016, 474, 475, 489, 524, 531, 533, 537, 542, 555, 558, 565, 575, 613
US relationship with, 613–614
unemployment, 153, 379, 380
unhinged opposition, 47–48, 49
United Nations (UN), 60, 62, 75, 77, 130, 464, 514, 589
Uranium One deal, 19, 39, 42
US Constitution
　Fifth Amendment, 189
　regard for, 9, 67, 147
　Second Amendment, 111
　Section 4, Article 2, 352
　Twenty-Fifth Amendment, 320, 321, 634
US embassies
　in Iraq, 617
　move of to Jerusalem, 63–64, 153, 155–157, 393
US Justice Department (DOJ). *See* DOJ
US Ninth Circuit Court, 415
USA Today, 47
useful idiots, 128, 129, 131–132, 134, 181, 182, 183, 202, 236, 246, 270, 476, 626
USS *John McCain*, 410, 412

V

Vance, Joyce, 541
Venezuela, Trump and, 377
Veselnitskaya, Natalia, 220
The View, 707
vigilantism, 159, 160
Vindman, Army Colonel, 531, 532, 535, 536, 591, 644, 645
violence
　bomb threats, 240
　condemnation of, 240

747

Dayton shooting, 439–440
El Paso shooting, 439–440
encouragement of/promulgating, 160–161, 241, 342, 426, 629
left-wing violence, 13
Parkland shooting, 107–108
Pittsburgh synagogue massacre, 241–244
right-wing violence, 4
Volker, Kurt, 485, 503
Vos, Robin, 714
voter fraud, 127. *See also* electoral fraud/election fraud
voter ID laws/voter IDs, 24, 127, 167
Vox, 305

W

Wall Street Journal, 21, 41, 82, 96, 143, 197, 269, 326, 396, 427, 454, 459, 463, 549, 563
Wallace, Daniel, 720
Warmbier, Otto, 327
Warren, Elizabeth, 299, 451, 452, 457, 461, 467–468, 519, 652, 705
Washington Post, 21, 69, 177
Wasserman Schultz, Debbie, 1, 7, 8
Waters, Maxine, 98, 207, 240
Weinstein, Harvey, 19, 20, 23, 29, 56, 229
Weissmann, Andrew, 291
whistleblowers, 455, 456, 459, 462, 465, 468, 469, 471, 474, 475, 482, 483, 485, 487, 489, 492, 493, 498, 504, 505, 510, 514, 525, 535, 538–539, 546, 548, 557, 561, 563, 573, 591, 613, 620, 625, 626, 627, 629, 630, 633, 634, 638
Whitaker, Matthew, 248–249
white supremacists, 10, 13, 24, 25, 75, 610
white-power hand gesture, 597

Whitmer, Gretchen, 690, 691
WikiLeaks, 31, 46, 253, 310, 371
witch hunts, 8, 116, 134, 136, 210, 211, 218, 340, 350, 354, 365, 567, 632
Woodward, Bob, 224
Wray, Christopher, 88, 92, 96

X

Xi Jinping, 488

Y

Yates, Sally, 57
Yovanovitch, Maria, 557, 558, 560, 604, 622

Z

Zeldin, Lee, 28
Zelensky, Vlodoymyr, 463, 468, 471, 487, 521, 535, 557, 562, 566, 584, 600, 605, 606, 622, 625, 628, 629, 630, 636, 644
Zimmerman, George, 188
Zinke, Ryan, 215